LORD LIVERPOOL'S ADMINISTRATION

THE CRUCIAL YEARS

1815–1822

LORD LIVERPOOL'S ADMINISTRATION

THE CRUCIAL YEARS

1815–1822

J. E. COOKSON
University of Canterbury, Christchurch, New Zealand

1975
ARCHON BOOKS

Library of Congress Cataloging in Publication Data

Cookson, J   E
    Lord Liverpool's administration, 1815–1822.

    Includes bibliographical references.
    1. Great Britain—Politics and government—1800–
1837.   2. Liverpool, Robert Banks Jenkinson, 2d. Earl
of, 1770–1828.   I. Title.
DA535.C66   942.07′4′0924   74–22080
ISBN 0–208–01495–0

First published 1975 by
Scottish Academic Press Ltd
Edinburgh
and in the United States of America
as an Archon Book, an imprint of
The Shoe String Press, Inc.,
Hamden, Connecticut 06514

Printed in Great Britain

To Pamela

PREFACE

THIS work is an attempt to explain British politics from the government side in the seven traumatic years immediately after Waterloo. It is essentially a narrative account of the shifts and expedients adopted, either separately or collectively, by the small group of men who comprised the Cabinet. If I have done nothing more, I hope I have rubbed at a small patch sufficiently to encourage others to strip the whole panel. But I have tried to show what response the most powerful men in the country made to an expanding and more assertive political public, which in the nineteenth century was crucial to the survival of aristocratic government.

Needless to say, I do not agree with those historians who maintain that the British governing class is not worth studying or that it has been studied enough. In particular, there is a great need to understand better the extent of ministerial power in the late eighteenth and early nineteenth centuries. At this time, it seems to me, the Cabinet occupied an exceptional place in government; the monarch was withdrawing from politics; the civil servant who advised was hard to find, he who was a 'states-man in disguise' had yet to appear, party feeling there was; but the machinery and discipline to produce and enforce views were virtually non-existent; the parliamentary opposition, by later standards, was unformidable, lacking cohesion, unsure of its role and uncertain of whether or how to use public opinion to its advantage. In other words, attack on the Cabinet from above was unlikely, from behind inconceivable, and both the parliamentary and public flanks were extremely difficult to turn. In these circumstances, relationships within the Cabinet assume singular importance.

Regarding terminology, it was sufficient for my purposes to borrow the expressions which were contemporary. Hence I use 'country gentlemen' and 'independents' as synonymous terms

vii

(though not all independents were country gentlemen and not all country gentlemen independents). I have not made a habit of referring to the ministerialists as 'Tories' because this was apparently rare. To impart a certain period flavour I have retained the original capitalisation, punctuation and spelling when quoting except where it would have grossly distorted the sense.

I wish to place on record my thanks to the staff of the following for their assistance: the University Library, St Andrews; the British Museum; the Public Record Office; the Library, University College, University of London; the National Library of Wales; the National Library of Scotland; Cornwall Record Office; Devon Record Office; Gloucester Record Office; Durham Record Office; the Archives Department, Leeds Public Library. In addition, I should like to recognise the generosity of the Marquis of Normanby, the Earl Bathhurst, the Earl of Harrowby, the Earl of Harewood, the Lady Mairi Bury, Mr G. Fortescue, and N. M. Rothschild & Sons for allowing me access to papers.

I cannot conclude without expressing my particular indebtedness to four persons. Miss Bridget Moore produced a very fair typescript. Dr I. J. Catanach read all but the last five chapters and was a scrupulous critic. Professor Norman Gash, who first saw this work in thesis form, has given helpful advice on all matters from the technicalities of publication to the art of writing history. My wife, Pamela, not only assisted with research but was uncomplaining when I often neglected the twentieth century for the nineteenth. In this task, as in so many others, she has been my helpmate.

                                                        J.E.C.

Christchurch, 1974

CONTENTS

ABBREVIATIONS

Add. MSS.	Additional Manuscripts in the British Museum.
Arbuthnot	*The Correspondence of Charles Arbuthnot* (ed. A. Aspinall).
Bathurst	Historical Manuscripts Commission. *Report on the Manuscripts of Earl Bathurst.*
Bathurst MSS.	Papers of the third Earl Bathurst in the British Museum.
Brougham	*The Life and Times of Henry, Lord Brougham* written by himself.
Brougham MSS.	Papers of the first Baron Brougham and Vaux, University College, London.
Buckingham, *George IV*	Duke of Buckingham and Chandos, *Memoirs of the Court of George IV.*
Buckingham, *Regency*	Duke of Buckingham and Chandos, *Memoirs of the Court of England during the Regency.*
Canning	Augustus Granville Stapleton, *George Canning and his Times.*
Canning MSS.	Papers of George Canning, Central Library, Leeds.
Castlereagh	*Correspondence, Despatches and other Papers of Viscount Castlereagh* (ed. Marquis of Londonderry).
Castlereagh MSS.	Papers of the second Marquis of Londonderry, Mount Stewart, Co. Down, Northern Ireland.
CJ	Journals of the House of Commons.
Coed-y-maen MSS.	Papers of Charles Watkin Williams-Wynn included in the Coed-y-maen deposit, National Library of Wales, Aberystwyth.
Colchester	*The Diary and Correspondence of Charles Abbot, Lord Colchester* (ed. Charles, Lord Colchester).

xi

Creevey	*The Creevey Papers* (ed. Sir Herbert Maxwell).
Croker	*The Correspondence and Diaries of John Wilson Croker* (ed. Louis J. Jennings).
Eldon	Horace Twiss, *The Life of Lord Chancellor Eldon.*
Fortesque	Historical Manuscripts Commission, *Report on the Manuscripts of J. B. Fortesque.*
George IV	*The Letters of George IV*, 1812-1830 (ed. A. Aspinall).
Grenville MSS.	Papers of the first Baron Grenville, Cornwall Record Office, Truro.
Hansard	*The Parliamentary Debates* published by Hansard.
Harrowby MSS.	Papers of the first Earl of Harrowby, Sandon Hall, Staffs.
Herries MSS.	Papers of John Charles Herries in the British Museum.
HO	Home Office Papers in the Public Record Office.
Hobhouse	*The Diary of Henry Hobhouse* (ed. A. Aspinall).
Liverpool	Charles Duke Yonge, *The Life and Administration of Robert Banks, Second Earl of Liverpool.*
LJ	*Journals of the House of Lords.*
Londonderry MSS.	Papers of the third Marquis of Londonderry, County Record Office, Durham.
Mrs Arbuthnot	*The Journal of Mrs Arbuthnot* (ed. Francis Bamford and the Duke of Wellington).
NLS MSS.	National Library of Scotland Manuscripts.
Peel	*Sir Robert Peel* (ed. Charles Stuart Parker).
Plumer Ward	Hon. Edmund Phipps, *Memoirs of the Political and Literary Life of Robert Plumer Ward.*
PP	Parliamentary Papers, House of Commons.
PRO	Public Record Office

Sidmouth	George Pellew, *The Life and Correspondence of First Viscount Sidmouth.*
Sidmouth MSS.	Papers of the first Viscount Sidmouth, Devon Record Office, Exeter.
Wellington Desp.	*The Despatches of Field Marshal the Duke of Wellington* (ed. Lt. Col. Gurwood).
Wellington Desp. (new series)	*Despatches, Correspondence and Memoranda of the Duke of Wellington* (ed. Duke of Wellington).
Wellington Sup. Desp.	*Supplementary Despatches and Memoranda of the Duke of Wellington* (ed. Duke of Wellington).
Wilberforce	Robert Isaac Wilberforce and Samuel Wilberforce, *The Life of William Wilberforce.*
WO	War Office Papers in the Public Record Office.

INTRODUCTION

Like many a patriarch of Adam's seed, the administration of the second Earl of Liverpool is most easily remembered by the fact of its longevity, as if to exist is a great achievement and all others of lesser importance. Perhaps this is a fair beginning for an assessment of its worth, but it is only a beginning. To survive fifteen years less a month or two is no trifling performance for any government. To survive fifteen years at a time of profound social change, when many contemporaries were prepared to contemplate revolution, lifts it into the category of the quite extraordinary. The mere fact of longevity matters little to the historian alongside the circumstances in which control of the state was retained and power possessed was applied.

Liverpool's administration was not one which followed Nature's course of growing strength then growing feebleness. It was at its weakest during its middle years, the period between Waterloo and the ministerial changes of 1822, when its popularity in the country was at its lowest and parliament represented the dissatisfaction to be its most unruly. In contrast, in its later years it had a robustness which was only seriously impaired by a degree of personal and political estrangement within the Cabinet not met with previously. It did not die gradually but suddenly with its prime minister's physical collapse and total incapacity. Nevertheless, it was undoubtedly at the peak of its strength in its infancy; and the circumstances of war mainly explained it. The conflict with France, the traditional enemy, and Napoleon, the Continental despot, stirred patriotic feeling in the nation as never before. Especially after 1812, the year the government took office, with the military fortunes of Britain and her allies obviously turning, men once again permitted themselves to think of ultimate victory and the war acquired a new popularity. Parliament cheerfully voted, with increasing generosity, the means to wage it; the Whigs added to their difficulty

1

of acting as a 'loyal' opposition by appearing unduly sympathetic to the enemy; and the ministers found a solidarity, which
would otherwise have been lacking, as Wellington and Castlereagh translated their efforts into a sequence of brilliant
successes.

This last point is perhaps deserving of special emphasis.
After five administrations in eleven years, political loyalties
were unusually atomised, as the negotiations to form a government on Perceval's assassination made only too obvious. The
great party the younger Pitt had gathered together had divided
in 1801, but as if by some strange chemistry the process of
fission had continued until it could be said that five lesser
parties represented the cellular remnants. These only gradually
achieved a fresh, and as it happened, shortlived, coalescence.
Where Pitt, with the American War at an end, was able to compound a government out of Shelburne's and North's followers
in a matter of months, his protegé laboured ten years to build
an equivalent broad bottom, such was the degree of estrangement. The attempt to reunite all or some of them in 1812 failed
abysmally. Sidmouth carried his reconciliation with the main
body of Pittites a stage further by exchanging the Presidency of
the Council for the Home Office, but Grenville refused to part
from the Whigs, Wellesley to serve under Liverpool, and Canning
to accept Castlereagh as his superior or equal. The result was
that the new administration was essentially a continuation of
Perceval's without Perceval. This fact was undoubtedly of some
advantage as far as the unity of the Cabinet was concerned, for
it enabled the unfamiliarity and awkwardness, present in the
opening period of a coalition at least, to be avoided. The abortive negotiations with other political principals also provided
the ministers with an assurance that for the moment no stronger
combination to carry on the war with vigour and resolution was
possible. But above all, at a time when personal hostility
obscured and often overcame political agreement, it was partnership in a great enterprise, carried on to ever greater success,
which produced a real solidification of loyalties. On the prime
matter of how to win the war, the ministers were never at
serious loggerheads, and they soon showed that they had
administrative and diplomatic talent equal to the occasion;

Wellington, on whose small British army so much depended, was supported to the full, while Castlereagh successfully set about remaking the Grand Coalition. The consequences of failure would have been the same as for North and Newcastle. Liverpool and his fellow ministers knew well that their charge to carry on the king's service meant in particular fighting the war, and that in the event of a run of defeats the confidence given them would soon be withdrawn, possibly amid a welter of anti-war feeling. To this extent, the government's future was beyond their control, at least where the supply lines ended in the Peninsula; and to this extent, Wellington, with his splendid victories, secured the administration he was later to join. Winning the war had both the positive effect of promoting the unity of the Cabinet and the negative one of curbing the efforts of its enemies.

The effeteness of the Whig opposition and the strength of the government was given additional emphasis by the absence of great domestic questions until the crisis of agriculture in 1814. Having lost the goodwill of the Court, the Whigs, though they seemed singularly reluctant to acknowledge it, had to place their hopes with the Country; but by the time an issue arose which, in view of their own unpopularity, could only have provided them with meagre leverage against the government, the ministers had the considerable capital of victory to draw on. The first two years of the administration's existence were, generally speaking, years of prosperity and order. The session of 1811 had settled the vexatious question of a return to gold while the war lasted; and the much-hated Orders-in-Council, which regulated the trade of neutrals with Napoleonic Europe, had been revoked a fortnight after Liverpool had taken office. This action by itself did much to free foreign trade; but in addition the culminating war effort stimulated industrial production; agricultural prices, and therefore incomes, remained high well into 1813; and, as the frontiers of Napoleon's Empire were pushed back, the country's markets on the Continent were re-opened. Even the outbreak of hostilities with America disrupted the economy minimally, mainly because compensating opportunities were not hard to find but also because an indirect trade through Canada continued. Prosperity notably reduced the problem of order. At home the Luddite disturbances reached their height in 1812, and thereafter the authorities had only to cope with occasional local outbreaks, the sort of violence which was endemic in Hanoverian England.

Ireland too remained as quiet as could be expected. Apart from the war's happy turn, this was probably the most important single circumstance in the administration's favour. For when trouble occurred in that part of the kingdom, the neutrality of the Cabinet on the question of Catholic emancipation was always tested to some extent. Neutrality had been adopted by successive governments in the knowledge that a purely 'Protestant' or a purely 'Catholic' administration, if formed, would have little chance of survival; but it was only an acceptable posture for as long as Irish opinion on the subject remained latent, diverse and ill-organised. The moment a protest against Catholic disabilities developed which was properly national, in the sense of embodying the grievances and aspirations of the various sections of Irish society, the 'Catholics' within the Cabinet would be under the severest pressure to end the compromise. Until then, frequently when Irish concerns were discussed, their conviction that emancipation would pacify had to combat the futility of expecting its enactment. Most of the parliamentary effort in favour of emancipation came not from them but from the Whigs, who naturally saw advantage in publicising as much as possible the Cabinet's divided opinion. This mischief making outside the government and the tender consciences to be found within it led a highly exasperated Peel to exclaim on one occasion that the consequence of neutrality was 'daily embarrassment'.[1] While the comment was an exaggeration, it was an indication of the administration's difficulty. But when Ireland was quiet, the strains and stresses were reduced to a minimum. Fortunately for the government, the tranquillity of 1812–13 was exceeded in the years which followed, until in the 1820's Irish dissatisfactions found a common outlet in O'Connell's Catholic Association.

Liverpool's administration, therefore, largely thanks to the fortuitous, consolidated its position remarkably in the first three years of its existence. Probably, in terms of popularity, parlia-

[1] Gash, *Mr Secretary Peel*, p. 140.

mentary goodwill and ministerial solidarity, it was at the peak
of its strength in 1815. This is not to say that its original endow-
ments were inconsiderable. The support of the Court, which
could be inferred from what had passed between the Prince
Regent and the Whigs in 1812, was of importance at a time when
the notional power of the Crown was being reduced at a much
slower rate than the real: a great number of 'parliament men',
possibly a majority, would have been prepared to argue that it
was unconstitutional for ministers to force a policy or any
action against the decided wishes of the king and that he was
entitled to dismiss them if there was a loss of confidence to this
extent; nor did many doubt that a new, viable administration
could be formed by him on the strength of the insult and the
needs of the king's service. The support of parliament, strongly
exhibited when the House of Commons met in November 1812
after a general election, had its guarantee in the general realisation that for the moment the king's business could be carried
on by no stronger combination, and further in the old Tory
repugnance for the Whigs who now demeaned themselves by
their attitude to the war, their preference for Catholic emancipation and the interest of some of them in parliamentary reform.
In spite of a decade of instability, the rivalries and reconcilia-
tions of which had baffled and often disgusted contemporaries, there had been a survival of party feeling mainly based
on the attribution of views concerning the power of the Crown
and the political worth of the people. In the Tory mind, the
Whigs bore a hostility to the prerogative which could not be
countenanced and shared an affinity for popular causes which
did not fall short of the dangerous. To the Whigs, the Tories
were too indulgent towards the executive power at the expense
of national needs and too unresponsive to popular demands—
they allowed confidence in and the reputation of aristocratic
government to be seriously eroded. This party feeling, in fact,
came into increasing prominence. The issue of what was due to
the monarch faded, because the Prince Regent was not as
politically active as his father had been and successive Cabinets,
on important matters, invariably mastered him. But the issue
of what was due to public opinion intensified greatly with the
agitations of the immediate post-war period. The Tories still

stood forth as the proponents of strong government, but they were much less concerned with defending the Crown against the aristocracy than with defending it against the people. The Whigs changed the object of their attack from the personal power of the monarch, now obviously diminished, to the power in the exercise of ministers. Liverpool and his colleagues believed in all sincerity that they were equipped and in the best position to judge the real interest of the nation, and it followed that the legislature should act on their recommendations rather than on public opinion's, whether the representations came from the 'rational' or 'irrational portion of the community'. In practice, of course, parliament could not be insulated from public opinion, and the executive from parliament. The actual question was to what extent the Cabinet should notice the people. The Whigs thought the Tories did not go far enough; the Tories thought the Whigs would go too far. It was the widely found aversion for 'popular government' which gave Liverpool's administration its main strength after 1815. But even in 1812 there was sufficient feeling against the Whigs to encourage a sense of unity among the ministers and to provide them with much goodwill in the legislature.

The new government was most vulnerable in its lack of parliamentary, as distinct from administrative, talent. Indeed, the front bench in the Commons continued to support too many mediocrities until as late as 1822, when Canning took over the leadership and had Peel, Robinson and Huskisson, to call to his assistance. Liverpool, it must be said, was painfully aware of this weakness. Writing to Wellington two months after taking office, he confessed that in the lower house the government would depend on 'the most promising of the young men' and went on to wish aloud for 'a second Pitt' to arise from amongst these novices.[2] The point was that talent was a more precious commodity than ever. The increase of parliamentary business which was correspondent with the increase of administrative business, largely but not wholly caused by the war, obviously required an administration to look to its efficiency. Every House of Commons minister had to take his share of committee work, which demanded a certain knowledge and a

[2] *Wellington Sup. Desp.*, vii. 402.

certain expertise. As well, the more who could hold their own in general debate the better, for the load, if it fell on one or two, could scarcely be endured—such was Castlereagh's fate, and in the end it was not the least factor which destroyed him. There was, not surprisingly, some tendency towards specialisation or for the lesser official men to play a part of greater prominence. The all-rounder survived particularly in the leader of the House, but in the normal course of events the departmental representative, who was naturally *au fait* with the subject, introduced business affecting his office into the legislature and supervised its passage.

However, talent was of greater value on the broader view of the prestige of the executive and aristocratic government generally. No politician needed to be told that the activities of ministers were being scrutinised by an expanding public, or that that public was mainly informed by the proceedings of parliament, given a generous amount of space in the metropolitan and provincial press. How an administration acquitted itself in the legislature was increasingly important. It was not enough for the ministers to enforce their superiority at division-time. Silence on their side, broken only by the tramp of marching feet into the lobby, had the effect of encouraging the belief that the basis of their power was something other than the true confidence of the House. A government needed to be able to 'speechify', to cut the opposition down to size, to justify itself before the nation, and to demonstrate its wisdom and capability. It was really a constant appeal to that part of the public which did not want the executive to be responsive so much as responsible, attending to national needs whatever the demands of the populace and the habits of the past. In the midst of the transformation of British society, the demand for strong government always made itself felt, if subtly rather than overtly. An executive which in its appearance did not govern with a sense of purpose, lacked initiative and was unassertive in the legislature was never in safe enjoyment of its power.

The problem was one which beset Liverpool's administration for much of its existence. Certainly at the outset Liverpool found his 'speechifying' resources woefully inadequate. On the Commons front bench, where they were of most account, there were

only Castlereagh, Vansittart and Bragge-Bathurst of the
Cabinet: the first could hold his own on what he called 'field
days'—though alongside the stars of the opposition side he was
a clumsy orator; but the second was even confusing on his own
speciality of finance, and the last barely articulate. Neither did
Wellesley Pole's admission to the Cabinet in 1814 redress the
balance of talent, for his contribution to general debate was
distinguished only by his intemperance. To be sure, the young
men of whom Liverpool had hopes slowly learnt their trade until
Castlereagh never ceased boasting that each department had
'persons able to repel any assailant on the details of the particular office'.[3] But this was as late as 1822. For a long time before
that there was a deplorable lack of heavy artillery, so much so
that in November 1814 the Prime Minister was beseeching
Castlereagh to hurry home from Vienna to bring the Commons
to some kind of order.[4] Liverpool, in his first years, was only
able to tackle the problem in a negative fashion. Canning, who
was probably the best speaker in the House, was an obvious
man to entice in this connection, and also for the reason that he
represented the constant threat of a third party or 'flying
squadron'. But both attempts to win him over failed completely. The first in July 1812, soon after Liverpool's administration had introduced itself to parliament, collapsed when
Canning in an evil hour insisted that he would never be Castlereagh's subordinate. The less-known second, made sometime
in 1813, depended on Melville leaving the Admiralty. When for
some reason this arrangement was not carried through, Liverpool magnanimously appointed Canning to the embassy at
Lisbon where he remained, reflecting on his folly, for two years.
There was, however, more to the Prime Minister's magnanimity than met the eye. With Canning abroad and Wellesley
cold-shouldered by government and opposition alike, trouble on
the administration's flank was unlikely for the moment; and,
with a firm promise to Canning that the next Cabinet vacancy
would be his if he wanted it, there was a fair chance that it
would be dissipated altogether. The government's bottom had
still to be broadened, the front bench in the Commons was still

[3] *Croker*, i. 231.
[4] *Castlereagh*, x. 239.

a sorry sight, but at least those who might have been against were rendered relatively innocuous.

The nearer Great Britain came to winning the war, the nearer came daunting problems of peace. War stimulated administrative energies and channelled them into the particular cause of carrying on the conflict. Peace, on the other hand, had the effect of releasing political energies, pent up during the war by the 'unpatriotism' of opposition, and which inevitably spent themselves mainly on domestic issues. The difference is perhaps best explained by Huskisson's reference to 'the old Remark that a Ministry enjoying the cordial good will of the Sovereign is best for War, but unfitted for Peace'.[5] The need for a strong executive, an administration of talent unobstructed by a king still with some power, was reduced in peace by the need for a strong parliament. Unless the dissatisfactions of the public, which gained freer expression without the distraction of war, were faithfully represented in the legislature, forcing the government to some compromise, the isolation of the ruling class from the people would reach dangerous proportions. The ministers wished to maintain their freedom of action, but parliament wished to keep on good terms with public opinion. The only solution was for the Cabinet to engage in the difficult exercise of acknowledging popular demands, to keep its popularity, without becoming subservient to them, to keep faith with itself. Too much concession would create as perilous a situation as too little, for where the first would encourage public opinion to make further trials of its strength, the second would perhaps bring disillusionment with the existing political order to a breaking point.

That there would be a revitalisation of politics with the coming of peace was further assured by a deteriorating economic situation. In many quarters, including the government, a depression was taken to be the inevitable aftermath of war, especially of a war which had extended over two decades and been sustained by unprecedented effort. The experience of the past indicated as much, most latterly in what had followed the war with America in the 1780's. It was obvious that war caused a diversion of resources, stimulating some sectors of the economy

[5] Huskisson to Lord Liverpool, 9 July 1818, Add. MSS. 38191, f. 114.

at the expense of others, and that the first years of peace were necessarily a period of painful adjustment. These fears were confirmed when the price of corn suffered a sudden slump towards the end of 1813; the landed interest responded with protectionist cries, the urban poor countered with violence, and the economists nodded knowingly that the war had given agriculture an artificial prosperity and the farmer would now have to pay for it. More depressing still, by 1815 trade and industry seemed to be heading in a similar direction. Where the farmer was in difficulty for over-producing and over-capitalising, the merchant was also over-extending himself by pouring goods into Europe for which there was no certain demand, with the result that the war industries were not alone in experiencing hardship. Instead of a depression localised in part of the economy, though being felt throughout, the greater evil occurred of a large area facing the direct impact and all its concomitant miseries. In the midst of final victory, therefore, the government could find few crumbs of comfort in the situation at home. Even the corn law of 1815, passed to quieten an indignant squirearchy, failed to achieve its purpose, for the price of wheat and other agricultural staples continued to fall regardless.

The periods of distress were, in fact, those when the administration was most endangered. The danger was the greater because the protests from the country that invariably resulted had a content that was more than simply economic. Hard times had the effect of pouring forth resentments and animosities that were being brewed in a rapidly changing society. A decline in agricultural profits, for instance, drew complaints from the agricultural community that the trading and manufacturing part of the nation enjoyed a superior protection from the state. Likewise a commercial depression aroused feelings that its rigours might have been reduced but for the mis-government of a landed aristocracy who were jealous towards or who under-estimated the importance of a different form of wealth. But above all, distress forced the government to tackle in an unequivocal fashion the deeply embedded, wide ranging suspicion that the holders of power would consult a narrower interest than the nation's. In its most refined form, the suspicion was that the ministers could not take a right view of the needs of the state because their attitudes and assumptions precluded it; they were too firmly wedded to the established order to see its imperfections, too incomprehending of the strength of the people to make a sufficient appeasement. At the lower end of the social scale, cruder arguments were invoked. The ministers were not so much misguided as wicked. They were the chief operators of a system of extravagance which secured their power by reducing the legislature to servility and by gratifying the Court and the aristocracy, a cancer of the constitution which could only be eradicated by the drastic surgery of parliamentary reform. Of course, popular opposition, in the broad sense, had become a potent political factor as the central government made inroads into local independence and parliament achieved frequent and regular meetings. The fact that the Country had a focus for its discontent in the Court and an institution to relay its grievances did much to develop the political consciousness of the nation and advance its political education. By the 1790's there was ample evidence that even 'the lower sort of people' were beginning to turn from the primitive protest of riot and rowdyism towards constitutional agitation on a national scale; ministers, rather than middlemen or masters, were increasingly pointed out as the real villains. It was this growing political sophistication of the lower orders which emphasised more than ever that 'politics remained an affair of two nations'; 'a tight political establishment' on the one hand, and 'an amorphous mass of political sentiment' on the other, with each striving for a preponderant say in the direction of the state.[6] In the early nineteenth century an executive which valued its independence highly had to cope with a public opinion drawn from an expanding catchment and flowing where the full force of the strengthening current was felt mainly by it alone.

Popular complaint was not only directed at the executive but its very existence condemned the ministers among their own kind, inasmuch as it signalled the discontent of the political nation outside the establishment and contributed to the growing disillusionment with the existing order to be found there. Liverpool and his colleagues soon had it brought home to them

[6] J. H. Plumb, 'Political Man' in *Man versus Society in 18th Century Britain* (ed. James L. Clifford), pp. 12, 20.

with the postwar troubles that popular agitation, far from consolidating support for them, rendered their position more precarious. The ruling class easily appreciated that it needed to
keep the goodwill of the 'rational' public, and it became
increasingly obvious that that could only be secured by respecting the fears and aspirations of the 'middling sort' who largely
comprised it. Parliament threw out the property tax, attempted
to coerce the 'lower sort' into silence and constantly berated the
executive for extravagant government in this knowledge. 'Respectable' opinion, which contemporaries saw as deriving from the
'middling sort', was the great fulcrum of politics in the early
nineteenth century. The government and the governing class
had an unassailable strength when they could apply themselves
with its support. This is not to say that it was ever totally available. Among the 'middling sort', whose economic importance
and political interest were rapidly growing, there was a certain
feeling against aristocratic exclusiveness and aristocratic power.
But it was invariably overwhelmed by a desire for order and
stability. If the passions of the 'inferior sort of people' were
aroused and given political direction, those immediately above
them in the social scale could be depended on to lend their
efforts to subdue them, whether by coercion or conciliation, out
of a fear that if popular indignation were not quelled they and
the aristocracy alike would be the victims. There were not many
who were prepared to call in the 'mob' to redress their wrongs
and create a world more to their liking. The 'middling sort' put
their faith in peaceful penetration of the constitution, and even
that penetration was hampered by the aristocracy's readiness
and ability to serve them well.

Lord Liverpool's administration, then, above all had to keep
the confidence of those great legions of 'property and intelligence' in the nation which were only meagrely represented in
the institutions of the state. The power of 'respectable' opinion
could no longer be denied on any account. A hundred different
newspapers helped to sharpen its focus, the platform in many
places, even in the counties, was under its control, and parliament paid it heed to the extent that the government found it too
dangerous to hazard a contest in the legislature over the Orders-
in-Council in 1812 and the property tax in 1815. The best

satisfaction the ministers could give the 'middling sort' was to maintain order and provide a government which was not oblivious to their needs and demands. With regard to the first, the administration did not for a moment anticipate the massiveness of the challenge which the lower orders were to present to the rest of society in the immediate post-war period. The suppression of the forces of disorder through the law and the traditional peacekeeping machinery had apparently worked in the 1790's and again in 1812, and there seemed to be no reason why a similar coercion would not succeed in the future. Probably the most important fact in the career of Lord Liverpool's administration was that it did not. Hampered greatly by the libertarian tradition of the English state and an antiquated administrative system, the government found it impossible to restrain more than minimally the expression of alien opinion. The result was that it had to learn to endure a politically active populace whose political intelligence it believed was much wanting, and come to terms with the 'middling sort' who were as fearful as the aristocracy that numbers would overwhelm property if some appeasement were not attempted. As it happened, the menace was at its greatest during the post-war depressions and the excitement of the Queen's trial. But the 'respectable' classes in this short time saw in the people a beast of unexampled ferocity which they could not slaughter and which they did not know could be domesticated, and this memory had its effect on political action for a very long time to come.

On the other matter of preserving the good name of aristocratic government before the 'middling sort' Liverpool's administration was perhaps better armed. It acknowledged, as previous administrations for a century or more had acknowledged, that the aristocracy's control of the state depended in the last resort on the consent of the governed. Every government had to be prepared to defend its acts in terms of the national interest and none could afford wholly to identify that with its own interest or the interest of a ruling class. The propertied had a duty to the propertyless at every station of power. Property also owed a respect for the law which embodied a wisdom far greater than any one generation could command. To speak therefore of 'a self-gratifying oligarchy that held power for its own profit', even with the age of Walpole in mind,[7] is to tender too harsh a judgement. The *ancien regime* in Great Britain always exhibited a certain responsibility and flexibility in that it looked beyond the aristocracy and took account of public demands. The fiscal system did not favour landed property excessively, if it favoured it at all; by the early nineteenth century commercial and industrial property was almost certainly contributing a less than proportionate share of the public revenue. The protection and encouragement of commerce was regarded as one of the chief functions of the state; in this respect the aristocracy assisted the growth of other than landed wealth and helped to promote the challenge to their social and political ascendancy. One might also mention the legal system which was developed and operated during the eighteenth century. The enactment of a penal code which dealt with crimes against property with particular severity redounded to the advantage of the mercantile as much as the agricultural community, and indeed it was not unlikely that the most stalwart opposition to its amelioration came from the former. Perhaps most important of all, the idea of the liberties of the individual was kept alive, so that even when the ruling class was confronted with the spectre of popular revolution it refused to resort to 'arbitrary government'. Undoubtedly the aristocracy created a congenial world for themselves, but it was also in many of its aspects not an uncongenial world for many others. Much to their advantage, Liverpool and his colleagues were the imbibers of a tradition of government which insisted that they exercise power in a national view.

Liverpool's Cabinet slipped the more easily into this tradition because its members were really less the representatives of the landed aristocracy than professional politicians. The only minister with impecable aristocratic credentials was Lord Westmorland who held an earldom bestowed in James I's reign and estates in several counties. Castlereagh and Wellington can be said to have had origins among the substantial Irish gentry because both their families were ennobled in the eighteenth century. Throughout the rest of the Cabinet, as it was both in 1815 and after 1822, the pedigrees were much dowdier. Harrowby and Robinson had had grandfathers who had prospered

[7] Ibid., p. 9.

in the law and in the diplomatic service under Newcastle. Liverpool, Melville and Bathurst had had fathers who had made a lengthy climb into political prominence during the reign of George III. Sidmouth, Canning and Vansittart had associations with the smaller gentry and to a large extent had made their own way in the world. Eldon and Peel (or his father) had thrust themselves out of the 'middling sort' into the political elite. Liverpool's Cabinet attested to the rich variety to be found in the ranks of the British ruling class, how the social order was able to accommodate the pretensions of leading county families, struggling gentry and *nouveaux riche* alike. But the point to be made is that in the case of most of the ministers the social progress of their families had been rapid within recent experience and that that progress had often been accomplished in the service of the state. Their notions of the excellence of the existing order must have been confirmed by their own success and by the society and education to which it admitted them. More important still, the world in which many of them moved from an early age was a political world. The sons of Jenkinson, Dundas, Bathurst and Grantham were in a real sense bred up to politics for they lived in the centre of political society; and the same is to a lesser extent true of the son of Dr Addington who inhabited its fringes. Even those whose families had little or no contact with magnates or ministers had an early start to their political careers —Castlereagh was elected a member of the Irish parliament and Peel of the Westminster parliament on their coming of age, and Canning, without their advantages of local power and wealth, was not far behind them. As a political system aristocracy is much kinder to young men than democracy. This explained above all the impressive amount of political and administrative experience which the Cabinet contained. While most of the ministers had family pasts which connected them with the gentry, often the not too affluent gentry, they were of a different world. The escape to London from the provinces which they or their fathers or grandfathers had made gave them an education in politics and statesmanship which left them something much more than representatives of the landed interest. Though they possessed or sought to possess land, though they retired into the country whenever the business of government permitted it, the appearance was deceiving as to their true character. They indeed were civil servants and politicians who maintained a front as landed gentlemen because these professions had yet to secure a status of their own.

A Cabinet of experience which could be expected to feel its way rather than plough it had undoubted strength when it came to deal with the problems created by the first industrial revolution. At the same time these qualities were no guarantee that it could keep its balance in the swift and turbulent currents which would certainly beset it. That the ministers would bend to them was never in doubt, but whether they would bend far enough remained to be seen. It is not difficult to accept that their pragmatism had definite limits in their affection for the existing order, an affection surely strengthened by success in war, and in some of the attitudes it incorporated. An executive which maintained that in the last resort the task of government remained to it and that its judgement was superior to parliament's or public opinion's would obviously have to make some sacrifices of its independence. One which would have the government do little other than conduct war and diplomacy, regulate trade, administer justice, maintain order and provide finance could find itself facing a demand that it extend its responsibilities. Furthermore, if reform became the price of survival, there was the possibility that in the hands of a government which made a virtue of expediency and had high notions of the justice due existing interests its progress would be too creeping, or appear to be too creeping, to make the rescue. The sort of bureaucracy which existed to put into effect the executive's desires compounded the difficulty. In the localities the unpaid, often indolent, often overworked justices of the peace were still its main representatives. At its centre it was ill-balanced and the more efficient parts were being overworked to the extent that they could barely handle the routine. In 1797, for example, about fourteen-fifteenths of an establishment of 16,000 was devoted to raising the public revenue or supervising its expenditure, while between them the three secretaryships and the Board of Trade employed eighty-one persons.[8] All the major offices were small enough to discourage initiative from

[8] *PP*, 1828, xvi. 531–3.

below, though the increasing burden of administrative and parliamentary business placed upon ministers was in a few places, notably the Treasury, beginning to have an opposite effect.[9] The most recent expansion of the bureaucracy was of a temporary nature because it was the result of war, and no other was likely as long as the public viewed the executive power with suspicion and condemned in particular its inevitable proclivity towards extravagant government. The increase of business in an administrative system whose proportions remained much the same had, without question, led to increased efficiency; but until it was generally understood that new tasks could not be undertaken merely by its continued rationalisation the executive was necessarily handicapped. Whatever will the Cabinet might summon up, a way often might not present itself so easily.

Lord Liverpool's administration, then, would place itself in peril as soon as it lost the goodwill of the public, especially the 'respectable' public, the most powerful force in the constitution. In the circumstances in which it found itself in 1815, the pragmatism, which perhaps came naturally to it out of an aristocracy's constant need to defend privilege, could only be an advantage. Whether by the same token its conservatism would be a disadvantage was a question which did not permit an answer. How radical English society would become depended on any number of obscure factors. It depended on the health of the economy because distress always had the effect of sharpening grievances. It depended on what threats to social order emerged because disorder could be guaranteed to strengthen conservative instincts. It depended on the continued openness of society because social pretensions which were not satisfied could be given a political direction. Old loyalties, old habits of mind could persist in spite of a changing world. In its essence the task of Liverpool and his colleagues was to nurture these to the best of their ability. In an age when the centripetal forces in society were strengthening, they stood forth as the foremost representatives of the old order, and therefore on them fell the greater responsibility to advertise what they believed was its indubitable excellence.

[9] See J. R. Torrance, 'Sir George Harrison and the Growth of Bureaucracy in the early Nineteenth Century', *English Historical Review*, lxxxiii (1968). pp. 52–88.

Chapter One

PEACE AND PARSIMONY

I. The Waterloo Months

Waterloo was a battle which not only won a war but conquered a nation. For most Englishmen it wrote history as they wanted it to be written: it exhibited the Duke of Wellington, so none could deny it, as the greatest captain of the age; it fulfilled Great Britain's destiny, as the most unremitting of Napoleon's enemies, to be the instrument of his final overthrow; it showed 'the firmness, and nerve, and independence of the British soldier, the stamina of his courage . . . which renders our armies invincible, and without which even the transcendant abilities of the Duke of WELLINGTON could not have saved the day. . . .'[1] Europe was served notice that God was on the side of Britannia and that the inestimable blessing of liberty was the foundation of that prosperity and military stamina which had made the nation great. Those with a sense of the past, however, had more cause to wonder at this sudden access of military glory. For never before, at least never since medieval times, had British intervention on the Continent been so successful. In the past, time and time again, the conduct of a land war had been hampered by any number of difficulties, among which the chief probably were obstreperous allies, a defective supply system and the enemy's greater professionalism. So true had this been, even recently, that in the early summer of 1815 while the armies were gathering it would have taken a brave man indeed to venture the prophecy that within three weeks of the first encounter Paris would open her gates to the Allies. Yet happen it did. Napoleon had been destroyed and his empire occupied more or less at one blow, and that a mainly British army had inflicted. Little wonder that the news of Waterloo as it spread over the country touched off rejoicing

[1] *The Times*, 24 June 1815.

after rejoicing. More than a war had been won; the greatness of
the British nation had also to be celebrated.

After victory, of course, it was safe to develop arguments of
its inevitability. But what if there had been defeat instead? what
if the war had lasted not a hundred days but a hundred weeks
or a hundred months? It is as well to ask these questions
because these were the possibilities the government of the day
had to contemplate and which necessarily determined many of
its decisions. Too often Wellington's words that Waterloo was
'a damned nice thing—the nearest run thing you ever saw in
your life' have been allowed to recall the man rather than the
situation,[2] as if victory was certain for the Allies and Napoleon
yielded his supremacy in Europe only after a suitably titanic
struggle. In fact, the British government, like every other
government, learnt the real significance of the battle by slow
degrees. On 20 June London knew that Wellington had sent the
French in headlong retreat from Brussels, but did not know
that he would march into France to meet virtually no resistance.
Some weeks later it was clear that the Allies were conquerors,
but by no means certain that the politicians would be able to
devise a peace settlement generally acceptable. By the end of
the year the plenipotentiaries had reached agreement and
departed from Paris, but not one of them could know that the
Napoleonic menace had been dispelled for ever, that the
Bourbon monarchy would survive another fifteen years or that
they had witnessed the beginning of a long European tranquillity. In short, the limited vision of the present has always to be
acknowledged. Some time after Waterloo Liverpool's government dared not discount the possibility of the war's continuation; and even with the formalities of peacemaking concluded
it could not assume that the peace would last.

The most urgent task the British ministers set themselves,
once it was obvious that France lay at the mercy of the Allies,
was to conserve the financial resources of the state. In 1815 men
to fight a war were not lacking (Great Britain had never had to
resort to conscription), nor was matériel; but when it came to
money—by many reckoned the essential sustenance of war—the
supply seemed likely to dwindle rapidly. While the exact cost of

[2] *Creevey*, p. 236.

the struggle against Revolutionary and Napoleonic France was impossible to calculate, everyone knew that during the last four years of the war the country's investment had reached unprecedented proportions; (figures presented to parliament half a century after the Peace of Paris showed that government expenditure from 1812 to 1815 totalled £550,000,000, an amount surpassing that spent from 1793 to 1796 by over three and a half times).[3] Mostly this huge outlay was seen as draining the country's real strength for the immediate purpose of military victory. In the counsels of government Adam Smith's maxim that defence required the sacrifice of opulence was clearly established. Waging war, the ministers firmly believed, checked rather than contributed to economic growth and therefore was detrimental to the increase of national wealth. War taxation had the effect of discouraging consumption, while war borrowing, by enlarging an alternative field of investment, took money away from trade and industry. Furthermore, a large portion of this revenue and these receipts was spent overseas in aid of allies and to supply the army and navy, with the result that there was a significant export of capital and the exchanges tended to remain permanently adverse to Great Britain. There was little recognition that expenditure abroad could stimulate foreign trade, that home producers could often acquire a measure of protection from foreign rivals, that new markets could be won as much as established markets lost, that war demands could hasten technological innovation and that the expansion of particular industries could contribute to the affluence of at least part of the population. The government, being without elaborate statistical devices to plumb the workings of the economy very deeply, preferred to believe that the country's wealth had increased in spite of war rather than because of it.

Peace, then, after a period of painful adjustment to a new state of things, was expected to accelerate the rate of economic progress and replenish the nation's resources to the extent that Great Britain could once again have power commensurate with her status. It was a conviction of the wastefulness of war which

---

[3] *PP*, 1868–9, xxxv. The figure cited includes money paid out for the reduction of debt as well as for the expense of current services.

made Castlereagh remark in one dispatch that seven years of quiet would be the least recuperation.[4] Of course, signs of a serious depression in the offing in the latter half of 1815 made a lasting peace even more desirable. As long as the energies of the state were directed towards war, leading to heavy taxation, heavy borrowing and heavy overseas spending, distress could only be exacerbated. By asking for money at a time when farmers were struggling to make ends meet with falling prices and merchants were beginning to suffer from the speculative overloading of the Continental market, the government would perform the dubious service of starving parts of the economy of badly needed credit in the interests of national security. Conversely, peace by permitting parsimonious government would positively encourage economic recovery. British capital instead of draining away in Europe would be available for the direct benefit of British enterprise, and as a result the exploitation of the favourable circumstances of peace—reopened markets, free navigation, lower shipping costs—would be that much facilitated. As the ministers saw it in 1815, money in good supply was what the domestic economy needed most, and the best way that they could help to provide it was to reduce the financial demands of government—in effect, the sooner a definitive peace was signed the sooner government could make a worthwhile contribution to the relief of distress and economic progress in general. In this sense the ministers must surely have applauded the opportuneness as much as the military finesse of Wellington and Blücher's swift advance towards Paris following Waterloo. So gloomy was the news from the home front that Vansittart, the Chancellor of the Exchequer, claimed that if Waterloo had not been the victory it was the country would have been hard pressed to foot the bill for a further year of war.[5]

Once victory in France was assured, it was obvious that economising could best begin by attending to expenditure abroad in the form of foreign subsidies and remittances to the army. Such outlay not only aggravated the credit situation at home but also depressed the exchanges by keeping foreign currencies in high demand, and though wholesale reductions were out of the question at this early stage it was felt that the

[4] *Wellington Sup. Desp.*, xi. 138.   [5] *Castlereagh*, xi. 5.

little that could be done should be to give an earnest of measures
to come—the pride of Englishmen that their country was 'the
paymaster of Europe' was equalled by a suspicion that Europe
had an insatiable greed for British gold. Thus in the period
immediately after Waterloo the subsidies to friendly powers,
many of them still being contracted, became one of the administration's foremost concerns. Most of the treaties engaged Great
Britain to pay either until 1 April 1816 or, if peace was signed
before then, until the armies had disbanded themselves, so that
notwithstanding victory in June she was still paying money out
at the end of the year. If paid in full the subsidies were calculated to cost the country in excess of £11,000,000.[6] Concerning
the expense, Castlereagh felt that it was better to be over-
generous rather than niggardly, making the point that, as long
as the other Great Powers kept more men in the field than was
required of them by the Treaty of Vienna and Great Britain
kept fewer, the subsidies were one way in which she could make
an equal contribution and maintain her standing in Europe.
Moreover, bearing in mind the fact that German troops made
up nearly half of the British army at Waterloo, to offend just
some of the German princes would possibly be to place in
jeopardy one of the country's vital military resources. Naturally
the finance ministers—Liverpool and Vansittart—could muster
up little sympathy for this 'European' point of view; with the
war over they saw no need to subsidise armies to march into
France and back again, and in response to or in anticipation of
their remonstrances the Danish corps and the Russian army in
reserve were halted in Germany and the Spanish army turned
back from the French frontier. In the end though, the saving
must have been trivial. The Danes lingered nearly two months
at Bremen—even if they had gone straight home their share of
Great Britain's largesse would not have been much less than it
was—and the Russians decamped only after they had been
promised over £400,000 to meet their expenses. All told, a war
in which the actual fighting lasted no more than a few weeks saw
nearly £7,000,000 paid out in reimbursement of foreign allies.[7]

[6] Ibid., pp. 107–8; *Wellington Sup. Desp.*, xi. 153.
[7] *Castlereagh*, x. 418, 473–4, 477–8, 481–2; xi. 1–3, 44; John M. Sherwig,
*Guineas and Gunpowder: British Foreign Aid in the Wars with France,
1793–1815*, p. 339 and n. 79.

When dealing with its own, the government could expect more attention to its wishes. As usually happens, peace was declared long after the fighting stopped. For over four months the British army, like the others, stood easy while the diplomats at Paris talked themselves into agreement, and in the meantime the Treasury had to accept the delay with the best grace possible as it added up the enormous cost; in July it was over £400,000.[8] Really annoying were reports that the British quartermasters were paying their way, as they had done when they last entered France in 1814. Then the quarrel had been with a man, but now it was with a people, and the government quickly reminded Wellington, needlessly as it turned out, that he should live upon the country like any other conqueror.[9] Once the requisitioning machinery was working properly, Great Britain found that her monthly expenses were cut by over a third.[10]

Heavy remittances abroad, whether payments to the forces or payments on account of foreign loans and subsidies, always did much to place sterling under pressure, and therefore a strong motive for economies in overseas spending was the relief it offered to the pound. The effect of adverse exchanges, of course, was noticed throughout the whole economy. Whenever sterling suffered the country's bullion reserves suffered as well, because the exchange rate for metal was steadier than that for paper and to purchase foreign goods and services became that much more expensive. Furthermore, the Bank of England was strongly tempted to respond to a fall in its reserves by contracting its issues of commercial paper, a move which if followed by other financial houses left large sections of the commercial community seriously incommoded. In 1815 peace was regarded as a fortuitous circumstance which could assist greatly in returning the exchanges to par, thus relieving a deteriorating economic situation. From the outbreak of war British commissaries abroad had mostly paid their way by drawing bills of exchange on London, but towards the end the government began to raise money on the Continent and used it to finance its foreign concerns. With sterling still weak throughout 1815 the same

[8] *Castlereagh*, x. 482.
[9] *Wellington Sup. Desp.*, xi. 23–4, 28; *Wellington Desp.*, xii. 557.
[10] *Castlereagh*, xi. 3.

policy was continued, this time even more assiduously; a clause was written into the new subsidy treaties allowing the powers concerned to draw upon funds in Europe instead of London; full advantage was taken of the credits accumulated on the Continent by renewed trading; and a large part of the issue of a £30,000,000 loan was successfully put up for sale in Hamburg, Amsterdam and other financial centres.[11] Under this protection the exchange rate of the pound continued to improve after its slight setback following Napoleon's sudden return, notwithstanding that at least £12,000,000 was remitted abroad in the course of the year.[12] Keeping roughly in step with the exchanges the Bank of England's bullion reserves also recovered, so that by New Year they were the highest they had been since 1809, cheering news when it was everywhere assumed that the Bank would soon resume cash payments. Of course much of the success was not the government's work; the agricultural depression and the collapse of the export boom had given the exchanges strong assistance, and the Bank was purposely replenishing its stocks of bullion in preparation for a return to the gold standard. But at least the government had helped and not hindered. To its way of thinking the money-raising on the Continent was eminently sensible finance, not only allowing it to let the London market well alone at a time when credit could be put to better use elsewhere but also discouraging a severe contraction, the effects of which did not bear contemplation. Possibly the unconventionality of the operation deserved to be noticed as well; according to Herries, who as Commissary-in-Chief was largely responsible for organising the sale, subscriptions to the loan floated by the government in the financial capitals of Europe represented the 'first successful attempt to raise money on British credit on the Continent for the public service'.[13]

Other than keeping clear of the loan market as much as possible and closely scrutinising foreign expenditure the government could do little to protect trade and agriculture from

[11] Sherwig, p. 342.
[12] Norman J. Silberling, 'Financial and Monetary Policy of Great Britain during the Napoleonic Wars', *Quarterly Journal of Economics*, xxxviii (1924), p. 227 says £11,900,000, but this figure only includes money remitted to foreign powers and the British army in Europe.
[13] Edward Herries, *Memoir of John Charles Herries*, i. 246.

the raw wind of economic circumstance. Admittedly on four
occasions after 1793 exchequer bills had been issued as a form
of loan to help merchants, manufacturers, and in one instance,
West Indian planters through difficult periods, but this time
the government preferred to redeem outstanding bills rather
than issue more. That it could afford to do so needed no
explanation because a handsome sum remained out of the supplies voted by parliament on the outbreak of war. It also happened to be a 'safe and unexceptionable' interference; there was
no superintending commission to appoint, the ministers would
not be bothered by squabbles about who or what should be
assisted, and a generous redemption of bills—the government
depended on them for its ready cash—might be expected to
thaw a channel of supply which was already frozen solid. This
way good turns were done all round. The government gladly
reimbursed the Bank, the largest holder of exchequer bills, in
the expectation that it would return the favour by increasing its
private advances as relief to the pangs of deflation; and the
Bank, always wary of over-extending itself, was grateful to be
repaid, for its advances, both public and private, had only once
before been as high as they were in the second quarter of
1815.[14] Usually reliable in crises of this sort, the directors did
all that the government required of them. For the quarter ended
30 June they had, on average, £13,846,000 in bills and notes
under discount: for that following the amount was nearly
£3,000,000 more.[15]

There was nothing very daring about the government's
tinkering with the economy, but solid and unoriginal finance did
bring results, and no doubt the ministers congratulated themselves on their good work as the exchanges kept improving,
bullion returned and the Bank had money to put to good use.
However, the achievement by itself was not enough to set their
minds at rest. Everything in the last resort depended on what
happened at Paris—whether agreement was reached, and if it
was, whether the peace was likely to last. No one knew better

[14] *Castlereagh*, xi. 6, 24. For a table showing the index number of the
Bank's advances 1793–1822 see E. Victor Morgan, 'Some Aspects of the Bank
Restriction Period, 1797–1821', *Economic History*, iv (1939). 206.

[15] Report on the Bank of England Charter, Appendix, p. 53, *PP*, 1831–2,
vi. 543.

than the Cabinet did that another armed truce—which on looking back was all 1802 and 1814 had been—was a state of affairs which the country would not accept and certainly could not afford. A breathing spell was essential. Indeed, Lord Liverpool wondered how the interest of the debt would be paid if the peacemakers failed or if another war had to be fought in the very near future.[16]

The Cabinet made certain that Castlereagh saw things as they did. There was no need to instruct him on the nation's security. Perhaps there was reason to remind him, for he did not care much for the money side of government, that Great Britain was neither able nor willing to pay a fortune to obtain suitable guarantees. From the beginning some kind of indemnity was insisted on, and once the Great Powers began to think that an army of occupation and counter-fortifications opposing the French frontier were further precautions worth taking, Castlereagh was sent strict instructions that France should be made to pay for both.[17] The government even went so far as to forbid France to borrow her way out of difficulties with British money. Vansittart reacted smartly when he learnt that the French government had the City's ear; Barings were told that a loan raised in London was out of the question, and Castlereagh was quickly briefed with arguments against it in case the French approached him directly.[18] In 1815 the ministers had no scruples about being as ungenerous as this. To them it seemed that France should be punished in some measure for her perfidy and that Great Britain should look first to her own condition; if wealth was the true source of national greatness and the country's finances were in a parlous state, then it was high time that Europe stopped being served with British treasure.

The treaties, signed and sealed on 20 November, bore out Vansittart's contention that his country was 'not making war for conquests, and much less for money'.[19] No more colonies were taken from France, and part of Great Britain's share of the war indemnity—100,000,000 francs—was given to the Dutch to help them fortify their frontier and reduce the chance of another French irruption into the Low Countries. At the same time the

---

[16] *Castlereagh*, x. 476–7.
[18] *Castlereagh*, xi. 22–3.
[17] *Liverpool*, ii. 195, 211.
[19] Ibid., p. 24.

government gave away only what it could comfortably afford. To be sure, the 30,000-strong contingent of the occupying army was not wholly supported by what France was ordered to pay for its upkeep, but the difference was scarcely worth grumbling about. If the troops had been brought home and disbanded there would have been a charge for their half pay and pensions, and this saving alone brought the actual cost down to £195,000 a year. In addition, however, with such a large army just over the Channel, the government felt it was safe to lower the home establishment by 5,000, which saved well over £100,000 more.[20]

The happy event at Paris signalled that it was time for the army and navy to reduce themselves, though of course this could not be done in a moment. When parliament next came together the government was to remind everyone repeatedly that the country was in an intermediate state between peace and war, and because it took time to work out troop movements on a global scale and more time to ship regiments where they were wanted, it was difficult not to agree. India, for example, the most remote station apart from New South Wales, was six months' sailing away for most vessels, but taking account of weeks spent at the Cape resting the men, twice as far for a troop transport. It was about October that the Duke of York, who was Commander-in-Chief, began to ponder the army's commitments. Altogether they made disturbing reading; Ireland had to be reinforced with regulars seeing that the militia could not be kept on duty there indefinitely, 30,000 men had to be left in France, many of the colonial garrisons were in dire need of men through sickness and long neglect, and not a soldier could be withdrawn from India while the Gurkhas remained in arms and when a showdown with the Marathas was imminent.[21] The most unpleasant fact was that once the militia had been disbanded the effective strength of the army was going to be less than adequate. Indeed, there was a grave danger that it would fall far short of a suitable peace establishment if the discharge of

---

[20] *Wellington Sup. Desp.*, xi. 205; undated memorandum, Castlereagh MSS, xxix. 352. According to 'An Account of the Sums received from France in respect of the Pecuniary Indemnity', *PP*, 1823, xiv. 125, £1,269,071 was paid to the army in France 'beyond the Sum received from the French Government', about £400,000 a year.

[21] *Wellington Sup. Desp.*, xi. 204–5.

invalids and short-service men, and reductions generally, were not countered by some vigorous recruiting.[22] There were no Germans for hire, as the princes had their own contingents to raise for service in France.[23] Unless, therefore, the army managed to scoop large numbers of militiamen into its net at the last minute, its embarrassment was almost certain.[24]

A tussle between the politicians and the generals over establishments was perhaps inevitable. The Cabinet, anticipating trouble in parliament if their pruning fell short of expectations, wanted to protect themselves by economising to the utmost;[25] while the Commander-in-Chief, for his part, was just as determined to check this incorrigible political instinct. Of course, all wanted an army equal to its responsibilities, but the Horse Guards could not forget the shambles of 1793 when the nation, finding itself unprepared for war, had embarked on the 'fatal System' and false economy of trying one expedient after another to raise the men it needed. On no account would the Duke of York see it happen again, and understandably so; his life's work had been the army's greater efficiency and he saw no sense in letting all be undone simply to ape the disastrous policy of wholesale reduction which followed the American War. There were sound political arguments, anyway, against going wild with the economist's axe. After the long contest with France the army was at the peak of condition, not lacking admirers on the Continent either; since for the first time in years Great Britain was not written off as a military power by the rest of Europe, the government had a valuable political asset which it was madness to squander lightly. Besides, the Duke continued, economy and efficiency were reconcilable. That the rationalisation of the organisation and administration of the army could be an exercise in economical government was what he had been trying to prove throughout the war, and peace, he assured the ministers, would not be taken as the excuse to lapse into the bad habits of the past.[26] In reply the government said little. Indeed there was

---

[22] Memorandum by the Duke of York, 3 November 1815, Add. MSS. 48427, ff. 117–31.   [23] *Wellington Desp.*, xii. 662, 669.
[24] *Bathurst*, p. 392.   [25] *Wellington Sup. Desp.*, xi. 205.
[26] Memorandum by the Duke of York, 3 November 1815, Add. MSS. 48427, ff. 117–31. This paper referred to another memorandum dated 17 May 1814 where the arugument was explored in more detail. See Sidmouth MSS.

little to say, apart from a reminder that the country had to be given an opportunity to recover from the tremendous exertions of the past two decades. Otherwise a huge army would be kept up for no purpose, for when war next eventuated the means to wage it would be soon exhausted.[27]

The dialogue itself began on a note of sweet reasonableness. In his first memorandum on the subject of establishments the Duke of York agreed to take 5,000 from the force to be kept at home as long as a British army remained near at hand in France, and to garrison the empire with 800 fewer than he had wanted in 1814, even though since then the Ionian Islands had become a new responsibility engaging about 3,000 more troops.[28] Here the ministers found nothing to quarrel about; or if they did they gave no sign of it, inasmuch as Sir Henry Torrens, the military secretary at the Horse Guards, was under the impression that 'some trivial details' were the only difficulty.[29] A fortnight later, however, things had changed completely; the mood of the Cabinet had hardened perceptibly, the Commander-in-Chief's number was no longer acceptable, and Torrens was warning his chief that whatever he shrank from would be done notwithstanding.[30] It was only now that the ministers apprehended that reduction would be a work of months not weeks. The December returns made it quite plain that before a single regiment had been struck off the list the number of effectives did not equal the establishment which the Duke of York had in mind.[31] Obviously, in these circumstances, care had to be taken not to let reduction outpace recruitment, which was bound to be slow so soon after the war and which the law itself hindered by prohibiting drafts from regiment to regiment. Once it was safe to disband, moreover, a further year could elapse, for some troops would have to be brought home from the remotest stations and others sent out—in itself a complex operation, involving the navy as much as the army. When pressed by demands out of the

---

[27] *Bathurst*, p. 399.

[28] Memorandum, 3 November 1815, Add. MSS. 48427, ff. 117–31.

[29] Sir Henry Torrens to Lord Palmerston, 16 December 1815, W.O. 3/610.

[30] Sir Henry Torrens to the Duke of York, 30 December 1815, ibid.

[31] On 25 December 1815 the effective strength of the regular army was 150,591. *PP*, 1816, xii. 419. The Duke of York asked for an establishment of 152,500. Memorandum, 30 December 1815, Add. MSS. 48427, ff. 141–61.

ordinary, an administration barely able to handle the routine had to do what it could in its own good time.

The ministers, then, had to face up to the unpleasant truth that in the current year the army was going to be more expensive than they had bargained on, and, not surprisingly, they began a thorough search for possible economies. Probably they had already resolved to keep the total establishment below 150,000, come what may, and when this mark was overstepped by making the force in France wholly British, it became impossible to shirk a revision any longer.[32] Once at work they did not stop at half measures: Canada and the Cape lost 1,000 men apiece; the West Indies 1,500; and Ireland, despite the very real fears for her future peace and quiet, 5,000. Only one increase was permitted. With the army abroad crying out for reinforcements, and in many cases in urgent need of relief, allowance had to be made for an exceptionally heavy traffic to and from imperial outposts throughout the year. On second thoughts, 8,000, instead of 5,000, were set aside in preparation, though it was by no means a generous provision, this number being merely 1,000 more than what the Commander-in-Chief calculated would ordinarily be required.[33] Still this meanness did enable the ministers to fix the establishment at 147,000, which was roughly the number they had been aiming for.[34] Only the Duke of York remained dissatisfied. As late as February, when discussion of the estimates was in full swing in the House of Commons, he was complaining that insufficient allowance had been made for a proportion of sick and wounded, and that the army at home could have done with 5,000 more men than it had been allocated.[35] But as his own secretary had warned him, the government insisted on having the last say.

The Admiralty was never handled half so roughly. The First Lord, unlike the Commander-in-Chief, held Cabinet rank, so that the navy always knew the government's views at first hand; and because politicians sat alongside professionals on the Board,

[32] 3,000 had to be added to the French establishment. Cf. memoranda, 3 November, 30 December 1815, ibid., ff. 117–31, 141–61.
[33] Memorandum, 18 February 1816, ibid., 38366, ff. 153–8.
[34] Memorandum submitted to the Prince Regent, 18 January 1816, ibid., 48427, ff. 162–4.
[35] Memorandum, 18 February 1816, ibid., 38366, ff. 153–8.

the issue could be fought out there without any need for outside interference. Fortunately a politician was in charge in 1815, one moreover who could be depended on, and the government was able to rest assured that the job would be done with a sufficient ruthlessness. Even if Lord Melville's loyalty had been questionable there would have been less need to check his work, for parliament always had a special affection for the navy and the rest of the country felt the same. Nobody was ready to grudge the so-called bulwark of the nation a certain favouritism, and it more or less got away scot-free while the army was the whipping boy on which any passion for economy spent itself. Nor were naval reductions as irrevocable as the army's. A regiment was disbanded for good, but ships which were not wanted for the moment were laid up with skeleton crews aboard, and provided they were kept in good repair they could be made ready for sea again at fairly short notice. The government knew, then, that if the Admiralty did make the mistake of moth-balling too many ships, it was no great bother to correct it.

The navy completed its post-war stocktaking in December, a full month before the army was finally brought to heel. Forty-four first to fifth-rate ships, which included everything from three-deckers to 36-gun frigates, were to be left in commission and two hundred and sixteen to be laid up, neither figure, of course, taking into account a vast flotilla of smaller craft—sloops, corvettes, bomb ketches and the like.[36] As for the establishment necessary to maintain this fleet, that had to be regulated according to the time it was going to take for ships to be called home and paid off. For the first year of peace the Admiralty intended to ask parliament to vote 33,000 seamen and marines. Thereafter it was hoped that 23,000 would be sufficient.[37] Nor was the exaggeration in numbers more than adequate. By the end of March 1816 there were still twice as many ships in commission as the peace establishment allowed for.[38]

The cost of the army and navy, unavoidably enormous, made

[36] J. W. Crocker, Secretary of the Admiralty, to the Navy Board, 8 December 1815, NLS MSS. 1044, ff. 158–63.

[37] *Hansard*, 1st ser., xxxii. 384.

[38] On 25 March 1816 there were 101 first to fifth-rates in commission and 138 others. *CJ*, lxxi. 672.

it impossible to balance the budget with the permanent taxes alone. The real difficulty was that the income of the consolidated fund was almost wholly devoted to servicing the debt—that is, to paying the interest and the Bank of England its management fee. In 1816 well over £32,000,000 was needed to meet this charge, £29,000,000 for the remaining expenditure;[39] and when a small surplus was all that the permanent taxes could provide, to make ends meet a large sum had to be commanded from somewhere. Usually there were three possibilities worth exploring, though this time, one way and another, the government felt diffident about each of them. The first of these was to raid the sinking fund. By 1815 the fund had been in operation for almost thirty years, and having been designed to accumulate money on the compound interest principle, a hard-pressed Chancellor of the Exchequer was bound to be tempted to help himself to its treasure.[40] Neither could the law, as it stood, stop him, for a clause in the original act expressly allowed the commissioners in charge to lend to the state. But no finance minister had ever plundered the fund, though it was true that once or twice a little money had been inveigled by some devious accountancy. Every government was anxious to have an ever-increasing sinking fund to show off simply because it advertised the state's determination to pay back what it had borrowed, thereby encouraging people to lend more when more was wanted on conveniently favourable terms. Throughout the war the fund was especially useful in this way. At the same time the belief in its intrinsic merit went from strength to strength. No one, or very few, worried about the absurdity of creating debt bearing a higher rate of interest to pay off debt bearing a lower. At least the public credit had remained unshaken and whenever the government had called out for money it had not been slow in coming.

This service seemed no less desirable once the war was brought to an end. After a generation of international turmoil

[39] See the Chancellor of the Exchequer's 'budget speech', 12 February 1816. *Hansard*, 1st ser., xxxii. 376–89.

[40] Briefly, the sinking fund operated thus: each quarter a payment of £250,000 was made out of the consolidated fund to the Commissioners for the Reduction of the National Debt. They used the money to redeem stock, and the dividends which accrued were use to redeem still more.

the government, like everybody else, found it hard to put its faith in a lasting peace, and the sinking fund remained one guarantee that huge sums could be commanded if the worst came to the worst. Except for Hamilton the economist, who in his *Enquiry concerning the National Debt* (1813) argued that a sinking fund was no more efficacious than an annual surplus of revenue, hardly anyone as yet thought there was a better way of paying off the massive debt run up in the last twenty-two years. The faults and failings the sinking fund did have were blamed wholly on the war and not on its own shortcomings. To all appearances, until the war had broken out in 1793 it had worked perfectly, Pitt redeeming £10,000,000 of the 3 per cents in under seven years, and there seemed to be no reason at all why it should work less well, even according to Hamilton's precepts, now that real surpluses were again attainable. Because the nation believed in it the fund had its own justification. If it needed any other the government did not have to look beyond the first few years of peace. For by 1815 the sum at the fund's disposal was approaching an amount equal to one forty-fifth of the total debt, which was when cancellation of the redeemed stock might begin, which was also when 'the accumulations of it will . . . be fairly at the disposal of the public . . . either for the purpose of peace establishment or of reduction of taxes.' [41] The climax of the whole operation, then, lay clearly in sight. To press forward was to arrive in a world of stable expenditure and progressively decreasing public debt. To turn about was to destroy the work of nearly thirty years and a system of proven merit and acceptability.

With the sinking fund the sacred cow of government finance, the alternatives left the ministers for raising money were a loan and continuation of part of the war taxes. To arrange the first was temptingly easy, despite talk that the nation's resources were near exhaustion. If the government advertised fresh stock on the loan market it was sure to sell because the depression had made the money world uncertain and over cautious; many

[41] In January 1815 Lord Liverpool thought this point would be reached in 1819. *Liverpool*, ii. 135. The war upset this calculation. More money was taken from the fund in the course of the year, and as a result on 1 February 1816 the actual sinking fund was slightly less than it had been the year before. *PP*, 1814–15, viii. 228–9, 1816, xi. 228–9.

would seize avidly the opportunity of investment with such security. But not for a moment was this contemplated. It was, so the ministers thought, a shabby trick to play on the country. They assumed, quite unreasonably, that a loan would aggravate the credit shortage, that interest rates would be encouraged to rise and that any money they took for their own use could be put to better service by the private sector. Obviously public spending on a large scale had yet to be recognised as suitable medicine for a deflating economy. Indeed in their ignorance the ministers threatened to do nothing right: if they refused to borrow to make up the deficit in their budget they had perforce to step up taxation, and lighter taxation to encourage heavier private spending was as good a way to ginger the economy as the other. Fortunately for them, they were bound to think twice before they fell back on the alternative of keeping up the war taxes, for they knew from the great furore there had been a year earlier, when they had been ready to use them to wind up the war expenses, that the country would never meekly accept their renewal. In the parliament to come Castlereagh was to chide the people for their 'ignorant impatience of taxation', and although the opposition made sure that he lived to regret the remark, it did sum up the government's dilemma. The people were impatient because they saw no need for war taxes once the war was won. They were ignorant because the government knew its responsibilities better than they did. But the ministers had to go some way to meet popular misconceptions. The question was how far.

A neat way was found out of the difficulty eventually. In the middle of December Vansittart confided his financial plans to Henry Bankes, a prominent independent in the House of Commons, 'the substance of which was an intended reduction of the Property Tax to five per cent, and a small loan of five or six millions.'[42] Most abhorred of all the war taxes, the property tax —more correctly, it was a tax on income—brought in over £14,000,000 in 1815.[43] At the new rate it would bring in half that, so it was by no means an empty gesture to popular feelings. On the other hand, the loan was a happy arrangement as far as the government was concerned. The Bank was asked to make

[42] *Colchester*, ii. 563.　　　[43] *PP*, 1816, xiv. 3.

the advance and the directors cheerfully complied, not least because the ministers had fallen in with their wishes earlier on by promptly reducing the public advances when they had become very uneasy over their amount. This promise of credit tidied everything up. The official letter to the Governor and Deputy-Governor had made the government's point of view clear, that it was 'of the greatest importance to the public interest, to provide for the expenses of the present year with as little pressure as possible upon the Money Market';[44] a small loan from the Bank could do this as no other could. Of course each measure had yet to be sent forward to receive parliament's blessing, and it was no use the government deluding itself that the opposition would stay silent when that moment arrived. Some of the objectionable war taxes remained, borrowing to make ends meet during peace always looked like shoddy finance and until the ministers justified the expenditure item by item there was no saying that either was really necessary. But Vansittart could look parliament straight in the face and say that he had tackled the problem of depression, and tackled it in an unexceptionable way. When it was believed that a shortage of money was the main trouble, to reduce taxes, to keep clear of the loan market and to keep repaying the debt was the right medicine for any government to prescribe.

II. WHIG FURY

There was no need at all for parliament to meet before Christmas, for enough was left over from the generous votes of the previous session, made in anticipation of a longer war, to ensure that the government would not run short of money before the New Year was well in.[45] As long as the negotiations continued at Paris a meeting would only have hampered Castlereagh anyway. More likely than not, parliament would never have checked its language sufficiently, leaving him the awkward job of explaining away the gaffes and gossip emanating from Westminster; and even if it did behave itself there was no saying what might follow if the negotiating parties once got it into their heads that

[44] 16 January 1816, ibid., xiii. 345.
[45] *Castlereagh*, xi. 24.

Great Britain was impatient to bring matters to a conclusion.[46]
Above all though, the government had to bear in mind the effect
of Castlereagh's absence abroad. Even if his fumblings for words
and his famous circumlocutions made him a laughing stock on
occasions, his authority in the Commons was quite beyond
dispute. As Thomas Barnes, soon to become editor of *The
Times*, recorded: '. . . his handsome person, his intelligent and
well-defined countenance, his conciliatory tone, his graceful
manners, his mildness, urbanity, and invincible courtesy,
ensure him popularity and even fondness from the House. . . .
Personal and even political animosity loses daily some of its
rancour, from the influence of that gentleness which never
irritates, and is as slow to be irritated; whose polish makes the
sharpest arrow, which anger can shoot, glide from him harmless,
and whose softness neutralizes the most acrid venom . . . he is
perhaps the greatest favourite, since the time of Lord North, in
an assembly consisting four-fifths of Englishmen.'[47] Nor were
impeccable manners, an even temper and a thick hide his only
parliamentary qualities. His hauteur may have been a sure
armour against the brilliant invective of Brougham and others,
but when aroused he could give back as good as he got with
his own sarcasm, one government man indeed likening him to
a top 'wch. spins best when it is most whipped.'[48] Certainly his
colleagues were of an altogether different calibre. On the last
occasion that Castlereagh had been away, Vansittart, deputising
as leader of the House, had cut a sorry figure, and the rest of the
front bench had been no better. What made matters worse was
that the promising young men, like Peel and Palmerston, had
yet to find their feet in general debate and were virtually speechless except on the business of their own departments.[49] There
was only Castlereagh, in the words of the journalist quoted
earlier, 'to fight the pitched battles with the armies of Whiggism,
or to ward off the desultory attacks from the adventurous
marauders who start up occasionally from all quarters of the

[46] 'You may rely upon me, if I am alive, for the meeting of Parliament,
whenever you may assemble, but for God's sake save us a session before
Christmas if possible. It is prejudicial to us in all shapes.' Castlereagh to
Lord Bathurst, 20 October 1815, *Bathurst*, p. 391.
[47] [Thomas Barnes], *Parliamentary Portraits*, pp. 18–19.
[48] *Hobhouse*, p. 92.   [49] *Castlereagh*, x. 239.

House. . . .'[50] Without him the government depended on sheer
weight of numbers to keep parliament in hand, the sort of control which gave extra force to radical arguments that the
executive used devious arts to manage the legislature into
obedience. Ministers constantly needed to deny the opposition
the honours in debate in order to keep their parliamentary supporters in good heart and to maintain their standing in the
country. By the end of October, once it was clear that Castlereagh would be busy in Paris for another three or four weeks,
the Cabinet arranged a further prorogation to the middle of
January.[51]

The government fully expected financial questions to be to
the fore when parliament did reassemble, especially that of the
property tax. Not two months after Waterloo Lord Liverpool
warned Castlereagh that it would cause much contention,[52] and
on the eve of the meeting of parliament he was just as gloomy,
finding it 'quite impossible to be certain, or even confident of
the issue'. Before an official announcement had even been made,
he noticed, the opposition had been spotted stirring up the
country, organising the petitions and meetings which by now
were their recipe for success after the triumphs over the
Orders-in-Council in 1812 and the war taxes three years later.[53]
A full muster of friends was imperative if this 'Clamour' was
going to be held at bay in the Commons. As it happened,
another item on the parliamentary agenda made a good attendance equally desirable. Lord Liverpool, his ear to the ground
as always, heard early on that the opposition was planning
mischief when the peace treaties were laid before parliament,
and if the contest came to a vote he wanted a solid majority to
show the world that Great Britain refused to find fault with
Castlereagh's work.[54] Probably his reasoning did not stop here
either. Inasmuch as the debate seemed likely to be the first trial

---

[50] *Parliamentary Portraits*, pp. 13–14.
[51] About the middle of October the signing of the treaties was expected to
take place before the end of the month. However, a hitch occurred and it
was not done until 20 November. *Bathurst*, p. 389.
[52] *Castlereagh*, x. 476.
[53] For example, *The Times*, 25 January 1816 included a report from the
Hull Advertiser that several meetings were planned in the West Riding.
[54] Lord Liverpool to Peel, 28 January 1816, Add. MSS. 40181, ff. 66–8.
The letter is printed in *Liverpool*, ii. 251–2, but is wrongly dated 20 January.

of strength in the country's new situation, it had an especial importance. When winning could perhaps put the opposition in its place for the rest of the session, a resounding success became all the dearer.

Castlereagh, as leader of the House of Commons, sent out the customary circular to the government's friends about three weeks before the meeting. It told them what date had been fixed and politely requested their attendance, vaguely going on to say that 'public business of importance will be immediately proceeded on'.[55] The summons was by no means peremptory. Nor could it be until parties consolidated and claimed an allegiance which at this stage many members owed only to themselves. The Irish members whom Castlereagh addressed certainly felt this way. They told Peel, who as Chief Secretary in Dublin had the job of whipping them in, that the note was 'a mere matter of course', and insisted on staying at home to mind other matters unless a more pressing invitation came meanwhile. Hurriedly Peel wrote off to London to find out how things really stood, and, learning from his chief that the opposition was already limbering up, he passed on an urgent plea for support which explained the situation far better than the official circular had done.[56] Perhaps if the government had kept its rank and file better informed in the first place there would have been less recalcitrance. But this again was the curse of politics without strong party associations. The Cabinet invariably led, and hoped that the rest, unorganised, leaderless and loyal to a degree, would follow.

If anything, the party tie in parliament was at this time showing signs of increasing slackness. Such lapse had little to do with the fact that in 1816 a great number of members owed their election to their own resources of rank or wealth, for the unreformed representative system in its setting amidst an hierarchical society had always produced and would always produce 'inevitable parliament men'. Rather the tendency away from party has its explanation in the content of the political debate. In the eighteenth and early nineteenth centuries, as long as the

[55] The circular was dated 11 January. A copy is to be found in *The Times*, 18 January 1816.

[56] *Liverpool*, ii. 249–50; circular letters, Peel to various Irish M.P.s, 30 January 1816, Add. MSS. 40290, f. 52.

political supremacy of the aristocracy remained largely unchallenged, the progress of party inside and outside the legislature mostly depended on the seriousness of the disagreements
affecting the old governing class. As Burke remarked: 'when
bad men combine, the good must associate'. Whenever genuine
issues emerged, members of parliament, indeed the political
nation as a whole, responded to the need to propound and
defend those views which seemed fundamental. On the other
hand, when the conflict of principle became muted or obscured
the opposite process occurred, with a marked deterioration of
discipline and organisation on either side. It was in parliament
that this ebb and flow was most readily recorded; a full tide of
party feeling saw few members willing to profess independence
an honourable course and the Westminster duty performed with
a new conscientiousness, while its turn was signified by renun-
ciations of 'thick and thin' support which found their practical
expression in lackadaisical attendance and increasingly erratic
voting.

The first fifteen years of the nineteenth century were years
when the passionate exchanges of the 1790s between 'Jacobins'
and 'Patriots' were rapidly forgotten in order to make a national
resistance against Napoleonic France. War, as is so often the
case, left much of the leaven out of politics; not only was it
necessarily the central preoccupation of the state, pushing other
matters to one side for the duration, but because it was seen as
a patriotic endeavour it also forced the political opposition into
timid and compromising courses. The result was that over the
period of a decade or more the contest for power lost much of
its earlier keenness and indeed became subdued to the point
where the area of agreement between government and opposition exceeded the area of dispute. Certainly concerns less major
than the war did little to provoke fresh quarrels or extend old
ones. The Whigs shared with their adversaries a dread of
popular protest, violent or non-violent; no administration,
whatever its hue, faltered in its pursuit of economical government or failed to take seriously its duty to protect and regulate
trade; and even Catholic emancipation and parliamentary
reform were hardly party issues, for stalwart supporters of the
first were found on both sides and the Whigs were far from

united on the second. By 1816, in fact, administration and
opposition were divided by the past rather than by the present,
by history rather than by policy. Where the Whigs still considered themselves to be 'friends of the people' in the sense of
being sympathetic to popular needs and aspirations, the Tories
held together out of fear of the consequences of 'popular
government'. Both were ready to admit the increased power of
the people and both wanted the minimal disturbance of the
traditional society and its institutions. But while one party was
determined to avoid change at the dictate of public opinion the
other saw in too great a resistance to popular pressures the
unnecessary jeopardising of stability and order; the Whigs
maintained themselves on what their opponents would not do,
the Tories on what the Whigs might do should they once be
given the opportunity. All this meant that by the time Liverpool's government came to tackle the problems of peace most
members of parliament professed a party allegiance, but many
among them paraded it only on those few occasions when the
administration's existence was manifestly at stake. Ordinarily,
on the routine business of the House of Commons and on a
multitude of issues, attendance and voting among the rank and
file of either party ranged from stalwart support to support
little more reliable than that offered by the relatively small body
of genuine independents. It was the casualness and sporadic
recalcitrance of many of the government's followers which
explains the ministers' perennial concern for their parliamentary
position. Circular letters sent out before the commencement of
the session were merely one device designed to cope with the
indiscipline resulting when parties had cohering principles which
were largely negative.

The attendance at Westminster on the opening day of the
first session of the peace (1 February 1816) turned out to be
little better than usual. In particular, the Irish reported for duty
sadly under strength, and in fact still were lacking in numbers
two months afterwards.[57] However, the ministers made no complaints. Any annoyance or disappointment they may have felt
must have been checked at once by the heartening sight of the
opposition in renewed disarray. As long as the war had lasted

[57] Peel to William Gregory, 27 March 1816, ibid., ff. 173–4.

and as patriotic ardour had gathered heat the Whigs had
occupied an uneasy perch. Out of honour they had had to make
some show of opposition, yet every act had seen them run the
risk of being stamped as averse to a conflict everyone else
thoroughly approved and admirers of a man, Bonaparte, who
was a European abomination. In addition, their partnership
with Lord Grenville and his small following had gone from bad
to worse. With the Grenvilles highly reluctant critics of the war,
and distinctly uncomfortable in the company of parliamentary
reformers like Whitbread, they and the Whigs had really pulled
together only when Catholic emancipation had come up for
discussion, both holding themselves irrevocably committed on
this issue. In 1816, though, all this lay in the past. Whatever the
record of incompatibility the government could not count on it
lasting indefinitely. The war largely explained the Whigs'
discomfiture. With peace there was no reason why they could
not make friends with the people again, and also enter into a
more cordial relationship with the Grenvilles. A rumour, therefore, of angry words and lost tempers at Brooks's just before
parliament met was sweet music indeed for the government's
ear, and sweeter still when the story proved to have some foundation. Romilly and others, impatient of what Brougham called
'half measures' and 'temporising plans', bludgeoned the leadership against its better judgement into trying an amendment when
the Address was brought up on the first day,[58] only to have the
Grenvilles hastening to advertise their complete dissociation.
Lord Grenville refused at once to commit himself or his friends,
being little inclined, he said, if he were in the Commons 'to vote
for an amendment at the close of a debate in which more than
half of the principles & opinions urged in its support would
probably be much more repugnant to mine than anything said
by its adversaries'.[59] His brother had a similar message for
Tierney, the acting leader of the opposition, telling him that he
doubted 'whether any amendment could be framed that would
not give a stronger appearance of resistance . . . than our friends
would or could concur in'.[60] As for Charles Williams-Wynn, the

[58] *Fortescue*, x. 412; *Creevey*, p. 247.
[59] Lord Grenville to Charles Williams-Wynn, 24 January 1816, Coed-y-
maen MSS.   [60] *Fortescue*, x. 412.

leader of their little party in the Commons, he ignored a summons from 'the anonymous Gentlemen who in Ponsonby's absence have taken upon themselves the office of Leaders', and remained at his estate in faraway Wales.[61]

The news that all was not well in the opposition's house was soon known of course. Huskisson kept Canning in his Portuguese exile fully informed, though to account for the puzzling absence of the party leaders he did a little embroidering of his own:

> The Opposition, I understand, are much divided; and in private not very sparing of their abuse of one another, which is not the best way to heal their dissensions. In public they still manage to keep up, tho' rather awkwardly, an appearance of cordiality and union. Grey is not come to Town. It is given out that He is ill— I believe He is sulky. Ponsonby had called a Meeting at his House for the 31st of last Month. The Whigs went according to Summons; but their Leader was not arrived, nor is He yet come. He too is said to be ill. I fancy He has caught Grey's Complaint.[62]

That matters were as bad as they looked became obvious when the opposition lined up to fire off its first volley at the government. The ministers deliberately made the Prince Regent's Speech as uncontroversial as possible, 'leaving it open to all who voted in its favour', so Lord Liverpool explained, 'to exercise a judgement, and to form an opinion more deliberately upon the details, when they are supplied from the offices of government'. All that was asked of parliament was 'a general congratulation on the restoration of peace', which was exactly what the Grenvilles thought should be the sum of the first day's business.[63] However, the opposition hotheads would not be reined in by their leaders. According to plan the party put forward an amendment in the House of Commons when the Address was moved; but 'the most considerable Members' intended to do no more than this, mindful as they were of the poor attendance on their side of the House and that the Grenvilles would never help out if it came to a division. When Tierney got up to speak he

[61] Charles Williams-Wynn to Lord Grenville, 27 January 1816, Coed-y-maen MSS.
[62] Huskisson to Canning, 6 February 1816, Canning MSS. Grey was ill and family concerns detained Ponsonby in Ireland.
[63] *Fortescue*, x. 412; *Hansard*, 1st ser., xxxii. 12.

declined a contest, which was the signal for a general exodus as
members from both sides rushed off home for an early supper.
Then came disaster. Hardly had he sat down before one of his
back benchers was on his feet calling for the division he had
just renounced, and to keep up some semblance of party unity
he ate his words without a murmur and trooped into the lobby
with a handful of diehards where they went down in defeat by
90 votes to 23.[64] It was hard for the Whigs to wring a drop of
consolation from this performance. Apart from the débâcle at
the end, when even the amendment's mover and seconder could
not be found, the Grenvilles had deserted them, there had been
annoying defections—among them Lord Milton, Fitzwilliam's
heir—and, most provoking of all, except for Vansittart and
Castlereagh, not one official man had bothered to open his
mouth. 'It was bad enough', wrote Tierney musing on his
party's disarray, 'to have brought up many from the country
who when they came into the house were told there would be
no division, but it made it a good deal worse when, after they
were gone . . . they found that one had taken place.'[65]

Yet the debate, rout though it had been, did warn the government to be careful in one respect. The Whig amendment sought
to pledge the House to undertake 'a careful revisal of our
Establishments, Civil and Military, with a view to such an
immediate reduction of the same as may be required by the
principles of a rigid economy, and by a due regard to the
Liberties of the Subject'.[66] Clearly the opposition, at least for
the first part of the session, intended to concentrate the fire of
its main armament on the old bogey of ministerial extravagance.
Indeed any doubts the ministers may have retained on this
score must have been removed by what their adversaries gave
out directly. When the news that the property tax would be
continued was squeezed out of Vansittart by Lord John Russell,

---

[64] *Hansard*, 1st ser., xxxii. 17–63; *Memoirs of the Life of Sir Samuel Romilly*
iii. 213–14. Of course the Grenvilles chuckled at the Whigs' discomfiture:
' . . . the final division after Tierney had announced that none would take
place is a good illustration of the degree of discipline & tactick which may be
expected from that party during the present Session. . . .' Charles Williams-
Wynn to Lord Grenville, 5 February 1816, Coed-y-maen MSS.

[65] Tierney to Lord Grey, 2 February 1816, Grey MSS., Prior's Kitchen,
Durham, quoted in Austin Mitchell, *The Whigs in Opposition*, 1815–30, p. 90.

[66] *CJ*, lxxi. 5.

Brougham at once asked the country for a repeat performance
of the petitioning so successful the year before. In the same hour
Tierney urged the House not to vote a penny until some idea
had been given of what would be spent *in toto*, in case the
government got an amount piecemeal which parliament would
have forbidden had it known better, and Coke, the member for
Norfolk, threatened a motion on the malt excise if the ministers
did not come to their senses and grant a generous moderation.[67]

The Whigs knew that here at long last there was promise of
a passage to office and power. There was no better cause than
economy and retrenchment for them to champion. The war was
over so that the government could neither use it as an excuse
nor as a distraction. The depression seemed to be worsening so
that the work brooked no delay. It was a cause sure to bring
them popularity and a chance of victory at Westminster, when
they could expect neither, for the moment anyway, from
Catholic emancipation and parliamentary reform. The point
was that the country, including the 'respectable' classes, continued to be convinced that the Crown, if left to itself, would
never embark on sufficiently frugal government. Partly, of
course, the providers of public money had a natural desire to see
it spent parsimoniously, but there was also a deep-rooted
assumption that the king's ministers would always be guilty of
more than casual extravagance. By systematic misappropriation
of the public revenues, it was believed, politicians in office were
able to strengthen their hold on power and its perquisites; an
over-generous civil list and a large standing army was a guarantee of the sovereign's goodwill, while large establishments
generally, together with a lavish bestowal of pensions, consolidated and extended electoral and parliamentary support. It
followed that somehow the executive had to be compelled into
better courses. In the eighteenth century the proponents of
ministerial perfidy had concentrated on ministerial usurpation
of the patronage belonging to the Crown; through placemen and
pensioners, 'wicked ministers' or 'wicked cabals' attempted to
reduce the legislature to such servility that it became unresponsive to popular complaint and incapable of performing its
constitutional function of checking and regulating the executive

[67] *Hansard*, 1st ser., xxxii. 33, 36, 39–40, 55, 59.

power. By the early nineteenth century, after a generation of steady economical reform, these fears were rendered quite ridiculous. Only the 'irrational part' of public opinion continued to insist that the influence of the Crown ought to be diminished for parliament to become properly independent. The 'rational public' accepted that the executive needed to be represented in the legislature to the extent that official business could be managed and the government's policy expounded and defended. Its complaint was of a different character, being concerned less with the power of the Crown than with the power of the people. By making uneconomical administration their interest what the ministers were doing was posing a threat to the constitutional balance from a different direction, inasmuch as distress, grievance and disorder followed in logical succession from higher taxation. Bearing in mind the immense war debt which the country in straitened circumstances had to support, and also the fact that the roots of popular radicalism had merely shrivelled and not disappeared, the situation in 1816 called for particular caution. Should parliament fail to brake adequately the excesses of the ministers there was every reason for the country to recall it to its duty in the time-honoured way of petitions. It was the Whigs who saw themselves able to assist in this service. They wanted to act as the spokesmen of that 'intelligent and independent portion of the community' which had an inherent distrust of the executive; and they were quick to appreciate that the issue of economy was one which could be regularly exploited and which would place the ministers constantly on the defensive. For the unreformed parliament of the early nineteenth century invariably attempted some appeasement of fractious public opinion, as events after 1816 were to show, even if it emanated from the 'inferior sort'. In turn, just as invariably the executive strove to come to terms with the fears and prepossessions of the legislature. Altogether the Whigs knew well what they were about. A bold showing on their part would make it difficult indeed for the government to avoid some appearance of dancing to their tune.

The first occasion on which the opposition could really take the government to task for extravagance was when the House of Commons went into committee of supply over the army estimates. According to the programme which the ministers had sketched out this was to take place immediately after the peace treaties were voted on 15 February.[68] Before then, however, Vansittart, a trifle grudgingly because 'the practice was unusual', had given the House a rough resume of the budget and the military establishment in response to a pert suggestion of Tierney's on the first day,[69] and the opposition members presumably joined battle well-armed with the facts and figures they had had a fortnight to pore over. The game they had in mind was an unusual one. At this juncture, it seemed that the ministers intended to foist the property tax on the country before it could speak its objections. On 26 February Vansittart suddenly announced that he would put the question to the House in two days' time, and the opposition was only able to wring a further two days' grace out of him before the evening was done.[70] This was the smallest of mercies. For the great flood of petitions which the Whigs were counting on was not yet in full spate. The day on which Vansittart made his surprise announcement only about fifty lay on the table in front of the Speaker's chair. Three weeks later it was to groan under the weight of four hundred. Somehow precious time had to be won, and, as it was the invariable practice not to go into committee of ways and means until a supply had been voted,[71] a filibuster over the army estimates was the line of attack to be preferred above all others. Yet to obstruct the king's service by obstructing parliamentary business was unusual because for a century oppositions had been doing their utmost to escape from the odious imputations of irresponsibility and disloyalty which attached to them. The difference this time was that the Whigs could easily claim that they were acting on behalf of the country. Most of the petitions either implied or stated directly that a large army and the property tax were one and the same evil. As the inhabitants of one ward in the City declared: '. . . this obnoxious and inquisitorial Tax can only be proposed, with a view of

---

[68] *Liverpool*, ii. 251.

[69] *Hansard*, 1st ser., xxxii. 376–89. Castlereagh promised such a statement on 5 February. Ibid., 311.

[70] Ibid., 834–5.

[71] John Hatsell, *Precedents of Proceedings in the House of Commons*, iii. 196–7. See also *Hansard*, 1st ser., xxxiii. 24.

maintaining an enormous Military Establishment in a time of
profound Peace, a measure hostile to the spirit of the *British*
Constitution, and highly injurious to the best interests of
society.'[72] The Whigs felt that a sufficient justification of their
conduct would be to act in a popular cause, a stand which would
force the government into the difficult argument that its per-
ceptiveness was far ahead of the country's. At the same time the
tactics of deliberate delay had a particular suitability. With their
decided superiority of talent the opposition could look forward
to good sport, certain as they were that the wretchedly inarticu-
late ministers had no hope of out-talking them.

It was on 26 February that Vansittart moved to refer the
army estimates to the committee of supply. Usually the occasion
was uneventful, a formality quickly passed by. That the country
should have a standing army was never arguable, and any
difference there was over numbers could be thrashed out best
in the question and answer of the committee proceeding and
later in debate when the report was brought up—if there happened to be dissentients who wished to go as far as this. Thus
as soon as Vansittart made his motion and the opposition rose
up in anger it became obvious what their game was. They were
not against a standing army because that was nonsense. They
were not demanding fresh estimates because that had no point
when the House of Commons could vote what money it
pleased.[73] They were playing for time by pretending 'that his
majesty's ministers recommended a system, which, if it did not
produce an immediate military despotism, had a tendency to a
state of things of which a military despotism must be the final
result . . . that because the proposed measures appeared to
them to be in their nature unconstitutional, they ought not to
be submitted for a moment to the committee for investigation'.[74]
As a result, for three days the rest of the House had to sit back
and listen to a tiresome harangue about how standing armies in
peacetime had been an abhorrence in the good old days of
William III, and how large ones assisted the Crown in its

[72] Petition of the Inhabitants of Farringdon Within, *CJ*, lxxxi. 95.
[73] However, if the government had been defeated, the House would have
addressed the Crown for new estimates. But this was unprecedented.
[74] The Master of the Mint, a Cabinet Minister, summarising the opposition's argument in the debate. *Hansard*, 1st ser., xxxii. 997

nefarious work of sapping the independence of the Commons while instilling into the people those bad habits of 'military insubordination' intolerable in a free country.[75]

Nevertheless, when all was said and done, the opposition came out of the debate very well indeed. The motion on the property tax had to be put off for five and later ten days, a delay which suited them admirably;[76] and just as pleasing was the government's poor showing both on the floor and in the lobbies. Except for the first night, when he was in the House but never spoke, Castlereagh remained at home sick in bed,[77] which left his side of the House to make do with a string of second-rate speakers and Vansittart's incompetent generalship. Up to the last night the government did not fare too badly. Lord Palmerston, never straying far from the facts and figures he had at his finger-tips as Secretary-at-War, made a good speech which did much to kill the notion that the army should be content with the establishment of 1792. Peel followed him the next day with a lengthy *exposé* of Ireland's critical state and made out an excellent case for a garrison of 25,000 regulars while about it. But after this fine start the government failed to hold its own. On the last night the opposition dominated proceedings by holding the floor for three-quarters of the time and by regaling the House with a succession of speeches from such capable performers as Lord Folkestone, Mackintosh, Burdett and Tierney. It fell to Vansittart as acting leader to sum up on behalf of the government and cut the Whigs down to size. In attempting it, so Peel reported, he 'made himself ridiculous'. He was too apologetic about going over the same ground twice to keep the House from getting restless, and asides about the produce of taxes and the sorry plight of midshipmen on half pay only made matters worse. That night, surely, Castlereagh was sadly missed. To cap a dismal performance the division shamed the government still further. The opposition 'divided very strong', with 121 votes against 241, over forty more than they had collected the week before on the peace treaties and as good a minority as they had made throughout the whole of the previous session. Economy was obviously a banner under

[75] Ibid., 845, 857–8, 860–1, 963–72, 988.
[76] That is, until 11 March. Ibid., 1051, 1060.   [77] *George IV*, ii. 150.

which radical Whigs, conservative Whigs, the Grenvilles and friendly country gentlemen would march happily together.[78]

In the committee the government could expect the going to be just as hard, if not harder. The procedure there allowed a member to speak more than once on a question if he chose, and this gave the opposition ample opportunities for more time-wasting and also for a thorough interrogation of the ministers. Nor was there anything to stop them from insisting on voting the estimates item by item, though during the war, partly in the interests of security, the practice had grown up of pro-posing a single vote to cover every branch of the army at home and abroad.[79] But whatever procedural tricks the opposition might try to pull off, it was the ugly mood the more independent members were in that most worried the ministers. They had one indication that all was not well at the end of the debate on 28 February when Stuart-Wortley, a backbencher of some stature, commended Tierney for a thought-provoking speech and went on to remind the government 'that the time for economy was come', as if hitherto its indifference had fooled nobody.[80] Clearly it was an admonition, and one which the ministers did not dare take lightly. If Stuart-Wortley and his friends thought so badly of them, a majority could no longer be taken for granted; and the possibility of defeat brought any number of unpleasant consequences—the worst was their over-throw—readily to mind. It was a vital moment. What the government needed most from the committee, especially when the session was young and economical questions so frequent as to threaten it with almost constant embarrassment, was a con-vincing exhibition of its parliamentary superiority.

The first vote which came before the committee of supply had nothing to do with money. The Mutiny Act pre-supposed a standing army, and the technicality had to be observed that until the House of Commons took formal cognizance of one by passing the establishment its renewal could never be enacted. A question of establishment was of course a question of num-bers, but in explaining their arithmetic—in saying what troops

[78] *Hansard*, 1st ser., xxxii. 843–74, 909–32, 955–1017; Peel to Lord Whitworth, 27, 28, 29 February 1816, Add. MSS. 40290, ff. 106–111.
[79] *Hansard*, 1st ser., xxxiii. 134.   [80] Ibid., xxxii. 1016–17.

were needed where—the ministers invariably found themselves defending their foreign commitments, colonial policy and much more besides.[81] It was an excellent chance for members to peer into many different corners and the Whigs might well have chosen to reserve their fire until this moment. That they did not was less a misjudgement than a shrewd appraisal of where their real strength lay, for in the committee, while the opposition could use delaying tactics, the government had opportunities for answering back which it never had in formal debate and could get down to details its adversaries knew nothing about.

As it happened, the 'country gentlemen' saved the Whigs the bother of having to repeat themselves. No sooner had Lord Palmerston moved the establishment than Bankes stood up to give the government a severe basting; and when he sat down Stuart-Wortley and Wilberforce, possibly by prior arrangement, were quick to follow his lead. Why, they asked, should the country depart from the old policy of a small army and a large navy when the ministers boasted each day that the Paris treaties guaranteed lasting peace in Europe? Why trouble about the land forces when supremacy at sea made it impossible for the colonies to come to any harm if the worst did happen? Why ape the Continental habit of keeping up a large standing army as a showpiece when it would only tempt Great Britain to meddle where she need not? Why not disarm since neither danger nor disadvantage could come of it? 'We had no enemies to fear abroad,' Bankes was reported to have concluded, 'but we had two great enemies at home—a national debt, and a most improvident expenditure. Let those be kept down, and the country would be saved. If that were not done, years of peace would not invigorate us, and on the breaking out of any new war we should be in a state, not of strength, but of exhaustion.'[82]

These prejudices of isolation and economy had long been the ordinary sentiments of the House of Commons but to hear them articulated as plainly as this was an unsettling experience for

---

[81] See Castlereagh's comment that such a question 'branched out into discussions so multifarious in their bearings, so mixed up with all the relations of the country. . . . ' Ibid., 1096-7.   [82] Ibid., 1091-6.

any front bench. The fact that Castlereagh, newly risen from a sick bed and still unwell, got up to answer Bankes showed how seriously the government viewed the situation, for usually he spared himself to deal with opposition giants like Tierney and Brougham. His speech on this occasion, together with another which closed the discussion two nights later, almost certainly saved his side from defeat or at best a marginal victory. As always he seemed to be prompted into a good performance by a hostile audience. He never made superbly eloquent speeches. He sought to inform rather than to delight, and happily he had the knack of making it an interesting exercise, being content to convey a few plain truths to the House and leave it at that. Now he took pains to point out that the estimates before it 'were the intermediate estimates between a state of war and peace', which left members perfectly free to take a fresh look at the position in a year's time when a permanent peace establishment could be decided. He scorned the idea, implied if not uttered, that Pitt could have done better had he been in charge. There could be no going back to 1792 because since then Great Britain had found herself a dozen new colonies and also had to meet a charge for half-pay and pensions amounting to little less than the total cost of the army in that year. Even if she made do with a third less troops, as Bankes wished, the saving would not nearly correspond thanks to this 'dead expense'. The figure for the establishment was an exaggeration anyway, in so far as what was an army of 99,000 on paper was vastly smaller in fact.[83] Castlereagh in this vein hounded the 'country gentlemen' from their attitude of penny-wise and pound-foolish, forcing them to acknowledge that the government knew best what the national interest demanded. Only Bankes, Stuart-Wortley and a few others remained impenitent enough to provoke a division, and though the opposition joined them in full array the ministers made good their ground with a majority of 72. Further encouragement came two days afterwards (8 March) when the report was brought up. This time a majority of 68 reaffirmed that the House was with them, Wilberforce talking in vain about how bayonets threatened the constitution and 'military habits' the country's morals.[84]

[83] Ibid., 1096–1109, 1257–63.   [84] Ibid., xxxiii. 99–102.

Even so, the government hardly romped home. Majorities of about 70 left much to be desired, as Castlereagh's reports to the Prince Regent at Brighton did not disguise. While he described the division of 28 February on the question of referring the estimates to the committee as 'a good one', he was sorry that the muster of barely 200 votes in support of the establishment a week later was 'not more considerable', a disappointment Peel too did not hide when writing to his chief in Ireland. As for the performance on 8 March when the report was brought up, the figures spoke for themselves; 190 in the government lobby and a majority of 68 indicated the persistence and strength of the feeling against the government.[85] Perhaps the ministers should have rejoiced to get off so lightly, but Huskisson interestingly hinted why a celebration was out of place. The official interest in the House of Commons could be counted on to contribute about 60 votes in an important division, and a majority roughly equalling that number was to be regretted, conveying as it did an impression that the government had used the Crown's influence to override the judgement of the free and independent part.[86] Times had changed. In Walpole's day no minister had been ashamed to parade a great army of placemen to get the king's business done. Now the government preferred to win by merit rather than by manipulation. Nearly forty years of reform propaganda had given influence an odium it could never shake off and the ministers hated to appear to make decisive use of it.

By the time the establishment was voted, the government's parliamentary timetable was again hopelessly out of date. What had been rushed through in two nights during the war years had already taken six and only a preliminary vote had been dealt with, which left Castlereagh exclaiming that 'the history of Parliament does not furnish an instance of so protracted and determined an opposition to the Army estimates'.[87] All too clearly the property tax could no longer be proposed on 11 March, though the ministers needed no reminding that

[85] *George IV*, ii. 150, 154, 155; Peel to Lord Whitworth, 7 March 1816, Add. MSS. 40290, ff. 125–6.

[86] Huskisson to Canning, 13 March 1816, Canning MSS. See also *Hansard* 1st ser., xxxv. 283.

[87] *George IV*, ii. 156.

precious parliamentary time was fast running out. On 5 April the authorising act expired and three weeks left them little time to get fresh legislation through if the opposition, as was more than likely, chose to harass it to the limit of their power. In the same way other important business was also being jeopardised. Easter, when a good many members went home and stayed there, was only a month away, and because Whig morale was high it was likely that the government would suffer most from the thinner attendance after the holiday. Not that the ministers faced actual defeat. It was simply that important measures brought forward too late were unlikely to pass through the House attended by the plumpish majorities any administration loved to parade, and for this reason alone the Cabinet may have begun to regret that parliament had not been called back into session a fortnight earlier. Certainly Castlereagh and Vansittart postponed their motion on the property tax for yet another week only because they had to.[88]

Of course money had yet to be voted for the army, and here the opposition could be as great a nuisance as they had been all along if they insisted on toiling through the estimates item by item. As soon as Williams-Wynn gave formal notice that he would move an instruction to the committee to consider the charge for the army under nine separate heads, the government knew that they were planning mischief of this sort. When the House came to decide the matter Lord Palmerston to temporise suggested three votes, while Castlereagh chimed in with a reminder that 'local inquiries' were an unprofitable and uninteresting way to occupy parliament's valuable time. However, the opposition were determined to go the whole distance. Specific deductions such as they had in mind, they said, required specific votes. Only at the last minute, after strangers had been ordered to withdraw, did Castlereagh concede the point,[89] no doubt to avoid the appearance of having something to hide and also in the hope of wearing the opposition out quickly by beating them as often as they brought a question forward. As it turned out, nothing untoward occurred. The opposition soon did tire of a game they seemed to have no

[88] *Hansard*, 1st ser., xxxiii. 132–3.
[89] *George IV*, ii. 155; *Hansard*, 1st ser., xxxiii. 134–5.

chance of winning. On the first night (11 March) they pressed
three divisions and lost them all fairly convincingly. On the
next (13 March) they were no longer game for anything.
Williams-Wynn while on his feet despaired of ever breaking
the ministerial majority and over twenty votes were hurried
through without the House being cleared once. Indeed shortly
after these resolutions had been reported and voted, the Whigs
formally announced their surrender. A few brave words from
Tierney, deploring 'defiance of the sense of the House and the
Country', wound up ten nights of bitter though often tedious
altercation.[90]

Not surprisingly, the opposition took their defeat very much
to heart. They knew they were right to take up the cause of
economy and were deeply disappointed that the government
had not been run harder when for the first time for years the
advantage had lain with them. So many tricks in the parliamentary book had been tried, and yet, as Tierney remarked,
not a farthing had been struck off the estimates in consequence.[91] Their only consolation—and word probably did get
around sooner or later—had to be that the government too was
mulling over the experience. For, while the House itself had
been unable to force any alteration of the estimates, the ministers, in the intervals between sittings, had furiously amended
the figures which they had first proffered. As some must have
realised, such fiddling was unlikely to be forgotten in a moment.
After repeated statements from the government that the estimates represented the greatest possible saving, people were
bound to think dark thoughts when the ministers under
pressure surrendered an additional £340,000;[92] and it was only

[90] Ibid., 138–55, 247–54, 384–8.
[91] Ibid., 387.
[92] This figure is arrived at by comparing the estimates with the sums voted.
The reductions only applied to the regimental establishments. i.e.

	Estimate (£)	Vote (£)
Household Troops	385,276	385,276
Dragoon Guards and Dragoons in Great Britain, Royal Waggon Train		333,693
Infantry in Great Britain	3,588,752	514,288
Infantry and Cavalry abroad		1,539,707
Cavalry in Ireland		142,872
Infantry in Ireland		718,188
	3,974,028	3,634,024

to be expected that the opposition, without taking exception to the reductions themselves, would make out a serious charge of double-dealing and inconveniently press it when a question of economy next arose. The net effect of what had been done was to nourish the popular impression of ministerial extravagance and perfidy. Huskisson certainly thought the move a clumsy one, calling it 'a concession which comes rather awkwardly after the general assurance in the Speech that the utmost economy had been attended to in all the Estimates. . . .'[93] But the truth was that the ministers were afraid, not dishonest. Although they had anticipated trouble, parliament's earnestness over expenditure and establishments surprised them by its vehemence, and, rightly or wrongly, they refused to take too high a view of the executive's responsibility to the legislature. At the bottom of it all lay the lack of communication between the ministers and those who sat behind them. The years of Whig eclipse, perhaps the emphasis the war had given to ministerial authority in parliament, had produced a complacency in official circles which at its worst threatened to become an arrogance. Ministers came to the House and more or less expected their supporters to take them at their word. As one backbencher of the period remarked: '. . . men in office . . . hold cheap the support of any man who will not go every length with them. Great men want adherents; passive obedience is the only qualification they desire in friends.' He added: 'For my own part I will retain the liberty to make my bow and retire when I please.'[94] In the early days of the session of 1816, when the 'great men' complained to the Prince Regent of 'unprecedented difficulties . . . in all financial discussions',[95] they were learning afresh that the party they headed was held together more by tradition and sentiment than by personality or particular measures. Many who counted themselves their followers were convinced that the independent assessment of the actions and propositions of ministers was the path of honour and duty for a member of parliament. Inevitably there was the constant prospect of an exchange with adminis-

---

[93] Huskisson to Canning, 13 March 1816, Canning MSS.
[94] 'Extracts from Lord Hatherton's Diary' (ed. A. Aspinall), *Parliamentary Affairs*, xvii. (1963–4). 16.　　　　[95] *George IV*, ii. 158.

trations which placed great value on their own knowledge and experience as 'more complete'. Indeed after 1815 a relationship increasingly abrasive seemed to be presaged. The end of the war together with the growing power of public opinion could be expected to render opposition from any quarter less diffident; while the increase of parliamentary business, which in the previous two decades had been very rapid, would make regular support all the more desirable.

The 'country gentlemen' preferred to stay away rather than vote against the popular mood and with a party they did not fancy. Probably in their eyes it was a convenient reconciliation of self-interest and loyalty, but it did embarrass the government and reminded everyone that a considerable number of 'parliament men' continued to make control of the executive their first responsibility. Though two calls of the House were enforced over the army estimates, to the extent of having two absentees placed in the custody of the sergeant-at-arms, the attendance throughout was remarkably poor; poor enough for Tierney to draw some solace from the fact that only about a third of the members had abetted the ministers in their wickedness.[96] The government's predicament is perhaps best explained by the figures for one division. On that of 8 March, when the establishment was finally voted, over 300, including the tellers, went into the lobbies. Forty-eight had been excused attendance when the House had been called over earlier that night, and another 48 already had leave of absence. Although 236 defaulters were named at the call, 101 turned up in time to vote, which left 135 who either had good reasons for being absent or who deliberately abstained. Even assuming that all were genuine absentees, which was quite impossible, there remained at least 100 who attended the House to answer the call but who did not bother to vote.[97] The paradox was that abstention on this scale was almost as good as a vote of confidence, for in stopping short of outright opposition the 'country gentlemen' showed

[96] *Hansard*, 1st ser., xxxiii. 387.
[97] Lists of the majority are to be found in *The Times*, 12 March 1816 and the *Morning Chronicle*, 11 March 1816. There are one or two discrepancies between them. The minority is listed in *Hansard*, 1st ser., xxxiii. 117–18. The names of defaulters when the House was called over are given in *CJ*, lxxi. 159–60, and those excused in the Colchester papers, PRO 30/9.

that their aversion for the measure was not matched by aversion for the men who produced it. Indeed, as long as the Whigs remained under suspicion as Catholic and Radical sympathisers, the government was likely to continue surviving in this fashion. All men who were Tories argued, with baffling logic, that a Whig accession to power would be an inevitable prologue to Radical tyranny. Caught between a desire to preserve an aristocracy and a desire to give government something of a popular basis, the 'country gentlemen' had no other way of marking their displeasure.

The vote on the property tax, however, which now loomed up, allowed these irregulars of party warfare to act with less retraint. In a way they had no choice. With the whole nation in a frenzy over the question and constituents everywhere badgering their representatives, the fence-sitters found their numbers steadily dwindling, and even members who dodged a commitment right to the end knew well that not to vote would never pass unnoticed. Such was the public's interest in the proceedings of parliament that almost every newspaper, metropolitan or provincial, could be depended on to publish an account of the debate and a list of the division. But while the people had members of parliament on the run, the 'country gentlemen' had fewer misgivings about going into opposition anyway, simply because this time the government's existence was not at stake. Over the army estimates it had been. If the House of Commons had rejected those it would have been discarding what the Cabinet thought was essential 'for the protection and safety of the Country'. If, on the other hand, the ministers were beaten on the property tax, parliament would merely veto a financial plan which they preferred and a proposal which did not bear so directly on the national interest. By the custom of the constitution such a defeat was not a resigning matter. How money was raised was not as important as how it was spent.[98]

From the beginning the government made little or no head-

[98] Huskisson to Canning, 13 March 1816, Canning MSS. The worst sort of defeat a government could incur was on a motion where the censure was explicit. But a succession of implicit censures—when a government proposition was defeated or an act of government criticised—could have the same effect.

way against the massive prejudice surrounding the tax. The idea that it was an impost inflicting 'inquisitorial vexations' and 'multiplied oppressions' was so firmly fixed in the public mind as to be scarcely eradicable, and the fact that the government had allowed the tax to lapse in April 1815 seemed to confirm that it was a war levy only. Not that the ministers ever deluded themselves that its renewal would be easy. Lord Liverpool admitted to being full of apprehension every time the subject was mentioned.[99] Sensibly though, the administration never tried to cram the objectionable old act lock, stock and barrel down parliament's throat. Apart from lowering the standard rate from two shillings to one shilling in the pound, the ministers offered a generous relaxation of Schedule B of the act— the so-called tenant's tax—and did their best to minimise the prying into private affairs which caused general indignation. The first was a sop to help keep the agricultural interest quiet throughout a lean year, and the Office for Taxes produced figures to show the government's beneficence to full advantage. Using the 1812 returns as a basis for calculation, it reported that 527,000 out of 589,000 occupiers would now have nothing to pay and that the Exchequer would collect £200,000 instead of £2,000,000.[100] The other major modification was equally handsome. It affected those chargeable under Schedule D; that is to say, those in receipt of 'annual Profits or Gains arising . . . from any Kind of Property' other than land or government stock. Under the old act, which except for one interruption had been in force since 1806, these persons made an annual return to commissioners who were local notables but responsible to the Tax Office through the 'bureaucratic curiosity' of paid officials. Understandably, disclosures of a private nature to either had always rankled. To mend matters the government proposed changes which made for less meddling and more confidential treatment. Henceforward each individual would have the option of paying according to his old assessment with no questions asked or appealing for a reduction. If he appealed only one commissioner instead of several would handle his case, and if he objected to this he himself might

<hr>

[99] e.g. *Castlereagh*, x. 476; *Liverpool*, ii. 251.
[100] *PP*, 1816, xiv. 101, 103.

nominate referees to look into his affairs on the commissioner's behalf.[101]

Without doubt these were welcome changes, certain to take some wind out of the opposition's sails. But if they were meant to save the property tax from the country's vengeance the ministers should have announced the good news much sooner than they did. Early on, as early as the second day of the session in fact, Vansittart mentioned that the government had in mind modifications 'to remove a part of the pressure from some classes of society'. Ten days later he gave out that they would apply to Schedule B; but until the beginning of March, when at last he got down to details, the House had no more to go on than this. By then the country was in a fine rage, and it was too late to do much good. As for the improvements in Schedule D, parliament knew nothing of them until the government deigned an explanation on the very night of its motion.[102]

If the truth be known, the ministers did not care much what the people thought. In their view the people might complain and parliament was bound to hear them out, but popular judgement was always suspect because it was passionate and partial, markedly so when a 'very natural impatience' of taxation asserted itself. By comparison parliament was a creature of reason, a parent over children, meant to take a parent's notice of these tantrums. As Castlereagh said, referring to the petitions against the tax:

> . . . no one would say that the deliberative faculties of parliament ought to be so limited or paralysed by them, that the legislature of the country was to look to the sentiments entertained beyond the walls of that House for the rule and guide of the course it had to pursue.[103]

This was wishful thinking. Parliament could never be so independent of the country. More than a convention of popular delegates, it was also less than the conclave of an oligarchy.

---

[101] See Vansittart's explanation of the different procedure in *Hansard*, 1st ser., xxxiii. 430–2.

[102] Ibid., xxxii. 65, 382–3, 1128, xxxiii. 431–2.

[103] Ibid., xxxiii. 443. See also ibid., xxxii. 897–8, xxxiii. 421–2.

Even members who had no reason to fear a scolding from their constituents disliked seeing the House get out of step with public opinion. Most believed that 'sympathy and mutual feeling' between government and people was part of the proper ordering of the constitution, and that if a rupture took place the people might take it upon themselves to exact retribution in some form or other—disorder and even revolution was an ever recurring nightmare. The art of government lay in reconciling administrative necessity and popular complaint. Partly because the opposition deliberately played the 'game of the country and the people', partly because the increasing power of the state was felt and resented and 'the voice of the people' (in accordance with the time-honoured doctrine of balance) was seen as a salutary check, public opinion was invariably hostile to the administration, making it necessary for the latter somehow to come to terms with it. This compromise it was parliament's special function to impose. When the issue was clear-cut, when the country was of one mind, as it was over the property tax, the legislature could never stand as firm as Castlereagh said it ought to.

Of course the government, though convinced that it and not public opinion was taking a 'national' view, saw no reason why it should busy itself with counter-petitions and meetings. An appeal to the platform was quite futile when feeling against the tax ran so high and when the executive power was regarded with such aversion. The days when the 'respectable classes' could meet in cosy convocation had long since passed. As public meetings had become properly public, so they had become demonstrative rather than deliberative, and usually the nobility and gentry, unless sympathetic, saw no point in turning up just to be shouted down. If the government had got its friends to exert themselves the results would have been a fiasco, not least because the meagreness of its support in terms of numbers would have become damagingly apparent. The Whigs, therefore, over a period of five or six weeks from the beginning of the session, were given a free run in the country. Out of over four hundred petitions only half a dozen admired the property tax 'for sustaining the Public Credit, for bearing with comparative lightness on the poorer and labouring classes of the community, and for reaching income in the possession of whomsoever it may be vested'.[104]

Strangely enough, the government was almost as indifferent in parliament itself. For weeks only a few murmurs came from the Treasury bench while the opposition, every time a petition was brought forward, held forth about government deceit, prying commissioners, ruined farmers and national bankruptcy. Even when ministers argued that the question was for the 'calm and deliberate consideration of parliament' alone, they should never have let such remarks pass unchallenged. Silent contempt may have been a brave front to put up against 'clamour' but it gave their supporters in the legislature no lead when they most wanted one, and at this time a majority had to be managed into existence as much as at any other. There was no excuse, or at best only the feeble one that for a few days sickness laid low many on the front bench.[105] Over the Orders-in-Council in 1812 Brougham and his friends had used the same stratagem to bully the waverers and address the nation, and their success then should have warned the ministers to make a reply whatever happened. In addition, their silence after Brougham had needled them for being 'ashamed to avow themselves' after 'the national wish had been so unequivocally expressed' made them seem abashed,[106] when in fact the continuation of the property tax had a number of arguments to commend it; not only did it secure the sinking fund, relieve the money market and place credit in private hands, but it procured a revenue from trade when land was disproportionately burdened and relieved the poor to the extent of making an increase of indirect taxation less necessary. Indeed, the opposition admitted its sense by saying as little as possible about the alternatives. Yet for all the government cared nobody needed to know it. Vansittart explained the good the tax would do when he summarised his budget on 12 February, but little else was said on the subject

[104] Petition of the Freeholders, Justices of the Peace, and Commissioners of Supply of the County of Perth. *CJ*, lxxi. 219.

[105] Castlereagh was absent from 27 February to 4 March. Bragge-Bathurst and Wellesley-Pole were also ill at this time. *Hansard*, 1st ser., xxxii. 1044–5. Vansittart did not attend the House on 29 February and 1 March. He wanted a short rest. Ibid., 1130.

[106] Ibid., 947.

until the motion itself came up for consideration, far too late to bring the House and the country to their senses.[107]

Within the government itself the deteriorating situation fostered speculation that the public would in the end prevail. Huskisson predicted a beating, and rather blithely at that, partly because he thought the government would survive it, partly because it would show him to have been right all along. In his view the ministers were foolish to try the tax, and his noncommittal remarks in parliament made no secret of his opposition.[108] Peel, without reason to wish the government ill, also anticipated defeat—after 'the toughest battle of the Session'.[109] The leadership, however, never doubting that they were right and the opposition wholly wrong, were not put off by ugly portents. 'Those who raise this Clamour', Lord Liverpool wrote to Canning, 'have a Narrow View of their own Interest, as the Restoration of Publick Credit, the Rise of the Funds, and the consequent Fall of the Interest of Money will afford more Relief to the existing Distresses of the Country, than any other Measure which could be adopted'.[110] 'Several Gentlemen of considerable weight' in the House of Commons, who waited on him to remonstrate, were given the same lecture, and to quash any rumours of a capitulation that might be getting abroad, he added that if the tax did go it would be parliament's and not the government's doing.[111] This was not bravado. Nor did it mean that the ministers were too jealous of their honour to back down with good grace. Rather, for them to see the matter through to the bitter end was in keeping with the accepted notion of their function. As has been said, most people considered that it was the duty of ministers to formulate measures of public necessity and the duty of parliament to

---

[107] Ibid., 381–3, xxxiii. 427–9, 448–9. Significantly, when the government on 5 and 6 March did make an effort to answer the opposition on other points, Castlereagh immediately reported an improvement in the temper of the House. *George IV*, ii. 154–5.

[108] Huskisson to Canning, 13 March 1816, Canning MSS. *Hansard*, 1st ser., xxxii. 1236–7.

[109] *Peel*, i. 210, 212; Peel to Lord Whitworth, 7, 13 March 1816, Add. MSS. 40290, ff. 125–6, 144–5.

[110] 13 February 1816, Canning MSS. The letter is printed with verbal mistakes in *Liverpool*, ii. 253–5.

[111] Undated memorandum, early 1819 perhaps, probably by Lord Liverpool, Add. MSS. 38741, ff. 270-6.

submit these to the test of public acceptance. Parliament in effect was the place where the expediency of what the government intended could be scrutinised for the last time. The executive used its experience and expertise to propose, while the legislature used its sympathy with the country to dispose. It was this view of parliament as a counter to ministerial insensitivity which really explained why those in power took their occasional defeat there as something less than disastrous. If a difference did occur between Crown and country, and sometimes it was unavoidable, parliament was the recognised arbitrator.

When at last the Commons came to settle the business of the property tax, the debate was a tame affair, despite the weeks of strenuous rehearsal. As Brougham reminisced years afterwards: '... it speedily appeared manifest that there would be a decision without any debate; for that had been anticipated, and indeed had taken place over and over again'.[112] Everyone was weary of the subject and impatient to be done, and the speakers gave up contending with a rude and restless House after about an hour and a half. Vansittart and Castlereagh were allowed to have their say, but the rest, including Brougham himself, had to be brief and to the point if they wanted to be heard.[113] On some nights, when the opposition had been in good form, the discussions on the petitions had lasted much longer. Yet though both sides arrived on the field to find a battle was impossible, the occasion created its own excitement. The House was packed with well over 400 members present, there was no standing room in the public galleries, and a mighty throng filled the corridors outside and spilled into Palace Yard. The rousing cheer this crowd set up when a majority of thirty-seven against the tax was announced was a fitting anthem to hail a victory of public opinion over official insensibility. For such a victory it undoubtedly was. From the start the ministers had been confident that parliament would acknowledge that they were right and the people wrong, as if the House preferred to be at variance with the country rather than with them. In the middle of February Lord Liverpool spoke of government notions 'gaining ground', three weeks later there was talk of a

[112] *Brougham*, ii. 311.   [113] *Hansard*, 1st ser., xxxiii. 421–51.

majority of twenty, and on the morning of the contest the Treasury checked its canvass figures and predicted one of forty.[114] The final result made fun of these forecasts. Far from swinging in the ministers' favour, the House had been coming to terms with the sentiment it had been told to ignore. About 80 government supporters crossed the floor to swell the 150–160 strong regular opposition, and possibly as many went away or never turned up.[115] Castlereagh in his report to the Prince Regent spoke of 'some going against, whose support had been calculated upon' and 'numbers . . . going away', which suggests that it was the abstentions which caught the government by surprise and were mainly responsible for converting the prognosticated majority of 40 into a minority almost as large.[116] Admittedly, not all of the abstainers were acting out of displeasure. A handful of Irish members, as Peel thought they would, balked at passing a tax which their countrymen would never pay, even though such reservations made the Union something of a mockery.[117] Nonetheless, *The Times* was still right. The House of Commons had 'felt with the feelings of the country'.[118] When the majority comprised twice as many county members as the minority, most men would have agreed that that was indisputable.

Whether or not the government had learnt a lesson remained to be seen. As always, public feeling had proved, in some measure, to be muddle-headed, short-sighted and ill-informed. Apart from a necessary and often quite timid invocation against the property tax, many petitions gave attention to other and what were regarded as more pertinent complaints like parochial taxation, the laws against distilling and even the duty on hair powder. Many too took the government to task for a

[114] *Liverpool*, ii. 255; *Creevey's Life and Times* (ed. John Gore), p. 100; *George IV*, ii. 160.

[115] About 150 members remain after voters, pairs and members with leave of absence have been accounted for. When the House was called over on 8 March 48 were excused attendance, but this number was almost certainly substantially increased when defaulters were ordered to attend on 11 March and again on 13 March. It is worth noting that 33 members who supported the government over the army estimates on either 6 or 8 March did not vote at all on the property tax.

[116] *George IV*, ii. 160.

[117] Peel to Gregory, 2 March 1816, Add. MSS. 40290, f. 116. The letter is partly printed in *Peel*, i. 212. See also *Hansard*, 1st ser., xxxiii. 198–9.

[118] *The Times*, 19 March 1816.

flagrant breach of faith, which was plain nonsense; a year before, when no one knew what Napoleon's next move was going to be, the ministers had been scrupulous not to pledge an end to the tax after twelve months.[119] Moreover, feeling against the 'damnable impost' may have been genuine enough, but the Whigs had coaxed and marshalled it to suit themselves. As Castlereagh was quick to point out, nearly a third of the petitions were from Devonshire and the metropolis because there each parish had produced its own, and out of eighty odd counties in Great Britain only nineteen had been called together in meetings regularly convened by the county sheriffs. If opinion could be managed in this way to produce desirable results, it did not mean much, it did not represent 'the unbiassed and collected sense of the people'.[120] Yet parliament had had the perspicacity to distinguish an honest protest behind the manipulation and the mummery, and the ministers had not. Here, if nowhere else, there was food for thought.

Some results of the defeat were apparent at once; it was obvious that the government would have to find alternative ways and means to meet the supply and that the opposition would strike more confidently than ever on issues of taxation and expenditure. But the other consequences worked at a deeper level. Within a year the 'inferior sort' in many places had taken up the cause of parliamentary reform anew and the rest of society had been terrorised by an unprecedented show of their strength. Much of their inspiration must have come from the successful onslaught on the property tax. To be sure, Brougham and the Whigs had appealed only to the 'respectable classes' to set the machinery of protest in motion, but once that had been done men of all conditions had responded. Even where the populace had been passive spectators, the lesson must have gone home that parliament could be brought to submission by strictly constitutional means. The 'clamour' of February and March 1816, to some extent at least, had its echo in the 'clamour' of the following winter. Taken together, these agitations had the important effect of endorsing the tradition of protest through public meetings and petitions at a time when an opposite tradition, that of protest through violence, had been

---

[119] e.g. *Hansard*, 1st ser., xxxi. 238.　　　[120] Ibid., xxxiii. 444–5.

shown by the recent Luddite disturbances to be very much alive.

The paradox of the defeat of the property tax was that in the long run it excited popular grievance more than it dampened it. Not only did many men see it as a success which could be repeated but an opportunity was lost to recast the system of taxation, a system which was to become increasingly out of plumb in relation to the new realities created by the Industrial Revolution. In part the property tax was a tax on commercial and industrial property. Had it been continued after 1816, the proportion of the public revenue contributed by the most rapidly expanding section of the economy would have corresponded more closely with its wealth. As it was, industrial Britain was favoured at the expense of agricultural Britain. This fact was not lost on contemporaries, though it was impossible to calculate the disparity precisely. The landed interest was always willing to believe that it paid more than its fair share into the public coffers on the grounds that it bore the brunt of direct and parochial taxation, and it became outspoken in its complaint when agriculture entered a long period of difficulty in the early 1820's. To the conventional protest that the real cause of excessive taxation was ministerial extravagance was joined a charge that the particular burden on land had become too great to be borne quietly, a stern attack being mounted on the so-called 'agricultural taxes'. Of course the retention of the property tax in 1816 would never have silenced irate agriculturists a few years later. But it would have taken a great deal from their argument and might have enabled the ministers to anticipate their opposition by surrendering gracefully what could have been more conveniently afforded.

In the same way the loss of the property tax, at first cause for congratulation, served only to strengthen the general complaint against taxation and government expenditure. The point was that the ministers thereafter had no option but to draw the major part of the public revenue from indirect taxation, and such taxation, because it attacked spending rather than incomes and concentrated on articles of general consumption, pressed heavily on the poor whose earnings were lower and less dependable. For a generation after 1815 the most strident chorus of popular 'clamour' was always that devoted to the charge of government. The demand for parliamentary reform was merely a logical extension of this protest, for taxation was taken by the people to be the chief evidence of that oppression which reform would bring to an end. The government, therefore, in 1816 was committed to a financial scheme which provided more for its future embarrassment than comfort. Indeed it might even be argued that with the defeat of the property tax the ruling aristocracy rejected, to some extent, policies it had upheld for over a century. Previously the state had levied money in strict accordance with economic realities; agriculture had been the foremost industry and land had contributed an appropriate portion to the Exchequer. But now, while the taxes on agriculture were reduced as agriculture's importance declined, the charge was transferred not to trade and manufacturing but to the heterogeneous mass of consumers of whom the poor made up the vast majority. Furthermore in Great Britain the aristocracy had always taken seriously the duty of the state to protect commerce, and had rarely hindered, had sometimes actively assisted, the onset of industrialisation. Yet after 1815, though some steps were taken to 'liberate' trade, it is not amiss to accuse the aristocracy of prolonging an obsolete commercial system for the revenue it provided. Convinced, by what had happened in 1816, that the alternative to indirect taxation was not feasible, every government chipped away at the mass of excise and customs with half its mind on the public purse. Not until Peel in the 1840's had the boldness to bring in an income tax did the aristocracy keep faith with its traditions with a sweeping attack on the indirect taxes in the name of 'freer' trade and the people's better condition. Even so, it is interesting to note that there were some in the intervening period who understood that parliament had made a wrong decision. The most persistent in denouncing what had been done was the same Herries who had so ably directed financial operations during the latter part of the war and who was later to become Goderich's and then Wellington's Chancellor of the Exchequer. As early as 1819 he pressed for the revival of the property tax though his colleagues were immovable, and in 1827 and again in 1830 he may have been mainly responsible for getting the Cabinet to take up the subject afresh, though nothing was achieved until Peel returned to office in 1841.[121] Perhaps there is an illustration here of how the Tory philosophy of political action differed from that of the Whigs. While the Tories with their keenly developed administrative sense always acknowledged the desirability of a property or income tax, eventually managing an enactment, the Whigs, seeking identity with the people and impressed with the power of public opinion, never considered such a tax even remotely practicable.

III. WHIG DISCOMFITURE

The opposition, in making what it believed good riddance of the property tax, had won a skirmish rather than carried an assault. Whatever the excitement at Brooks's concerning arrangements for a Whig administration,[122] the vote on the tax had never been an outright vote of confidence; and the fact that parliament and the Cabinet had happened not to see eye to eye on policy was of little account since in those days no one construed such a difference as a censure. There was no need for the ministers to resign, and in obedience to constitutional proprieties they did not contemplate it for a moment. Yet while defeat of the men may not have mattered, defeat of the measure did. It was not a setback soon got over by honeyed phrases and smart accountancy but a misfortune which dogged the ministers for the rest of the session and long after that. For a start the loss of the tax completely upset their financial plans for the immediate future. Keeping in mind the extra if temporary expense which would follow the war, they had counted on it providing £12,000,000 over a two year period. Now part of the sum, at least, had to be borrowed whether the economy could stand it or not. As Castlereagh ruefully remarked, what with the Bank advance and the surplus grants carried over from 1815, the government was left with £12,000,000 of 'clear revenue' to meet an expenditure of £30,000,000. Even supposing spending was cut by a third a year later, there would still 'exist a serious deficiency of means to meet the charge'.[123]

[121] W. D. Jones, *Prosperity Robinson*, pp. 173–4; Gash, *Mr Secretary Peel*, pp. 613–18.
[122] Arthur Aspinall, *Lord Brougham and the Whig Party*, p. 61.
[123] *George IV*, ii. 160.

An easy way out of the quandary did not exist. The ministers continued to insist upon the inviolability of the sinking fund, they were reluctant to apply to the money market for aid, and they had no intention of playing the fool with parliament and the country by suggesting new taxes in lieu of those discarded.[124] Once again the Bank came to the rescue. After earnest consultations with the Treasury throughout April, the directors agreed to lay before the proprietors a proposal for a loan of £3,000,000 at a modest 3 per cent in return for a substantial increase of capital; and with Bank stock paying handsome dividends time out of mind the proprietary Court offered a ready acquiescence.[125] Indeed, every party stood to gain from the bargain: the proprietors were given a chance of gilt-edged investment, the government obtained money on the cheap, and the public saw with satisfaction its bankers expand their capital to keep pace with increasing credit issues.[126] Of course the amount of the loan was a paltry sum against the produce of the property tax, more so when a further £2,700,000 of revenue was written off with the dropping of the war excise on malt. But by really scraping the barrel the government was able to make up the difference. Enough Exchequer bills were to be retired to make a fresh issue feasible, unclaimed dividends on public stock held by the Bank were appropriated, the Exchequer was raided for several small balances of bygone grants, and Vansittart had the good fortune to find that £3,000,000 was a gross under-estimate of the 1815 surplus.[127]

The budget may have balanced, out of the ways and means only the issue of Exchequer bills may have pressed the money market and the exchanges, but in the long run makeshift finance like this was bound to cause disquiet. Had there been the taxes to support it, a policy of debt redemption such as the government continued to uphold would have been unexceptionable. As it was, the theory of the sinking fund demanded a real surplus, and to sell Exchequer and Treasury bills to redeem funded debt just to fund them a year or two later was a

---

[124] See Vansittart's declaration to this effect, 25 March 1816, *Hansard*, 1st ser., xxxiii. 553–4.

[125] Sir John Clapham, *The Bank of England*, ii. 55–7. For the precise terms of the proposition see *CJ*, lxxi. 396.

[126] *Hansard*, 1st ser., xxxiv. 823–5.   [127] Ibid., 833–4.

conjuring act which in the end everyone could see through. Even so, the ministers hardly deserved the opprobrium heaped on them then and since for 'cowardly public finance'.[128] As Lord Grenville, putting himself in their place, said: 'the distress of the Exchequer . . . arises from an Expenditure of Debt & Establishment which can only be defrayed by taxation so enormous that in the evasions & retrenchments it produces, it defeats itself'.[129] Parliament was too intimidated to allow the war taxes to remain, yet the proper operation of the sinking fund was impossible without them; and it seemed by far the lesser evil to borrow to tide over a difficult period than assault the public credit. After all, distress was seen as the direct result of the war, a temporary phenomenon at most; and the huge war establishment carried over into the peace was just as unavoidable. As trade picked up and as the army and navy were reduced, the situation would right itself by an increasing revenue and a decreasing expenditure. Grenville had a short answer for the government's critics and it applies equally well to those who have imitated them: 'Tierney & those who talk with him', he told his brother in successive letters, 'would I think do well to remember that they might very suddenly be called upon, & by more than one event, to *act* in the very same situation in which they are now inveighing against poor Van's helplessness. . . . The whole question is not what we could wish to do, but what we can do.'[130]

Unfortunately for the government it was expected to achieve more than the possible. The ministers played along with the country by giving up taxes and conscientiously tended the sinking fund, but what commendation came from the monied interest for securing the public credit and assisting the funds was spoilt by the continual reproaches of the rest. Large loans in peace were resented because they made it seem that the nation was living beyond its means, and uneasiness at home and sneers abroad were the inevitable result. The Bank, too, used the government's importunities to explain away its dithering

---

[128] The phrase is Clapham's. Clapham, ii. 64.
[129] Lord Grenville to Charles Williams-Wynn, 23 December 1816, Coedy-maen MSS.
[130] Lord Grenville to Thomas Grenville, 11, 15 January 1817, Add. MSS. 41853, ff. 340, 342–3.

over the resumption of cash payments, not without reason since the advances assisted a credit expansion which in turn brought down the exchanges. Worst of all, as Vansittart warned parliament, the defeat of the property tax deprived the government of a chance to overhaul the ill-balanced tax structure which was so closely connected with an increasingly anachronistic commercial system.[131] To make a thoroughgoing job of fiscal and commercial reform was impossible when parliament had dedicated itself to the remission of taxation, for administration and legislature would, in some measure, work at cross-purposes, one intent on making method out of muddle, the other on getting maximum relief. Needing every penny it could get from existing sources of revenue, the government merely made plans to squeeze as much as possible from the hotchpotch of duties by thoroughly checking the apparatus of collection and management. In 1817 a commission was set up 'to inquire into the existing Regulations for the conduct of the Business' in the customs and excise 'with a view to suggest such alterations therein, as may be considered necessary for facilitating the dispatch of Business, for affording accommodation to Trade, and for securing and improving the Revenue'.[132]

Of course, following their beating over the property tax the ministers' first thought was to save their majority not salvage a policy. What they wanted above all was a victory to shake off the stigma of defeat, a victory which would reassert their authority in the Commons, restore the waverers to their proper allegiance and place the whole matter in the context of an occasional defeat any government had to learn to endure. Unfortunately for them, a now cock-a-hoop opposition was not to be repulsed easily, especially one which was more than prepared to follow up its success by having ready yet another 'economical motion' at exactly the right moment. The Whigs' latest device concerned the Admiralty Office. In 1800 it had been decided to pay the two secretaries and their clerks a special wartime increment as compensation for their loss of sundry fees and perquisites under economical reform, but when the arrangement failed to find favour either inside or outside the navy an Order-in-Council of June 1815 authorised a return

---

[131] *Hansard*, 1st ser., xxxii. 1127–8.   [132] *PP*, 1820, vi. 561.

to the principle of fixed salaries applicable in every other department. Had the new salaries fallen short of the war charge, the matter would have ended there, but a pay increase was involved, which did not look at all well alongside the government's oft-repeated professions of irreproachable economy.[133] The opposition said as much when they asked for information a few days before the property tax came on,[134] and with the government sent reeling by parliament's unexpected onslaught they were quick to see the advantage of pursuing the matter further before their adversaries could collect their senses and supporters. A day after the defeat of the property tax (19 March) Methuen, a county member with firm opposition leanings, gave notice of motion for the following evening.[135]

The government's reaction showed that the ministers fully acknowledged the peril of their situation. The sum involved was hardly an extravagance to be sure—not £2,000—but when peace would bring about a rundown of business in the office concerned, when living was cheaper and a search for economy was in full swing it was too much to expect a sympathetic hearing from the House of Commons. The ministers, in fact, spurred themselves in the knowledge that the administration was fighting for its life; they could never remain in office with honour after an act of government had been discredited by parliament and after defeat had been inflicted in two consecutive divisions. No sooner had Methuen given his notice in the House than a Cabinet meeting was arranged for the following afternoon.[136] At it the decision was made to drop the war excise on malt and the idea of new taxes to replace the property tax was finally abandoned.[137] As far as the ministers were concerned it was time to humour parliament, and with the malt tax past saving, it being one of the hated war levies, they assumed they lost nothing by discarding it for the benefit of farmers and indeed the populace as a whole. There were no fine feelings to hold them back. Now that the property tax was gone, the money market would have to help the government out sooner

[133] Ibid., 1815, xiii. 167–80.   [134] *Hansard*, Ist ser., xxxiii. 219–32.
[135] *The Times*, 20 March 1816.   [136] Ibid., 21 March 1816.
[137] *Peel*, i. 216.

or later, and whether the loan was for £6,000,000 or £8,000,000 made little difference in the circumstances. 'There being little hope of carrying the war malt tax through,' Castlereagh explained to the Prince Regent, 'your Royal Highness's Ministers thought it better to add two millions to the amount of the loan, than to make perhaps an ineffectual attempt to force this tax upon the agriculturists and upon the poor, when the rich had deliver'd themselves from the property tax.'[138] To concede something seemed the best way out of present difficulties.

Yet though the ministers shrewdly announced the welcome news shortly before the House set to on Methuen's crucial motion,[139] it did not save them from yet another disappointment. The opposition's attack was a plain enough charge of extravagant government. The pay rise at the Admiralty Office, they declared, was a deplorable departure from 'wholesome Regulation' and 'an unnecessary expenditure of Public Money'. 'He called upon every member who heard him', said Methuen, 'and who was anxious for the prosperity of the country, and who knew its distresses, to prove by their vote . . . that the resources of the nation were not to be squandered away by the improvident prodigality of ministers.' When many loyalties were being sorely tested, Castlereagh did not dare meet the censure head on with a direct negative. Instead, he moved to read the other orders of the day, urging the House to let the matter rest until the estimate came before the committee of supply. This was a shuffling excuse at the best of times and the government was lucky indeed to get away with it. A long monologue from Castlereagh on reductions department by department probably had little effect because he had more progress to promise than report, and on the issue itself the general feeling was that the increase had been ill-timed and over-generous, however much paperwork the Admiralty now had to handle and however important it was for the Crown's servants to be adequately remunerated. Determined on economy, parliament was quite prepared to haggle over a sum as trivial as £1,500. Had Brougham not had the colossal impertinence to reprimand the Regent for 'blind and profligate expenditure', a charge which naturally stunned the whole House, Castlereagh

---

[138] *George IV*, ii. 161.   [139] *Hansard*, 1st ser., xxxiii. 457.

admitted the ending would probably have been 'a decision unfavourable to the Government'. As it was, the ministers scrambled home with a majority of 29, though the result was less an acquittal than a remand, inasmuch as the committee of supply was certain to continue where the House had left off. Such a prospect was disconcerting, to say the least. Brougham's extraordinary gaffe may have helped the government once but it would never happen a second time. And about a dozen friends had been voted on the opposition side in spite of it.[140]

At this stage the ministers really believed that the government could not stand in greater peril. In their view the Whigs had been thwarted more by good luck than good management, and to avert what seemed to be an inevitable defeat they waived the point of the salaries,[141] which meant that for the third time in three days their adversaries got their own way. No government could go on like this, as the ministers well realised. For the next few days there were frenzied comings and goings. Arbuthnot of the Treasury was sent off post-haste to Brighton to brief the Prince Regent on the situation, and a letter from Lord Liverpool seems to have preceded him, one which urged the Prince to return to Town immediately so that his ministers could confer with him daily and even hourly if need be.[142] The Duke of Rutland and Lord Lonsdale, and probably other prominent supporters, also heard from the Prime Minister. These particular peers had fifteen votes at their command and when the government hung by a thread every one was needed.[143] Finally, the officeholders were ordered to attend *en masse* at Fife House, Lord Liverpool's place in Whitehall, to learn what was expected of them in the crisis.[144] The next parliamentary question of importance would concern the navy estimates. The sea service, the charge of ships in commission, had already been provided for, but apart from that nothing, and there were rumours about that the Whigs would make their next move when the rest of the estimates were presented.[145] Yet the

[140] Ibid., 476–513. See also accounts of the debate in *George IV*, ii. 161; *Peel*, i. 217.
[141] Parliament was told of this on 22 March. *Hansard*, 1st ser., xxxiii. 534.
[142] *Liverpool*, ii. 270–1.
[143] Lord Liverpool to the Duke of Rutland, Lord Lonsdale, 23 March 1816, Add. MSS. 38262, ff. 323–6.   [144] *The Times*, 26 March 1816.
[145] Aspinall, *Lord Brougham and the Whig Party*, pp. 66–7.

conference at Fife House must have involved more than the
usual appeal for regular attendance and support. Such a lecture
would never have kept the party behind closed doors for over
an hour one evening and for another two the afternoon following. Moreover, the Duke of York attended the second session
which was something quite out of the ordinary.[146] His presence
in fact explained much. If the Commander-in-Chief was
needed, almost certainly the army estimates were discussed,
and if this was so, the navy estimates and the civil list must
have been too, for the government had equal reason to fear
parliament's animadversion on those. The purpose of such a
briefing was obvious. No doubt there were appeals for loyalty
and a stricture or two, but the Cabinet's real concern was to
reassure the rank and file that they had the situation in hand,
that reductions were in progress and more were contemplated.
They could be relied on to spread the news outside. When the
party had no formal organisation to speak of, when none of the
ministers headed a connexion in the old style, this was the best,
perhaps the only way to pass the message on.

The talk around Town of an onslaught on the navy estimates
did turn out to have foundation. When parliament met on
25 March the opposition rushed immediately to the assault; no
sooner had the House been asked to refer the estimates to the
committee than Tierney was on his feet racing through the
figures. Thanks to forgetfulness on the part of someone, his
attack was given an additional chance of success. 'Facts,
positive and clear facts' Tierney demanded of his opponents,
but when Castlereagh called Croker of the Admiralty to his
side he found that the papers giving them had been left behind
by mistake. It is not too much to say that for the next few
minutes the government's existence was as precarious as it
had ever been during the previous week. At all costs Tierney
had to be answered, for the time had come for the government
to show its parliamentary strength or resign. Indeed, the very
nature of his argument forced the ministers to rely on a point
of official information. When he said that in the year to come
the administration of the navy was going to cost £20,000 more
than in the last year of war, he was not fabricating figures to

[146] *The Times*, 26 March 1816.

suit himself but repeating the amount given in the estimates. Warrender, therefore, one of the civil Lords, was given the task of extemporising as best he could to stall off a division, while a whip raced round to the Admiralty Office for the memorandum on which so much depended. Croker only had to read it out to humiliate Tierney completely and make the whole opposition appear disingenuous and dissembling. The vote for the sea service, he explained, carried the charge of ships in commission, the 'establishment estimate' that of ships in ordinary, and in peace when most of the fleet was laid up the latter was bound to be as large as the other was small. Tracing the figures back over the period of a century he showed it to be invariably true. This statement, Croker recalled years afterwards, 'changed the face of the House in a moment'. Quite caught out by their own chicanery, the opposition tried to salvage some self-respect by moving an adjournment. It availed them nothing. On being brought to the decision, the House did not even bother to divide.[147]

This success brought the crisis to an end. The estimates caused the government no further trouble and a week later they were safely through the committee of supply. The majorities which attended them 'have put us all in Spirits', Peel wrote in great relief.[148] Indeed three years were to pass before parliament and Peel's colleagues were again at such loggerheads. What needed to be shown had been shown, that the 'country gentlemen' were not out to destroy the government or even to control it, only to nudge it on those occasions when the situation seemed to demand as much. When the ministers were manifestly in the right, as they had been this time, their loyalty could never be placed in question. But it had not always been so. Over the property tax parliament had chosen to relieve the people before it relieved the money market when the government would have done the opposite. Over the Admiralty salaries what one had felt was a fair and reasonable remuneration the other had called exorbitant. The difference was resolved in the only way it could have been, by the ministers acknowledging that parliament existed to pronounce on the policy of the

---

[147] *Hansard*, 1st ser., xxxiii. 567–91; *Croker*, i. 80–5.
[148] Peel to Lord Whitworth, 30 March 1816, Add. MSS. 40290, f. 182.

executive and to regulate its particular acts. Seeing that this idea of the constitution was still current, the greater part of the Commons would have looked upon the Cabinet's resignation as unnecessary and even irresponsible. Any act which needlessly landed the country with the nuisance of a political interregnum would have been widely condemned, especially one which brought the suspect Whigs to power; and most members could not care less about the contradictions and inconsistencies of government policy if they meant that the Cabinet fell in with their wishes. Inevitably the opposition sought to provoke the ministers into going by all manner of ridicule, but, since no censure or vote of no-confidence had been carried, it was perfectly proper to treat these efforts with disdain. In 1816 there was a crisis because what was convenient from the administration's point of view happened to conflict with the susceptibilities and prejudices of parliament. As long as the ministers continued to be regarded as the representatives of the executive power and not leaders of a parliamentary party these minor collisions of will were only to be expected.

In parliament economical government was long to remain the dominant issue. Mainly this was because the country had an abiding conviction, which the legislature shared, that extravagance was the natural inclination of all governments. But it was also because questions of expenditure came constantly before the House, allowing the opposition to keep up a running attack on ministers, and because the search for economy was a subject in which most members laid claim to some expertise. How much to spend was a much repeated and relatively simple contest between ministers who recommended one figure and a House of Commons which wanted it justified to its satisfaction. Sometimes, with parliament playing to a gallery of public opinion, and the most timid animal in the chamber, the country gentleman on the hindmost bench, fancying he could smell out extravagance wherever it existed, these struggles developed into battles royal over what must have seemed mere trivialities.

In the session of 1816 a good example of this was provided by an item of Irish business—the so-called consolidation of the exchequers. By the seventh article of the Act of Union Great

Britain and Ireland undertook to contribute to the common purse in the proportion of fifteen to two, each country keeping its own revenue departments to raise its own taxes. However, the same legislation scheduled these separate administrative structures for demolition as soon as the national debts of both countries were in roughly the same proportion as their revenues. In 1811 a select committee of the House of Commons noted that this point had been reached; four years afterwards another recommended immediate action; and in May 1816, in a series of resolutions, parliament gave its formal consent to proceed. No sweeping reorganisation of the financial departments was needed to consummate this fiscal union, but as usual the 'economical mono-maniacs' investigated the matter until they found something to confirm their suspicions of government prodigality. Ireland's finances were presided over by a Treasury Board of six and two secretaries, and as in Great Britain the debt was administered by specially appointed commissioners. In the transfer of responsibilities which the government had in mind the British commissioners were to take over the Irish debt, a vice-treasurer was to replace the Irish Treasury and two of those dispossessed were to be added to the Board in London. With reason the ministers considered the arrangement an exemplary 'economical reform'; eight places were to be done away with and only three erected in their stead. But many 'country gentlemen' in the House of Commons stumbled over one detail. When told that for the routine chore of counter-signing warrants the vice-treasurer was to receive a salary of £3,500 and a deputy to boot, they refused to be convinced that an office of trust and political reward, which was what the government made out it was, deserved so generous an endowment. In the end, after four sittings on the authorising bill, the ministers were beaten down to £2,000 on the salary and the deputy saved only by passing the clause permitting the principal a parliamentary seat.[149] Here parliament faced the usual dilemma of serving the king or serving the people. It was quite ready to allow the Crown a moderate influence to facilitate the conduct of the king's business in the legislature. At the same

[149] *Hansard*, 1st ser., xxxiv. 588–617, 1045–8, 1109–22, 1128–9, 1225–1230.

time, out of respect for the strong and less reasonable feelings
of the public, it felt a need to advertise frequently its concern
for economical government, in this instance by insisting that
the pay of public office be commensurate with its duties. A
certain number of members no doubt were as prejudiced as
public opinion on the subject of influence and establishments.
A great many more, however, knowing better than the country,
were only anxious to make an occasional gesture to avoid the
appearance.

The matter was of no great moment to the government;
nevertheless the reverse rankled. Fully aware by now that when
it came to economy parliament would be difficult to handle, the
ministers had done their best to satisfy its earnestness on
questions of this sort ever since the difficult days before the
Easter recess. Shortly after the defeat of the property tax
£318,000 had been lopped off the army, navy and ordnance
estimates,[150] while behind the scenes the Treasury had gone
to work with a will, ordering reductions on the departments
and setting up commissions to inquire into civil list expenditure
and offices of wartime creation.[151] Such overt zeal—overt
because the news of these doings soon got about—had seemed
to pay off handsomely. Satisfied that the government was not
playing them false, the 'country gentlemen' had refused to run
in harness with the opposition from then on. Within the space
of a month motions deploring the enormous peace establishment, the charge of public offices and the retention of three
secretaries of state had all been baffled by their willingness to
wait and see.

The sight of a diligent Treasury was not all that softened
parliament's dangerous mood. The work itself also provided
abundant information which the ministers paraded with great

[150] See Lord Palmerston's memorandum in Add. MSS. 48429, f. 104 and
Paper supplementary to the Ordnance Estimates, 29 March 1816, in PP,
1816, xii. 91–3. In addition, £40,000 was saved on the navy extraordinaries
and a further £3,000 on Admiralty salaries.

[151] Huskisson to Canning, 20 April 1816, Canning MSS. A copy of the
Treasury minute of 5 April appointing the commission into offices created
since 1793 is found in PP, 1816, xiii. 97. According to Lord Binning the
Treasury had circularised the departments concerning reductions before this.
Hansard, 1st ser., xxxiv. 321. The reports submitted by the Treasury commission on eighteen offices and departments are printed in PP, 1817,
xv. 11–21.

effect whenever the Whigs tried to vilify them for unfeeling extravagance. Before about 1780 the various offices within the government had been subject to little interference from outside. Nothing like an integrated civil service existed, every office being almost regarded as a demesne the lord of which was the principal; he largely decided appointments, remunerations and promotions, office hours, discipline and leave. But with the commencement of 'economical reform', reform which was carried out relatively systematically, this magnum of independence was lost for ever. Because the attack on the administrative system was mostly inspired by a demand for 'public economy', the Treasury, within the government, found itself captaining the onslaught. It assumed responsibility for enforcing obedience to parliament's commands and for acting in anticipation of them whenever possible. In the process it became familiar with the abuses which existed, with the practical difficulties of reform and with what had been accomplished. By the early nineteenth century, in fact, the Treasury was making the first attempts, none of them very successful, to lay down regulations for the whole of the civil service. It was a storehouse of knowledge about the administrative system, but there had been a natural progression from inquiry to control and supervision, in principle at least.

The importance of these researches and the Treasury's increasing authority was well illustrated in 1816 by what occurred over the civil list. Here the government was able to push its investigations much further than parliament, with the result that the only danger it faced was if parliament preferred to consult its anti-ministerial prejudices. The great problem of the civil list was an ever-recurring deficit of income, the product of a bad bargain made by George III at the time of his accession. For by exchanging most of his grandfather's revenues for a fixed parliamentary grant, the king had unknowingly signed away one of the last vestiges of the Crown's independent power, a civil list supervised by the sovereign and by him alone. 'To an Expenditure necessarily increasing', a committee of the House of Commons explained in 1815, 'a fixed Income was applied, and though that Income was at different times augmented, it was never increased beyond an Amount sufficient to meet the Expenditure at the time the Augmentation was made. . . .' As a result a monarch of simple tastes was dogged by debt for the whole of his reign. The more the king kept living beyond his means, the more parliament was called on to help him out, and in the circumstances it was not long before a balance sheet accompanied the royal message as a matter of course. The opposition had set the precedent by worming some accounts out of Lord North in 1770, but after the turn of the century the practice had begun to be regularised. An act of 1804 had insisted that accounts should be presented forthwith if any class of the civil list was in arrears for more than two quarters, and one of 1812 the same immediately the overall deficit exceeded the average of the past eight years. For a while the Crown had managed to put a stop to the snooping by using its remaining hereditary revenues to pay its way, but though war boosted the yield of these, after 1812 even they had been insufficient and once again parliament had the advantage. When the House of Commons came to consider the civil list in 1816, the accounts of 'the King's own' made fairly familiar reading.[152]

Of course a financial statement told so much and no more, for it said nothing definite about how debt had been incurred or who was to blame. Here, however, Burke's reforms in 1782 had done parliament an inestimable service. That cleansing of the Augean stable, as the Whigs liked to regard it, had irrevocably established the principle of casual interference, and in obedience to it six committees had sat above stairs from 1802 to 1815, poring over the accounts and any other evidence the Crown had been gracious enough to give them. Nevertheless, though they had laboured hard, their inability to save their sovereign from embarrassment showed what little they could really do. Always parliament was handicapped by its own loathness to pry too far in defiance of the much-venerated notion that the civil list was the king's exclusive property. While only part of the list was for the maintenance of the royal state, as late as 1815 when Tierney asked for a committee with power to send for persons, papers and records, the usual ministerial protest against 'violating the delicacy and deference

[152] Report on the Civil List, *PP*, 1814–15, iii. 91–175.

due to the Crown' brought him to defeat.[153] Thus a commission such as the one the Treasury appointed in 1816 could
carry its researches much further than any committee of the
House. The private nature of the inquiry set the Crown at
ease and even compelled it to co-operate when the choice lay
between the two, which was precisely what happened in 1816.
By then the Prince Regent was in dread of being called to
account, while his ministers were certain he would be, and
purely to save his feelings they suggested a small commission
under Treasury auspices. For a time there was a tussle, but
when they pointed out that parliament would otherwise interfere whether he liked it or not, he waived his objections and
gave his permission.[154] Not often did the ministers have the
run of the Household, and, propriety or no, they made the
most of it. After questioning officials the House dared not send
for, after checking accounts the House was never allowed to see,
the government had inside information no parliamentary committee was ever likely to obtain.

The main task the Treasury set its three-man commission
was to settle a new estimate for the civil list, one which would
spare the government the nuisance and the Crown the embarrassment of another application to parliament for the rest of
the reign. Admittedly, a select committee of the House of
Commons had already arrived at a figure, but this was no
reason for the ministers not to go one better if they possibly
could. Probably parliament expected as much anyway. The
ministers had taken a fresh look at all their other estimates
immediately after the defeat of the property tax, and presumably no exception was to be made of the civil list. Certainly,
when the commissioners—Charles Long, Huskisson and
Arbuthnot—were done, they handed in a report of exemplary
thoroughness. The fourth class (the allocation for the Household departments) was marked down £20,000 and the contingent or occasional payments £90,000, both categories
including charges of a civil as well as of a personal nature.
With the savings in the third class (payments to the diplomatic service) which the Foreign Office found itself able to

[153] *Hansard*, 1st ser., xxx. 616–44.
[154] Huskisson to Canning, 20 April 1816, Canning MSS.

recommend, the reduction was little short of £140,000 altogether.[155] That this much could be gleaned after a parliamentary committee had been over the ground underlined the ineffectiveness of parliamentary as opposed to official inquiry, even if the largest reduction had to be discounted as following from a state of peace and not from any administrative resourcefulness.

Despite the good work, the question of the civil list still gave the government great anxiety. 'Upon this subject', Huskisson gloomily reported to Canning, 'we are forewarned not to expect the support of many who are generally our friends in the House; and out of doors public opinion is still more decidedly against us.'[156] In the past there had frequently been glimpses of parliament's displeasure at extravagance in high places, most notably over the Brighton showpiece, but this time there was reason to fear that the members would feel even less inhibited. As Liverpool and two colleagues thought it their duty to warn the Regent: '. . . no subject is viewed with more jealousy and suspicion than the personal expenses of the Sovereign or his representative at a time when most of the landed gentlemen of the country are obliged to submit to losses & privations as well as to retrenchment'.[157] Unhappily the latest accounts were least likely to keep this feeling at bay. Those for the April quarter showed a deficit of £140,000, which brought the total debt outstanding to over £400,000. To complete the government's discomfiture the whole of it had been incurred within a year, because in June 1815 when the civil list had been £534,000 in arrears parliament had obliged the Crown to the full amount.[158] For this state of affairs the ministers would bear the responsibility, but many believed one much greater than they to be the real culprit. George III's parsimony still stuck in the nation's mind, and his high-living son paid dearly for the memory. Yet in fact the country was much too ready to condemn the Regent. If the Crown had run up so large a debt in the space of twelve months, the discrepancy between the income parliament had seen fit to grant and an

[155] *PP*, 1816, xiii. 52–3.
[156] 20 April 1816, Canning MSS.   [157] *George IV*, ii. 158.
[158] See the accounts in *PP*, 1814–15, iii. 158, x. 171; 1816, xiii. 15, 41.

expenditure no one could anticipate adequately explained it. As soon as it became more expensive to live, govern or diplomatise, the civil list was almost certain to run into arrears, and with the war, one way and another, all three had happened. Throughout the reign, indeed, the story had been the same, an indigent Crown living from hand to mouth with parliament reluctant to see the fault in its preference for a fixed grant adequate for the moment.

Typically, a small item concerning Brighton worried the Ministers most on this occasion. The Pavilion being a royal residence, not a royal palace, was never the property of the Crown, but early in 1816, having run out of private funds, the Prince Regent applied for Crown money to continue the building and furnishing. Discreetly, the Treasury chose to act on what it called the 'just and reasonable' principle that wherever the Crown chose to reside there the trappings of royalty should be provided at the public expense, and, not wishing to add to the civil list debt, a meeting of the Board ordered £70,000 to be made over from the hereditary revenues with the proviso that furnishings should remain the property of the Crown.[159] Needless to say, serious objections could scarcely be avoided. Strictly speaking, public money was being put to private purposes, and that which was used—the revenue from the Admiralty droits—was a fund which the government habitually drew upon when it wanted to discharge the civil list debt without recourse to parliament. Hence there was a danger that a notion would go abroad that the Crown bargained on the House of Commons paying its debts regardless, a notion perhaps vaguely formed already, for by a regrettable oversight no formal message had been sent in acknowledgement of the previous year's settlement. Nor was this the only questionable part. A transaction under the counter such as this was also made nonsense of any estimates the Crown saw fit to produce in respect of the civil list; if parliament could vote so much while the Crown with the ministers' connivance spent more on the side, the Commons' overlordship of financial concerns was far short of what it ought to be. Either objection, then, was likely to place the government in an awkward position. It was not just

[159] Copy of Treasury Minute, 23 February 1816, ibid., 1816, xiii. 63.

that parliament wanted frugality in the royal household as much as anywhere else; the dignity of the sovereign had equally to be protected from the humiliation of frequent parliamentary solicitation. With good reason every administration feared the consequences of bringing 'the king's own' into public discussion because a charge of lese-majesty inevitably accompanied the charge of misgovernment. Whenever the Crown made application for the nation's charity the Commons no less than the Court felt an irreparable insult, though how the former could satisfy its economical urgings without detracting from the royal state remained an impossible contradiction.

As it was, on this occasion the ministers handled the issue with considerable adroitness. The difficulties at the start of the session may have shaken them after the politically serene years of the war period, but seemingly it did not take them very long to learn the steps of parliament's dance. The House of Commons was told the amount of the civil list debt on 26 March. Almost in the same breath Castlereagh divulged that the hereditary revenues would pay it and that to prevent a recurrence the estimates would be revised and a bill introduced to carry out the recommendations of the last committee. As was only to be expected, Tierney professed himself dissatisfied, and at once promised to propose a committee of inquiry, again one not hamstrung by being without the power to send for persons, papers and records.[160] Such a committee had no precedent. Hitherto, the House had had to be content with whatever information the Crown saw fit to give it, but if Tierney was allowed to have his way, that security would finally vanish and parliament's invasion of the royal privacy would be virtually complete. The proposal, of course, was repugnant to the Prince Regent. The ministers perhaps had an additional reason for their hostility. For while parliament had persistently held the Treasury responsible for civil list expenditure, the Household, like many other departments, had just as persistently resisted Treasury control, and Lord Liverpool and Vansittart would have had no desire to be blamed for others' mistakes more than they could help. Somehow the ground had to be cut from under the opposition's feet, preferably by satisfying the House that a select committee would be an unnecessary impertinence. But that meant forestalling Tierney, and on 10 April he had entered his motion in the order-book for 6 May. Hastily Castlereagh reserved 3 May on the government's behalf.[161] On a motion asking for leave to bring in a civil list bill he could say all that needed to be said.

When the day arrived the ministers had left nothing to chance. They had the Prince Regent's word that building at Brighton would be brought to a standstill,[162] they had an estimate to present which undercut parliament's by £139,000, and they had a bill ready based on a report the House had previously commended. To 'dish' the Whigs even a little skulduggery was not thought amiss. A comprehensive view of the Crown's resources necessarily included both the hereditary revenues and the civil list, and though the opposition asked for accounts of the Admiralty and other droits a month in advance, the government produced nothing until after Castlereagh had spoken. This left Tierney with a weekend to do the essential homework on his motion. Lest the House should feel itself slighted—there was no chance of getting the papers printed in time—Castlereagh called representatives of the 'country gentlemen' round to his house to make any explanations necessary.[163] One last precaution was taken, a whip sent out to official members.[164] Even when the government was likely to be hard pressed apparently, the most loyal of its supporters were still not dependable enough to make a reminder unnecessary. As it happened, Tierney's request for a committee was turned down out of hand. When a division was called for, only opposition stalwarts were found to favour the idea and those on the government side outnumbered them nearly two to one. As Castlereagh pointed out, with five reports on civil list expenditure since 1802 and other accounts and papers besides, the House had ample information. If it wanted more, it had only

[161] Ibid., 1133; *The Times*, 25 April 1816.

[162] See the correspondence in *George IV*, ii. 158–9; Sir Benjamin Bloomfield to Lord Liverpool, Lord Liverpool to Sir Benjamin Bloomfield, 16 March 1816, Add. MSS. 38262, ff. 317–20.

[163] Tierney mentioned the meeting in his speech. See *Hansard*, 1st ser., xxxiv. 256.

[164] Castlereagh refers to it in a letter to Peel, 8 May 1816, Add. MSS. 41810, f. 202.

to address the Crown in the usual way without disparagement
of the royal dignity. Over Brighton the ministers also escaped
the drubbing they had feared. Tierney insisted that the droits
should pay the Crown's debts before all else, and later on he
tried to make it mandatory by inserting a clause in the preamble
of the government's bill. Had there been a second application
for parliament's largesse in consecutive years, the House
would have certainly taken a different view of the matter.
However, the droits, thanks mainly to prize money, afforded
enough to pay debts public as well as private. If any doubt
existed over the transaction, the ministers received the benefit
of it.[165]

On this as on other 'economical' questions the Whigs could
in large measure attribute their defeat to the fact that parliament, despite its representative character and the idea that
it existed to contain and regulate the executive, was not without
feelings for efficient and well conducted government. In practice Crown and parliament in permanent partnership pursued
a course which weighed carefully the needs of the executive
and the reproaches of the country. It was the Whigs' great
weakness that they were forced to emphasise parliament's
responsibility to the country because their only hope of office
was to ride a wave of popular indignation. In 1816, having
found one which held great promise, they preferred to forget
that parliament's mania for cheap government had its limits.
Sometimes they seemed to err on the side of stinginess, to set
too low a price on public service by denying responsibility a
proper reward. At others—and their attack on Lord Bathurst's
secretaryship was an example—they appeared to throw efficient
government to the winds, by ignoring the increase of public
business and by wanting to limit too severely the representation
of the executive in the legislature. Their final embarrassment
was over the civil list when they found to their cost that most
members of parliament were still unwilling to subordinate the
honour and dignity of the Crown to the financial exigencies of
the state. The Whigs seized on the issue of economy as a short
cut to popularity and even power, but the ministers always had
the advantage of them. Provided the administration made an

[165] *Hansard*, 1st ser., xxxiv. 185–206, 255–99, 789–806.

honest job of retrenchment, which it showed every sign of
doing, the most the opposition could expect to achieve was an
occasional triumph of little or no significance. And even if
public discontent deepened to bring greater pressure to bear
on parliament, the reluctance of many 'parliament men' to see
the Whigs installed in power had still to be overcome.

Chapter Two

THE DELUDED PEOPLE

I. Distress

The summer which members of parliament and the rest of high society went home to enjoy was one of the worst in living memory. Throughout July and August the thermometer remained anchored in the fifties and sixties, and a long sequence of grey days and drizzle was relieved only by torrential downpours and hailstorms. Everyone's first thoughts were for the harvest. 'A cold backward spring' had already stunted the young grain, and a wet summer 'with a singular absence of solar heat' on top of it seemed catastrophic.[1] When the harvest failed the whole community felt the consequences; parochial taxation had to succour a starving populace, hungry people posed a threat to social order and emergency imports played havoc with the exchanges and the balance of trade. Europe, moreover, had fared no better than Great Britain weatherwise, so that the danger this time was magnified by an international shortage. Anticipating a calamity, the corn wholesalers began to conserve their stocks while the fields were still green. In the maritime counties, which were fairly representative of England and Wales, the average price of wheat shot up from 65s. to 80s. a quarter in May alone, and though there was a slight easing in June and July, it was again that high in the middle of August.[2] It was almost a certainty that by the time the nation's representatives began to retrace their steps of the summer 'the condition of England' would be the most pressing problem awaiting them.

Granted that a lean year was in prospect, the government's attitude, on the face of it, was puzzling to say the least. While

[1] See the meteorological figures and descriptions in the *Annual Register*, 1816, pp. 112–13, 355; *Gentleman's Magazine*, 1816, 11, pp. 94, 173, 190, 194; Thomas Tooke, *Thoughts and Details on the High and Low Prices of the Last Thirty Years*, 111, p. 78; E. I. Jones, *Seasons and Prices*, pp. 160–1.
[2] *PP*, 1821, ix. 381–2.

the rest of the nation was indulging in morbid reflections on the upward price of corn, the government was using evidence of its own to arrive at a happier, altogether different appraisal. The fact was that the ministers measured the economy's fluctuations in crude fashion using the revenue returns, the excise and the assessed taxes in particular being reckoned 'the true Criteria of Internal Prosperity'. If they were down in any one quarter the assumption was that people were spending less and therefore were less well off, but after keeping a close eye on the figures coming in during the October quarter, Lord Liverpool came to the conclusion that the situation was not as bad as most were making out. At the beginning of September he bade Lord Sidmouth be of good cheer, and what he said then held good later on when the quarterly account was finally drawn up:

> The Revenue looks better. The Excise (which is the most material Branch) good, the Customs still very low, but the great falling off is in the Port of London, which is a proof that it does not arise from Smuggling or diminished Consumption, but from want of Speculation growing out of Want of Confidence. We may trust therefore that this Evil will in a short Time be removed.[3]

If this was a comfort, so was the state of the money market. In the same letter the Prime Minister went on to say: 'Money is in Abundance, and I have no doubt that in a few Months the Market will be glutted with Gold and Silver.' Throughout the war a good part of the profits of economic growth had been funnelled into government loans, and when these suddenly ceased compensating opportunities proved hard to find. At home the sluggishness of trade and industry was discouraging, the canal boom was over and enclosure was a poor proposition in view of the distresses of agriculture. Abroad it was too early to say what the prospects were. Meanwhile Europe's straitened circumstances and exchanges consistently around or above par were bringing a tidal wave of treasure into the country. In February 1816 the Bank's bullion reserves totalled £4,600,000.

---

[3] Lord Liverpool to Lord Sidmouth, 3 September 1816, Sidmouth MSS.; Lord Liverpool to Lord Castlereagh, 11 October 1816, Castlereagh MSS., xxx. 514–17. The second letter is printed with mistakes in *Liverpool*, ii. 281–2.

Eighteen months later they were two and a half times as much. [4]
From the government's point of view the best that could come
of money in plenty was the return to prosperity of the landed
interest. Distress invariably brought the country gentlemen to
Westminster in an ugly frame of mind, petty about public
spending and clamorous for the redress of their own grievances.
Now, for the first time since 1813, agriculture seemed on the
verge of better things. It was not just that corn was going to be
in short supply. An agriculture nourished on capital, as Great
Britain's was, depended as much on easy credit as on a relatively
high return, which meant that low interest rates were no less
important than good prices. What made 1817 so promising was
that a momentary lull in investment was making money cheaper
while the prospect of a bad harvest was making corn dearer.
No farmer could ask for more; and in view of parliament's
recent peevishness no government could either.

Thus in Great Britain there was reason enough for complacency, not least, it might be added, because the labouring
classes, generally speaking, were protected from the full blast
of distress by the fact that wages had fallen less than prices
since the war. But Great Britain was only part of the kingdom.
In Ireland Nature's waywardness could never be taken with the
same equanimity. There a season in which the crops failed and
the peat did not dry was the fore-runner of certain starvation
and misery, for living nearly at subsistence level the Irish
peasant tragically had no escape. However remote from the rest
of Ireland it may have seemed in other respects, the Irish
administration was never insensible to this danger. Throughout
the summer Peel and Gregory, his under-secretary, were in
constant touch with the localities, and after the equinoctial
gales had brought more rain at the beginning of October they
felt that the situation was serious enough to warrant the attention of the government in London; both Peel's immediate
superior, Lord Sidmouth, and the Prime Minister were told
that nothing less than famine lay around the corner. [5] It was
generally agreed that when a moment like this arrived there was

[4] Report on the Bank of England Charter, *PP*, 1831–2, vi. 511–12.
[5] Peel to Lord Liverpool, 9 October 1816, Peel to Lord Sidmouth, 10
October 1816, Add. MSS. 40291, ff. 186–7, 196–7.

not much the government could do. To have it feed half the population was asking the impossible, and to hand out charity at any time had the disadvantage of encouraging the people to turn to the state when they ought to rely on their own frugality and industry. Peel was emphatic that it was far better to do too little than too much:

> ... the Government might in case of *extreme necessity* administer relief by direct interference, but if half the population is in this state we cannot help trembling to think of the consequences of the first precedent. I must say, however, that if there were within the reach of the Government a number of persons *actually starving, & without the hope of relief from other quarters*, I would overleap every difficulty & buy food for them at the public expence. I would only do this under Circumstances of the extremest necessity, and I would do it even under those circumstances with every possible precaution, and with every effort to prevent its being known that the relief came from the hands of Government.[6]

During the really bad weeks of famine in the spring and early summer of 1817, when the scanty supplies of the previous year remained unreplenished by a new harvest, the government stuck faithfully to this policy of limited assistance. An act of parliament authorised a commission to keep an eye on the situation and to advance small sums, but only where local subscriptions were underway. Self-help was to be rewarded not displaced by state charity. As it was, an attempt to distribute seed oats in the famine area showed that anything more grandiose was beyond the government's capabilities: three out of every four shiploads arrived in a rotten condition thanks to double-dealing on the part of the suppliers and the negligence of the government's agents. In condition and disposition alike the government was far from ready to take a generous view of its social responsibilities. Altogether the relief operation probably cost Dublin Castle a little over £40,000.[7]

Even so, Whitehall's effort was pigmy in comparison. In

---

[6] Peel to Lord Whitworth, 8 March 1817, ibid., 40292, ff. 174–8. The letter is printed with mistakes in *Peel*, i. 241–2.

[7] *Peel*, i. 244–5; Norman Gash, *Mr Secretary Peel*, pp. 219–24. According to the public accounts £40,015 was advanced to the commissioners in charge of famine relief. *PP*, 1818, xii. 117.

Ireland the state had to interfere more than it liked because of the colossal nature of the problem and because absenteeism hampered private initiative, but in Great Britain the old-fashioned idea that the poor should look to the parish was still very much in evidence. One parliamentary committee of the period referred to an 'insuperable' difficulty if poor relief became a national responsibility, 'the impossibility of devising any adequate means to check the demands upon such a fund, when every excess in parochial disbursements would be merged in the general expenditure of the empire'. Charity too freely given, it was felt, by diminishing the 'natural impulse by which men are instigated to industry and good conduct' would be the ruination of the poor, and under the old system the rate-payers at least got best value for their money since they supervised its spending directly.[8] But basically, throughout the eighteenth century and well into the nineteenth century, distress was widely believed to be the consequence of economic forces before which the government was almost completely powerless. When parliament reassembled in January 1817 the ministers made a frank confession of their impotence. 'These evils upon this Country,' they had the Prince Regent declare, '. . . are of a nature not to admit of an immediate remedy.'[9] Lord Liverpool was clear in his own mind that the trouble arose 'from the unavoidable Circumstances which grow out of a Change from a state of Expensive War to Peace'.[10] An article in *The Quarterly Review* (incidentally one he admired greatly[11]) elaborated this argument:

> Peace was a great and sudden change, and such a change, however desirable, however necessary, however beneficial at last, could not occur without much immediate inconvenience. It was not our military departments alone which were upon the war establishment, it was every branch of trade, and every kind of industry which was in any way connected with the war or influenced by it. The ordnance, for instance, employed the foundries, the gunsmiths, &c. &c. these manufactories called

[8] Report on the Poor Laws, *PP*, 1817, vi. 4, 11.
[9] *CJ*, lxxii. 4.
[10] Lord Liverpool to Lord Redesdale, 5 September 1816, Gloucester Record Office, D2002, C23.
[11] Lord Liverpool to Lord Sidmouth, 17 November 1816, Sidmouth MSS.

upon the iron and brass works, and the furnaces kept the colliers in activity: thus it was in every part of the great political
machine, (the most complicated that ever existed,) wheel within
wheel, and when one was checked, the obstruction was felt
through all. The whole annual war expenditure to the amount
of not less than forty millions was at once withdrawn from
circulation. But public expenditure is like the fountain-tree in
the Indian paradise, which diffuses in fertilizing streams the
vapours which it was created to collect and condense for the
purpose of more beneficially returning and distributing them.
A vacuum was inevitably produced by this sudden diminution,
and the general dislocation which ensued may not unaptly be
compared to the settling of the ice upon a wide sheet of water:
explosions are made and convulsions are seen on all sides, in one
place the ruptured ice is disloged and lifted up, in another it
sinks; sounds inexpressible by language and wilder than the
howlings of the wilderness, are emitted on every side, and thus
the agitation continues for many hours till the whole has found
its level, and nature resumes in silence its ordinary course.[12]

There had to be then a large readjustment of supply and
demand, a readjustment which would come in its own good
time and no quicker. By improvement and expansion agriculture had snared itself in over-production, and though the Corn
Laws offered a generous protection the farmers still had to pay
the penalty for their 'great and imprudent speculations' in the
past. So too with industry. Peace was always held to be a mixed
blessing inasmuch as depression was its inevitable companion.
Throughout every part of the economy falling prices and
tighter credit would necessarily force a return to normal levels
of production and consumption, but the greater the effort and
therefore derangement of war the greater the pangs of peacetime recovery.

Unavoidable as these were, what the government could offer
in the way of relief was negligible; resistance to what was
thought to be an inexorable economic process was pointless and,
similarly, assistance to hasten it could have little significant
effect. All that was worth doing was to reassure the country that
distress was a temporary aberration and that despite it the

[12] Op. cit., xv (1816). 566. For Huskisson's views see *Hansard* 1st ser.,
xxxvi. 1360–2.

national resources remained largely unimpaired. 'I see no immediate or adequate Remedy which Govt can apply,' wrote Huskisson, an acknowledged expert in such matters. 'Their Game must be patience, temper and great discretion in all that is done or said.'[13] Many would claim that such an attitude stemmed directly from deep-rooted *laissez faire* convictions, from the ideas which Adam Smith had produced or retailed in the *Wealth of Nations* forty years earlier. But this is to grant economic theory an importance it did not possess and never had possessed. Before the 'age of *laissez faire*' the state had always done little in the event of distress, mainly because it lacked the administrative means to conduct a large scale relief operation and because its thinking on these occasions was dominated by the problem of order. It might also be true that the fluctuations of the economy were gentler or distress less severe compared with what came later. Certainly during the period when the principles of Adam Smith were held in high esteem there are many signs that the state was more ready to intervene. While it still relied mainly on what could be achieved at the local level and while it still insisted that the poor should be left to their own devices as much as possible, its humanitarian impulse when an emergency did arise was notably stronger, as was its fear of the excesses to which a distressed population might be driven. Probably the new watchfulness can mostly be explained by the growing evangelical influence in government and by the aristocracy's realisation that popular agitation, being better organised than ever before, was capable of making coherent demands and a sustained protest. The government found both a greater urge to do something and a greater urgency.

All this does not mean that the ideas of the classical economists counted for nothing in the economic policy of the state. The administrations of the early nineteenth century indeed generally subscribed to them. To ignore this fact is to misunderstand how easily the eighteenth century tradition of limited government could absorb the economic theory formally enunciated towards its end. When in 1816 Squire Western, the champion of the agriculturists in the House of Commons, demanded a bounty on the exportation of corn to draw off what he conceived was a

[13] Huskisson to Lord Granville, 13 October 1816, PRO 30/29.

permanent surplus, Robinson, then President of the Board of
Trade, gave him a straight free-trade answer: 'no trade which
could stand by itself needed the assistance of a bounty, and . . .
no bounty could uphold a trade which required artificial support'. Likewise Robinson saw a protectionist policy as essentially evil; as he told parliament on more than one occasion,
to adopt 'the principle of an universal prohibition' or that of
protection to a greater or lesser degree would certainly penalise
those industries dependent on imports and probably others if
retaliation was the foreign response.[14] But the point was that
laissez faire was 'a rule of expediency, always subordinate to the
principle of utility, and never a dogma'.[15] Adam Smith and
those who followed him freely admitted that there were certain
aspects of economic life over which the state had to exercise a
permanent control and many occasions when it had to interfere
albeit temporarily. In the matter of distress the classical
economists generally agreed that in the face of widespread social
misery the state could not afford to remain rigidly non-
interventionist, and it is more than likely that the politicians
reached a similar conclusion from a similar humanity and
expediency. Clearly, should the situation deteriorate, so that
popular discontents jeopardised the government's existence, or
worse the state's, the ministers would be forced to sponsor
relief measures whatever economic faith they subscribed to;
and even supposing things never got as bad as this they could
conceivably be forced to act out of compassion if nothing else.
The theoreticians admitted that the government could not
afford to be doctrinaire. Whether the ministers read or misread
them, their political sense told them the same. Lord Liverpool
and his colleagues had an accepted duty to maintain law and
order, they had sufficient humanitarian feeling to try to prevent
a social catastrophe and they owed a loyalty to themselves, being
in their own eyes the men best fitted to hold the reins of power.
Any administration has to keep loosely anchored to its principles

[14] *Hansard*, 1st ser., xxxiii. 695–8, 1082–3, xxxv. 1045–51.
[15] Jacob Viner, 'Bentham and Mill: The Utilitarian Background', *The
Long View and the Short* (Glencoe, 1958), p. 330 quoted in Edward R. Kittrell,
' "Laissez Faire" in English Classical Economics', *Journal of the History of
Ideas*, xxvii. (1966). See also R. L. Crouch, ' "Laissez Faire" in Nineteenth
Century Britain: Myth or Reality', *Manchester School of Economic and Social
Studies*, xxxv. (1967), pp. 199–215.

in order to cope with the ebb and flow of circumstance. In view of the paucity of its administrative resources and the idea that the state normally should not interfere, if the government did venture to intervene it would immediately betoken a critical situation.

The grim progress of distress throughout the winter of 1816–17 soon convinced most people that extraordinary measures would be required. Though the ministers kept up a cheerful patter in public, by the end of the year their first confident predictions had not been borne out at all. In the half year ending 5 April 1817 the excise was down nearly £1,000,000 on the 1815–16 figure,[16] and this the government, as was its wont, took as evidence of real hardship. Lord Liverpool's forecast of corn in fair supply,[17] too, was upset by a massive exportation to France, promoted after August by exemptions and bounties. Strange to relate, in 1816, a year of wild talk about famine, Great Britain's exports of wheat meal and flour exceeded imports and for every seven quarters of wheat brought in two were sent out.[18] The worst of this was that after a poor harvest nothing was better calculated to send prices soaring. At the beginning of August wheat was fetching 77s. 4d. a quarter in the maritime counties, but by Christmas it was selling at over 100s. and remained as high well into the summer.[19] Naturally the poorer classes were the hardest hit. Just how hard is difficult to say, though the statistics of poor relief give some indication. Between 1812–15 about £6,000,000 a year was spent on average in England and Wales; in 1816 this figure jumped to £6,800,000 and a further £1,000,000 the year following, so that even taking into account high food prices the pauper population must have shown a marked increase.[20] This seemed to afford a glimpse of the Malthusian doom awaiting the country. 'We must always bear in Mind,' Lord Liverpool wrote when the distress was reaching its height, 'that if our Commercial Situation does not improve, Emigration, or Premature Deaths, are the only Remedies. Both must occur to a considerable Extent. It would be most inhuman in

[16] *PP*, 1817, xiv. 14–15.
[17] Lord Liverpool to Peel, 18 October 1816, Add. MSS. 40181, ff. 77–9.
[18] *PP*, 1818, xiv. 184–5, 188–9.   [19] Ibid., 1821, ix. 381–2.
[20] Ibid., 1818, xix. 627–30, 1820, xii. 40–3.

such Case, to encourage the latter, by prohibiting the former.'[21]
A committee which was at work on the poor laws agreed
wholeheartedly, merely adding that from an imperial point of
view the colonies were a preferable dumping ground to foreign
states.[22] But however much emigration was looked upon as a
salutary traffic, the government, in the meantime, was content
to stick to tacit encouragement. All that was done in 1817 was
to relax many of the restrictions and penalties of the Passenger
Act so far as they applied to the insignificant migration to
British North America. By allowing ships to carry more passengers and less food, the government apparently accepted the
pleas of shipowners and would-be emigrants that additional
berths and cheaper fares would fulfil an urgent social need.[23]

If it was true that the better-off among the poor tended to
emigrate, these inducements contributed almost nothing in the
way of immediate relief. Certainly one other piece of legislation,
the Poor Employment Act, which was hurried through parliament in the early summer of 1817, was a more conspicuous
example of the government's concern. About the middle of
1816 Vansittart began to toy with the idea of loans to land-
owners, either by Bank mortgages or an issue of exchequer
bills, but on the grounds that mortgage business was outside
its department and that credit was being conserved in view of a
return to gold the Bank firmly refused to co-operate.[24] The
objections to direct government assistance proved to be no less
insuperable. The principle of advancing public money for
private purposes was not without precedent in times of distress,
but suitable securities were absolutely essential, as was responsible and honest management, and on both these counts
the government was never completely satisfied.[25] Since

[21] Lord Liverpool to Lord Sidmouth, 5 April 1817, Sidmouth MSS.
[22] PP, 1817, vi. 20. See also Sidmouth, iii. 155.
[23] Oliver MacDonagh, A Pattern of Government Growth, 1800–60,
pp. 64–5; K. A. Walpole, 'The Humanitarian Movement of the Early
Nineteenth Century to Remedy Abuses on Emigrant Vessels to America',
Transactions of the Royal Historical Society, 4th series, xiv. (1931). 202–3.
[24] Clapham, p. 60.
[25] According to Lord Liverpool 'the best Professional Opinions' were
consulted, and also those 'well acquainted with the Money Market'. The
general conclusion was 'that such a measure was not practicable, upon any
sound principle, and if practicable would have been productive of more evil
than good', Lord Liverpool to Lord Kenyon, 27 May 1817, Add. MSS.
38267, ff. 12–13.

agriculture was showing signs of recovery with higher prices, the plan was no great loss anyway. Vansittart, however, did not give up entirely. Now that landlord relief no longer headed the list of priorities he proceeded to recast his scheme to mitigate the chronic unemployment in the manufacturing districts. In the past *ad hoc* commissions had often administered loans for public works on parliament's behalf, so in this respect a proposal which offered exchequer bills to corporations and private individuals for the same purpose was nothing out of the ordinary. But previous loans had been economic rather than social in intent. They had been designed to promote the liquidity of capital in crises and to finance various development projects which frightened away private investment. Vansittart's primary consideration was humanitarian, even moral if it was true that idle hands soon found mischievous occupation. He made it quite clear that the commissioners in charge 'would particularly consider the influence the prosecution of any public work would have on the employment of the present unemployed population', and here indeed the short title of the bill spoke for itself. Nonetheless, conscious of the novelty of the plan, the ministers went about its promotion with some diffidence, continuing to insist that 'time was the only effectual remedy' for the nation's troubles, that public works were better carried on by 'commercial speculation', and that 'a combination of circumstances which peculiarly called for the special interposition of parliament' was their justification. Yet the consequences of their action could not be denied, for henceforward it was impossible for a government to disavow an obligation to tackle serious unemployment. Neither, it might be added, was compassion all that prompted the ministers to interfere. Hard times were times of political insobriety among the poor, as the events of the winter had made only too plain. The sooner they were put to work, so the argument went, the sooner they would simmer down and leave the affairs of government to those whose province they were.

As a palliative to the prevailing unemployment the new act was without doubt of little consequence. Brougham's insinuation that Birmingham's redundant population could use up half the sum allotted to Great Britain in just over a

year may or may not have been an exaggeration, but it fairly
called to mind the immensity of the problem. And rural
parishes, as the government fully intended, had no hope at all
of qualifying for loans. Only in the towns, where the labour
fluctuation was enormous, was poor law spending likely to be
up the necessary fifty or seventy-five per cent, and even there
the response was discouraging. All in all, few local authorities
were prepared to run into debt when the choice lay between
higher rates and jobs for the workless, while as far as private
enterprise was concerned the stringent securities, the short-
term nature of the loans and the preference given to works
already in progress killed much of its interest. The disappointing result was that despite the government's earnest
professions of concern the worst-hit areas in the North and the
Midlands went very short indeed. Possibly the measure came
a little too late to be of any real use. Though the ministers
hurried the bill through parliament as fast as they possibly
could—at one point it required a severe redrafting—it was
mid-June before it entered the statute book, and by then, with
a good harvest in prospect and trade and industry stepping up,
the worst of the depression was over. Nevertheless, applica-
tions did come in thick and fast immediately the commission
opened for business. Within two months over one hundred
were on file, which at once disproved the opposition's con-
jecture that capital was freely available for most 'promising
undertakings'. But even if the plan did little to alleviate economic ills or made a meagre contribution to economic development, the gesture alone was worth much. For months the
government had had an authoritarian look about it, had had to
appear so to keep the peace which was its first and foremost
responsibility. A measure like this one was a welcome reminder
that it regarded the people's affection, not the superior power
of the state, as the best guarantee of social order. If the coincidence of prosperity made the Poor Employment Bill seem more
important than it really was, so much the better.[26]

[26] *Hansard*, 1st ser., xxxvi. 27–48, 569–74, 818–19, 928–32; M. W. Flinn,
'The Poor Employment Act of 1817', *Economic History Review*, 2nd series,
xiv (1961–2), 82–92.

II. DISAFFECTION

The violence which accompanied the depression took nobody
by surprise. The tempo of trouble always quickened when 'the
inferior set of people' were or imagined themselves to be
hardly treated, for rowdyism and riot were a traditional form of
protest and social revenge. In October the Prime Minister
spoke of 'a Stormy Winter' ahead, and in the same breath
blamed 'the evil of a high Price of Bread coming upon us before
we have got rid of our Commercial & Agricultural Distresses'.[27]
Yet the idea that the greater the distress the worse the disorder
is quite untenable. Ireland enjoyed peace and quiet throughout
months of famine or near-famine; strangely enough, there the
people's wretchedness and their dependence on the charity of
government and landlord was in itself a surety of good behaviour.[28] In Great Britain the appetite for violence varied
immensely from place to place. Throughout the countryside
the tradition of protest through destruction and intimidation
remained very strong, but there was much that could prevent
an explosion in any one part, from an active magistracy and the
menaces of landlords to charity freely bestowed and sheer
isolation from the centres of disturbance. A similar situation
prevailed in the towns. In some—Birmingham is perhaps the
best example—there was a guarantee of order in the close
relationship which existed between employer and workman, a
relationship strengthened by the growing tendency of the
latter to blame his grievances on the political system and seek
their redress through constitutional agitation. In others, most
notoriously Manchester, there was a long history of street
rioting, often explained by the presence of a large immigrant
element which either was struggling to come to terms with a
new environment or, as in the case of the Catholic Irish,
periodically provoked the latent prejudices of the rest of the

[27] Lord Liverpool to Lord Sidmouth, 21 October 1816, Sidmouth MSS.
See *Sidmouth*, iii. 148, 150–1 for Sidmouth's and Lord Eldon's apprehensions.
[28] *Peel*, i. 235. See also Sir Henry Torrens to Peel, 2 January 1817, Add.
MSS. 40220, f. 160: 'It is the idleness arising in a plentiful harvest of potatoes
and the cheerfulness with which the Irish Peasant lives upon that fare, rather
than work, that create the turbulence of Winter meetings.'

populace. Some towns had a reputation for wildness; some produced movements rather than mobs; some were hardly disturbed by either. The wonder was that the mushrooming towns of early nineteenth century England were as peaceful as they were; the vanished expectations of the newcomers, the tendency for social divisons to harden, the often appalling deficiencies of municipal administration, the lack of an adequate police force—all were fuel for social conflagration. That the amount of violence was slight must be ascribed mainly to the developing political sophistication of the common man there, who if he did feel resentment preferred petitions to pikes and paving stones. It is in cause more than in character that we are reminded of 'the sheer human diversity, complexity and in the best sense of the word, eccentricity' of popular protest.[29] The most robust roots of agitation were local. Even in the event of widespread distress, when feeling ran as high as it ever did, the response of individual places varied enormously. Attempts were inevitably made to harness the disparate agitations so that there could be a measure of central direction and to provoke protest where there was none, but always with limited success. Whatever the ruling class thought, 'clamour', non-violent as well as violent, remained essentially spontaneous and disorganised.

In 1816 the most serious violations of law and order occurred in the spring and autumn, interestingly enough when the line of economic wellbeing was just beginning an abrupt downward trend. Violence as the most primitive form of protest flared up in the old rural society at the first indications of hardship. The worst outbreak was in East Anglia, which for most of May was in a constant state of emergency. What began with isolated cases of midnight arson and angry demonstrations against flour mills and bakers' shops ended with rioting in two market towns in the Isle of Ely, and a special commission ordered twenty-four offenders to the scaffold, though a late reprieve saved all but five for varying terms of transportation and imprisonment. Another frightening disturbance came in October when the iron-workers and colliers of Glamorgan went on the rampage, putting out the blast furnaces from Merthyr

[29] Angus MacIntyre, introduction to Frank Ongley Darvall, *Popular Disturbances and Public Order in Regency England*, p. xvi.

Tydfil to Llanelly, presumably to intimidate the proprietors and also to pick up recruits. Clearly, the protest was less against present distress than distress to come, for the trouble began with foundrymen in employ who took the law into their own hands after a wage reduction had brought home the unpleasant truth that the war boom was over. The same happened in East Anglia where there was talk of starvation and ruin when the corn was half grown. People cried out, so it seemed, before they were really hurt.[30]

Lawlessness like this was exceptional. In the towns and even in the metropolis, the mass meetings and street marches which were the predominant form of urban protest passed off without incident, though thousands were often involved. The December meeting at Spa Fields may have been the occasion for an attempt at armed insurrection, but a few constables were able to round up the madcaps and the huge concourse came and went in perfect peace. There was, in fact, a diminishing preference for violence. Doubtless the presence of the yeomanry and the establishment of a permanent garrison in the 'disturbed districts' after 1812 meant that the army was better equipped to and did take a livelier sense of its responsibilities as 'the police force of industrial England'.[31] At the same time the stern suppression of the Luddites and the success of the agitations against the Orders-in-Council and the property tax must have taught the 'lower sort' the futility of violence and the potential of constitutional protest. Many factors were stimulating their political interest, and their yearning for effective political action was in consequence becoming all the stronger. Certainly the prevalence of outrage was markedly less than it had been five years earlier, even though the price and wage indices (which are not very meaningful in view of the variation in local circumstances) suggest that the plunge from prosperity to distress was as great if not greater. The opposition, quite rightly, gave the people full marks for good conduct. 'No other country in the world,' Burdett claimed, in this instance in full accord with his party, 'could exhibit a population, suffering under such

---

[30] *Annual Register*, lix (1816), Chronicle, pp. 61–2, 66–8, 69–73, 165–7. A.J. Peacock, *Bread or Blood* is a detailed account of the East Anglian disturbances, sympathetic to the labouring class.
[31] Darvall, pp. 260–1.

accumulated distresses, where so much forebearance and temper were manifested.'[32]

To the government, however, these appearances were totally deceptive. Radicals, in its book, were 'revolutionists', and if they employed legal or peaceable means this was a deliberate design on their part to draw attention away from the monstrous evil they would perpetrate. The limitations of the evidence that violence against the state was being plotted mattered little. Constitutional reform leading to 'popular government' was revolution, and it seemed reasonable and safer to assume that what the government did not know or could not know definitely would be towards the same end more directly and viciously. As the ministers expounded the conspiracy for the benefit of parliament, the first meeting at Spa Fields in the middle of November was in the nature of a dress rehearsal when the 'revolutionists' mustered their mob and tested its fervour. After this, plans for a rising a fortnight later went on apace. Ways of recruiting soldiers, sailors and felons were decided, shops and warehouses containing arms and explosives carefully noted, provincial towns warned to hold themselves in readiness, and large supplies of tricolour ribbon ordered in advance. On the appointed day a crowd which came to hear the usual patter about constitutional remedies heard instead the heady language of sedition and half an hour of this rallied a hundred or so for a march on the City, a march which saw shots fired in Cheapside, pillaging in the Minories and one gentleman severely wounded. Nothing more nor less than 'a traitorous conspiracy' formed 'for the purpose of overthrowing . . . the established government, laws, and constitution . . . and of effecting a general plunder and division of property' thus came to light. And it was by no means the end of the danger. Frustrated once, with some of their best men under lock and key in the Tower, the 'incendiaries' went underground to plot and plan afresh. The admonitions against disorder which prefaced every public meeting had been a precaution against premature action. Now they became a blind behind which every conceivable wickedness was carried on—the peddling of penny parodies on church and state, the intimidation of magistrates and other law officers, even an assassination

---

[32] *Hansard*, 1st ser., xxxv. 854, 856, 1084, 1098, 1112.

attempt on the Prince Regent himself. Indeed, the climax of this
continual incitement was a further attempt at insurrection,
evident in the Manchester meetings at the beginning of March;
for though the Blanketeers who set out for London were un-
armed and ostensibly seeking redress by petition, in their ranks
there lurked scoundrels who hoped to take the capital by sheer
weight of numbers. Whatever the opposition said, therefore,
the right of public meeting was being perverted before their
very eyes. One sacred liberty was insidiously becoming the
destroyer of the rest, and when this happened securities and safe-
guards needed no other justification.[33]

The period of greatest menace, so the government felt,
lasted as long as 'tumultuous assemblies' were tolerated. Once
the Seditious Meetings Act put a stop to the rabble-rousing, 'the
party of sedition' fell back on hare-brained schemes which
government agents had knowledge of from the start. A rising
at Manchester at the end of March was thwarted by the last-
minute arrest of the ringleaders. Another taking in much of the
North and Midlands two months later was equally abortive,
though more of a powder and ball affair; while most of the high
command was surprised at a rendezvous, two small bands
marching on Huddersfield and Nottingham fell in with cavalry
patrols and they broke up only after shots had been exchanged.
Dispossessed of the people, the 'revolutionists' were seen to be
in no position to challenge the power of the state or 'the great
body of his majesty's subjects'.

The real terror had come earlier when the demagogues had
had thousands under their spell. Though they accepted the
'advance of popular knowledge', the 'march of mind', the
ruling class found it difficult to believe that the common people
possessed a rationality or wisdom equal to their own. Government and legislation, they argued, echoing Burke, were matters
of reason and judgement, and both qualities were best developed
by moving in a world whose horizons were more than local,
by knowledge which extended beyond mere literacy, and by the
experience of power handed down from generation to generation. The 'lower sort' were incapable of good government

[33] Reports on the State of the Country, *PP*, 1817, iv. 1–14; *LJ*, li. 40–2,
285–7.

because of their very lowliness. What was dangerous about the 'diffusion of knowledge' was that it gave them a confidence in themselves without their realising how little primitive passions and impulses remained uncorrected by full intellectual refinement. 'It might reasonably be questioned,' a contributor to *The Quarterly Review* declared, 'whether the misinformation of these times be not worse than the ignorance of former ages. For a people who are ignorant and know themselves to be so, will often judge rightly when they are called upon to think at all, acting from common sense, and the unperverted instinct of equity. But there is a kind of half knowledge which seems to disable men even from forming a just opinion of the facts before them—a sort of squint in the understanding which prevents it from seeing straightforward, and by which all objects are distorted.[34]

This unfitness for power because of irrationality was held to be exemplified in the susceptibility of the people to the blandishments and intrigues of a designing few. The lower orders easily became the tools and dupes of agitators more cunning than themselves, and the French Revolution provided an awful example of what happened when an unthinking, vicious and easily-led multitude was allowed its head. History seemed so near to repeating itself. In 1789 there had been cries for bread and the political system had been held responsible for the distress. Now British people were being told that parliamentary reform would right all wrongs and cure all ills. To the 'intelligent and propertied' in general, it really did seem as if the meetings at Spa Fields were the precursor of revolution, just as the street corner harangues which had incited the Parisians had been in 1789. Even if what had gone before could be overlooked, a very great danger was inherent in any situation where the appetite for violence was so obviously being sharpened. Should the demagogues, who were the real villains of the piece, turn 'the deluded people' on the soldiery there was no saying where it would end, for the military could not hold out indefinitely against the superior numbers of the populace. An army 12,000 strong—almost half the size of the home garrison in 1817—had been required in the North when the

[34] Op. cit., xvi (1816–17). 226

Luddite disturbances were at their height, and in 1780 when the
Gordon Riots broke out, though thousands of troops had been
stationed in and around the capital, it had taken fully a week
to drive the mob from the streets. The worst which could
happen in view of the government's limited peacekeeping
resources was simultaneous or nearly simultaneous trouble in
several different places. This the Radical genius was seen as
quite capable of organising. For a few months, in fact, the
'respectable' classes lived in fear and trembling. If once the
rest of the country was given a lead by London and followed it—
and evidence of co-operation did exist—the prospect was all
too horrible to contemplate.

The government, then, was in a genuine state of alarm when
it asked the House for secret committees on the state of the
country. No matter how well-behaved the crowds which came
to hear 'profane and miserable sophistry' were, no matter how
much the poor were bearing their privations 'with exemplary
patience and resignation', a few desperate men were trying to
and conceivably could poison the public mind to bring about
the worst of catastrophes. In stating the case thus, the ministers
were merely repeating the assumptions of their age. Englishmen,
not only high-born Englishmen, had long appeared to sub-
scribe to the conspiracy theory of revolution; time and again a
malignancy in the body politic was declared to exist and exposed as the work of a wicked cabal, a wicked minister or the
'enemies of order'. It would be interesting to know whether
such a view was mainly derived from the classical historians,
whose writings educated contemporaries were steeped in and
who emphasised the precariousness of political stability and
exalted the individual as the fashioner of events. On this
occasion had the government had better information to act
upon it would have been less prone to alarm, but, as always,
those who represented it in the country—the justices of the
peace—dwelt too much in isolation from the rest of the
populace to assess the situation realistically.[35] Only spies and
informers could penetrate the counsels of the disaffected and
they told tales which made everyone's hair stand on end.

[35] It may be that some magistrates exaggerated the danger in order to get
troops sent to their localities.

Doubtless, some of what they passed on to the Home Office
was pure fabrication. More must have been tavern talk or
second-hand gossip. The trouble was that the typical agent
did not know his trade, desperately wanted to prove himself
and earned money by results; and the more dastardly the plot
the informer divulged the better it was for him. The secret
committees of 1817 felt bound to say that due allowance had
been made for 'questionable' testimony, and this comment
spoke for itself.[36] No doubt the final result of misinformation
was that the ministers exaggerated the danger; but they did so
out of fear, not out of any need to buy support in parliament or
out-of-doors. To be on the safe side the government had to
credit stories about secret arsenals, lists of proscribed persons
and committees of public safety. Too much was at stake not to.
The French Revolution had had small beginnings but they had
led inexorably to the total subjugation of Christianity, property
and law—the three great pillars of civilised existence. Seeing
that in Great Britain these were present almost to perfection,
whereas France, in one sense at least, had been well rid of
Romanism, an idle aristocracy and an omniponent king, there
was all the more reason for an unrelenting vigilence. 'I rely
with the utmost confidence,' the Prince Regent told parliament,
'on your cordial support and co-operation, in upholding a
system of Law and Government, from which we have derived
inestimable advantages, which has enabled us to conclude,
with unexampled glory, a contest whereon depended the best
interests of mankind, and which has been hitherto felt by
ourselves, as it is acknowledged by other Nations, to be the
most perfect that has ever fallen to the lot of any People.'[37]
It was a hymn of praise in which few of his listeners would not
have been disposed to join.

With so much to lose, and within an ace of losing it for all
the government knew, there was no stopping at half measures, a
resolve if anything strengthened after Lord Liverpool had
become convinced that the 'conspiracy' of 1794 had been small
beer in comparison.[38] Strangely enough though, it was the

[36] *PP*, 1817, iv. 13; *LJ*, li. 285.
[37] Speech on opening the Session, 28 January 1817, *CJ*, lxxii. 4.
[38] Lord Liverpool to Lord Sidmouth, 21 October 1816, Sidmouth MSS:
Peel, i. 237; *Hansard*, 1st ser., xxxv. 573.

end of March, almost four months after the incident at Spa
Fields, before the government had the emergency powers it felt
it needed, and the delay was a quite deliberate decision on the
part of the Cabinet. Over this, Sidmouth by no means saw
eye to eye with the Prime Minister. As the minister responsible
for keeping order, not only did he want the armoury of the
law brought up to date as soon as possible, but he also saw
parliament as a platform from which the government and
others so inclined could rally the loyal and harass the seditious.[39]
But Liverpool wanted to act the libertarian as long as he could.
'I have never known,' he confided to Peel, 'any Period of
Internal Distress arising from defective Crops or Stagnation in
Trade, in which the Discussions of Parliament did not do more
harm than the Measures of Relief proposed afforded Benefit.'[40]
The moment the liberty of the individual was tampered with,
he saw, the opposition was sure to make a scene, which would
hardly calm the country; and the more evidence the government
had, the more desperate the situation seemed, the better its
chances of coming away morally and legally supported. Meanwhile, at a time like this when the magistracy had its hands full,
there was much that peers and members of parliament could
usefully do in their counties.[41] Thus to his mind inaction was
clearly preferable. Those of his colleagues who could be collected together in the holidays must have been equally convinced because on 4 November the Cabinet put off parliament's
meeting until the beginning of January. Of course, the difference with Sidmouth was nothing serious. The Home
Secretary, above all, wanted tools for the job. His fellow
ministers wanted to make certain he was not refused them, and
so they held back until the existing laws had been tried and
found wanting.

Probably work was begun on the new bills sometime during
January. From all accounts a decision to seek extraordinary
powers was pending after the Spa Fields trouble, and the go-

[39] Lord Sidmouth to Lord Liverpool, 5 November 1816, Sidmouth MSS;
Sidmouth, iii. 161. The Home Secretary seems to have had second thoughts
on the subject. On 16 September he had written to Admiral Frank 'that, on
public grounds, an early meeting of parliament ought rather to be avoided
than desired.' Ibid., p. 149.
[40] Lord Liverpool to Peel, 18 October 1816, Add. MSS. 40181, ff. 78–9.
[41] Hansard, 1st ser., xxxv. 571.

ahead was given once spine-chilling evidence, good enough to
satisfy parliament's scruples, had come to hand early in the
New Year.[42] The ministers themselves were quite emphatic
that the attack on the Prince Regent on the opening day of the
session had nothing to do with it, and since they had discussed
the state of the country twice in the preceding fortnight there
can be little doubt that they were speaking the truth.[43] It was
on 21 February that the government began bringing its measures
forward. In these could be read in full the fears which had been
their inspiration. One bill, to be sure, merely corrected an
oversight which had deprived the Prince Regent of the protection of the Treasonable and Seditious Practices Act, but the
others hammered home the idea that a distressed population
had regrettably fallen prey to the wicked machinations of 'an
active and enterprising minority'. To destroy this revolutionary
underground the licensing of 'every House, Room, Field, or
other Place' used for public lecture or debate was ordered, any
form of federation absolutely prohibited, the Spencean societies
—supposedly hotbeds of sedition—were banned by law and
habeas corpus partially suspended.[44] The right of assembly was
also restricted to put the common people out of harm's way.
Henceforth, with certain exceptions, a meeting of fifty or more
required what amounted to official permission, and the magistrates had power to intervene the moment they imagined insult
had been done to the king, the government or the constitution.
Finally, since plans to win over soldiers and sailors had come to
light, the incitement of mutiny was made a capital offence.

Though the secret committees remarked on 'seditious and
inflammatory' publications, 'marked by a peculiar Character of
Irreligion and Blasphemy', the press was hardly touched.[45] A
proposal to license reading rooms as well as political clubs got
no further than the committee stage of the Meetings Bill,[46] and
in only a few instances, it seems, did the magistrates act on
Sidmouth's famous circular of 27 March 1817 which conveyed
the law officers' opinion that a person selling seditious literature

[42] Ibid., 570–1.   [43] Ibid., 193, 209; Darvall, p. 226.
[44] Partially, in the sense that it applied only to persons arrested for treason
or suspicion of treason.
[45] *LJ*, li. 42, 286; *PP*, 1817, iv. 6, 13.
[46] Compare the Bill as introduced and reported, ibid., i. 71, 87.

could be arrested and held pending bail.[47] Some people perhaps wondered why the authorities did not make do with the powers they had. The keeper of a public house who allowed 'Publications of a seditious or immoral Nature' to be read on the premises could be deprived of his licence. By law a printer had to register his presses, keep a record of who commissioned work and display his name and address on every copy he produced, the last regulation applying equally to booksellers who were forbidden to keep stock which did not comply. Moreover, anyone publishing a writing tending to a breach of the peace could be prosecuted for criminal libel, and the act of publishing was taken to involve printers and vendors, and their assistants, as well as authors. In such cases the Crown possessed special and important privileges. The Attorney General could threaten a journalist with legal action by filing information *ex officio* against him. This enabled the authorities to dispense with a preliminary hearing of the case before a grand jury, and therefore to evade the influence of a possibly differently disposed public opinion. A prosecution might or might not follow this sort of indictment. Should a trial for libel come on, the defence was likely to have to contend with a jury chosen from a specially compiled list; but even if the matter was not pressed beyond the laying of a charge the accused paid a fine in effect because he could not avoid incurring heavy legal expenses.

Yet in practice these powers amounted to very little. At the local level the justice of the peace often had considerable qualms about exercising the jurisdiction which belonged to him. For instance, a magistrate who arrested a news vendor or who closed a public house or reading room took upon himself to declare what literature was seditious, profane or immoral, and unless a previous judgement had been handed down regarding a particular work this was ample reason for leaving well alone for fear of an action for wrongful arrest. Few, too, were ready to enforce a law which was matter of doubt in important respects. Precisely for this reason Sidmouth's letter to the lords lieutenant evoked a negligible response in the country. On the narrow ground of the decision of the Court of Common Pleas in Wilkes'

---

[47] Aspinall, *Politics and the Press*, 1780–1850, pp. 49–54. For a copy of the circular and the law officers' statement see *PP*, 1817, xv. 7–8.

case (1763), where the defendant charged with publishing a libel was able to plead his membership of parliament, it presumed to declare that persons not so privileged could be apprehended and a surety demanded. However, before taking on a discretionary power of arrest in such cases, which could amount to a power to silence for long periods whoever caught their attention, the magistrates understandably wanted to hear what weightier authorities than the advocates of the Crown had to say. Fox's Libel Act of 1792 had appointed juries, not the judiciary, to decide what was permissible public language. There were similar difficulties with the Hawkers and Pedlars Act mentioned in the same circular. Dating back to the reign of William III this prohibited hawking and peddling without a licence, but whether street vendors of books and pamphlets came within its purview was arguable inasmuch as one clause specifically exempted those who sold 'acts of parliament, forms of prayer, proclamations, gazettes, licenced almanacks or other printed papers licenced by authority'.[48] In view of the expiry of the Licensing Act, the implication was that any writing could be freely sold until such time as it was proved libellous in the law courts. So dubious were the provisions of this act, in fact, that though the Home Office in this instance vigorously defended its applicability, not one successful prosecution, if the Whig opposition is to be believed, was carried in consequence.[49]

Because of these reservations at the local level, it was usually the government which sought to bring 'blasphemers' and 'sedition-mongers' to book. Sometimes prosecutions were the result of some direct provocation, sometimes they stemmed from a natural desire to make some exhibition of authority. But what is most interesting is that they showed the government to be almost as inhibited and powerless as the justices in the counties. The Attorney-General, for example, used his prerogative to file information *ex officio* sparingly because with a free press the common boast of Englishmen a careful line had always to be drawn between necessary and excessive regulation.[50] He

[48] 9 William III c. 27.
[49] *Hansard*, 1st ser., xxxvi. 1186.
[50] Brougham brought in a bill to curb the Attorney-General's powers in 1816. Five years earlier the opposition had called for an account of their exercise.

was also loathe to prosecute every libel which came to his notice, for a court demanded that he prove not only publication, often difficult thanks to the dodges employed, but the malice of the act as well. Cobbett, arch-villain in the government's eyes, put out his twopenny *Political Register* for four months without once being called to account, while Hone the parodist and Wooler of the *Black Dwarf* escaped five libel charges between them, one on the technicality that articles set up in type without a manuscript could not be described as written. All in all, the government was in an astonishingly feeble position. It could not stop the production of Radical 'trash' by censorship because that form of control was viewed with total repugnance; the offence lay only in the act of publication, which meant that the sole deterrent the law provided was a law of libel whose practical effectiveness amounted to very little. Nor could the government do much to check the circulation of writing it found objection-able. To tax penny parodies and suchlike out of existence was a difficult exercise inasmuch as it could destroy the virtuous along with the wicked, the antidote along with the poison. And pro-secutions, however successful, often gave obnoxious works a publicity they could never have enjoyed otherwise and made martyrs of disreputable authors, stimulating them to fresh excesses instead of silencing them. In short, the press laws as they stood were wholly inadequate for the purpose of suppressing writing which the government believed was calculated to throw into contempt the existing social and political order. The fact that Cobbett could outsell every other journal with his *Political Register*, while his opponents relied on subsidies, Post Office facilities and free propaganda, was ample testimony that the government could never force the public to read what it alone considered good and wholesome. Any significant change to harsher laws and harsher enforcement was out of the question. The ministers might bemoan the abuse of the freedom of the press, but as long as they and the country saw a connection between traditional English liberties and national greatness the principle mattered more than the perversion. Not tempted to assume the powers which a totalitarian state commands, the administrations of the early nineteenth century had to learn to endure a growing tide of public criticism as best they could.

Once they had come to a proper appreciation of their helplessness, 'gagging acts' and all other means to browbeat alien
opinion became steadily obsolescent.

Not for one moment did the government expect parliament
to question its assessment of the country's situation. After the
opening encounter on the Address, Peel described the attitude
of the Commons as 'good, excellent with respect to reform and
seditious societies'. Lord Melville, looking back a few weeks
later when all was nearly done, admitted that he and his
colleagues had 'had little doubt of being enabled to carry such
measures as we might deem expedient'.[51] The point was that
parliament had no information to go on other than what the
government gave it. Even those who attended from the disturbed districts made vague assertions and little else. Only one
member, Philips, a Lancashire manufacturer, spoke of what he
had seen with his own eyes and, significantly, he went on to
suggest the credulity of everyone.[52] But with parliament
confronted with evidence of the government's choosing, it was
impossible to expect that it would play down 'the nefariousness
of certain designing persons'. The Whigs laboured in vain
against this engrossment in gunpowder, treason and plot. Had
they had information of the sort the *Leeds Mercury* later provided, after it had done detective work on Oliver the spy's
activities, they might have disputed the government's findings
with telling effect and put things in better proportion. Without
the facts, they fell back on wholesale accusations and tried to
make a splash as the lone defenders of civil liberties. The
government, they said, was secretly nursing authoritarian
ambitions and using the present scare to distract attention from
the economical reform which had hitherto frustrated these
heinously wicked designs. Why else would fundamental free-
doms be withheld when no war was being fought and the people
were peaceably disposed? This was nonsense at any time, but
now such assertions went down even more miserably because it
was seen that half the party did not hold with them. While election by ballot gave the ministers a majority on the secret committees as a matter of course, the few Whigs who were voted did

---

[51] *Peel*, i. 238; Lord Melville to Charles Hope, 2 March 1817, NLS MSS.
10, f. 1.   [52] *Hansard*, 1st ser., xxxv. 702-5.

not prevent unanimous reports being returned. The Duke of Bedford stayed away in disgust, but the rest publicly avowed that the ministers were right—'evil-minded and insidious men' were subverting everything the country held dear.[53] After this, the opposition inevitably faltered. On the Habeas Corpus Suspension Bill they amassed about one hundred votes or two-thirds of their regular strength in the House of Commons, on the others never more than thirty or forty. All the measures were through parliament within three weeks except the legally complex Seditious Meetings Bill, and that passed a fortnight later. Much the same happened when the further suspension of habeas corpus came up at the end of the session; Grenville and Elliot accepted the reports in their entirety, Lamb remained uncommitted, while the others only jibbed at 'extraordinary powers', Piggott and Ponsonby refusing to attend when they read the government's play. Again legislation was hurried through both Houses, this time in barely two weeks. If one member of the Commons' committee is to be believed, 'at the conclusion of their work there was not a single difference unadjusted, except the practical recommendation that grew out of the facts and observations in which all concurred'.[54] The statement summed up the extreme weakness of the Whig position. Even those who agreed there was cause for alarm balked at severe counter-measures, and in this way the party as a whole failed to come to terms with the general feeling of parliament and the country. It seemed wiser in the circumstances to take extra precautions and be sure than leave the government's power as it was and be sorry.

III. 'RIGID UNSPARING ECONOMY'

The problems of distress and order by no means destroyed let alone weakened parliament's obsession for economical government. Throughout the session the opposition persisted

---

[53] The opening remarks of the Commons' report attested unanimity. *PP*, 1817, iv. 3. Lord Milton, Piggott, Ponsonby, Elliot and Lamb sat on the Commons' Committee, and, apart from the Duke of Bedford, Fitzwilliam and Grenville on the Lords'. For their statements in the House see *Hansard*, 1st ser., xxxv. 491, 586, 605, 614, 616, 730, 805.

[54] Lord Lascelles. Ibid., xxxvi. 1086.

with the thesis that every affliction proceeded from the original sin of ministerial extravagance, that distress was the child of bad government and trouble its grandchild. In the words of Burdett's celebrated quip, 'the Expenceans' in their ignorance were perpetually aiding and abetting the villainous, treasonous, godless Spenceans. 'Prompt and effectual reductions' in all departments, Lord Grey's amendment to the Address declared, were 'the first step to relieve the distresses, and redress the grievances of which the people so justly complain.'[55] From the government's point of view such accusations could never be taken lightly. Stories of ministerial perfidy always appealed to the country's deep-rooted suspicion of executive power, and the Whigs, by relaying them afresh, helped to give them greater credence. As Huskisson said, however much the administration might talk of 'inevitable difficulties', the people were all too ready to lay the blame on 'systematic misrule'.[56] In this instance too the greater the trumpetings about sedition the greater the suspicions of 'sensible and moderate men'. Not inconceivably they would conclude that the government wished 'to magnify a mob into a rebellion, in order that a tub may be thrown to the whale, the public attention diverted from economy, and a pretext made for maintaining the military'.[57] In these circumstances what had to be done was never in doubt. With an election in the offing, members of parliament were already being assailed in their counties by reformers and the general outcry against exorbitant public spending. A plan of thoroughgoing economy would not only arm them with a suitable reply but also nerve them to take a tough line with 'treason under the mask of reform' in the meantime. Better still, the Whig argument would fall to pieces; for if the legislature stood forth as advocate of both economy and repression it would openly repudiate the connection between expensive government and civil commotion. Or to use Lord Castlereagh's words: 'the elements of mischief and of embarrassment . . . much blended at the outset' would begin to decompose rapidly.[58]

As it was, difficulties over the budget would have forced a

---

[55] Ibid., xxxv. 57–8.
[56] Huskisson to Lord Granville, 13 October 1816, PRO 30/29.
[57] *Peel*, i. 236.   [58] *Wellington Sup. Desp.*, xi. 660.

cut in government spending regardless of these other considerations. Once again the problem was to balance an abnormal
expenditure with a revenue unsupplemented by new levies or
large loans, a revenue moreover which was falling off alarmingly
as the economy slowed down. At the outset the ministers made
a firm resolution to keep the charge of government, which
excluded the charge of debt, below £18,000,000 if they possibly
could,[59] but, even with this considerable reduction, by the time
ways and means came to be discussed it was obvious that taxation
would contribute little or nothing. Indeed, the revenue returns
for the year ending 5 January 1817 were described as 'a severe
blow'.[60] Making allowance for taxes discontinued in 1816, the
net produce appeared to be down £4,000,000—the excise ten
and the customs nearly 20 per cent. Not surprisingly, there was a
deficiency on the consolidated fund which amounted to
£600,000.[61] Since 1815 had been a year of 'extraordinary
Produce' these figures were not as bad as they looked,[62] but it
still had to be borne in mind that economic recovery would be
slow which made a drastic improvement wholly out of the
question. Without a surplus accruing on the consolidated fund
not one penny of current taxation would be available for the
supplies, and this meant raising the entire £18,000,000 by some
other means. Here most options were ruled out immediately.
The sinking fund could not be tampered with because in the
aftermath of war and during economic doldrums the public
credit was seen as requiring particular support. For the same
reason the ministers would not borrow and increase the
funded debt. All they could really do to make ends meet was
scrape together a little money from tax arrears and surpluses
from previous grants, and cover the rest by an issue of exchequer
and treasury bills while interest rates were dropping and the

[59] Compare the memorandum in Castlereagh MSS, xxxii. 33–4, 37–8
where the charge is first given as £19,321,000 and then as £17,880,000. 'In
order to be *quite sure* of getting Our Expenditure below £18,000,000,' the
latter paper continues, 'and to allow for such unforeseen Expences as never
fail to occur, it seems absolutely necessary that the Army Ordinaries should
not exceed £6,600,000, the Navy £6,000,000 and the Ordnance £1,100,000.
By such further Reductions our supply would stand better by £250,000. . . .'
[60] Lord Melville to Charles Hope, 2 March 1817, NLS MSS. 10, f. 2.
[61] PP, 1817, iv. 182–4, xii. 52–77.
[62] Lushington, one of the Treasury Secretaries, argued this point at length
in a memorandum dated 20 February 1817. Castlereagh MSS, xxxii. 414–54.

demand was good. As the debt to be incurred would roughly equal the debt which the sinking fund would redeem, the year, as Castlereagh put it, would 'be at best Stationary'.[63] But this was better than nothing. Had a larger loan been required, it would have seemed that the traditional policy of paying off the debt in time of peace had been rejected and the public credit sacrificed for a momentary advantage. The search for reductions did not take place simply to satisfy the public's demand for cheap government but to maintain a financial system which had yet to incorporate the idea of a perpetual national debt. 'It was quite clear', Lord Melville wrote in March 1817, 'that unless we could satisfy the country, & particularly the monied people in the City, that at least we were not getting deeper in debt, & that we could so far cut down our expences as to make the two ends of the year meet . . . the most serious consequences were to be apprehended, & at any rate no administration could stand against the despondency & discontent which a different state of things would produce.'[64]

The largest single item in the supplies was of course the army. The previous year parliament had voted over £10,800,000 to support an establishment of 149,000, but as these figures were inflated by the special circumstances of the transition from war to peace, and the demand for economy had intensified, everyone took it for granted that the 1817 estimates would be considerably lower. Certainly throughout 1816 reductions had gone on apace. The returns from the Adjutant-General's office on 25 December 1816 listed the number of effectives as 146,994, almost 30,000 less than twelve months earlier.[65] One of these economies—the reduction of the cavalry establishment at home and in Ireland—was particularly notable because it was unscheduled and because it was achieved in spite of strong representations from the Commander-in-Chief. When parsimony became the order of the day, the cavalry, as the most expensive branch of the service, was more vulnerable than the rest of the army. But the Duke of York had never ceased insisting that

[63] Lord Castlereagh to Charles Abbot, 13 January [1817], PRO 30/9.
[64] Lord Melville to Charles Hope, 2 March 1817, NLS MSS. 10, ff. 1–2. See also Peel to Lord Whitworth, 29 January 1817. Add. MSS. 40292, ff. 115–16.
[64] PP, 1816, xii. 421, 1817, xiii. 193.

the government would reach the height of folly and irresponsibility if its reductions took no account of the army's efficiency. On this occasion, because he saw the cavalry as specially useful in peace as a force to harry smugglers and put down disturbances,[66] he pressed his opposition as far as he could, so far that there was another head-on collision of political and military arguments. Needless to say, once again the politicians worsted the generals. Though the Duke sent a 'very strong remonstrance' to the Cabinet and when that was rejected persuaded his royal brother to intervene, the government by this time was too set in its pursuit of economy to be put off its stride.[67] The real significance of the episode was that it made both parties resolve to avoid such encounters in the future; the Commander-in-Chief fully understood the Cabinet's determination, and the Cabinet, disliking confrontations with the Court, was prepared to appeal to the Commander-in-Chief's tact and discretion.

As this tussle had taken place in August 1816, memory of it must have still been fresh when the new estimates came up for discussion just before Christmas. By then the ministers had made up their minds to be thoroughly ruthless. A meeting at Fife House on 18 December fixed the establishment for 1817 at 130,450, and soon afterwards this figure was further whittled down when Dublin agreed to a reduction after March and the Allied powers to be a partial withdrawal from France.[68] These reductions went to the absolute limit. To have gone further,

[66] See his 'Memorandum Relating to the Cavalry', 29 December 1815, Add. MSS. 48427, ff. 133-5.

[67] Lord Bathurst to the Duke of York, 20 August 1816, Bathurst MSS; *Bathurst*, pp. 423, 425-6; *Wellington Sup. Desp.*, xi. 469-70. According to *The Times*, 4 September 1816, the Duke of York saw the Prince Regent on 3 September. Lord Bathurst had written on 29 August that 'the measure is considered as decided'. The second report of the select committee of finance mentions the reductions as having been carried through. *PP*, 1817, iv. 44.

[68] Memorandum, 18 December 1816, Add. MSS. 48430, ff. 73-4. The establishments in 1816 and 1817 compared thus:

	1816	1817
Great Britain	28,000	26,000
Ireland	25,000	22,000
France	30,000	25,000
India	20,000	17,000
Other overseas stations	46,000	33,000
	149,000	123,000

the government felt, would have been wantonly to jeopardise the security of the nation and the empire. Castlereagh had to admit in the House that it had been found 'necessary in a great measure to put out of view the military defence of the colonies against any external attack', and in private the Prime Minister called it 'an Army not more than sufficient certainly for the Protection of the British Dominions'.[69] The disturbing thought was that in view of home disturbances and the defencelessness of the colonies the Prince Regent might again prove awkward, especially if the Commander-in-Chief had his ear and advice of his own to offer. Fortunately, this time everything went smoothly. The Duke of York promised not to make a nuisance of himself, even agreeing to say nothing on the subject until the day before Liverpool and Castlereagh presented themselves at Brighton. By then the Duke of Wellington, on furlough from France, had himself won the Prince Regent round, telling him so he said, 'that after the Reduction he would still have the means of bringing into the field a better & more efficient Army than I had ever seen in the British Service.'[70] Naturally the drastic reduction of the establishment made possible considerable savings on the estimates. Once serious work began on these, however, the ministers found to their disappointment that their original figures had to be amended upwards. Where one paper hopefully suggested £6,700,000 for the ordinaries and a total charge of £8,730,000—exactly £500,000 less than the amount tentatively held out to the Commons—the estimates in their final form required a vote of about £9,000,000, equal to half the supply. There was some consolation in that that represented a saving of nearly £1,750,000. But what mattered above all was parliament's reaction, and it obviously approved of the government's effort by passing the ministers' proposals with little further ado.[71]

For once, the navy got rougher treatment than the army. It too had busily reduced itself, being in February 1817 half the

[69] *Hansard*, 1st ser., xxxv. 257; Lord Liverpool to Peel, 20 December 1816, Add. MSS. 40181. f. 87.

[70] Lord Bathurst to Lord Castlereagh, 25 December 1816, Duke of Wellington to same, 29 December 1816, Castlereagh MSS, xxxi. 1066-7, 1078-9.

[71] Undated memorandum, ibid, xxxii. 37-8; *Hansard*, 1st ser., xxxv. 258-9, xxxvi. 1101.

size it had been ten months earlier.[72] But this time the ministers took full account of the fact that a fleet could be made ready for service far more quickly than an army. The establishment of seamen and marines barely exceeded the number voted in 1792 and this was irrespective of a growing merchant marine, a larger empire and the rise to prominence of the seventy-four with its proportionately heavier complement than the older sixty-four or fifty. Futhermore, exclusive of money put aside to pay off debts, the estimates for the year were £4,000,000 down on those of 1816. The biggest reductions took place in the seagoing part of the service, for in the administrative and technical branches peace created an enormous backlog of paper and dockyard work as crews were paid off, ships laid up and claims for half pay and pensions sorted out. The wear and tear estimate, for instance, which calculated per man covered the expense of the force afloat, was £1,350,000 less; that for the transport service, a composite charge for troop and supply ships, seamen casualties and prisoners of war, about £1,600,000. Since it was pointless to cut down the civil establishment while the business remained in arrears, the real economies were made in the dockyards. The huge bill run up by ships in ordinary was reduced by keeping smaller crews aboard and by selling or breaking a vast number of vessels beyond reasonable repair. Despite the fast deteriorating condition of the fleet, the sum available for building and repair was cut by a quarter and that for dockyard and harbour improvement by fully one half.[73] Even so, with only 150 battleships and frigates fit for immediate

---

[72] On 25 March 1816 the number of ships in commission was given as 239 and on 1 February 1817 as 185. However, at least 55 of the latter were vessels in the revenue service newly come under Admiralty orders. *CJ*, lxxi. 672; *PP*, 1817, iv. 269, xiii. 339.
[73] See the report of the Finance Committee on the navy estimates, *PP*, 1817, iv. 203–25 and undated memorandum, Castlereagh MSS., xxxii. 274–85. In round figures the estimates for 1816 and 1817 compared thus:

	1816	1817
Ships in commission	£2,911,000	£1,556,000
Ships in ordinary	922,000	687,000
Civil establishment	1,842,000	1,788,000
Shipbuilding and repair	1,565,000	1,139,000
Dockyard and harbour improvements	577,000	252,000
Transport service	1,858,000	261,000
	9,678,000	5,685,000

service,[74] against a supposed strength of 240, most naval men soon concluded that skimping and scraping to this extent could not be defended. They insisted that it was time to call a halt, and well before the year was up they were loudly calling for increases.[75] Never again, indeed, was the financial straitjacket drawn as tight as this. Yet the daring and preposterousness of the reductions showed clearly what frame of mind the government was in. In the second year of peace, as far as both the army and navy were concerned, the cheeseparing was done in earnest.

Hard as the ministers laboured, their work received scant acknowledgement. The public's complaint that government was extravagant focused not on the estimates but on the placemen and pensioners supported by the civil establishment. Most of the politically active among the 'lower sort' argued that these dependents of the executive made up a sizeable host and were the chief means by which the ministers subdued the Commons to the extent that it could not perform capably its function as the popular part of the constitution. Almost every reform petition sent in from the country in 1817 made a set at 'useless sinecures and unmerited pensions, the excessive salaries paid to the higher Officers in the State, and the unexampled magnitude of the Civil List'. Such allegations were derived from the habitual assumption that misgovernment lay at the heart of the nation's troubles, though their absurdity was obvious when pensions, places and civil list expenditure had been under regulation for years and politicians went out of office little richer than they went in.[76] The 'rational part of the community', the 'middling sort', were much less inclined to regard ministerial influence in the House of Commons as excessive or

[74] Navy Board to the Secretary of the Admiralty, 16 January 1817, NLS MSS 1044, ff. 192-201.　　　　[75] *Bathurst*, pp. 436-9.
[76] Canning made some interesting remarks in this last respect. In 1821 when he was deciding whether to seek office at home or the Indian viceroyalty he noted that the salary of £6,000 allowed the Home Secretary hardly met his expenses and that much the same applied to the First Lord of the Admiralty and the President of the Board of Control. The next year too on Castlereagh's death he was torn between the glory but penury of high office and the lavish emoluments of Bengal. Neither the Exchequer nor the Foreign Office, he declared, offered enough 'to provide for the proper performance of the duties of the Leader of the H. of C.' Canning to Mrs Canning, 16 April 1821, 3, 8 September 1822, Canning MSS.

aristocratic government as oppressive. They wanted the last
stages of economical reform to be carried through in order to
bring the influence of the Crown to the strict limits of what was
'just and necessary', and they saw all the more reason to hasten
the work because of the desirability of checking the progress
of radical ideas among the lower orders. Thus whether the
ministers liked it or not the assertion that the Crown's influence
was excessive had to meet with some notice, not least because
the parliament was old, and popular pressures greater in
consequence. An inquiry into sinecure offices had been hanging
fire for years, anyway. Twice when the government was in its
infancy the Lords had provocatively thrown out bills which
would have made a clean sweep of them, and, certain that
sooner or later the Commons would try again, the ministers
since then had anxiously waited every vacancy. The sudden
death of the Earl of Buckinghamshire in February 1816, which
rendered an exceptionally lucrative sinecure in the Irish Court of
Exchequer disposable, finally brought matters to a head.
Should the House of Commons act up to an earlier resolution
to regulate the office, the government saw an 'inconvenient
precedent' in the making, for if one sinecure could be swept
away regardless of the need to reward long and loyal political
service, so could the rest. Fortunately, a lawsuit between the
Crown and the Chief Baron over the right of appointment
provided an excuse to impound the fees and emoluments, and
thus gratified parliament swallowed its impatience. In any case,
until the amount of these was precisely ascertained nothing
could be done. But the whole question of sinecures was only
shelved for the time being.[77] As Castlereagh reported, the week
before Christmas he and his colleagues were all back in Town
going over it anew.[78]

Always the ministers were haunted by fears that the House
of Commons would go too far with economical reform, that
having begun the work it would not call a halt until the in-

---

[77] The office was the Clerk of the Pleas, worth about £8,250 a year to the
principal and £10,000 to his two deputies. *PP*, 1817, xi. 6. For details of the
question see Peel to Lord Whitworth, 8, 11, 15 February 1816, to Lord
Sidmouth, 16 February 1816, Add. MSS. 40290, ff. 56, 63-4, 78-80, 83;
Peel, i. 212; *Hansard*, 1st ser., xxxii. 331-2, 337-8, 546-7, xxxiii. 939-40,
xxxiv. 5-9, 91-6.   [78] *Castlereagh*, xi. 330.

fluence of the Crown had been reduced to negligible proportions and rendered utterly useless for the purposes of efficient government. Somewhere the line had to be drawn between saving money and undermining the relationship between executive and legislature. The right formula or principle in this instance was a complicated one, mainly because a distinction had to be made between offices of wartime creation, now become moribund, and old sinecures representing a traditional influence. The former, recent appendages, were indefensible where the latter were indispensable, and an indiscriminate attack on inefficient offices would have ignored this important difference with perhaps catastrophic results. As the Prime Minister told Lord Palmerston: 'Some of the Lords of the Treasury & of the Admiralty might on this Principle be reduced—Many Political Situations might be expected to be consolidated & in short there is no saying where such a System of Reform & Innovation might stop or what wd. be the result of it when carried into execution.' This did not mean that the ministers were ready to defend sinecures to the last against an increasingly hostile public opinion; in other words, that they would 'rest upon the Principle of a Recurrence to a State of Things wch. had been known & tried & which had not been considered either as profusely extravagant or as dangerous to the Constitution of the Country.'[79] It did mean that they were to be left alone until an equivalent system of political reward had been devised. Seeing that the House of Commons had already insisted upon this, such a condition seemed fair, reasonable and safe.[80]

The weeding out of redundant war offices was completed without difficulty. In April 1816 the Treasury entrusted the work to a small commission of official men headed by Lord Binning, and, as proof of a job well in hand, a memorandum summarising its reports on eighteen different offices and departments was laid before parliament early in the next session.[81] On the other question, though, that of the sinecures, the ferocity of the Commons caught the government quite by surprise. The ministers, as far as economy went, came to the

[79] Lord Liverpool to Lord Palmerston, 30 December 1816, Add. MSS. 38264, ff. 72–6.
[80] See the resolutions of 31 May 1810, *CJ*, lxv. 436–40.
[81] *PP*, 1817, xv. 11–21.

House full of fair words and fine promises. They proposed a select committee to scrutinise their estimates, offered a voluntary tax on official salaries, and in the Prince Regent's name struck £50,000 off the civil list, the privy purse and the Duchy of Cornwall revenues. This was straight-forward window-dressing, probably not altogether sensible, for the House could ponder estimates as much as it liked as it was, and any voluntary austerity in high places could suggest that previous grants had been over-generous.[82] However, for the moment parliament's interest lay elsewhere. Apprised of the government's plans, the opposition immediately demanded a separate inquiry into public salaries and emoluments, and, though the 'country gentlemen' were unenthusiastic, their spokesmen, Wilberforce and Acland, made a damaging affirmation of the Crown's increasing influence and the unsuitability of all-powerful ministerial representation on a committee intended to check it. Divisions much too close for comfort followed the nomination of Huskisson and Lord Binning—two official men—for places.[83] 'The Ministers disconcerted by this apparent temper of the Ho[use],' wrote the Speaker in his diary that night.[84] On the subject of sinecures, the government reluctantly saw no option but to fall in with parliament's and the country's wishes. Probably all along, since the political importance of sinecures was taken for granted, a faint hope had remained that parliament would come to its senses and let them be. The first task of the finance committee was to have been an open acknowledgement of official parsimony through the trenchant examination of estimates and public accounts; its second a consideration of 'further measures' of relief, which might or might not have included the abolition of sinecures.[85] Now, however, with placemen again parliament's pet aversion, the priorities had to be reversed. Sir Matthew Ridley, a Whig stalwart, already had a motion on the Admiralty lords down in the order book, and if this was a taste of things to come, the whole of the Crown's

[82] See Peel's criticisms. Peel to Lord Whitworth, 12 February 1817, Add. MSS. 40292, ff. 141–2.
[83] *Hansard*, 1st ser., xxxv. 252–308.
[84] 7 February 1817, PRO 30/9, 36. The entry is misprinted in *Colchester*, ii. 601.
[85] See the committee's terms of reference, *CJ*, lxxii. 37.

'just influence' was immediately jeopardised.[86] How could sinecures survive if the House in its wrath refused to spare the so-called 'parliamentary' or 'political' offices? Lord Melville fairly stated the seriousness of the situation:

> All our confidential friends in the H. of Commons, without exception, on whom we could most depend, were decidedly of opinion that unless we could come to some understanding & compromise by which we could give the Country Gentlemen a plausible reason for being fully satisfied, we ran great risk of being beat in detail, office after office, & though we might not feel ourselves called upon to resign after losing one or two of those questions, it would be impossible for us to go on with credit to ourselves or with advantage to the Public if the House were to get into the *habit* of beating us, even with many of the persons engaged in that course thinking perhaps very innocently that there was no harm in it, & not wishing to drive us out.[87]

The ministers, then, acted to save not only the government but also a system of government. A decision to surrender sinecures was taken, albeit reluctantly, because it alone was the sop that would do, gratifying the people and therefore those about to face them on the hustings. Not that the Crown suffered any loss of 'constitutional power and patronage' as a result, for a pension scheme reserved for politicians of the highest rank was to come gradually into operation over a twelve-year period as existing interests expired one after another.[88] Needless to say, the government made its proposals public at the earliest possible moment. Ridley's motion stood for 18 February. On Monday, 17 February, after a weekend of Cabinet meetings, 'about forty of the most discontented' country gentlemen were invited to Fife House and told the good news.[89] The next day,

[86] He gave notice the same day the government announced its economies. *The Times*, 8 February 1817.

[87] Lord Melville to Charles Hope, 2 March 1817, NLS MSS. 10, f. 4. See also *Wellington Sup. Desp.*, xi. 660–1.

[88] The Crown to some extent lost its discretionary power of reward, for only those who had served in certain offices for a certain number of years were eligible. Still, the few sinecures that were left had been mostly reserved for deserving cases anyway.

[89] The Cabinet met on Saturday and Sunday afternoon, on each occasion for over two hours. *The Times*, 17 February 1817. For mention of the Fife House meeting see Lord Melville to Charles Hope, 2 March 1817, NLS MSS 10, f. 5; *Colchester*, ii. 604.

presumably, the finance committee sat down to a different agenda. A saving of a few thousand had suddenly acquired more importance than a saving of millions.

After this the rest of the session was plain sailing. 'The language of the Country Gentlemen,' Peel reported right at the beginning, 'is that if the Government can show that they have done the work of Retrenchment honestly—that they will be as firmly supported as any Govt. ever was.'[90] It was soon obvious that they meant what they said. The government having obliged them they obliged the government, so much so that long before the Easter holidays some of the opposition were slinking off into the country. In the finance committee a few days after the Fife House meeting a 'sweeping resolution' on sinecures failed nineteen to two. Thereafter it was as 'reasonable & manageable' as the ministers could wish.[91] The army and navy estimates passed through the House without once encountering serious opposition. So did the Civil Service Compensation Bill, though pensions in lieu of sinecures were a trivial saving and instead of having fewer offices in its gift the Crown ended up with more.[92] Nonetheless, the ministers regarded Ridley's motion as the real test of parliament's goodwill, for an Admiralty lordship was an 'efficient' if 'secondary' office and there was at stake the principle of the smooth and proper working of the constitution through the modicum of influence which it and others like it supplied. It being idle to pretend that the office had an administrative *raison d'etre*, on this ground alone they made their defence. The Whigs, Canning told the House, 'would pull down the building to obtain possession of the ruins'.[93] The majority which followed, therefore, was more than a tactical victory for the ministers. It was the legislature's vote of confidence in a government which refused to admit that the system was amiss. Both reiterated their belief that the

---

[90] Peel to Lord Whitworth, 30 January 1817, Add. MSS. 40292, f. 118.

[91] Lord Melville to Charles Hope, 2 March 1817, NLS MSS. 10, f. 6.

[92] The charge of the sinecures was roughly £100,000 and the pension list at its maximum £42,000. However, many of the offices were reduced, not abolished, and the estimated charge of these reformed establishments was little short of £50,000. Since the subordinate positions were transferred from the principals' to the Crown's patronage, the influence of the latter was actually increased. 'You will perceive the change is more nominal than substantive,' Castlereagh told Wellington. *Wellington Sup. Desp.*, xi. 667-8.

[93] For the debate see Hansard, 1st ser., xxxv. 654-94.

representation of the Crown in the Commons was 'salutary' rather than invidious, that power was being sensibly used and was in no way responsible for existing economic difficulties. It followed that because government was reasonably economical and sensitive to national needs, popular agitation could be only the contrivance of a few wicked individuals. Castlereagh's boast at the end of the session was quite permissible: 'We separated the question of economy from that of seditious reform, and we became masters of both.'[94]

[94] *Wellington Sup. Desp.*, xi. 661.

Chapter Three

THE POWER OF THE PEOPLE

I. RETREAT

TO the ministers, the economy, like the Deity, moved in mysterious ways; and even when they admitted as much few among the 'respectable' classes appeared to hold it against them. By far the larger part of 'intelligent' public opinion was or became as fatalist as parliament, wanting no more than vague assurances of inevitable recovery to bolster up a belief that sooner or later the fundamental laws governing the employment of capital would overcome any abnormal circumstance. Such an attitude was not without significance. For because most of the 'rational public' believed that it was beyond the wit of man to manage the economy, the ministers were not held responsible for the quirks of its behaviour. Squire Western's resolutions on agricultural distress in 1816 cast no aspersions on the government. Brougham's on trade and manufacturing and his address on the state of the country the year following did, but even his friends grudged him their support and he was soundly caned for his presumptuousness as a result.[1] No government yet had shown signs of succumbing to economic adversity. Indeed, the experience of Lord Liverpool's administration from 1815 to 1819 indicates that even in the midst of deepening despair the state of the economy was never anything more than a serious embarrassment. In contrast, a century to come, as soon as governments accepted a responsibility for permanent prosperity, a depression became a political disaster which those in power counted themselves lucky to survive.

Political issue or no, controllable or uncontrollable, the economy's vagaries had to be observed, and this the ministers did in rough and ready fashion. The usual indicators of distress or wellbeing were the revenue returns, the trade figures, the rate of exchange, the state of the funds and the price of corn.

[1] *Hansard*, 1st ser., xxxiii. 55–6, xxxv. 1044, xxxvi. 1392–6.

These were given much greater weight than they actually
deserved. The official value of imports and exports, for example,
based on prices current at the end of the seventeenth century,
bore little relation to their real value, so much so that in the
period 1815–18 exports and re-exports were underestimated
by 10 and imports by 100 per cent. In 1817 an official trade
surplus of £19,000,000 was really a deficit of almost £8,000,000.
Without the government knowing, it was the invisible earnings
of banking, shipping and insurance which were keeping the
country out of the red.[2] Nor was the cost of living indexed by
the price of corn as the ministers were wont to believe. They
spoke of an 'Approximation, which must take place, of the
Price of all Articles of Consumption to that of Grain', when in
fact the opposite might occur. In the latter half of 1817 some
agricultural and most industrial prices continued to rise notwithstanding a spectacular slump in the price of wheat.[3] The
consequence of inadequate statistics, or no statistics at all, was
that the ministers remained interested observers of the
economy's fluctuations, incapable of measuring them accurately or reaching sound conclusions as to their cause. In
1817, certainly, the government's information confused the
expectation of recovery with the fact. As soon as good harvests
seemed assured both at home and on the Continent, the mercantile world went into a frenzy of buying and selling, banking,
of course, on a resurgent demand. This made the trade figures
and revenue returns look deceptively favourable. Imports and
home exports went up 12½ per cent on the previous year while
the net revenue for the last two quarters produced over
£3,000,000 more than the first two.[4] Throughout the prorogation members of the government joyfully bandied about the
latest bulletins of the economy's glowing health.[5] No one

[2] Albert H. Imlah, 'Real Values in British Foreign Trade, 1798–1853',
Journal of Economic History, viii (1948). 148; 'British Balance of Payments
and Export of Capital, 1816–1913', *Economic History Review*, 2nd series,
v (1952–3). 234.
[3] Lord Sidmouth to Lord Sheffield, 21 January 1816, Sidmouth MSS;
Gayer, Rostow and Schwartz, *The Growth and Fluctuation of the British
Economy, 1790–1850*, i. 140–3.   [4] *PP*, 1818, xii. 252, xiv. 11.
[5] See Huskisson to Lord Liverpool, 19 September 1817, Lord Liverpool
to Huskisson, 9 August, to Peel, 30 September 1817, Add. MSS. 38191,
ff. 106–8, 38741, ff. 112–13, 40181, ff. 122–3; Lord Liverpool to Canning,
20 September 1817, Canning MSS.

thought for a moment that the spur, being speculative, would peter out within a year, that the country was riding for a fall through overproduction and overtrading. The figures were taken as accurate because no other yardstick existed.

However, as far as the ministers were concerned, fortune had smiled on them and at no better time. Had the country faced yet another year of distress, issues like the poor laws, parliamentary reform, public order and public spending would have made parliament incorrigible, if not openly rebellious. With a solitary exception, no parliament had lasted more than six years since 1768, fifty years before, which made a general election almost certain in the months to come; and a House waiting on a dissolution always took some handling as members were anxious to gratify their constituents at the last possible moment.[6] Prosperity, on the other hand, drained any popular complaint of passion and purpose. Equally propitious was the way events appeared to bear out the government's earlier perspicacity and confidence. Almost the first words parliament heard when it reassembled was a smug reminder that the ministers had repeatedly ascribed the depression to 'temporary causes' and that now they were proved right.[7] Furthermore, the Pentridge rising in June, to all appearances, had been the last attempt at revolution, and while the improving economic situation may have done more than anything else to settle the country it was still fair to say that extraordinary powers had helped. Certainly, the failure of the prosecution at the trials of Watson, Thistlewood and other miscreants showed only too plainly the inadequacies of the normal legal process.[8] Perhaps the ministers had worked no miracles themselves, but they had not been the false prophets many had made them out to be.

A development of a different sort made the government's joy complete. On the best authority, that of Lord Buckingham

---

[6] The exception was the parliament of 1784–90 which lasted six years and a month. The existing parliament had been elected in November 1812.

[7] See the Prince Regent's Speech, 27 January 1818, *CJ*, lxxiii. 3–4.

[8] True bills of indictment for high treason were found against five of the Spa Fields conspirators, but when the first brought up for trial was acquitted, the Crown declined to produce evidence against the others. At York assizes in July 1817 ten rioters charged with burglary, robbery and aiding and abetting attempted murder were all found not guilty. Prosecutions in Scotland were equally unsuccessful.

himself, the ministers learnt for sure that the Grenvilles and the Whigs had finally parted company. The news, admittedly, must have come as no great surprise. The two had never run well in harness, each being hopelessly out of step with the other over the war, parliamentary reform and domestic disorder; and though the return of peace and parliament's subsequent preoccupation with financial questions temporarily disguised this incompatibility, it was again apparent immediately the national security became an issue in 1817. Like the ministers, the Grenvilles were too impressed with the threat of revolution to have faith in half measures, and the habit of political co-operation with the Whigs was forgotten the moment their conservative instincts were aroused. 'I cannot but think,' Lord Buckingham told his uncle, 'that the moment is arrived when as honest men we are bound to state our concurrence in one set of principles, and our difference from another, upon the adoption of the one or the other of which in these difficult times depends as *we all* believe the safety of the Country.'[9] In fact, the difference of opinion was not as serious as he liked to believe. There were plenty of moderate Whigs who felt the same about sedition as he did, and in the past the party had had to learn to live with its dissensions or perish. Indeed, Lord Grenville was reassuring Grey that they were still political allies soon after the secret committee on which he sat reported back to the House of Lords.[10]

It was Buckingham, a restless grandee with few qualifications for the political glory he thirsted for, who sought the break, and circumstances so favoured him that in the end he got his way. As early as July 1815 his mood was not to 'conscientiously embark again in systematic opposition to Ministers', being convinced in his own mind that the variance with the Whigs over the Bourbon restoration was 'a vital distinction upon public principles' and 'a disunion of political party'. A year and a half later he came to the conclusion that the Grenvilles and their allies were in total disagreement: '. . . surely,' he argued, it would be better at once to take our line, than to sustain the odium attending principles which are abhorrent to our own,

[9] Lord Buckingham to Lord Grenville, 9 February 1817, Grenville MSS.
[10] Austin Mitchell, *The Whigs in Opposition, 1815–30*, p. 106.

and the giving apparent sanction & support to a party with which upon *every* point now of policy we differ!'[11] None of his relations put up a strong resistance to the idea of separation. Charles Williams-Wynn, the leader of the coterie in the House of Commons, who might have been expected to know the state of the parties best, regarded himself as a political tenderfoot who could do no better than take the advice of his maternal uncles, Lord Grenville and his brother Thomas. They for their part took the view that the day of younger men had arrived, that Buckingham, as the succeeding paterfamilias, should be allowed to play the game his own way. 'I am sure I have no right, & I know not why I should have any wish, to restrain him from doing what he thinks best,' Lord Grenville wrote in April 1817.[12] It was probably this sudden spasm of self-assertion by his nephew which finally persuaded him to announce his retirement from serious politics.[13] Always punctilious of honour in public life, he was the last person to want accusations of desertion bandied about, and the death of Ponsonby, who as leader in the House of Commons had been the choice of both Grenvilles and Whigs, banished what few inhibitions remained about compromising old loyalties. Though Buckingham had seen little future in 'a party of occasional support and occasional opposition' at the beginning of the session, before its close the whole family was enthusiastic for a declaration of political independence. This was done at the first possible opportunity. Immediately parliament resumed in January 1818 Williams-Wynn seated his tiny following on a bench apart from the rest of the opposition. Whether his army, as Buckingham jocularly called it, with its 'general, five men & a drummer of great experience' could attract recruits, remained to be seen. Certainly, the new party, in Williams-Wynn's words, had no distinguishing principle other than 'general disapprobation of rebellion & want of confidence in Ministers'.[14]

[11] Lord Buckingham to Lord Grenville, 16 July 1815, 9 February 1817, Grenville MSS.
[12] Lord Grenville to Thomas Grenville, 16 April 1817, Add. MSS. 41853, f. 359.
[13] *Hansard*, 1st ser., xxxvi. 1013.
[14] Lord Buckingham to Lord Grenville, 13 February 1817, Grenville MSS; Lord Grenville to Charles Williams-Wynn, 2 July 1817, Charles Williams-Wynn to Lord Grenville, 1 July, 19 November 1817, Lord

The government, of course, took a lively interest in reports of Grenville discontent, because while occasional cooperation could provide no great addition of numbers or speaking talent, it was bound to be a constant reminder of the opposition's disarray, even of its immoderation if the departure of the conservative Grenvilles allowed 'the Mountain' a larger say in Whig counsels. From time to time discreet inquiries were made to find out how matters stood. Lord Buckingham reported one such conversation in April 1817, but what he was sanguine enough to believe was an offer of office his uncle called 'some co[a]rse wishes ... expressed to him as matter of compliment, or thrown out without any meaning at all'.[15] A few days later, however, Grenville himself was favoured with advance copies of the government's place and pension bills, and some time during the summer he was drawn into a discussion on the financial situation by a Treasury official he had come to know while premier in 1806–7. An account of the conversation was duly passed on to Lord Liverpool, who no doubt was interested to see how Grenville's ideas largely coincided with his own.[16] Towards the end of the year the government definitely made up its mind to co-operate with the Grenvilles whenever possible. Probably the decision was reached in December, when the old flirtation with Buckingham was renewed, for he could keep no secret and made it quite clear that the rupture with the Whigs was beyond repair.[17]

Once begun, the new friendship looked immensely promising. Harrison of the Treasury, the same intermediary of the summer, had a long interview with Buckingham on 24 January 1818, and after going over government policy for the ensuing session in general terms they found themselves in almost perfect agreement.[18] In all likelihood the ministers interpreted

Buckingham to Charles Williams-Wynn, 2 July, 15 September 1817, Coed-y-maen MSS.; Buckingham, *Regency*, ii. 211–13.

[15] Lord Grenville to Thomas Grenville, 16 April 1817, Add. MSS. 41853, f. 357.

[16] Lord Liverpool to Lord Grenville, 25 April 1817, ibid., 38266, ff. 53–4; Lord Buckingham to Lord Grenville, 26 January 1818, Grenville MSS.; Buckingham, *Regency*, ii. 207.

[17] Lord Buckingham to Charles Williams-Wynn, 17 December 1817, Coed-y-maen MSS.

[18] George Harrison, Assistant Secretary to the Treasury, 'Memorandum

this, as Buckingham's relations angrily did, as an 'implied *pledge* of co-operation'.[19] There certainly was no reason to think that Buckingham had spoken out of order. Lord Grenville's explanation that having retired from active politics the overture was unacceptable to him personally, while protecting his nephew from a public embarrassment, made it natural to conclude that the latter had acted on his own good authority as party leader.[20] As a result, the government had every right to rejoice. If the Grenvilles were willing to compromise their independence by accepting confidential communications from official men, they were never likely to become a formidable third party. Dissociated from the main body of the opposition, but still professing to be in opposition, they needed to oppose to survive, and then on principles not merely details. From 1801–5 Grenville had kept his connection intact by denouncing the pacific inclinations of Pittites and Foxites alike. From 1818 his successor wasted his inheritance on general support of the ministers interrupted by an occasional petty opposition. To suggest, as Williams-Wynn suggested, that 'general disapprobation of rebellion & want of confidence in Ministers' gave the Grenvilles a separate identity was nonsense. Sedition was an issue which cropped up only now and again, and irregular voting on the government side hardly manifested a grave dissatisfaction or displeasure with those in power. The fact of the matter was that the Grenvilles never did and never could have become an effective third party because they had neither a cause nor leaders to inspire one. Their true sympathies lay with the government and inevitably they drifted into its orbit, so that apart from an occasional confidence their support cost the ministers nothing. 'It is much more for the interest of the Ministers,' Grenville had written in April 1817, 'to receive the sort of assistance which naturally results from our acting upon

---

of a Conversation with the Marquis of Buckingham, Saturday 24 Jany. 1818', Add. MSS. 38367, ff. 235–41; Lord Buckingham to Lord Grenville, 26 January 1818, Grenville MSS.

[19] Charles Williams-Wynn to Lord Grenville, 28 January 1818, Coed-y-maen MSS.; Buckingham, *Regency*, ii. 204–8.

[20] Lord Grenville to [George Harrison], 28 January 1818, Grenville MSS. For his anxiety to avoid appearing to reprove Buckingham see Lord Grenville to Charles Williams-Wynn, 28 January 1818, Coed-y-maen MSS.; Buckingham, *Regency*, ii. 209.

our own notorious, & unchanged, opinions, without any junction, real or apparent, than to have to make arrangements for
admitting & satisfying the claims of a new set of adherents.'[21]

The Whigs themselves shed no tears at the Grenvilles'
going. If there were regrets they were sentimental rather than
serious, for in this case the loss of a dozen votes in the Commons
was well worth the corresponding gain in party accord. Indeed,
in one respect the separation perhaps seemed almost provi-
dential. With an election close at hand, and preparations already
underway, a spirited showing in parliament was eminently
desirable, and this an opposition of friends had a much better
chance of doing than a coalition of fellow-travellers. Fortunately for the government, the Whigs, bedevilled by inept
leadership and thoroughly out of sorts after long years in the
political wilderness, still searched in vain for an explicit
identity. In 1818, having exhausted, it seemed, the potentialities
of the new situation created by peace, they lapsed into a state
of supineness and indifference, content to live on past glories
and wait on events. Before the Easter recess they were lucky to
get sixty votes in a division, and in the dog days of the session
half that number. Thwarted in their main line of attack by the
government's readiness to lift the suspension of habeas corpus,
which they might easily have guessed would happen, their
opposition to the bill indemnifying magistrates and others for
their use of emergency powers and their motions against spies
and informers became little more than a stultifying repetition
of the previous session's debates.[22] Even economy seemed a
horse scarcely worth flogging, for once again a select committee
told parliament all it wanted to know. Significantly, when a tax
on leather did come under heavy fire from interested parties, a
stern appeal to save the revenue succeeded, despite an initial
government defeat and parliament's notorious sensitivity to
questions of this sort in an election year.

Even so, the ministers did suffer one major setback in the

[21] Lord Grenville to Thomas Grenville, 16 April 1817, Add. MSS.
41853, f. 358.
[22] See Williams-Wynn's comment, Buckingham, *Regency*, ii. 236: 'The
House is very dull, and the debates flat. We have nothing but the hashed-up
Habeas Corpus and Indemnity, which really is stewed and devoured to the
bare bones.'

session, and it did concern expenditure, the old problem of
royal expenditure at that. But as they brought it wholly on
themselves the success was hardly the opposition's. The birth
of a stillborn child to Princess Charlotte, followed shortly
afterwards by her own deeply lamented death, left George III's
twelve surviving sons and daughters without a single legitimate
heir. Worse still, while the Prince Regent's bachelor brothers
appeared to lack none of the voracious sexuality of the Hanoverian ilk, even the youngest were well in their forties. 'We are
thrown quite out to sea,' Lord Liverpool wrote in dismay, 'and
there is no expedient to which we can look with real satisfaction.'[23] The least that could be done was to find matches for the
unmarried royal dukes without undue delay, and in this connection the ministers lost no time in impressing each with a
proper sense of his responsibility to the state, Lord Liverpool
going so far as to urge the Prince Regent to a brotherly intervention.[24] The one who was most contrary was the Duke of
Clarence, the eldest and therefore the nearest to the throne;
Cambridge, who was already paying addresses to a German
princess, was accepted at once, and Kent was equally successful
with another not long afterwards. Fifty-two years old, up to his
ears in debt and the devoted father of ten illegitimate children,
Clarence, as he himself quickly found out, was hardly Europe's
most eligible bachelor, and he stubbornly refused to put public
duty before private comfort. A memorandum of his terms, which
the Prince Regent's private secretary passed on to the Prime
Minister, included a town house, an allowance of £40,000, an
outfit of £22,000 and the writing off of £17,000 of debt. These
demands, made shortly before Caroline of Denmark was
selected from the catalogue of Protestant princesses, forced the
Cabinet to make what in retrospect must have seemed a regret-
fully hasty decision, for in conceding all of them except the house,
and agreeing at the same time to allowances of £30,000 for the
younger princes, the ministers committed themselves in
advance on a highly delicate question.[25] Since the death of
Princess Charlotte and the final liquidation of the Prince
Regent's debts saved the consolidated fund from any additional
charge, the economy of the proposal was irreproachable. Nor

[23] *Liverpool*, ii. 322.   [24] *George IV*, ii. 225.   [25] Ibid., pp. 227, 236–8.

was it lacking in precedent. When the Duke of York had been in much the same situation Clarence was now in, Pitt had treated him even more generously. The great trouble was that parliament shared a pronounced dislike of George III's disreputable brood with the rest of the country, and the excuse that the times were exigent and that an election was near was an opportunity of paying off old scores too good to miss. Wellington's exasperated comment must be accepted as typical: 'They [the royal dukes] are the damnedest millstone about the necks of any Government that can be imagined,' he told a Whig acquaintance. 'They have insulted—*personally* insulted—two-thirds of the gentlemen of England, and how can it be wondered at that they take their revenge upon them when they get them in the House of Commons?'[26]

Not that the government threw caution completely to the winds. After polite refusals at two foreign courts and a brief infatuation for a rich Oxfordshire heiress which the ministers and his brothers bullied him out of, Clarence was able to announce his engagement to Adelaide of Saxe-Meiningen, and the morning before the royal message was sent down to the Commons about eighty 'office men' and 'country gentlemen' were invited to Fife House to hear what it was proposed to vote him and his brothers. The purpose of the meeting was not that of a party caucus. The sixty or seventy who turned up listened in silence and departed in silence. Because governments mostly depended on the support of those whose loyalty to party was sometimes less than their loyalty to parliament as critic of the executive, the ministers used such meetings not to reach a consensus with the rank and file on policy but to sample the likely reaction of the House regarding specific and controversial measures. Plans were merely disclosed, never formulated, for that was the task of the Cabinet. Parliament indeed remained deliberative in the best sense of the word, for there Cabinet decisions usually ran the test of supporters and opposition at one and the same time. On this occasion rumours of disapproval had been making the rounds and the government was anxious to ascertain the feelings of the 'country gentlemen' to avoid the embarrassment of a parliamentary defeat. As it was, the cool

[26] *Creevey*, p. 277.

reception, which greeted the proposals, together with private hints from friends who stayed behind, left the Cabinet in no doubt. The allowances had to be reduced, whatever insult was done the royal dukes by a public admission of their unpopularity.[27]

The suggestion, then, that the government was browbeaten into submission on the night the message was brought down is quite untenable. Enough opinions had already been collected to show that friends whether in or out of office were in two minds, and the fighting talk of half a dozen backbenchers on the floor of the House only strengthened this conclusion. On moving the address of thanks to the Crown, Castlereagh was deliberately non-controversial, saying nothing of measures arising, ostensibly because the courtesy was a mere formality. Nor was it shameful, as the opposition tried to pretend, to have to revise measures which parliament officially or unofficially already knew about. This sort of shuffle was inevitable when the executive could not come to the legislature in command of a firm party majority. The real embarrassment occurred when the House of Commons rejected the Cabinet's amendments. A meeting at Fife House on the day after the message was presented agreed in principle to reduction, but waited to hear from the Duke of Clarence before going further. In itself this was an awkward delay because the usual practice was to take royal messages into immediate consideration. As soon as he consented to an additional allowance of half the original sum, however, the ministers needed no other excuse to treat his brothers likewise, and since this would save £22,000 on the consolidated fund they had fair grounds for assuming parliament's gracious acquiescence. Where they went wrong was to forget or underestimate the unpopularity of the royal family, always excepting the pathetic old king and his redoubtable consort. Clarence, who retired after an undistinguished naval career to preside

---

[27] *Colchester*, iii. 43; *Peel*, i. 262–3; Buckingham, *Regency*, ii. 254–5; A. Aspinall, 'English Party Organisation in the Early Nineteenth Century', *English Historical Review*, xli (1926). 393. A list of members among the Liverpool Papers is almost certainly a list of those invited. It contains 79 names including 20 official members. Add. MSS. 38366, f. 133. It is interesting to note that Charles Williams-Wynn is not included, though Tierney told the House he had been sent a letter of invitation. *Hansard*, 1st ser., xxxviii. 42.

over a *menage* of illegitimate children, was regarded as something of a buffoon, and, though he had special claims for
distinction as the eldest of the unmarried dukes, parliament
flatly refused to grant the larger allowance which the government
urged on his behalf. Cumberland also felt the full weight of
parliament's disapprobation. In 1815 he had married a princess
whom the Queen declined to receive, and now, as then, the
Commons on the strength of this snub denied him any marital
income whatever. Only Cambridge and Kent were treated as
generously as the government wished. All in all, on the eve of
an election it was a very unfortunate episode. Because the House
in this instance necessarily professed more interest in economies
than casting aspersions on 'illustrious persons', the impression
remained that the government had fallen back into old errors of
extravagance all too easily. 'If the public necessity interposed,'
a prominent country gentleman had thundered during the
debates, 'the royal dukes, in common with every other description of persons in the country, must yield to the pressure of the
times.' This the ministers had not seemed ready to concede,
with the result that for the first time since the defeat of the
property tax they had been beaten on a point of economy in a
full House.[28]

How serious the mistake really was, probably dawned on the
government after the election in June. For that exhibition of
summer madness, despite improving economic prospects and
thoroughgoing retrenchments, made it plain that many people
were still wont to see the country's misfortunes as aggravated
if not caused by bad government. Such was the alarm and
exasperation of public opinion that in Great Britain the election
saw more contests than any other before 1832, even though one
object of a premature dissolution was to avoid precisely this
nuisance. Canning, fresh off the hustings at Liverpool, could
not help wondering whether the parliament ought to have been
allowed to die a natural death: 'I thought & think that those of
our friends who may have had to fight battles as hard as mine,
but with less certainty & at more expence, will feel that they
have been exposed to popular obloquy & violence by twelve

[28] *Bathurst*, pp. 447–8; *Hansard*, 1st ser., xxxviii. 1–13, 23–31, 40–7,
51–74, 76–154, 725–34.

months *unnecessarily too soon*—not to mention the chance that *in* twelve months the publick mind might have become more tranquilized.'[29] Not that a waning popularity could be read in the actual result. When most of the English returns were in, Arbuthnot counted twenty-five gains and thirty-five losses, while about a week later, after the government's better showing in Scotland and Ireland, Croker calculated a net loss of seven or eight.[30] Of course, with over 150 maiden members and some others professedly non-party, it was all very much a guessing game. Arbuthnot's opposite number, Lord Duncannon, estimated a Whig gain of twenty to twenty-five, which led Tierney to declare '175 members so decidedly in opposition as to desire to have notes sent to them'.[31] Only the first trial of strength in the new House would begin to determine the actual state of the parties.

It was what Canning called 'the spirit of the general return' which was particularly disconcerting.[32] Except at Liverpool where he and General Gascoyne held off a determined Whig assault, the government made little or no impression in the largest constituencies. The City of London displaced two friendly independents, Southwark showed scant mercy to a renegade Whig who had supported the suspension of habeas corpus, and for once, even a naval hero—a protégé of Admiral Hood, a former member, moreover—retired baffled from Westminster. Most provoking of all, a contest in Devonshire saw a Whig stalwart head the poll, and Acland, a leading country gentleman, beaten into third place. Huskisson, pondering the results at his country retreat in Sussex, came to the conclusion that the government was sadly out of touch. As he told Lord Liverpool in successive letters:

> . . . I cannot be indifferent to what the Opposition (not the Whigs but the high popular Party) will consider as a triumph in

[29] Canning to Lord Liverpool, 25 June 1818, Canning MSS.
[30] *Fortescue*, x. 441; Croker to Peel, 9 July 1818, Add. MSS. 40184, f. 233. For other progress reports and surmises see Lord Liverpool to Lord Talbot, 18 June 1818, ibid., 38272, f. 160; Croker to Peel, 1 July 1818, ibid., 40184, f. 210; Lord Liverpool to Huskisson, 2 July 1818, Canning to Huskisson, 5 July 1818, ibid., 38741, ff. 226, 229–30; Buckingham, *Regency*, ii. 265.
[31] *Fortescue*, x. 441, 442.
[32] Canning to Lord Liverpool, 25 June, 2, 5 July 1818, Canning MSS.

so many populous indications of their strength. It is a bad symptom, and will, I am afraid, have an influence with many of our well disposed Friends on all trying questions. The low periodical press has everywhere done more mischief than many are disposed to admit. I can trace it among our yeomanry in this County. They despise the Whigs; but they are no longer what they were ten years ago in their attachment to the old Tory interests and principles which are prevalent in the Nobility & Gentry.

Be assured that the feeling is strong in the Country, that we have not done enough.... The old Remark that a Ministry enjoying the cordial good will of the Sovereign is best for War, but unfitted for Peace, and especially with the present Sovereign, is making way among many well meaning People, notwithstanding all their apprehensions of the other possible consequences of not supporting the present Administration. I venture to say this much to you generally; because I am convinced that without great prudence in the Regent's Expenditure, and something more than has hitherto been done to diminish that of the State, you will feel the bad consequences in the new Parlt—and in public opinion, which is after all the power to which we must look for any durably prevailing influence in P[arliamen]t itself.[33]

Huskisson cannot have been alone in this heart-searching, of course. Doubtless there were many others who would have read Lord Liverpool the same lecture, for anyone could see that the government's standing in the country was a shadow of what it had been in the years of glory and victory. The truly sobering thought was that 'economy and reduction' continued to be 'the passions of the day', and that on this score the people had been much less easily satisfied than their representatives. The 'middling sort', especially, who made up a significant portion of the electorate, were still greatly disturbed by the phrenetic and unruly radicalism exhibited by the urban poor the previous year. As the complaint against extravagant government had gone so far, they felt that it was vital that the ministers apply themselves even more diligently to the task of economy to keep subdued the passions of an ignorant populace. These

---

[33] Huskisson to Lord Liverpool, 3, 9 July 1818, Add. MSS. 38191, ff. 112, 113–14.

fears, in fact, suggested a wavering of confidence in aristocratic government. Lord Liverpool knew well, as did the rest of the Cabinet, that possession of the power of the state by his class mainly depended on its performance as judged by the rest of the nation. If it was once widely believed that the aristocracy was the servant of something other than the nation and therefore incapable of taking a national view, the extinction of its hegemony could be only a matter of time. Government in the early nineteenth century involved a constant reference to the demands of the public, which were all the time becoming more explicit and more direct, and the needs of the state as these were defined by an oligarchy; it was a constant search for solutions which would have the approbation of the small portion who exercised power directly and the much larger portion who exercised it ultimately. In the particular circumstances of 1818 such a formula required the ministers to conciliate the 'lower sort' as far as was safe in order to calm the fears of their betters; one section of public opinion insisted that aristocratic government was extravagant and partial, another wanted the falseness of the assertion to be tangibly demonstrated. Despite the honest labour of the administration since 1815, economy continued to be an issue mainly because the administration's deeds never matched the gross and unrealistic expectations of that part of the public which was quickly coming to an awareness of its political might. In view of the alarm of 'respectable' opinion at a popular radicalism of unprecedented strength and aggressiveness the new parliament could be expected to prosecute the inquiry into extravagant government even more zealously than its predecessor. It was a situation fraught with danger for the ministers. A general election having been held, they needed to demonstrate as soon as possible that their hold upon the House of Commons had not been appreciably weakened;[34] and yet such a trial of strength had obvious risks when it was likely that a large number of members would come to Westminster with fewer illusions about the power of public opinion. A parliament which leaned towards the people necessarily pulled the government in the same direction.

Work began on the estimates in the middle of July, im-

[34] *Bathurst*, p. 456.

mediately Lord Castlereagh arrived back from electioneering in Ireland. There was no time for delay because in September he was due to attend the conference of European powers at Aix-la-Chapelle, and not knowing how long he would be away the Prime Minister was anxious to have the most important decisions settled before he left. Both agreed that the best way to enforce reductions was to set each service an arbitrary maximum—£6,000,000 for the navy, £8,700,000 for the army and £1,100,000 for the ordnance, the last sum excluding whatever might be fetched by the sale of unwanted property and old stores. Fortunately, in no instance did the departments prove uncooperative. The Master-General of the Ordnance was uneasy about the size of the sums allotted for works and the reduction of depots in the West Indies, but he was enough of a politician to appreciate the necessity of the times even if his professionalism was outraged by the suggestion that superiority at sea permitted some neglect of local defence.[35] The Duke of York, too, was no less compliant, perhaps surprisingly so, because remembering previous tussles on the subject the ministers frankly admitted their chariness in broaching it anew.[36] On this occasion what differences there were merely concerned the relative strengths of the cavalry and infantry, not the reduction itself.[37] Where the Commander-in-Chief argued the cavalry's greater usefulness and the difficulty of replacing a corps once broken, the ministers pointed to its disproportionate expense; a regiment of dragoons with 288 mounted and 80 dismounted rank and file, such as he wanted, cost £6,400 more than an infantry battalion of 650. Agreement was reached eventually by dismounting a further five men from each troop and reducing another regiment. This left the army with eleven more regiments and battalions than the 1818

[35] *Wellington Sup. Desp.*, xii. 860–3.
[36] Lord Liverpool to Lord Sidmouth, 6 August 1818, Add. MSS. 38273, ff. 14–20.
[37] There was a meeting between the ministers and the Duke of York on 7 August 1818. At it he was told the sum which the estimates were on no account to exceed, 'from the absolute necessity of a great diminution in the general expenditure of the Country' and irrespective of 'the Force which might be deemed necessary to secure these Realms and the Colonies from Foreign Insult'. He replied that he thought it 'His duty not to intrude upon Them any opinion of His own upon that head.' Memorandum, 28 August 1818, ibid., 38368, ff. 25–32.

establishment had borne, but 9,000 fewer men, an arrangement which saved £268,000 on the estimates and also made any sudden augmentation comparatively easy.[38]

Of the three services the navy alone found it impossible to keep within the sum prescribed by the government. For that no fault lay with the Admiralty. Lord Liverpool was the first to admit that Lord Melville had been his usual obliging self.[39] The insuperable difficulty was the fast deteriorating condition of the fleet, a problem Melville was still wrestling with in his last days as First Lord. Inferior workmanship in the haste of war, aggravated by constant seagoing and less durable Canadian timber, brought home hundreds of rotting ships which the overworked and probably inefficient dockyards had no hope of coping with. Rather than attempt such a mammoth repair job, between 1814 and 1820, 552 ships were sold or broken up, and in roughly the same period only 70 were launched.[40] Little wonder that at the beginning of 1818 the Navy Board reported 146 frigates and ships of the line in a seaworthy condition where two years before the Admiralty had planned on having 260.[41] Any economy under the head of building and repairs then was wholly out of the question as far as naval administrators were concerned, and Melville was not wide of the mark when he thought parliament would never condone it either. 'There is no object upon which the House will be less disposed to call for a parsimonious expenditure' was the Finance Committee's comment on plans for 'a complete renovation of the Fleet'.[42] In the other estimates impressive cuts were equally impossible: war or peace the transport service had to shift stores, convicts

[38] For the discussion see memoranda by the Duke of York, 20, 28 August; Arbuthnot to Huskisson, 3 September; memorandum probably by 'Mr Hill of the Treasury' [October]; Lord Bathurst to Lord Liverpool, 8 October; Lord Liverpool to Lord Bathurst, 9 October; memorandum, 12 October; Hill to Lord Liverpool, 13 October; memorandum submitted to the Prince Regent, 21 October 1818, ibid., 38273, ff. 297–9, 314–18; 38368, ff. 25–32; 38741, ff. 253–4; 48434, pp. 86–136; *Bathurst*, p. 457.

[39] Lord Liverpool to Lord Sidmouth, 6 August 1818, Add. MSS. 38273, f. 17.

[40] C. J. Bartlett, *Great Britain and Sea Power, 1815–53*, p. 24; *PP*, 1825, xxi. 331–9.

[41] Croker to the Navy Board, 8 December 1815, the Navy Board to Croker, 18 February 1818, NLS MSS. 1044, ff. 158–63, 224–6.

[42] *PP*, 1817, iv. 221; Lord Melville to Lord Liverpool, 28 July 1818, Add. MSS. 38272, ff. 334–42.

and troops; dockyard and harbour improvement while costs were down was to be commended; and the civil establishment was already pared to the bone thanks to parliament's special jealousy. The most that could be done was to reduce the number of seamen, even though merchant bodies were constantly petitioning for better protection and complaints of undermanning kept coming in from admirals on foreign stations.[43] The fact that the establishment of 19,000 voted in 1817 had not lasted beyond the year was itself an earnest of the difficulties involved. Still, with Sir George Cockburn's assistance, Melville did go so far as to draw up a plan, only to discard it when its impracticability became more and more obvious.[44] After this, the government, however loath, had to admit defeat and glumly make the most of estimates £500,000 above what was wanted. There was a will, but simply no way.

One other saving, important in effect rather than amount, was brought into discussion by the death of Queen Charlotte on 17 November 1818. An act of 1812 had ordered £10,000 to be paid her out of the civil list for the expense and responsibility she would bear as *custos* of the King's person, and her decease, without making it possible to dispense with the appointment, did give the ministers a welcome opportunity to moderate the grotesque and pathetic pantomime which had been carried on at Windsor throughout the Regency. By this time, when George III's doctors wholly despaired of a return to reason, a household of twelve officers of state and one hundred and thirty other servants seemed ludicrously large for a lunatic king living in absolute seclusion and, worse, at £10,000 a year, a deplorable waste of public money. Already, particularly with respect to the cost, murmurings had been heard, notably during the debates on the ducal allowances in April 1818 when the opposition dared to point out that cold mutton and no company were realising an immense private treasure which could be used to offset the extraordinary expense of two royal establishments.[45]

[43] Ibid.
[44] Lord Liverpool to Lord Sidmouth, 6 August 1818, ibid., f. 17. In 1819 20,000 seamen and marines were voted, the same establishment as the preceding year's.
[45] *Hansard*, 1st ser., xxxviii. 63, 70, 109–13.

Nevertheless, it was George III's fortune which constituted the chief stumbling block to drastic reductions at Windsor. The moment the government suggested the appropriation of part of the Privy Purse the Prince Regent and the Duke of York objected strenuously, refusing to see their inheritance wasted on what they conceived was a public responsibility. In their view the Purse's annual receipt of £60,000, not forgetting £10,000 more from the Duchy of Lancaster, was and 'has ever been considered the private property of the Sovereign of these realms, perfectly at his own disposal and free from the control and cognizance of Parliament', though equally cogent for them as the nearest in line to the throne was the almost certain knowledge that their father had left no will.[46] Whether in fact constitutional proprieties was against the ministers was difficult to say. Whatever the other encroachments on the royal revenue, up to 1811 the Privy Purse had indubitably remained 'the king's own'. The Regency Act of that year, however, gave the Keeper of the Purse authority to pay out a limited sum and invest the rest in government securities. That of 1812 went even further. It declared the King's medical expenses to be a legitimate charge and ordered previous surpluses to aid current deficits should the need ever arise. Some contended that this established parliament's 'whole dominion' for all time, since in effect the legislature had taken upon itself to say how much was to be spent and for what purposes. Others, including the ministers, construed it as the right of the nation to disburse Privy Purse money if the sovereign's will and pleasure is 'unfortunately not only for a time suspended, but in fact for ever closed'. Others yet again argued that parliament could do no more than interpret the King's wishes in the strictest possible sense, only spending where he had spent in full possession of his faculties. This last, of course, was the safest ground. Both Regency Acts stated categorically that the Privy Purse was to be put to accustomed uses, and doctors' fees had been included in its charge and surpluses given over to commissioners of the King's property accordingly. Moreover, since strictly speaking the maintenance of the royal state was the concern of the civil

---

[46] 39 & 40 Geo. III c. 88 provided that if the King died intestate his private property passed to the Crown.

list, in trying to meet the expense of the Windsor establishment from the personal revenue of the Crown the government was departing from a time-honoured rule which it itself had confirmed, implicitly at least. Probably for this reason Lord Liverpool from the start showed an unwillingness to argue the point. All he and his colleagues could really urge in extenuation of their impertinence was the likely hostility of parliament to any laying up of treasure and the construction of personal interest which public opinion was sure to put upon it. But not surprisingly, when the Prince Regent stood his ground they soon capitulated. If rumours of the King's intestacy were indeed true, the accumulations of the Privy Purse were left to George IV's future enjoyment.

Inasmuch as nothing was forthcoming from the personal funds of the Crown, the ministers became more determined than ever to make savings on the civil list proper. The termination of the Queen's annuity released £58,000, less the appropriate pensions and allowances to officers of her household and old servants. So vague were the precedents in this connection—only one Queen Consort had died in the previous century, and after her death salaries had been continued in full—that the Cabinet was quite happy to let a select parliamentary committee settle the precise amount. As for the establishment at Windsor, the ministers bluntly demanded an estimate of £50,000 per annum from the Master of the Household, exactly half the sum fixed in 1812. Predictably, Carlton House responded by accusing them of denigrating the essential dignity of the Crown. The Regency Act, it was maintained, had assumed the remote possibility of the King's recovery and for this reason alone he ought to continue surrounded by the full panoply of his exalted station: as the Duke of York asserted, 'painful sensations . . . must . . . be created in His Majesty's breast should he upon his recovery find that any great alterations had taken place during the time that he was alleged to be released from the care of public business'. To this the ministers made the obvious retort. After seven years it was safe to say the King would live privately for the rest of his days, and if nothing was recommended in the way of reductions parliament would take the work into its own hands. It did not take much to make the Prince Regent see reason. He himself held no illusions about his personal unpopularity and fully understood the necessity for public economy, and, having made his point over the Privy Purse, no doubt at this time he felt discretion to be the better part of valour. The last details of the Windsor estimate were settled shortly after parliament reassembled.[47]

II. STAND

The great issue of the session, the government anticipated, was going to be over not money in sums but money as a value. While sweeping reductions at Windsor and elsewhere were guaranteed to spoil the opposition's usual party piece, on the further restriction of cash payments public feeling was running much too high for parliament to stay quiet. Originally, or rather after five successive re-enactments of the suspension, the law had implied a resumption six months after a peace had been ratified. But one way and another the Bank and the government had secured postponements until July 1819, not least because in the Bullion Committee's famous report of 1810 their opponents themselves seemed to admit that the necessary preliminaries would take two years. To many, however, the delay was a flagrant breach of faith and a monumental injustice. As long as paper had remained inconvertible into gold a disparity in their values had always been apparent. When the galloping inflation of the war period had reached its height in 1813 the paper pound had been worth 14s. 2d. in terms of gold. Three years later an equally severe deflation had returned it to

---

[47] For these two paragraphs see *Bathurst*, pp. 460, 461–6; *George IV*, ii. 262–3, 265. Particulars of the King's establishment are to be found in *PP*, 1819, ii. 53–9. It is difficult to say exactly when the government finally decided not to touch the Privy Purse. Bankes, who sat on the select committee, said Castlereagh proposed to charge it with the allowances of the princesses and the pensions of the Queen's servants. Williams-Wynn, on the other hand, got an altogether different impression. There were certainly a number of ministerial meetings on the Windsor establishment just after the committee was appointed. Canning, at the Prince Regent's request, made a special trip to Brighton to talk over the matter as well. *Colchester*, iii. 69–70; Buckingham, *Regency*, ii. 327; Canning's diary, 4–8 February 1819, Canning MSS. Perhaps it is worth adding that in January the government vetoed the Prince Regent's plans for extending Buckingham House, Queen Charlotte's old residence. *Liverpool*, ii. 402–3; Sir Benjamin Bloomfield to Charles Arbuthnot, 17 January 1819, Add. MSS. 38275, ff. 78–9.

19s. 10d. Any number of people were hurt by such a fluctuation, for mortgages, rents, insurance, any money transaction contracted while prices were high now had to be paid for in an appreciated currency. Naturally the victims vented their spleen on those who stood to profit, especially 'the Old Hag of Threadneedle Street' and the investors in government stock. In parliament the opposition was for ever alluding to the Bank's record profits, and accusing the directors of having a vested interest in restriction which in return for credit unlimited the government was too cowardly to resist by itself. In the Radical press fundholders and bankers appeared a clan of extortioners whose rapacity knew no equal. Having lent money at one rate, they were being paid back double while the rest of the nation languished under a debt and taxes only nominally the same. Cobbett and his like even declared the execution of forgers to be a slaughter of innocents, inasmuch as it was the monied interest alone which drove men to such extremes. In the main the protest against the fluctuating value of money had ample justification. As Lord Grenville remarked, as long as the instability continued, 'no class of society, from the highest to the lowest, could know what were their means, what their income, or their wages'.[48]

The ministers' misfortune was that they agreed to a man that a return to the gold standard was desirable, but differed irreconcilably over how to set about it. The bullionists and antibullionists in the government had taken up public positions on the question long before, and since a theoretical point was in dispute this made it next to impossible to find any middle ground. Canning and Huskisson refused to recant one word of the heresy they had embraced in 1810-11, emphatically maintaining that an uncontrolled expansion of credit depreciated the paper in circulation, raised the price of gold and turned the exchanges. Vansittart, Harrowby and others stuck just as stubbornly to the old ministerial view that bullion prices and the rate of exchange kept strictly in step with overseas spending and the balance of trade. For them the right conditions for resumption—exchanges at or above par, a substantial reserve of bullion, and the market price of gold reduced to the Mint price

---

[48] *Hansard*, 1st ser., xxxviii. 928.

—could occur only naturally, not by the Bank checking note issues or by contracting credit generally. Hitherto these traditionalists had had the better of the argument. In 1816 there was bullion in plenty and the exchanges were near enough to par for the government to authorise the necessary preparations during a two-year extension of the restriction. Not a murmur came from Downing Street twelve months later when in complete defiance of the quantity theory of money banks everywhere began to increase their note issues regardless of the pound's weakening position. Indeed, the ministers seemed to encourage the Bank in its folly by their uninhibited borrowing which added a substantial amount to its public advances. It followed that when the period of grace finally expired with resumption again postponed, the government placed the blame not on an 'excess of circulation' but on an adverse balance of payments, largely caused by heavy corn imports and the floating of foreign loans in London.[49]

Nevertheless, some heed began to be taken of the bullionists' views, because in May 1818 the government commenced a drastic reduction of the unfunded debt and the repayment of advances from the Bank. These preliminaries not only supplied the right deflationary dose but also provided for a replenishment of treasure in anticipation of a renewed demand for gold. Yet it was far short of being a total conversion. At £66,000,000 the unfunded debt was much too large for any government's liking; with money in abundance and the funds holding well there could be no better moment for a funding operation; and the Bank was always wanting to check its holdings of public securities in the belief that they precluded a proper assistance to the commercial community.[50] If the truth be known, by 1819 the Cabinet was still much divided on the question but increasingly conscious of the country's demand for action of some sort. In this respect the bullionists, in possession of a plan, had the advantage of the antibullionists, who would wait until the economic and monetary situation was favourable.

[49] Ibid., xxxvii. 1232–7, xxxviii. 922–4, 939, 944.
[50] 'Memorandum enclosed in a letter from Lord Liverpool and Mr. Vansittart dated Fife House, 22 May 1818', PP, 1819, iii. 29. Huskisson listed the necessary preliminaries for resumption in a memorandum of 4 February 1819. Liverpool, ii. 382–4.

Lord Liverpool, to their further advantage, showed himself willing to be persuaded of his errors, a typical openmindedness which had important results. The mood of the public was sufficient to convince the ministers that positive measures would have to accompany the further postponement of resumption, but of all the Cabinet he, as the expert in such matters, had the largest say in deciding their character and extent. It was mainly thanks to the Prime Minister that the government, while prolonging the Bank restriction, first made a tentative move in a bullionist direction by approving sterner regulation of Bank lending to the state and then promoted an exhaustive and fully impartial inquiry into the whole question of returning to a gold-based currency.

The Bank itself was not under the thumb of monetary conservatives as many liked to believe. Just how much bullionist fancies had caught on there was shown by the evidence later collected by secret committees of each House and in the debates which followed; of nine directors whose views became known six appeared to admit and three to deny that the Bank's issues affected the exchanges.[51] On the other hand, they and 'the Chairs' were men who had a practical rather than an academic interest in economic policy, and as such, whether bullionist or antibullionist, they had ample grounds for urging caution and restraint at the beginning of 1819. Notwithstanding a reduction in note issues and repayments totalling £5,000,000 by the government, the exchanges continued unfavourable with no sign of improvement,[52] the pound at Hamburg actually receiving its lowest quotation in February 1819. To return to the gold standard in these conditions, when it was profitable to convert sterling into gold for foreign transactions, was unthinkable. No one could forget the unfortunate experiment at partial resumption in 1817, when exchanges below par had created a demand which had been steadily emptying the vaults of the Bank ever since. At the moment the insufficiency of its treasure was enough to forbid a precipitate end to restriction. Even worse, an

[51] J. K. Horsefield, 'The Bankers and the Bullionists in 1819', *Journal of Political Economy*, lvii (1949). 442–8.
[52] For the note circulation see *PP*, 1819, xvi. 375. The secret committees later discovered that the Bank's issues of commercial paper offset this diminution to a certain extent.

exceptional demand for gold would result in a 'diminution of circulation', because bankers invariably responded to a fall in their reserves by contracting their issues of paper. The state of the commercial world was such at the beginning of 1819 that it seemed impossible that it could accommodate a monetary deflation of even moderate severity. With a considerable amount of British capital tied up in Europe, when the Paris *bourse* had displayed symptoms of panic towards the end of 1818 the nervousness had been transferred inevitably across the Channel. At the same time trade had started to slacken off as merchants found that they had again over-estimated the demand of foreign and domestic markets. In these circumstances there was a real fear that a 'diminution of circulation' would cause 'stagnation in trade and manufactures, depreciation of property, and general distress'.[53] The same cheerless prospect was seen from every window. Though the bullionists argued that the exchanges could be made favourable, the only conceivable way these could be turned was by pursuing a 'tight money' policy which was objectionable in itself and possibly too gradual in its effect. Not only was there little time left before the restriction was due to end, but payments on Baring's latest loan to France would continue to influence the exchanges throughout the year as would other foreign investments, for such was their attraction that British capital was unlikely to be deterred until the very last moment. Altogether, when the choice lay between a continuation of the restriction and a course of action which might succeed at tremendous cost or not at all, the Bank was strongly inclined to let things be.

In general, the government's assessment of the situation was no different. The decision to prolong the restriction, of course, was the Cabinet's not the Bank's, though the directors had every reason to expect that their advice would be sought. Unbeknown to them, however, politicians and bankers had come to the parting of their ways. It was true that on 12 January 1819 the question was put to 'the Chairs' whether the Bank could control the exchanges by July, but at the same meeting they were told that resumption was postponed for a further seven

---

[53] For petitions from merchants and bankers to this effect see *CJ*, lxxiv. 52, 59, 71, 72.

months. Three days later the directorate's first representation on the subject merely tendered an answer—a negative answer—to the government's inquiry.[54] Since the restriction would now continue until February 1820, the Cabinet intended to insure themselves against parliamentary retribution by repaying as much of the advances as possible, by placing a statutory limitation on their future amount and by promising an inquiry in the event of yet another postponement.[55] The Bank slightly upset these plans on 15 January when the Governor insisted on renewing the Restriction Act until April 1820. As a compromise the ministers proposed March, though the change gave any inquiry an annoyingly late start.[56] Worse was to come however. On 20 January the Committee of Treasury, the committee of the Court of Directors which handled government business, 'considered the Improbability that the Foreign Exchanges will be turned and permanently settled in favour of Great Britain by March 1820' and came to the astonishing conclusion that 'the Consequences of a Parliamentary Enquiry' were preferable to a bill 'inadequate to the Circumstances in which the Country may be placed'.[57] This resolution was confirmed and slightly altered on the following day and taken round to Fife House on the morning of 22 January. Not surprisingly, the deputation met with a cool reception. To tell the Prime Minister that it was 'a Matter of the highest Importance that the Public shall not be deluded with an Expectation which is not likely to be realised' was bad enough.[58] To have the government inaugurate an inquiry it had little taste for added to the insult the chance of serious injury. The ministers had always regarded an investigation into the feasibility of resumption as the least desirable expedient, inasmuch as the Cabinet itself was divided between bullionists and antibullionists and there seemed to be little hope of them coming to agreement. But now the government's hand was forced. Once the Bank had publicly demanded inquiry, after

[54] See the Governor's evidence to the Common's committee on the resumption of cash payments. *PP*, 1819, iii. 28, 29.
[55] For Huskisson's exposition of the government's views see T. F. Lewis to Lord Grenville, 21 January 1819, Grenville MSS.
[56] *PP*, 1819, iii. 33.
[57] Ibid., p. 394.
[58] It was rumoured that the expression had given 'deadly offence'. T. F. Lewis to Lord Grenville, 25 January 1819, Grenville MSS.

having stoutly resisted such a discussion for years, it would have looked both churlish and suspect on the government's part to refuse. Deprived of a real choice in the matter, the Cabinet determined on 25 January, to take the directors at their word.[59]

Since Tierney had previously announced a motion for a committee 'into the state of Public Credit',[60] the government's chief concern from now on was to thwart the Whig opposition in its attempt to get command of the question and to keep politics out of the inquiry as much as possible. In his endeavours to have the case examined on its strict merits, Lord Liverpool played the premier's role with skill, though as usual a trying period drove him into one of his 'grand fidgetts'.[61] Having twice denounced the 'speculations' of the Bullion Committee in the House of Lords, he was as strongly committed as any of his colleagues, but not for a moment did he manoeuvre to defend his consistency or declare himself inconvincible. Indeed, in January 1819 he freely admitted the justice of his adversaries' arguments, where eight months before he had called them 'now *per force* abandoned'.[62] Doubtless it was he who arranged for each point of view to be fairly represented on the parliamentary committees, or in Huskisson's words, for 'a large sprinkling of Opposition, and a good deal of the talent of the House, with a less proportion than usual of Country Gentlemen as make weights'.[63] Certainly Peel, whose professions of neutrality none could asperse, was his nominee for the chairmanship of the Commons' committee,[64] and likewise with his connivance Lord King found a place on the Lords', though as the landlord who had ordered his tenants to pay their rents in gold he was the most notorious bullionist of all.[65] It is surely

[59] Canning's diary, 25 January 1819, Canning MSS.
[60] *Hansard*, 1st ser., xxxix. 65.
[61] Huskisson to Mrs Huskisson [23 January 1819], Add. MSS. 39949, ff. 37–40. A few days later he wrote: 'Liverpool beats Binning at figitatis. He ought to be the Grand Cross of the Order.' Ibid., ff. 41–2.
[62] See *Hansard*, 1st ser., xxxiv. 574, 578, xxxviii. 924, 948–9, xxxix. 32.
[63] Huskisson to Mrs Huskisson, 3 February [1819], Add. MSS. 39949, f. 59.
[64] Gash, *Mr Secretary Peel*, pp. 240–1.
[65] Lord Grenville to Lord Liverpool, 27 January 1819, Lord Liverpool to Lord Grenville, 30 January 1819, Add. MSS. 38275, ff. 133–4, 167–8.

significant that when Canning made mention of his opponents
the Prime Minister's name was never among them.[66]

The opposition was kept in hand with equal aplomb. Since
both Vansittart and Tierney were proposing committees, the
discussion was confined to the mundane matters of terms of
reference, constitution and membership. The government
favoured a comprehensive but confidential inquiry, for such
would get to the heart of the problem while avoiding what might
otherwise be imprudent disclosures of the Bank's true condition.
At first there was here a discernible difference with the Whigs.
Vansittart's motion specifically sought an inquiry into the feasibility of resumption, where Tierney's referred with peculiar
vagueness 'to the state of public credit as connected with the
circulation of Bank paper'[67]—Williams-Wynn was probably not
alone in thinking that the generality would 'introduce such a
variety of topics as to divert the public attention from the one
most important to which it should by every means be steadily
directed'.[68] On second thoughts, however, Tierney rewrote his
notice in the order book, and then a committee 'to report
whether any, and what reasons exist for continuing' the restriction became scarcely distinguishable from one 'to consider of
the State of the Bank of England with reference to the expediency of the Resumption of Cash Payments'.[69] Even so, a
withdrawal on the government's part was quite out of the question. Though Tierney had got in first, this was no reason for
giving way, especially when a division to sort out the allegiances
of new members had not yet eventuated. To have the opposition
capture the initiative on the first important question could do
untold damage to the government's parliamentary supremacy.
Both sides in fact were impatient for a trial of strength, the
Whigs to prove their new-found solidarity, the ministers to
parade their majority; and after four or five hours of skirmishing
over trifles, in which speaker upon speaker strained to produce

[66] Canning's diary, 1–3 April 1819, Canning MSS. T. F. Lewis, a staunch
bullionist, got the impression 'that Lord Liverpool and Huskisson are very
sincerely in Earnest to do what ought to be done'. T. F. Lewis to Lord
Grenville, 21 January 1819, Grenville MSS.

[67] *Hansard*, 1st ser., xxxix. 65, 72, 104, 131–3.

[68] Charles Williams-Wynn to Lord Grenville, 26 January 1819, Coed-y-
maen MSS.

[69] See Tierney's motion and Vansittart's amendment. *CJ*, lxxiv. 64.

disagreement, they finally got what they wanted. In some respects the result was disappointing to all concerned. The opposition had been sanguine enough to expect almost 200 votes, but in the event only trooped 168 strong into the lobby against the government's 277. Even so, on what was a division on straight party lines the ministers found the minority sufficiently large to be disquieting. The more the opposition perfected its association, which a muster of nearly 170 seemingly indicated, the more the government was obliged to follow suit. Yet, as long as so many members were inclined to resist the centripetal pull of party and Crown, that was a task fraught with any number of difficulties.[70]

As it turned out, by the end of the session the weakness of the executive in the legislature had been so well demonstrated that the administration was driven into retrieving the ordinary relationship by showing that its power to command was not exhausted. Time and time again the caprices of the 'country gentlemen', and official men as well, muddled the government's plans and made a mockery of its parliamentary authority. With a new parliament, and over one hundred and fifty new faces,[71] probably the trouble was not unanticipated, for it invariably took a year or two for the members to adopt settled postures, and a few defied categorisation long after that. However, whether this made the ministers more sinned against than sinning, as they themselves were apt to declare, was highly doubtful. Under Castlereagh's gentle regime the attendance of official members had often left much to be desired, and even in the face of a resurgent opposition the old habits of desultoriness died hard, especially after a session which had been easy going throughout. The slackness, of course, was infectious. No 'country gentleman' could be blamed for not sitting out a debate which front-benchers appeared to disdain; and neither was he likely to comprehend the growing pressure of committee and depart-

[70] For the debates see *Hansard*, 1st ser., xxxix. 213–75. It is interesting to note that the ministerial speakers received explicit instructions to avoid 'the principles of the question'. Huskisson to Mrs Huskisson, 3 February [1819], Add. MSS. 39949, ff. 58–9.

[71] The number of members without previous parliamentary experience totalled 157, nearly a quarter of the House. In the period 1734–1832 only the elections of 1768 and 1802 returned more. Gerrit P. Judd, *Members of Parliament, 1734–1832*, p. 28.

mental work which to some extent lay behind the casualness. As Arbuthnot once had to be told, 'they wd. not try to support those in office who wd. not take the trouble of trying to support themselves'.[72]

On the other hand, the incorrigibility went deeper, much deeper than the failure of 'office men' to set a good example. Fundamentally it was related to the persistence of the notion that a certain independence was an honourable political course inasmuch as parliament existed to check the Crown's inimical acts and propositions. As the government apprehended, the House of Commons was having grave thoughts about its estrangement from the country. The need to make repairs to the relationship between government and subject seemed to press with increasing urgency; and since institutional renovation was out of the question, the best way, perhaps the only way this could be done was by parliament doing something to match the hostility of public opinion. The legislature, in other words, took occasion to emphasise its supervisory and its critical capacities in order to restore the faith of the country in existing arrangements. Probably this was not all. It is hard to resist the conclusion that by 1819 many members of parliament were beginning to blame the situation on the government rather than on circumstances beyond the government's control. The ministers had not appeased public opinion as much as they might have done; too often when they did attempt it their efforts looked like last minute temporising or appeared to embody too great a readiness to accept instruction from parliament. Here, in fact, lay the crux of the matter. Most 'parliament men' had a high view of the executive's function. It was the responsibility of the Cabinet to recommend to the legislature those policies and measures which could sustain best the safety, prosperity and order of the nation. This it was manifestly failing to do. Administration and parliament were losing the initiative in government to public opinion. Every capitulation to public opinion had to be regarded as an acknowledgement of its power, and every acknowledgement was likely to subject the executive to fresh pressures. Instead the ministers should use to the full the authority which the constitution granted them. They should

[72] *Arbuthnot*, p. 15.

act up to the aristocratic tradition of responsible leadership; they should act with greater awareness of the strength of popular complaint, if necessary to the extent of rejecting the old-fashioned concept which made the army and navy, diplomacy, trade and finance the sum of their concerns. That way the descent towards popular government could be effectively arrested. As it was, the pace downhill was quickening. Many in parliament were beginning to agree with opinion out-of-doors that the administration had proved itself in war but had yet to prove itself in peace. Huskisson had reported this feeling after the general election in 1818. In 1819 and afterwards the government's parliamentary comfort mainly depended on whether he, and any others who had spoken with him, had been heard to good effect.

The first signs of recalcitrance in the Commons were not slow in coming. Because in the past Brougham had been found too domineering to be a good committee man, the government made a firm resolve to exclude him from the Bank inquiry despite his well-known predilection for economic subjects and their own eager concern to appear openminded. Shortly after the committee was balloted, however, a motion for his election was beaten by only 42 votes, prominent 'country gentlemen' like Wodehouse of Norfolk and Davenport of Cheshire joining the Whigs while many others pointedly abstained.[73] The next day the rebelliousness was carried into the committee sitting above stairs on the Windsor establishment. Though the ministers confidently expected 'to carry thro' every part of the arrangement',[74] two out of six equerries were discarded, a second defeat on the same question was only narrowly averted and the salaries of the officers of the late Queen's household, customarily continued to them in lieu of pensions, had to be immediately given up.[75] Even the reduced establishment was mildly reprobated by the 'country gentlemen' when it came before the House, for twenty or so, including four county members, sided with the opposition on a motion to charge the Privy Purse with the Duke of York's allowance as *custos*. As Williams-

[73] Buckingham, *Regency*, i. 328.
[74] Huskisson to Canning [5 February 1819], Canning MSS.
[75] *Colchester* iii. 69–70; Buckingham, *Regency*, ii. 302.

Wynn told Lord Buckingham: 'the striking *feature*—to use a Castlereaghism—of the day, is the unwillingness of most of the new members to be considered as belonging to Government, to receive notes or answer whip.'[76]

Perhaps on questions of economy the hostility could be shrugged off as the established complaint of a large portion of the legislature. Not so on a question of law reform, and at the beginning of March Sir James Mackintosh confounded the government by carrying a committee to consider 'so much of the Criminal Laws as relates to Capital Punishment in Felonies'. Interest in this subject was by no means new. The problem of crime and its punishment was one which had long caught the attention of intellectuals, humanitarians and lawyers; the first explored the theoretical imperfections of the system, the second the misery it inflicted; the last had direct experience of its practical deficiencies. In a sense all these influences came together in Sir Samuel Romilly. He, until his tragic suicide in November 1818, had kept reform of the criminal law constantly before parliament with a series of bills abolishing the death penalty wherever it seemed grossly disproportionate to the crime. More often than not, his efforts had come to naught in the House of Lords; but the cause had been publicised and the sympathies of many engaged, which promised greater success in the future. By 1819, too, much of the spadework of reform had been completed. The members of parliament, mainly from the Whig side, who gathered around Romilly and later Mackintosh, had acquired a practical knowledge of the abuses which existed, to give their righteous indignation and intellectual convictions an important sense of direction. In 1816 parliament began a lengthy investigation into the policing of the metropolis, and in the process a mass of evidence was collected on the causes of crime as well as on the impotence of those charged with combatting it. The concentration of the reformers on the issue of capital punishment also drew attention to the nature and efficiency of so-called 'secondary' punishments, particularly transportation and imprisonment. From 1811 until 1818 no fewer than six committees of the House of Commons conducted the inquiry, systematically exploring the

[76] Ibid., p. 315.

evils of over-crowded gaols, overcrowded hulks and struggling convict settlements.

But parliament's interest in reform, manifested so strongly in the session of 1819, cannot be attributed only to the few who had been diligent informing and instructing. There was a feeling abroad in the country that the incidence of crime was rapidly increasing. Why men had come to this conclusion is a question which has not had the attention it deserves. Some argued that the malefactor was inadequately deterred by the law; others, taking a more recognisably modern view, placed the blame on social conditions, especially the growth of the towns where many people were able to escape from the discipline and also security of the old society. In one respect, however, the feeling seemed to be solidly based on fact. An act of 1815 had ordered annual returns of the prison population in each town and country to be laid before parliament, and these statistics, after appearing for three years, told a dismal tale of increasing committals and convictions. Indeed, the point can be made best by reproducing the figures themselves. At the beginning of 1819 these actually covered the period 1805–17. In 1805 4,605 persons had been committed for trial in England and Wales and 2,783 had been convicted. By 1814 the numbers were 5,390 and 4,025. These increased to 7,818 and 4,883 in 1815; 9,091 and 5,797 in 1816; and 13,932 and 9,056 in 1817.[77] In other words, there was every reason to believe that the amount of crime had increased by about half in the decade 1805–14 but had tripled or even quadrupled in the thirteen years 1805–17. All this without any real change in either the law or the machinery for its enforcement. When criminality was added to political disaffection, it did not take some men long to conclude that there was a serious breakdown of morality among the lower orders.

However unpleasant the facts were, the ministers at least faced up to them, though in doing so they have never been given the credit they undoubtedly deserve. With or without the Whigs, they would have taken action. They, in effect, acted in the best traditions of aristocratic government, responding to a national need regardless of whether the matter was a conventional

[77] See *PP*, 1818, xvi. 190.

concern. Their involvement in 'law improvement' which began at this time was an important advertisement that the government still knew its responsibilities, was not so out of touch with the nation as some had feared. It is certain that the subject was being pondered as early as 1818. When Lord Lansdowne just prior to the dissolution in June requested information on the state of the gaols, Sidmouth 'cordially concurred', agreed that 'a subject of greater importance' did not exist and disclosed that 'it had been his intention, in the interval between the close and meeting of parliament, to make inquiries to the same effect'.[78] Possibly this seemed nothing more than an attempt to keep up appearances. If so, the sceptics were soon silenced. About Christmas Harrowby was describing 'the prisons' as one of 'many difficult questions before us'. 'Upon several of these points,' he went on to argue, 'even if it should be decided that Government will do nothing or at least do nothing early, it seems very important that we should so far understand one another, as to know what line is to be held in conversation with friends. It is hardly creditable to continue longer without an opinion at least, if not a measure, upon some of them.'[79] There is no reason to suppose his advice went unheeded. Though no record of a Cabinet discussion appears to exist, it is fair to assume that the subject came under consideration at two meetings at the Lord Chancellor's in January 1819.[80] Certainly Canning—in Castlereagh's absence—and Sidmouth both announced inquiries into 'the state and discipline of the various prisons' soon after the session's commencement.[81]

The government's immediate aim was to capture the initiative from the Whigs and the reformers on what had now become a question of great public moment. Its failure to achieve this until Peel came to the Home Office in 1822 was due less to its own inadequacies than to the fact that its labours passed largely unnoticed. Ironically Romilly's influence as a law reformer was greatest in the years immediately after his death, at the very time that he administration was beginning to patronise the

[78] *Hansard*, 1st ser., xxxviii. 1186–92.
[79] *Bathurst*, p. 466.
[80] Canning's diary, 12–13 January 1819, Canning MSS. Cabinet meetings on foreign policy were usually held at Castlereagh's or the Foreign Office.
[81] *Hansard*, 1st ser., xxxix. 71, 79–80.

issue seriously. Mackintosh and others on the Whig side continued to concentrate their attention on the number of capital felonies, and it was their argument that the reduction of these would increase the legal deterrent by bringing the law into closer accord with the moral feelings of the community which proved most persuasive with parliament and public opinion. Only gradually was it accepted that this approach was too simple, that the government's way of attacking the problem was more realistic. The differences between the ministers and men of Mackintosh's stamp centred not on the desirability of change but on its practical aspects. The view of the first was altogether broader. They referred frequently to the social causes of crime, if only to admit that these were beyond the power of the state to remove, and, necessarily forced back into considering prevention by punishment, they took account of the reform of the malefactor as well as of the need to deter him. Granted that 'the fear of death was the strongest moral sanction that could be applied to the human mind', there could be no permanent dismantlement of the scaffold. The question then became what offences were deserving of the ultimate penalty. Here the government insisted that the nature of the crime was of less importance than the means of preventing it. Crime had to be deterred by sufficiently severe penalties, and if that penalty were not to be death it had to be an effective form of 'secondary' punishment. The reduction of the number of capital offences could not by itself reduce the amount of crime, even if it produced greater certainty of punishment, because crime had many and varied causes. Therefore the strain on the system of 'secondary' punishment would not be relieved, and as long as abuses remained there the law could neither deter the criminal nor provide for his reformation adequately. As the ministers saw it, Mackintosh and his kind were blinded by their humanity. There seemed to be little point in a generous repeal of capital statutes when gaols were universities of crime and when transportation was regarded almost as state-assisted emigration. A reform to be useful had to embrace the system of punishment in its entirety. Indeed, any which did not was likely to be positively harmful because it would indicate without correcting the abuses which existed. As Castlereagh warned the Commons:

'It is not wise in any state, and least of all in this state, at the present moment, to arraign its own administration of justice, in the eyes of its own people and of the world, without at least presenting, at the same time, a remedial resource.'[82]

The ministers, then, went forth well-prepared for an encounter with the Whigs. What they mistook was the pitch of public emotion on the issue of capital punishment and parliament's reluctance—understandable enough after years of inaction—to attach the label of genuineness to their efforts. The precise wording of the government's motion in 1819 was for an inquiry 'into the state and description of Gaols, or other places of confinement, and into the best method of providing for the reformation, as well as the safe custody and punishment of Offenders'. One critic, and his view was typical, called it 'a hodge-podge committee on Penal Laws, Prisons, Botany Bay and Forgery' which would drag on indefinitely, submit the occasional report and never reach a single significant conclusion.[83] Castlereagh himself appeared to admit the immensity of the subject by suggesting 'one committee divided, if they would, into sections', a novel procedure which the Speaker promptly ruled out of order.[84] A warning of parliament's disillusionment came on 18 February when Henry Grey Bennet submitted a motion on transportation and the penal settlements. Though a committee was avoided, a display of honest indignation by the ministers to the effect that the mover was poaching on their preserve did not prevent several startling defections from their side of the House.[85] The ultimate test, however, was Mackintosh's proposal for a committee on capital felonies a fortnight later. The government carried its 'hodge-podge committee' the day before with little bother, but once again, this time decisively, the 'country gentlemen' refused to be convinced that a narrower inquiry would do more harm than good. Nearly thirty contributed to the opposition vote of 147, an ample muster so it turned out for a majority of 19.

The defeat had almost catastrophic repercussions. Coming hard on the heels of a series of sorry performances, a fresh

---

[82] Ibid., 483.   [83] Buckingham, *Regency*, ii. 323–4.
[84] *Hansard*, 1st ser., xxxix. 752, 776–7.
[85] Buckingham, *Regency*, ii. 314–15.

reverse resulted in a complete breakdown of parliamentary
discipline. Night after night the government whips came to
the House to find the opposition benches packed to the gang-
ways, and night after night they tried in vain to stop the early
departure of friends and colleagues from their own. In these
circumstances Castlereagh's absence was particularly unfortunate. His sister, Lady Ellenborough, died just three days
after Mackintosh's triumph, and though the most important
business was put off a week while he attended the funeral,
during such a trying period his personal authority was sorely
missed. Twice Arbuthnot wrote to the Prime Minister telling
him that the official members were not attending and the
'country gentlemen' playing coy as a result, and eventually in
desperation Long and Huskisson accompanied him to Fife
House where as usual they heard a long monologue about what
politics were like in the good old days. Liverpool, however,
perhaps knew Castlereagh better than they did. Not wanting
to assume his authority as Leader of the House, he would do
no more than summon a meeting of officeholders in both his and
the Prime Minister's name.[86] Almost certainly the reprimand
was delivered before 18 March, to which date a renewed motion
of Ridley's for the reduction of the Admiralty Board had been
postponed. Even so, it had little visible effect. While 'office men'
no doubt were called smartly back into line for the occasion,
the waywardness of the 'country gentlemen' continued to sap
the government's strength. Despite every effort on the part of
the whips—'since the Walcheren question I never exerted myself so much,' Arbuthnot wrote[87]—the ministerial majority
barely exceeded eighty and at least twenty recalcitrants voted
with the opposition.

The decisive blow, curiously enough, occurred on a Scottish question. Usually such business interested an English-
dominated House of Commons even less than Irish concerns.
Scotland supported a system of local government, endorsed
and guaranteed by the Act of Union, whereby the burgh councils were virtually self-electing. Only in the event of an invalid
election or no election could the Crown restore the franchise
to the burgesses at large. Following a law suit over the parlia-

[86] *Arbuthnot*, pp. 15–16.　　　　　[87] Ibid., p. 18.

mentary return of 1774 and subsequent disfranchisement, Stirling's constitution had been permanently 'democratised' in 1781, and it was largely on this precedent—the Court of Session having upheld the illegality of the council's election—that Montrose was granted the same privilege in 1817. This modicum of reform had important repercussions; for no sooner was it known than strenuous attempts were made to find similar technicalities to overthrow other councils, or failing that, to draw up petitions complaining of the varied iniquity of oligarchic exclusiveness. At this stage the government saw fit to intervene. Much of the trouble lay in financial mismanagement, Aberdeen's bankruptcy being particularly notorious, and in 1818 Maconochie, the Lord Advocate, brought in a bill to control this misapplication and in some cases malversation of public money. Though a fresh shower of petitions forced its withdrawal after only one reading, the ministers would on no account go further. If once the magistracy was opened to popular influence, they said, the whole state of the representation might be called into question, for in Scotland the burgh members were elected indirectly by the councils themselves. They might have added that as the government had over three-quarters of the Scottish seats firm in its grasp it did not intend to sell that ascendancy on the cheap. However, in the last resort the problem became one of parliamentary management. Confronted by a spirited and well-organised opposition, the ministers could not afford to take any minor question lightly, but as always it remained difficult to collect a good House on a subject of predominantly Scottish interest. The petitions which had come in from nearly all the burghs insisted that a return to popular elections was the only worthwhile reform, and when soon after the Easter recess Lord Archibald Hamilton, the Whig member for Lanarkshire, moved to refer them to a select committee it became essential for the government to resist. There had already been an unhappy augury in April 1819, a request for information relating to the Aberdeen scandal being turned down by a mere five votes, and this time so poor was the attendance on the ministerial side that even with negligible assistance from the 'country gentlemen' the opposition carried their proposal 149 votes to 144.

The next day Canning was round at Fife House arguing 'the necessity of a *vital* question'.[88]

Appropriately, for it was on taxation and expenditure that the administration had been most hard-pressed, the ministers chose to stake its existence on a financial issue. Vansittart and Liverpool's advisers had long felt uncomfortable about the pusillanimity of official policy in this connection, though in a sense the temporising which was their chief complaint sprang from the conflicting advice they themselves offered. At the beginning of the session Huskisson made a scathing attack on the shifts and expedients adopted since the peace, describing 'selling exchequer bills daily to redeem funded debt daily, then funding those exchequer bills once a year, or once in two years, in order to go over the same ground again' as a mystery which deceived no one.[89] William Hill, whose importance was greater than his position as principal clerk in the commissariat suggests, and Herries, were equally disillusioned.[90] Indeed, only the Chancellor remained unperturbed, for the Prime Minister himself admitted that 'a Debt of between 7 & 8 hundred millions without any Sinking Fund, or at best with a Sinking Fund of a million constitutes a State of things too appalling to be presented to a new Parliament and too critical with a view to the permanent Welfare of the Country to be permitted to continue without an Endeavour to improve it'.[91] In a way it was the reports of the Bank committees which clinched the argument in favour of a thorough reappraisal. These were in the government's hands by the middle of April and the repayment to the Bank of 'a large amount at an early period' was strongly recommended in each. Since the deficit of ways and means was already estimated at £14,000,000, to pay off £5,000,000 of exchequer bills, which Vansittart stood pledged to, and £10,000,000 of the Bank debt, roughly £30,000,000 would have to be borrowed to bring the budget

---

[88] Canning's diary, 7 May 1819, Canning MSS.
[89] *Liverpool*, ii. 382–4.
[90] *Arbuthnot*, p. 17.
[91] Lord Liverpool to Lord Sidmouth, 6 August 1818, Add. MSS. 38273, f. 16. Arbuthnot described Vansittart as 'proceeding with all the unwary simplicity of honesty & truth ... and should the storm of general dissatisfaction burst upon him, it will find him totally unprepared'. *Arbuthnot*, p. 17.

into balance.[92] In peace no government dared go a-begging to parliament for this amount.

The alternatives were to reimpose the war taxes or appropriate the entire sinking fund for the service of the year, the unpopularity of the one being fully met by the ignominy of the other. The reintroduction of the property tax was never seriously considered. Only Herries was bold enough to suggest it, and he was soon shouted down by those who had richer memories of the furore of 1816.[93] There were, anyway, definite advantages in keeping the tax a 'war resource' only, not to mention the fact that the administrative machinery which assessed and collected it had been largely broken up. The depredation of the sinking fund was by far the more attractive alternative. While there must have been a sentimental attachment to this pillar of Pittite finance, and after so many years considerable reluctance to admit its fallacy, even among the government a feeling of disillusionment was at least weakening the time-honoured principle of its inviolability. In three years of peace the nominal capital of the funded debt had been reduced £24,000,000 while the unfunded increased £4,000,000,[94] a performance which made a mockery of the arithmetical magic by which it was supposed to eliminate the whole debt within forty years. Early in 1816 Castlereagh spoke shamelessly of ministers helping themselves to its treasure once the public credit had fully recovered, and by 1818 Huskisson was scarcely deigning to hide his impatience to begin.[95] Inevitably, attention was being drawn to the thesis, first expounded by Hamilton, the Scottish economist, that the only real sinking fund was a surplus of income over expenditure. Huskisson, in a memorandum of February 1819, championed this view with some feeling:

> Whatever surplus of revenue we possess must be our real sinking fund. The growth of the revenue and the interest of the debt *really* diminished, will improve that sinking fund year after year whilst peace continues. Should it require further improvement,

[92] Undated memorandum, Castlereagh MSS., xxxv. 1024-5.
[93] Memoranda book, 23 April 1819, Herries MSS. Herries, who was Auditor of the Civil List, was not a member of parliament until 1823.
[94] *PP*, 1868-9, xxxv. 788-91. Contemporaries could not be certain of the figures because the consolidation of the British and Irish debts after 5 January 1817 made a precise calculation exceptionally difficult.
[95] *Hansard*, 1st ser., xxxii. 1108, xxxviii. 232-3.

I am sure that we should find in Parliament and the country a better disposition to submit to any moderate sacrifice for that purpose than we can possibly expect so long as the present system is persevered in. Our sinking fund (it is the only fund deserving of such a name) would then be whatever surplus of revenue the country can afford without too much pressure; and, be its amount great or small, it will do more for the real reduction of debt, for the real stability of public credit, for the character of England abroad, and the strength and ease of Government at home, than ever can be hoped for by continuing in a system which has all the inconveniences without any of the advantages of concealment, and is liable to all the derangement and expense incidental to complicated machinery, without producing any beneficial result, even whilst its movements meet with no interruption.[96]

The advice here proffered was accepted with little or no reservation. In 1819 the only conceivable way to obtain a surplus was by bringing the entire sinking fund of £15,500,000 to the service of the year, for the supply of £20,500,000 was almost three times as much as the revenue itself could contribute. The question then followed whether or not the country could afford any beyond this. Though Lord Liverpool eight months before had emphatically reaffirmed the policy of fiscal relief,[97] the Cabinet now summoned up sufficient courage to demand £3,000,000 in new taxes, about half of it to come from a lighter variation of the old war excise on malt. This, it was calculated, would produce a surplus of £5,000,000 over the next three years. While almost £50,000,000 would have to be taken from the sinking fund to realise such a sum, the ministers must have concluded that the advantages would not be slow in revealing themselves. They looked forward to the rapid accumulation of stock in the hands of the debt commissioners, to a rise in the funds which would facilitate a conversion operation later on, and to the 'natural tendency' of the revenue to augment itself, which by producing larger and larger surpluses would accelerate the whole process.[98] The new policy was not a

---

[96] *Liverpool*, ii. 384.

[97] Lord Liverpool to Lord Sidmouth, 6 August 1818, Add. MSS. 38273, f. 16.

[98] In 1820 and 1821 the government predicted surpluses of £5,800.000 and £6,037,000. Undated Memorandum, Castlereagh MSS., xxv. 1026.

defiance of the theory of the sinking fund; rather it marked a new determination to make practical arrangements to produce the results that that theory promised.

The actual decision to change course was taken a fortnight before the parliamentary crisis came to a head at the beginning of May.[99] At that time Herries alone strenuously opposed the plan, preferring to go on the market for the whole of the loan and not at all happy with the incidence of the new taxes.[100] However, when the question of a vote of confidence arose, the ministers normally unconcerned with financial matters began to echo his doubts about its expediency. Bloomfield, who flew to Town immediately upon the arrival of a despairing letter from Castlereagh, made a point of seeing Sidmouth and Eldon before even the Prime Minister, and while both blamed the trouble on 'the *heretofore* example of supineness in the official attendance which disquieted the independent members', it is more than likely that one or other of them conveyed apprehensions of a further defeat on the budget resolutions.[101] The Lord Chancellor certainly felt the government was inviting its downfall, and told Liverpool so in a letter he sent him the day after the Cabinet decided to stand or fall by parliament's decision.[102] That the Prince Regent, 'though unwilling to give a decided opinion at this distance', sounded a similar caution suggests that Bloomfield heard dire predictions somewhere in Town.[103] Nevertheless, Liverpool, and presumably Canning and Castlereagh also, was in no two minds about the desirability of a showdown. The dismal run of defeats or near defeats was making the government appear a government by sufferance not choice, weakening its ability to carry on the king's business and therefore not without dishonour to the ministers themselves. As the Prime Minister answered Eldon's expostulations:

After the defeats we have already experienced during this Session, our remaining in office is a *positive* evil. It confounds all ideas of government in the minds of men. It disgraces us

---

[99] Canning's diary, 24 April 1819, Canning MSS. Canning later asserted the same in the House. *Hansard*, 1st ser., xl. 971.
[100] Memoranda book, 27 April 1819, Herries MSS.
[101] *George IV*, ii. 288–9.
[102] Canning's diary, 10 May 1819, Canning MSS.
[103] *George IV*, ii. 290–2.

personally, and renders us less capable every day of being of any real service to the country, either now or hereafter. If therefore things are to remain as they are, I am quite clear that there is no advantage, in any way, in our being the persons to carry on the public service. A strong and decisive effort can alone redeem our character and credit, and is as necessary for the country as it is for ourselves.[104]

Nor was defeat anticipated on a vote of confidence. Lord Liverpool remained firmly convinced that 'the evil temper and disposition' of the 'country gentlemen' stemmed from no deep-rooted antipathy. Though further taxes on malt and spirits were bound to upset them, inasmuch as they did just this they would constitute a real test of their true loyalties. All that had to be done was to afford the least reliable of the government's supporters 'the opportunity of manifesting by their conduct, the nature and degree of support which they are prepared to give.[105]

As it happened, by a not altogether wise manoeuvre, Tierney himself silenced the pessimists. On the same day as the debate on Scottish burgh reform, but interestingly enough before it, he suddenly announced a motion on the state of the nation.[106] Such a proposal, in spite of its inferences of incompetence and mismanagement if carried, did not necessarily at once decide the government's fate, as the most recent precedent, that of 1778, made only too clear. On the other hand, there was nothing to stop either side making it a question of confidence if they so desired, and when Tierney at one point in his address frankly admitted 'that the motion he was about to submit did go to produce a change of administration' the ministers had no choice but to stake the government's existence on the result. Though the Whigs ranged far and wide in their search for brickbats, from the poor laws to European politics, the division at the end of the four hour marathon was an unqualified triumph for their adversaries. A two to one majority in a record House amply justified Lord Liverpool's earlier sanguineness. If Tierney had been 'determined to have a grand field day, and to parade his troops', as Castlereagh tauntingly suggested, the brave sight had stirred none to join his colours. Some earlier

---

[104] *Eldon*, ii. 329.   [105] *George IV*, ii. 290.   [106] *Courier*, 7 May 1819.

remarks of Buckingham, who was for ever trying to win his
cousin from opposition ways, plainly pointed out the hopeless
endeavour of the Whigs: 'the Country Gentlemen,' he had
written the previous February, 'delight in seeing [the ministers]
dragged through the dirt at the tail of said Country Gentlemen's
waggons or Carts. But depend upon it, were any question to be
brought forward the result of which would go to decide upon
the fate of the Govt. you would see those very Country Gentlemen flock to the standard of Ministers to save them & themselves from the opposition of which they entertain as cordial a
dislike as I do.'[107]

Predictably, a thoroughly chastened opposition caused little
bother for the remainder of the session. The military and naval
estimates, which had been subjected to the usual scrutiny of a
select committee, were rushed through in a matter of days, and
in the renewed discussion on the resumption of cash payments
the only serious dissentients were a Bank director who happened
to be an unrepentant anti-bullionist and a Norwich banker
whose currency views were unorthodox to the point of being
outlandish. Moreover, the resolutions stating the government's
financial requirements, avowedly a second vote of confidence,
were carried by a majority little short of 200. Sidmouth truly
remarked that 'the close of our parliamentary campaign is far
more satisfactory than its commencement'.[108] What was
heartening above all was the appearance that the administration
had regained the initiative in government from a parliament to
some extent under the tutelage of public opinion. The events of
the winter of 1816–17 had made it plain that a political consciousness existed at all levels of society and that henceforth
power would have to be exercised by the governing class on
these terms. Because the belief persisted, not only among the
aristocracy, that the aristocracy ought to have possession of the
state, the central problem in government, how to maintain the
existing order without defying the nation, came into sharper
focus. Clearly the ministers' main task was to represent popular
desires and yet at the same time avoid subservience to them.
An administration which was seen to be coerced would lay

[107] Lord Buckingham to Charles Williams-Wynn, 10 February 1819,
Coed-y-maen MSS.   [108] *Sidmouth*, iii. 246.

itself open to further instruction from public opinion. It was preferable that the aristocracy conceded out of wisdom rather than out of weakness, which meant that popular complaint had to be anticipated rather than ignored. The great danger of popular feeling on any subject was that it implied some disillusionment with aristocratic government and could be made to challenge its whole concept by the argument that the old oligarchy was no longer responsive to national needs or capable of taking a national view. Therefore, to restore the confidence of the country in a political elite, of which they were the most prominent representatives, was the first object of Lord Liverpool and his colleagues in 1819.

How successful they were it is difficult to say, but parliament, which since the peace had never been more unruly, seemed to be reassured at least, and this was an achievement of some significance bearing in mind that the legislature was a more sensitive mechanism for measuring public discontent than has often been allowed. It was true that in the matter of law reform the ministers were still making a lesser impression than the Whigs. Yet even here it was most unlikely that they would long be denied the credit that was their due. Sooner or later the intricacies of the problem would be revealed and Mackintosh's effort disparaged, and when it happened they would be able to pose as wiser than public opinion and parliament though not out of sympathy. But it was on finance—an important issue every session—that the ministers showed most clearly that they had managed the transition from war administration, with its emphasis on executive action, to peace administration, with its emphasis on executive accountability. While, once again, they were unable wholly to convince their constituency that expenditure, especially expenditure on establishments, had been cut back as far as was sensible and realistic, they did find new and promising ways of breaking the plier-like grip of state necessity and public grievance. Their plan for a return to monetary stability was a bold one which promoted both the 'public credit', not least by providing for some reduction of the debt, and the confidence of the business community. The change in their financial policy mainly made their operations more intelligible, clarifying their determination to attack the debt and holding out the prospect of reduced taxation in the event of a large surplus. That all this involved a change of mind regarding the cause of inflation and also regarding a 'real' sinking fund is some indication of the Cabinet's concern at the signs of fading public confidence.

Yet if it did seem at the end of the session that the government had come more fully into its role, there was one other development, a growing awareness of estrangement within the Cabinet, which precluded any excessive complacency. Partly the cause of the trouble was the strain and stress of the Cabinet's situation, but only partly. Ancient and fresh enmities particularly centred on Canning. In many respects, latterly over his return to office from a Portuguese exile, Lord Liverpool's partiality for him had become patently obvious. On that occasion, though the concerted dislike of Sidmouth and others was only too evident in their refusal to assist an arrangement by shuffling places, the Prime Minister faithfully remembered the 'understanding and expectation' he had given Canning shortly before he left England in 1814, an offer of first refusal on any vacancy that might happen to arise in his absence.[109] Canning himself was eternally conscious of his colleagues' dislike and distrust, and he also knew that in 1812 he had been cast into the political wilderness by rating his importance much too highly. In his first years at the India Board, therefore, the office which was finally allowed him, he was inordinately careful to appear a model of propriety and let bygones, mainly his celebrated quarrel with Castlereagh, be bygones. To a great extent the circumstances the government found itself in at the beginning of 1819 were the freak of fortune which forced him back into notice and led to renewed fears that once again as a rogue elephant he would terrorise the political jungle. He alone of his fellow ministers had taken a liberal stand on the reform of the criminal law, making a speech of some renown in support of Romilly's

[109] For details of Canning's admission to office see Canning to Huskisson, 25 January 1816, Huskisson to Lord Liverpool, 5 February [1816], Add. MSS. 38740, ff. 278–80, 38741, ff. 4–5; Lord Sidmouth to Lord Melville, 8 February 1816, Sidmouth MSS.; Huskisson to Canning, 6, 14 February 1816, Lord Liverpool to Canning, 13 February 1816, Canning to Lord Liverpool, 8 March 1816, Canning MSS. It is not generally known that in 1813 Lord Liverpool endeavoured to open the Admiralty for Canning, another instance of his cordiality and friendship.

Privately Stealing Bill in 1810. Huskisson it was, his closest political friend, who saw an actual surplus as the only efficacious sinking fund and financial policy. Above all, both had long been confirmed bullionists, and in recommending the repayment of a large portion of the Bank advances and the convertibility of notes into bullion beginning at 61s. per ounce with progressive reductions to mint price, the secret committees on resumption fully supported their earlier professions.

Easy it was, then, to attribute the changes of 1819 to the influence Canning was insidiously exercising at Fife House. In a way Vansittart appeared the chief victim of the restored favourite; for the country blamed him more than any other minister for the financial difficulties of the post-war period and no one could forget his famous resolution of 1811 that 'Promissory Notes . . . are . . . equivalent to the legal Coin of the Realm' which the findings of the Bank committees now positively refuted. On the other hand, and no doubt his proud and sensitive nature exaggerated the danger, Castlereagh could not help feeling his own position was none too secure. On financial subjects of which the House these days had more than its fill he frankly confessed to being all at sea,[110] Canning's superb oratory inevitably stole much of the glory from him on the floor, and as leader of the Commons he bore some responsibility for the parliamentary unruliness of the government rank and file. Moreover, Peel had become a force to be reckoned with. In his six years as Irish Secretary a considerable number of Irish members had attached themselves to his train, and his assumption, by tacit agreement, of the leadership of the Protestant cause, together with his maturing talents as a parliamentarian, brought others as well. No longer was he merely a departmental

[110] Lord Castlereagh to Lord Clancarty, 2 April 1816, Castlereagh MSS., xxx. 951-9. In *Hansard*, 1st ser., xxxiv. 165 there is an interesting example of how the opposition, in this case Horner, took him to task for his ignorance: 'The noble lord had thrown out such a mass of language and ideas, and had made such a novel combination of twisted expressions, that it was difficult in the many theories he had urged, to understand that one which applied to the resumption of cash payments, or to the manner in which they might be most speedily effected. (Hear, hear!) It was possible that the noble Lord held the thread which would guide him through the labyrinth of theory and phraseology into which he had gone; but as that thread was not visible to him, he would not venture to plunge into the inextricable abyss. (Hear, hear!)'

spokesman; he was also an able contributor to debates in general.
On one occasion even Canning was pleased to see him roughly
handled when Brougham turned on him smartly for attacking
his inquiry into endowed schools and colleges.[111] Sensing these
ambitions and frustrations the politicians sent conjectures
flying thick and fast. Some spoke of a new administration along
Protestant lines, others simply of Vansittart's dismissal and
Peel's promotion in his stead.[112] One thing was certain, though.
As soon as people began talking thus, the argument in favour of
recasting the Cabinet, already strong in view of the administration's recent tribulations, was significantly reinforced. Within
little more than a year, it turned out, Canning had pressed his
claims for promotion, Vansittart had offered to relinquish the
Exchequer and an approach had been made to Peel.

[111] Canning's diary, 23 June 1819, Canning MSS.
[112] *Arbuthnot*, pp. 16–17; Buckingham, *Regency*, ii. 303, 324–5.

Chapter Four

AGAIN THE REVOLUTIONISTS

I. Alarm

Parliament broke up for the summer holidays on 13 July, after quite the longest and most arduous session since the end of the war. Much to the ministers' annoyance, no doubt, the Prince Regent chose this very moment to raise yet again the highly delicate question of divorce, and the whole Cabinet had to linger in Town for another fortnight before making good their escape into the country. In all likelihood only six remained in or around London when news arrived that Orator Hunt's reform meeting at Manchester had been dispersed by the military with an alarming number of civilian casualties.[1] The fact alone is an apt comment that politics were still less a profession than a gentleman's occupation. For weeks reports had been flooding in to the Home Office that the Radicals were once again preparing for a day of reckoning, and a succession of 'tumultuous assemblies' throughout the Midlands and North, the reappearance of political societies seeking national affiliations and the usual rumours of secret arsenals and midnight drilling on the moors seemed to corroborate all that they said. Sidmouth, who was in the best position to judge, definitely thought the situation as serious as in December 1816. On that occasion he had wanted the law strengthened, and the day before Peterloo he was writing in much the same vein to a Devonshire friend.[2] Yet his colleagues refused to deny themselves accustomed pleasures. Though there was no reason not to believe the warning of the Lancashire magistrates 'that some alarming insurrection is in contemplation',[3] they blithely went

---

[1] *Eldon*, ii. 336, 338. On 12 August Liverpool, Castlereagh, Vansittart, Wellesley-Pole and Canning attended a meeting of the Cabinet. Canning's diary, 12 August 1819, Canning MSS. Canning sailed for the Continent two days later. [2] *Sidmouth*, iii. 249.

[3] Papers relative to the Internal State of the Country, no. 1, *PP*, 1819–20, iv. 219.

their separate ways, some like Canning to the Continent and others to hearth and home in the four corners of the kingdom.

Ironically, the incident at Manchester, which brought them and eventually parliament itself hastening back, was the climax of the gathering storm. Before Peterloo economic disillusionment, a daring press and exuberant platforming had recaptured the interest of the lower orders in parliamentary reform, and the magistrates, uncertain of the law regarding public assemblies, afraid to use the military before violence was actually done to life, limb or property, found themselves powerless in the face of the orderly demonstrations which 'the reforming crew' were only too capable of organising. But after the 'massacre' the tables were turned. Assisted by 'loyalist' associations and the like, the authorities were emboldened to do their duty; and not least because the Radicals' best men were snatched from them at the moment of greatest need, their challenge proved effete and short-lived. The first reaction of the hot-heads was to meet violence with violence. In and around Manchester there were a number of ugly scenes when street crowds swore vengeance on the perpetrators and joined battle with the military. Sticks, stones and imprecations, however, only persuaded the civil power to redouble its efforts, for if this was the mood of the people, the stories of pikes smelted and pistols smuggled seemed very near to the truth. The response, once tempers had simmered down, was a return to constitutionalist forms of protest; to subscription funds for the victims, legal actions against the yeomanry and public meetings all over the country. But even this sort of campaign, whatever names and numbers it managed to attract, had an essential weakness. Its whole accent was on inquiry, parliamentary inquiry, which meant that the chances of success depended in the last resort wholly on the Whigs. In coming forward when they did, Fitzwilliam and others pushed the popular leaders ignominiously into the background. After Peterloo it was not the system but the ministers who were denounced, and they could not be brought to book until parliament met. Immediately the initiative was taken from the people, the drift back to apathy commenced, as Thistlewood, who in November and December attempted the old trick of simultaneous meetings, soon found out for himself. And throughout 1820, a steadily improving economic situation completed the return to normality.

Radical dissensions, a run of successful prosecutions, and the stout exertions of the 'well-disposed' only gradually dissipated the government's alarm. Ill-informed and misinformed as Sidmouth was, it took a long while before things were seen in proper proportion. Towards the end of October, even, he was telling Eldon: 'the clouds in the North are very black, and I think they must burst'.[4] This did not stop the ministers freely admitting that the ramifications of Radical plotting did not extend much beyond Lancashire and Glasgow. At the beginning of September Lord Liverpool made a short tour of the South and came back convinced that 'the agricultural counties are in a state of progressive prosperity'. Indeed, outside the disturbed districts, where 'nothing can be worse or more alarming', he thought the country's condition had never been better since the end of the war, perhaps since his entry into public life almost thirty years before. Certainly, assuming disorder to be the consequence of distress, the available statistics painted a rosy picture: poor rates and criminal convictions were down, the excise up, and corn prices in general decline.[5] Unlike in 1816–17, the trouble seemed very much localised, the metropolis showed no inclination to lead the provinces and the economy was already taking a favourable turn.

What disturbed the government in 1819 was not an evident threat of insurrection—nothing like the Spa Fields conspiracy was ever discovered—but the apparently irresistible progress of disaffection. While Lord Liverpool understood that Great Britain's growing dependence on 'foreign demand' was intensifying the movement of the economy, and also how much easier it was to organise protest in the new industrial towns, he shared with his colleagues an ineradicable conviction that 'if the events of the French Revolution had not directed the attention of the lower orders of the community, and those immediately above them, to political considerations' the grisly prospect of class war would never have arisen.[6] No government could expect the people to bear privations with stoic indifference,

---

[4] *Eldon*, ii. 348.
[5] *Wellington Desp.* (new series), i. 76; *Liverpool*, ii. 408–9.   [6] Ibid., p. 431.

but at least in the good old days the protest had been essentially local and largely unpremeditated. The problem now was vastly different. By playing on 'the worst passions of the lowest orders', by deliberately exploiting every tittle of discontent, 'the promoters of general confusion' were systematically destroying 'all respect for established authority and ancient institutions'. Under the aegis of a free press, church and state were being openly damned and defamed. Under the banner of parliamentary reform, local dissatisfactions were being lumped together and paraded as a national sentiment. Most alarming of all, under the immemorial privilege of petitioning and public assembly, the common people were fast discovering the confidence which comes of discipline and large numbers. To the magistrates, and 'loyalists' generally, the very orderliness of the proceedings was more frightening than liberty caps and other 'seditious' accoutrements. The drilling beforehand, the exhortations against premature violence, the march past in contingents all seemed conclusive evidence that Hunt and his kind were actively preparing for nothing less than revolution. One of the Grenvilles was quite sure in his own mind of the imminent danger:

I utterly deny that any large body of men are authorised by the Law or can be safely suffered by the government to meet in the alarming & menacing manner in which [the Manchester] meeting took place, for the purpose of operating by force & terror a change in the laws & constitution of the country; if it once be permitted that under the pretence of discussing Parliamentary Reform, large bodies of men may learn the military exercise, may march with seditious banners, & with all the emblems & tunes of the French revolution, & may take undisturbed possession of the city of Manchester, menacing thereby the peace & property of all its respectable inhabitants,—& that all this must be suffered without resistance on the part of the Government, because this rebel army proclaims that it meets to consider of Parliamentary Reform, if such a pretence be once admitted & recognized, there is an end of all existing law & government, & the population of this country must be set loose to frame a new order of society through the same bloody practises which have attended the French Revolution.[7]

[7] Thomas Grenville to Charles Williams-Wynn, 1 October 1819, Coed-y-maen MSS.

Most others who represented 'respectable' opinion would not have disagreed. Despite his liberal inclinations, even Canning advised new laws for a new age: 'what is wanted,' he told the Prime Minister, 'is not a sudden & temporary measure ... applicable to a pressing but passing emergency: but a well-considered addition to the means which the present laws afford, for repressing Evils not in their contemplation, evils of modern growth, but too apparently of deep root & thriving malignity.'[8] With the army's reduction, with war no longer a major distraction, disaffection had truly become a permanent problem to be tackled as never before with permanent powers. In 1817 two of the four acts then passed had had a temporary validity. In 1819, if the government had had its way, only one among six would have.

In the Cabinet the necessity of strong measures went without saying. Sidmouth, who of course had first hand information of the law's, inadequacies, was continually representing the invidious position the magistrates occupied; Canning was all eagerness to find 'an effectual & permanent remedy'; and Eldon spent his holidays thumbing through his books and pondering possible improvements. The great question which the ministers had to settle among themselves was whether or not parliament should be called into special session. Sidmouth wanted no delay. As soon as the law officers had ironed out the legal complications, the new legislation should be hurried straight into the statute book to show that the government would not be cowed and to encourage the magistrates to even greater exertions. Lord Liverpool was more inclined to wait on events. He must have appreciated that to strengthen the law when feelings were running high was to invite accusations that the government was being needlessly antagonistic. At best, coercion which extended as far as this revealed that the forces of order were on the defensive. At worst, it produced, splits in the timbers of society which would do irreparable damage. Unlike Sidmouth, the Prime Minister realised that large and important sections in the community were coming more and more to question the wisdom of counter-revolution, and he did not take for granted parliament's ready response to the government's cry of alarm.

[8] Canning to Lord Liverpool, 14 October 1819, Canning MSS.

It was an elementary point with him, and with some others, that until the sentiments of the 'country gentlemen' were known, and known to be in favour of wholesale measures, there was a risk that few would turn up leaving the opposition too strong for comfort. Moreover, as Canning pointed out, even if they came in good earnest if the government had nothing substantive to propose, either new legislation or an increase in the army, the Whigs were bound to while away the time with searching and perhaps awkward questions on the Manchester incident.[9] In short, what was wanted for a meeting before Christmas was 'some New Explosion' which would justify the regulation of 'liberties' and the Lancashire magistrates as well.

At first the arguments in favour of delay preponderated. Liverpool, Wellington, Castlereagh and Sidmouth, who were the only ministers close at hand, met at the Home Office to discuss the situation on 15 September, but probably because the latter had just heard from the Grand Jury of Lancashire that the magistrates were 'unable to preserve the public peace under any circumstances of peculiar agitation',[10] a decision was taken to summon a full Cabinet for the following week.[11] This second meeting, which, as Sidmouth expected, produced 'much difference of opinion',[12] put off a proclamation in the meantime, though the ministers went away fully aware that much depended on developments in the next three weeks as protest meetings got under way.[13] If the Whigs in particular tried to ride waves of indignation and dismay over Peterloo and failed, there would be little need for the ministers to go early to parliament to uphold themselves and, more important, the credentials of the aristocracy to govern. Needless to say, such chariness highly exasperated Sidmouth. 'I wish those Members of the Government, who entertain that Opinion,' he told one of the absentees, 'were to pass Seven Hours every day for one Week at this Office & read all the Correspondence & hear all the

[9] Ibid.
[10] Papers relative to the Internal State of the Country, no. 43, *PP*, 1819–20, iv. 246.
[11] Lord Sidmouth to Charles Bragge-Bathurst, 14, 15 September 1819, Sidmouth MSS.
[12] Lord Sidmouth to Lord Eldon, 18 September 1819, ibid.
[13] *Liverpool*, ii. 410–11; Lord Liverpool to Lord Melville, 24 September 1819, Add. MSS. 38279, ff. 365–6.

communications which are received from various parts of the Kingdom.'[14] Perhaps it was only to be expected that the constant flow of alarmist reports would nurture his pessimism, until, shackled to a desk while his colleagues sported in the country, he could remain silent no longer. The letter he penned to Lord Liverpool at the end of the month was unusually frank, though no more so than he intended:

> ... hitherto my Colleagues have remained unconvinced of the imperious and urgent necessity of advising the adoption of the only Measure, which would, of itself, animate the loyal and awe the Disaffected, and by which alone effectual Means can be provided to meet and overcome a Danger, greater, as I am firmly and deliberately convinced, than any to which the Country has been exposed since the Accession of the present Royal Family to the Throne.
>
> I write to you on this subject, as I have repeatedly spoken, in the fulness of my Heart—Health and Comfort I have willingly sacrificed to a Sense of private Honour and Publick Duty; and there is no further Sacrifice, be it what it might, that I am not ready and determined to make, if required by such Consider-ations.—But I feel, and have felt for some time past, and whilst the Country is suffering, from the want, as I conceive, of those decisive and efficient Measures, which the Crisis calls for, my Reputation is suffering also. . . .
>
> I have, however, said more than I intended, tho' less, far less, than I feel.—It is a satisfaction to me to reflect that, in the various official Relations in which we have stood to each other, I have invariably proved myself
>
> > Sincerely yours,
> > Sidmouth.[15]

Here was the merest hint of resignation. As he confided to Eldon, 'on the subject of assembling Parliament, I have felt it incumbent upon me to express my Sentiments in a manner which I wish I could have thought myself justified in avoiding'.[16] The Prime Minister, however, was less moved by Sidmouth's fervency than by the altered circumstances of the case; for three

[14] Lord Sidmouth to Lord Melville, 29 September 1819, Sidmouth MSS. See also Lord Sidmouth to Lord Eldon, 26 September 1819, ibid.
[15] Lord Sidmouth to Lord Liverpool, 1 October 1819, ibid.
[16] Lord Sidmouth to Lord Eldon, 1 October 1819, ibid.

days earlier he had noticed reports in the London papers that
Fitzwilliam and other prominent Whigs had sent a requisition
for a county meeting to the sheriff of Yorkshire. Up to this
time 'the respectable part of Opposition' had shown a marked
reluctance to champion the people. In private almost all of them
agreed that 'the Manchester massacre' was a calamitous error of
judgement on the magistrates' part, but in public very few
seemed ready to argue that the Radical menace was being taken
too seriously. The grand juries of Cheshire and Lancashire,
with men of opposing political views among their number, both
put out alarmist statements; Brougham in a speech at Kendal
disapproved meetings on the Manchester model; and the latest
edition of Erskine's *Defences of the Whigs*, just published,
firmly averred that no 'practical and useful Reformation' could
come of 'violent unmeasured attacks upon the character and
constitution of Parliament'.[17] The first inkling the government
had of a swing away from passivity was Lawrence Dundas's
appearance at York Guildhall on 20 September when he
publicly demanded a Peterloo inquiry.[18] Since he had strong
connections with Wentworth Woodhouse, it was hard to
imagine that he was not working hand in glove with Fitzwilliam, a surmise soon verified when the signatories to the
county requisition were advertised a few days afterwards.

As Lord Liverpool maintained, this gave 'an entire new
Character to the whole Business'.[19] If the Whigs meant to
press for inquiry wherever they were sure of their strength on
the platform, not only would it 'afford a strong handle to the
disaffected' but leave the government's friends in the invidious
position of being powerless to make an effective reply. The
ministers had to answer Whig criticisms, however veiled they
were by the call for inquiry, and this they could only do in
parliament. There it would not be to their disadvantage that
they could accuse the opposition of bringing the law and those
who administered it into disrepute at a time when the machinery
of order never had greater need of the lubricant of confidence

[17] See Papers relative to the Internal State of the Country, nos. 41, 43,
PP, 1819–20, iv. 245, 246; *The Times*, 5 October 1819; *Pamphleteer*, xv.
287–316.   [18] *The Times*, 23 September 1819.
[19] Lord Liverpool to Lord Sidmouth, 28, 29 September 1819, Sidmouth
MSS.

and co-operation. In a sense the ministers were now paying the penalty for their precipitate approbation of the authorities' conduct on 16 August. While Canning may have been right, that 'to let down the Magistrates would be to invite their resignations & to lose all gratuitous service in Counties liable to disturbance for ever',[20] the fact remained that after congratulating them and the military on 'their prompt, decisive and efficient measures for the preservation of the public tranquility' the government could on no account admit any need for further inquiry. Had the ministers been able and willing to proselytise the country like their adversaries much of their embarrassment could have been avoided: but they took the view that parliament was the place where the calumnies and falsehoods the Whigs were circulating might best be rebutted,[21] a view which soon persuaded hard-pressed ministerialists to urge an early meeting.[22] Thus it was not the 'revolutionists' who brought parliament into session in November, but the Whigs. Had Fitzwilliam and others not stirred up the country, it is even conceivable that the Six Acts would never have been passed: by the beginning of 1820 the situation in the 'disturbed districts' was much improved and the ministers would have had a few months more to contemplate the expediency of coercion and the difficulty of framing 'adequate' legislation. But the decision to call parliament, once made, was also a decision to 'strengthen the laws'. The Whigs were as much the intended victims of the Six Acts as the Radicals, because these were to emphasise the awful necessity under which the Manchester magistrates and the ministers had acted. Indeed, as a political device the legislation was probably more effective than as additional horsepower for the engine of government. In 1819, over the issue of sedition, the Whigs cut a sorry figure, but before the next year was out the Radicals were acting with new vigour and new daring.

[20] Canning to Huskisson, 14 September 1819, Add. MSS. 38741, f. 315. Canning dated the letter 14 August by mistake.
[21] In Norfolk, Edmund Wodehouse, a county member, feared a Whig meeting and applied to the Home Office for more accurate information concerning Peterloo. Sidmouth replied that such details were 'unnecessary'. See Wodehouse to Lord Sidmouth, 29 September 1819, Lord Sidmouth to Wodehouse, 3 October 1819, Sidmouth MSS.
[22] *Liverpool*, ii. 412–13.

The Prime Minister agreed to a further Cabinet on the subject of an extraordinary session on the same day that he received Sidmouth's expostulatory letter.[23] This meeting took place on 8 October when perhaps seven or eight ministers attended. Though Lord Liverpool still had some doubts about the wisdom of an early session, especially now that party feeling was running high with the Whigs already active in a dozen counties, a decision to assemble parliament in November was adopted as by far the safest course.[24] Indeed, there was probably more argument over the precise date. Liverpool wanted towards the end of the month so that Canning would have time to return from Italy, and Sidmouth immediately interpreted this as the cause of the delay all along.[25] The announcement of an extraordinary sitting by no means cut the ground from under the opposition's feet. In nine counties, and in numerous towns besides, Whigs and Radicals went ahead with protest meetings, which with the steady fire kept up by a partisan press gave the case against the magistrates ample publicity. The government made virtually no attempt to retaliate in kind. Eldon had the bright idea of republishing eighteenth century tracts on the law of public assembly but nothing was ever done,[26] and the only advice Sidmouth could offer 'Friends of the Constitution' was to circulate a loyal address wherever a Whig meeting was threatened. 'To call a county meeting unless they had a well-grounded confidence in a favourable result,' he told one gentleman, 'would . . . be improvident; and how can such a confidence be entertained at the present moment when the struggle is between those who have property and those who have none, of which latter description there would be an immense influx, it being next to impossible to exclude from a county meeting inhabitants not being freeholders.'[27]

[23] Lord Liverpool to Lord Sidmouth, 1 October 1819, Sidmouth MSS.

[24] Since the Cabinet had last met, reports of mass meetings at Leeds, Birmingham and Halifax had come in.

[25] *Liverpool*, ii. 411–12; Lord Liverpool to Lord Sidmouth, 1 October 1819, Lord Sidmouth to Lord Eldon, 17 October 1819, Sidmouth MSS.

[26] Lord Eldon to Lord Sidmouth [20 September 1819], ibid.

[27] *Sidmouth*, iii. 275. Lord Grenville was critical of the Government's inactivity. After asserting the illegality of the Manchester meeting, he told his nephew: 'The Government seems to me to have been much wanting in their own cause & that of the Public, in not taking that ground openly, justifying it themselves, & shewing their adherents, who are now in many

Neither did alliance with the Radicals sorely tax Whig consciences. While plenty in the party admitted to having reservations, such co-operation at least exhibited its traditional concern for popular causes and from experience an appeal to public opinion offered the best chance of parliamentary success. The campaign in the country had hardly begun, anyway, when Fitzwilliam was dismissed from his lord-lieutenancy. This was not wholly an act of political vindictiveness, but it was one which immediately closed the Whig ranks and brought the stragglers running. In ordering him removed, the government, it must be said, fully anticipated as much. Sidmouth first raised the question the same day as the Yorkshire meeting, forty-eight hours before news of the proceedings arrived in London. Viewing his office as more than honorific, Fitzwilliam's offence had already been grievous. As the King's lieutenant he was perfectly free to make representations of his own accord, but 'to take a Subordinate Part in a Publick Meeting' at once disgraced his dignity and necessary influence. Less serious, his conduct could have been taken as disrespectful to the Prince Regent personally. The latter in his reply to the City of London address had sternly admonished the country not 'to institute an extrajudicial inquiry', and after this any meeting constituted a public defiance of the warning. The only consideration which made the government hold its hand was the hope that Fitzwilliam would deepen his offence, making his dismissal more defensible from a parliamentary point of view.[28] As it happened, in this respect he quickly obliged. Where the requisition for the York meeting had been temperately worded, professing uncertainty of the facts, the resolutions adopted there straightly accused the ministers of prejudging the case and approbating a proceeding 'which has the appearance of being illegal and highly criminal'.[29] 'He has now,' Lord Liverpool declared, 'so

---

places frightened & dumbfounded, that this is the doctrine which may be, & must be, maintained. Had this been done at first, the necessity of now prematurely calling Parliament together might I think have been wholly avoided.' Lord Grenville to Charles Williams-Wynn, 18 October 1819, Coed-y-maen MSS.

[28] Lord Sidmouth to Lord Liverpool, 14 October 1819, Add. MSS. 38280, ff. 137–8; *Bathurst*, pp. 479–80.

[29] For the requisition and address see *Courier*, 9, 16 October 1819.

entirely identified himself with the whole transaction, without
even any qualification that can be admitted as an excuse, that I
think our forebearance would be ascribed to nothing but timid-
ity, and would discourage our best friends.'[30] Hastily, a summons was sent out for a Cabinet meeting to which half a dozen
ministers repaired. All that could be urged in favour of restraint
was the present disarray of the Whigs and the possibility of a
mass resignation if a tough line were taken, but even these
advantages lost much of their pertinence when it was pointed
out that the instinct of an opposition to oppose would assert
itself in time and that only one lord-lieutenant was likely to
make a martyr of himself. Since the West Riding as a persistent
trouble-spot needed a dependable man in command, the result
of the deliberation became a foregone conclusion. Fitzwilliam
was given notice the very next day.[31]

Though his removal helped bring erring and faithful Whigs
together again, the escalation of the party war did their adversaries much the same service. One of the government's greatest
anxieties throughout this period of resurgent radicalism was
whether the 'country gentlemen' would be prepared to act as
toughly as they talked. Of late they had felt more than the
ministers that parliament should bend its course to that of
public opinion, and doubts about their attachment to 'our
happy Constitution' followed inevitably. Wellington was inclined to think that they would shrink from strong measures,
Peel too appreciated the force of popular enthusiasm,[32] while
Lord Liverpool did not even presume to guess their real sentiments: 'until our Friends come regularly to Town', he wrote,
'it will be impossible to determine to what extent we can venture
to go with a prospect of being supported in our Legislative
Enactments'.[33] As soon as the decision to reconvene parliament
was made, however, it became imperative to sample backbench opinion, and Arbuthnot was given the job of writing away
to thirty or more of 'the most important & *ticklish*'. The letters
were in the form of the usual circular sent out to request

[30] *Bathurst*, p. 480.
[31] Vansittart to Lord Harrowby, 23 October 1819, Harrowby MSS., 16,
ff. 186–8.   [32] *Plumer Ward*, ii. 22, 25.
[33] Lord Liverpool to Lord Melville, 24 September 1819, Add. MSS.
38279, f. 366.

attendance, but coming so early and at such a juncture they naturally evoked more than the usual cursory reply. Lord Liverpool, for one, found the response exceptionally gratifying. Forwarding a packet of letters received to Canning, he remarked: 'you will see that the Spirit in which they are written is excellent. I have not as yet heard of any Person on whom we have a right to depend, likely to fail us.'[34] The followings hovering on the government's flank were equally friendly. Bankes and Wilberforce were well-content with the Cabinet's proceedings. Wellesley had already pledged himself 'under so dreadful a peril' to offer every support, and the Grenvilles were as ultra-alarmist as ever.[35] In these circumstances the ministers could safely look forward to what Sidmouth unabashedly called a united front of 'honest and intelligent minds'.[36]

Apart from gauging the mood of allies and friends, the government's chief preoccupation throughout October and November was the drafting of measures appropriate to the crisis and acceptable to parliament. The necessity of legislation was taken for granted. Sidmouth was desperate to augment the magistracy's power, and the Prime Minister's only concern, one Canning also shared, was that the legal intricacies should be properly understood and political possibilities fully explored.[37] The warning, then, against 'a mere unavailing relation of plots & treason' which Lord Melville sent down from Edinburgh was needless and perhaps a trifle infuriating.[38] Time, in fact, was the government's main enemy, for the law officers had just six weeks to prepare suitable measures, no easy task when their superiors were wanting 'the means of permanent security'. Lord Liverpool, indeed, truly regretted the haste, and in this respect Eldon's coming to Town eleven days before the rest of the Cabinet must have been especially welcome.[39] The

[34] Lord Liverpool to Canning, 10 November 1819, ibid., 38568, f. 74; Canning to Mrs Canning, 16 November 1819, Canning MSS.

[35] Henry Bankes to Lord Sidmouth, 24 October 1819, Lord Liverpool to Lord Sidmouth, 27 October 1819, Sidmouth MSS.; Buckingham, *Regency*, ii. 337–8; *Liverpool*, ii. 418–30.

[36] *Sidmouth*, iii. 297.

[37] *Liverpool*, ii. 413; Canning to Lord Liverpool, 14 October 1819, Canning MSS.

[38] Lord Melville to Lord Sidmouth, 8 October 1819, Sidmouth MSS.

[39] *Liverpool*, ii. 413; Lord Sidmouth to Lord Kenyon, 31 October 1819, Sidmouth MSS.

deficiencies in the law which the Crown lawyers laboured so
diligently to correct almost went without saying. Peterloo and
preceding and subsequent events made some limitation of the
right of public meeting indispensable; Hunt's release on bail
and traverse to the spring assizes argued a need for speedier
justice for political miscreants; and the problem of Radical
propaganda with its agnostic and seditious overtones was as
great as it had ever been.

To know what improvements were called for, however, was
one thing. To translate them into good law quite another. The
ministers' reservations about coercion, reflected in their
anxiety to out-manoeuvre the Whigs and sample parliamentary
opinion, must have been strengthened by what happened
when they came to draft the appropriate measures. The law
relating to public meetings, for example, was a bewildering
amalgam of common law and later legislation, enough to
tax the sharpest legal brains let alone the average magistrate.
The great difficulty, but one the authorities on the spot could
never escape was at what moment a meeting convened for
a legal purpose became either an unlawful assembly or riot,
dispersible if necessary by force. While the people had an inalienable right to petition parliament or address the sovereign,
they had none to assemble *in terrorem populi*—'in Disturbance
of the Public Peace, to the great Terror and Danger of His
Majesty's loyal and peaceable Subjects'. But how could orderly
demonstrations, though their real object was revolution, be
designated a breach or threatened breach of the peace? Could
banners be taken as a species of seditious utterance? Could
applause at one remark? Could martial music? The essential
point was that the government would only act within the broad
framework of the law to defend the established order. 'English
liberties' were so revered by the nation that the ruling class
would and could not bring itself to condone censorship, a large
standing army, a police force, or a ban on public meetings even
to cope with the politically abhorrent. At first Eldon was confident that legislation could be drafted declaring that meetings
were 'dispersible by reasonable application of force',[46] but
eventually he was driven to conclude that there was no

[46] Lord Eldon to Lord Sidmouth, 4 October 1819, ibid.

alternative to the magistrate's discretionary power, and the government fell back on the difficult to enforce 'limitation of locality' which allowed parochial meetings only.[41]

Concerning the press, there were similar complexities. A seditious or blasphemous libel was perhaps definable in general terms but in the last resort—thanks to Fox's Libel Act and the absence of censorship—it was left to juries and public opinion to set the standards of decent expression. If the government felt the liberty of the press was being abused, all it could really do in the way of new law was to check the publication—publication in its widest sense—of 'the Minor Jacobin Prints' it so bitterly reprehended. The difficulty here was parliament's touchiness on the subject of the press's freedom, and more particularly, the need to avoid penalising the virtuous along with the wicked. Those 'very mischievous cheap publications' which masqueraded as pamphlets to avoid the stamp duty on newspapers could conceivably be taxed so as to reduce their number and influence, but if the job were done indiscriminately many exemplary works on manners and religion would also disappear. An explicit reference to political literature was absolutely essential, though even this would destroy much wholesome reading, for 'loyalist' papers would go the same way as the rest of the 'pauper press'. As for occasional works very little could be done without reintroducing some form of censorship. To increase the penalties for seditious or blasphemous libel had dubious advantages owing to the inconsistencies of the jury system. If the sentence of imprisonment, fine and security for good behaviour which the law at present imposed was extended, or some new punishment devised, there was every likelihood that juries would be harder to please, and the greater the uncertainty of punishment the less effective the deterrent. Any attempt to restrain circulation was similarly frustrated. Invariably, as soon as a libel action commenced, the offending work gained a notoriety it would never have had otherwise, and yet an injunction against its further sale was unknown in law either before or after conviction. Legal technicalities, especially the traverse allowable in cases of misdemeanour, aggravated the evil tenfold by delaying the court's

[41] *Liverpool*, ii. 433.

decision. In Lord Grenville's words, 'as great profit often attends the multiplied sale, fine becomes nugatory, and imprisonment cannot be repeated in any proportion of the number of offences committed'.[42] To impound copies of an alleged libel was considered too strong a measure. To suppress a work which had secured a conviction was open to the objections that only part of the whole was declared libellous by the court and that one man could be acquitted, on technical questions of publication and malice, for what another was found guilty. In the end it had to be admitted that the most that could be done was the confiscation of those copies which were in the convicted person's actual possession or use.

By wholly giving up their holidays the law officers managed to complete their task just in time for the Cabinet's return. Lord Liverpool moved to his seat near Kingston, Surrey at the beginning of November and asked to see the drafts a day or two later to 'apprise ourselves of the real State of any Difficulties which might occur'.[43] Since the Cabinet had agreed to reassemble on 8 November and definitely discussed the bills on the 10th, he cannot have found them much in arrears. Six measures, in Radical parlance soon to become the infamous 'Six Acts', were decided on. Three sought to curb the means of intimidation and violence, two its incitement through the press, and one the instigators themselves. Within the first category came the Seditious Meetings Bill, the Training Prevention Bill and the Seizure of Arms Bill. By confining public meetings, except those called by 'known constituted authorities', to a parochial level, and by prohibiting the slightest semblance of martial array, the government hoped to check 'the great evil of itinerant orators, and of all artificial means of excitement'. Great care was taken to preserve the right of assembly as much as possible. Only meetings deliberating on 'any public Grievance or any Matter in Church and State' was to come within the act's purview, and though notice of time and place was made obligatory so that the magistrates might alter both at their discretion, the power was very limited, just sufficient, it was hoped, to make an insurrection through simultaneous meetings

[42] Ibid., p. 426.
[43] Lord Liverpool to Lord Sidmouth, 28 October 1819, Sidmouth MSS.

next to impossible. Bills prohibiting unauthorised military training and permitting the seizure of arms 'dangerous to the Public Peace' were a natural corollary.

The measures affecting the press, short-titled the Newspaper Stamp Duties Bill and the Blasphemous and Seditious Libels Bill, were devised to restrict 'twopenny trash' while sparing the unobjectionable, unoffending majority. To deter 'irresponsible' or 'positively evil' argument, the Radicals' main weapon Liverpool and Sidmouth agreed,[44] the first bill ordered the publishers of periodicals to enter into recognizances as a guarantee of payment if ever they ran foul of the libel laws, and the other made banishment or transportation for fourteen years the maximum penalty for a second conviction. The economic war against 'political poison' was extended a step further by a redefinition of what constituted a newspaper. Only publishers whose works contained 'Public News, Intelligence or Occurrences, or any Remarks or Observation thereon' were to give sureties for good behaviour, and such papers if they appeared at least once every twenty-six days and sold for less than sixpence now became liable to a fourpenny duty Vansittart had imposed in 1815. This made a price rise inescapable for the proprietors of cheap weeklies, if they were to keep within the law. On pain of £20 fine no periodical outside the definition of a newspaper could be sold for less than sixpence, and with the exorbitant stamp duty twopenny papers like Carlisle's *Republican* would cost at least this and probably more. A new line of attack had been opened up by the authorities. The attempt to form a political consciousness at the lowest levels of society was to be frustrated by taking account of the fact that those most susceptible to obnoxious opinions were also the economically deprived. It was in many ways an acknowledgement that the other resources of the state had been found inadequate, though it was soon apparent that taxation was equally ineffective. One last 'insult' was offered a free press. Ironically enough, the court proceeding which declared a work to be libellous advertised it to the world when the law had no power whatever to check its circulation. By giving the magistrates authority to search for and confiscate all copies in the convicted's possession, the

---

[44] *Liverpool*, ii. 434; *Sidmouth*, iii. 297.

Libels Bill partially corrected this shortcoming, establishing a
principle which still remains extant.

The last bill of the six, the so-called Misdemeanours Bill, was
to some extent an alternative to a further suspension of habeas
corpus. As far as the government was concerned, demagogues
and scribblers were the masterminds of the British revolution,
and the sooner they were placed where their public was lost
to them so much the better. With due observance of the legal
process this was extraordinarily difficult to achieve. Charged
with a misdemeanour like seditious conspiracy or seditious libel,
the accused could demur his plea, traverse the indictment and
even postpone his trial to a later assizes, all the while being
released on bail. Since the suspension of habeas corpus was
perforce a temporary measure, and one which parliament only
grudgingly allowed at the best of times, these procedural delays
were ever a bane and curse, leaving undesirables at perfect
liberty and allowing them, if anything, to win the good offices
of public opinion in the interval of waiting. By stopping im-
parling on several points of law, therefore, notably on the
indictment and plea, the Misdemeanours Bill was a valuable
addition to the judicial armoury.

Not one of the ministers expected to have all six measures on
the statute book before Christmas. Liverpool himself was
under no illusion that the Whigs would manage 'to make common cause' somehow, however painful a subject sedition was
for them, and he set the government the modest target of
passing some while the rest got acceptance in principle—
another way of saying as far as the second reading.[45] Such
discreet confidence was fully justified by the debate on the
address. Predictably, since they had been urging the same from
the hustings for the past month, the Whigs made a formal call
for an inquiry into 'the Manchester massacre'. Equally predictably, the Grenvilles and the 'country gentlemen' joined forces
with the government to lay the subject to rest. Tierney managed
to gather 150 votes into the lobby, an opposition which was
nearly a full muster and which said a great deal for the party's
morale. But, basically, the Whig position was embarrassingly

[45] Lord Liverpool to Huskisson, 15 October 1819, Add. MSS. 38280,
ff. 146–7.

weak, and remained so throughout the whole of the session. With
regard to Peterloo it was difficult to argue the illegality of the
magistrates' action. As Eldon stated the law: 'numbers constituted force, and force terror, and terror illegality,'[46] which left
the onus on the opposition to prove that forty thousand people
marching past with drums beating and flags flying caused the
King's liege subjects no apprehension or alarm. That it had
done had already been admitted by the Grand Jury of Lancashire when true bills were found against Hunt and his ac-
complices and nothing against the yeomanry. Inasmuch as this
was the considered verdict of a bench 'composed of Persons of
all Parties in a Co. divided in Political Sentiment',[47] the case
seemed a clear-cut one, particularly when under common law
the magistrates could disperse an unlawful assembly whether
the Riot Act had been read or not. The only question concerning
Peterloo which admitted of real doubt was the extent of force
used, but this was more a political than legal issue. If no felony
was committed, and unlawful assembly was no felony, the
magistrates were bound to use a 'reasonable application of
force', neither too much nor too little. Obviously, where to
draw the line was always a problem. With a casualty list of
eleven killed and some four hundred wounded, Peterloo did
seem an example of unnecessary brutality, though the government was quick to point out, as if it really mitigated the case,
that the people had inflicted a third of these casualties on themselves. The effusion of blood, however, mattered less than the
circumstances which had provoked it. Because the country was
on the verge of revolution it was enough that the magistrates
had done their duty, and to have drawn too fine a distinction
between reasonable and unreasonable force would have
seriously inhibited the future exertions of the entire civil power.
The need to protect the magistracy, in fact, was the essential
weakness of the Whig argument. To cast reflections on their good
sense at a time when, as the Speech had it, 'a spirit is now fully
manifested, utterly hostile to the Constitution of this Kingdom',
was comparable to dismissing the general staff the moment war

[46] *Hansard*, 1st ser., xli. 38.
[47] Lord Liverpool to Lord Somers, 20 October 1819, Add. MSS. 38280,
f. 176.

was declared. Altogether, allegations of illegality and mis-judgment came hard indeed from an opposition most of whom accepted the danger meetings like that at St. Peter's Field represented.

Whatever the incongruities of the opposition's case, the defeat of the amendment calling for inquiry did not quite end the discussion of 'the Manchester business'. Further exchanges took place when the petitions of victims were brought up, and incidental references were continually made in debate. More-over, the 'Papers relative to the Internal State of the Country' which the ministers laid before parliament soon afterwards, included eye-witness accounts by a magistrate and the military commander, and in both Houses the opposition lost no time in proposing to have this information referred to select committees, their game being to have the Peterloo inquiry made incidental to a general inquiry into present discontents. In attacking on a broader front, however, in trying to press home the govern-ment's responsibilities for disorder and threatened insurrection, the Whigs unquestionably did themselves more harm than good. In the first place, they could not help being accused of making party war to the knife at a time when sedition represented a common enemy. By challenging the Prince Regent's approba-tion of the Manchester magistrates they had seemed to be willing to do irreparable damage to the authority of the civil power, and now it was easily alleged that they were endeavour-ing to drag the government through the same mire. In this sense bickering which took up valuable parliamentary time became irresponsible, even criminal if it deliberately obstructed the passage of measures vital to the country's security. 'What was parliament called upon to do by gentlemen on the other side?' taunted Castlereagh at the suggestion of a select com-mittee. 'To postpone those necessary measures of safety until a period when, in all human probability, they could be of no avail.'[48] Secondly, and even more unforgivable, their case against the government was feeble, poorly developed and based on out-worn arguments. Had the ministers, so their argument ran, not pursued a corrupt and extravagant system, had they been as zealous in retrenchment as repression, the people would never

[48] *Hansard*, 1st ser., xli. 558-9.

have taken the heady wine the Radicals offered them. But agreed that distress was the basic cause of disaffection, could depression really be ascribed the government's fault? In the view of parliament and much 'intelligent' opinion, not so. The derangement of the economy was a consequence of peace, and if the country's agony was the worst it had ever experienced it was only because of the magnitude of the war effort, a rapidly growing population, industrialisation and a slackening of world trade, all circumstances beyond any government's control. Moreover, the ministers had not entirely ignored present discontents. With the army and navy greatly reduced, with £14,000,000 in taxes remitted and all sinecures condemned to extinction, they had done something to meet the charge of extravagant government though it had no foundation. Confronted by a threatened 'Subversion of the Rights of Property and of all order in Society', what a majority of 'parliament men' expected of the opposition was not party rant but willing cooperation and, where necessary, temperate and useful criticism. After the impressive strides the Whigs had made in regaining the 'country gentlemen's' favour in the previous session, all was lost by their absurd and disingenuous performance in this. In accepting the Address *in toto* the party as a whole fully acknowledged the country's peril, yet failed to adopt the posture and attitude of a loyal opposition; and the vague declarations in favour of reform which Grey, and those who followed his example, made may have given them popularity of a sort but also incurred the long enduring displeasure of parliament and the 'respectable' classes generally. The events after Peterloo, as those of 1817 had done, did much to revive the distinction between Whigs and Tories, because once again the former appeared to act up to their character of being too ready to concede to popular demands regardless of the real interest of the state. As a result they alienated further a vast body of influential opinion which was not persuaded to look kindly upon them until the crisis over parliamentary reform a decade in the future.

Since everyone but the Whigs apparently accepted the seriousness of the situation, the government's measures had a relatively easy passage through both Houses. Indeed, by Christmas four had passed into law and one other only required the Lords' consent to the Commons' amendments. Though predictable noises came from the opposition side avowing the effectiveness of existing law, the rights of Englishmen and an exaggerated alarm, the 'country gentlemen' jibbed at no more than a permanent restraint on public meetings, a controversial point Castlereagh neatly evaded by proposing a trial period of five years. Otherwise they willingly allowed 10,000 to be added temporarily to the military establishment, and regulated, though with little practical effect, much vaunted British liberties from the freedom to arm to the freedom to opine. To say the least, the ministers found their ardour pleasantly reassuring. In the previous session the government could not help sensing a fading attachment to the established order of things, what Peel a few months later called the 'more liberal' tone of England, 'a feeling . . . in favour of some undefined change in the mode of governing the country'.[49] So strong was the impression that the ministers remained half afraid that parliament would grapple with Radicalism with little stomach for the fight. Canning for one thought its spirit had flagged, and even Eldon refused to take for granted its 'due & efficacious Aid'.[50] Gratifying indeed then, was the alacrity with which the 'country gentlemen' sprang to the constitution's defence. It seemed a welcome confirmation that the government was steering the right course, avoiding the twin dangers of outright capitulation to the people and outright defiance. Some 'liberalising'—Peel thought the new word 'odious but intelligible'—there had to be, and the abolition of sinecures, penal reform and professions in favour of freer trade had already made it plain that the ministers were not held fast in the ultra-conservative straitjacket. Over parliamentary reform, however, there could as yet be no compromise, no concessions. By spreading their sails on this issue the Whigs were blown far out to sea while the government continued to cruise in safe water.

[49] *Croker*, i. 170.
[50] Canning to Huskisson, 14 [September] 1819, Add. MSS. 38741, f. 315; Lord Eldon to Lord Sidmouth, [20 October 1819], Sidmouth MSS.

II. The Prospect of a Queen

After a brief adjournment over the Christmas weekend, parliament finally broke up on 29 December with the intention of resuming in the middle of February, somewhat later than usual in view of the special sitting which had gone before. To the ministers the New Year seemed full of promise. The revenue —the criterion of internal prosperity—was showing progressive improvement, the harvest had been good enough to close the ports while keeping prices relatively high, and, except in Scotland, where the Radical trouble culminated in the celebrated clash at Bonnymuir, the situation in the disturbed districts was quieter than it had been for months. With things in this healthy state, even the most pessimistic in the Cabinet could rejoice. No one foresaw, no one could foresee the imbroglio which was to bring the royal family into universal contempt, the administration its greatest test and the country near to what could well have been the constitutional crisis of the century. Just when the ministers were beginning to congratulate one another on the prospect before them, the savage perversity of fortune set in motion the train of events which led to the extraordinary spectacle of the Queen's trial. On 29 January 1820, attended by his usual retinue, George III quietly expired.

The Princess of Wales' conduct had been cause for rumour and speculation almost as long as she had been consort to the heir apparent. From the beginning the marriage had been a disaster, one of those instances of absolute incompatibility which were inevitable when, to quote Wilberforce, matches 'contrary to the laws of God and of nature' were contracted among royalty.[51] Since the couple had agreed to live apart barely a year after the wedding, gossip had come naturally, the more so when the husband had made no attempt to conceal his loathing and Caroline had seemed oblivious to the dignity of her exalted station. Despite the open scandal attending her peccadilloes, successive administrations had studiously ignored the world's idle chatter, until in 1806 Grenville and his Talents had reluctantly concluded that reports of her misconduct were

[51] *Hansard*, 2nd ser., i. 1391–2.

serious enough to warrant formal inquiry. The result of this
'Delicate Investigation', as it soon became known, had blasted
her character forever, for though the commissioners had
acquitted her of the gravest charge, that of having reared a
bastard child, they had been far from admitting her complete
innocence. 'Other particulars respecting the conduct of her
Royal Highness', their report had maintained, 'necessarily give
occasion to very unfavourable interpretations [and these] must
be credited, until they shall receive some decisive contradiction.'[52]
For a short time, by granting her a palace apartment and receiving her at court, the King had saved her from the full impli-
cations of the verdict, but after 1811, with her husband's
assumption of the sovereign's prerogatives, nothing had saved
her from his loathing and vindictiveness. Forbidden to visit her
daughter without permission, denied the entree to the Queen's
drawing-room, publicly exhibited as a woman in disgrace when
the Continental despots had visited England, she had at length
resolved to quit the country indefinitely. On 9 August 1814 she
had sailed for Cuxhaven and Europe. It is not inconceivable
that her husband toasted her departure as rumour reported:
'To the Princess of Wales's damnation and may she never
return to England.'[53]

At this early stage, divorce had been in nobody's contemplation, simply because a *prima facie* case of adultery did not exist.
Undoubtedly the Prince Regent had seen divorce as the ultimate
solution, especially when the constitutional relationship between
king and queen presupposed a public relationship between both,
but not for a moment could he have deluded himself that one
law existed for him and quite another for the rest of His
Majesty's subjects. The most he had been able to do was to
hope that, freed from the conventionalities of royal state, the
Princess would shortly destroy herself by her own indiscretion.
Almost as soon as she had landed on the Continent, this had
seemed very likely. From Brunswick and Strasburg, Geneva,
Milan and Naples reports had come flitting back of midnight
romps, daring costume parties and countless other vulgarities;

[52] *Fortescue*, ix. 445–8.
[53] Alice Drayton Greenwood, *Lives of the Hanoverian Queens of England*,
ii. 328 n.1.

and, not surprisingly, the Prince Regent had lost no time in ordering the collection of corroborative testimony. Probably about the middle of 1815, Ompteda, the Hanoverian envoy at the Vatican, had begun taking down depositions and recruiting spies,[54] the information passing to the Foreign Office through the British embassy in Vienna.

At this stage the Cabinet had taken no cognizance of Caroline's conduct, and indeed could have taken none until the Prince Regent expressly commanded it. The information which arrived in the diplomatic bag had been forwarded direct to Carlton House for the attention of the Prince of Wales' law officers without the ministers once seeing it. Even so, the government could not have long ignored the dangers and difficulties arising from Ompteda's inquisition. Provided that nothing could have been traced to its agency, there could have been no objection to the inquiry itself, for the incrimination of the Princess would not only have deterred her from returning home in the event of her husband's accession but have justified her exclusion from the honours and privileges of Queen Consort if she had dared to venture.[55] What the ministers had mostly feared was a proceeding for divorce beginning in the law courts and ending in parliament. Had it been simply a private issue between injured husband and erring wife the case would have been full of complication, because the defending party in extenuation of any offence had an inalienable right to produce recriminatory evidence, which the Prince's profligacy made only too easy. As it was, inasmuch as the nation had an interest in the monarchy's honour and dignity, any proceeding in which the heir apparent was concerned necessarily became an affair of state. No one could answer for the royal majesty if the Fitzherbert marriage of 1785 became public knowledge or if Caroline's lawyers allowed the country to feast itself for months on smut and sex put out by the first family in the kingdom. Moreover, it had been vain to hope that politics could be kept out. If the Prince Regent had wanted a divorce *a vinculo matrimonii*, a complete dissolution of his marriage, a bill embodying the annulment

---

[54] Brougham knew of a spy in her household in August 1815. Chester W. New, *The Life of Henry Brougham to 1830*, p. 117.

[55] Sir Archibald Alison, *Lives of Lord Castlereagh and Sir Charles Stewart*, iii. 217 n.

would have had to have been carried through parliament, and there it would have been certainly contested by the friends of Princess Charlotte, for she had no desire to be displaced in the succession, and also by those Whigs who could never forgive his desertion of the party in 1812. No good then, the ministers had soon concluded, could come of pandering to the Prince Regent's private wishes. Rather let Caroline compromise herself still further than risk the public weal with a shameful exhibition of royal infidelity. 'The only prudent course', Castlereagh had told his brother, the British ambassador at Vienna, 'is to augment and confirm the proofs the Prince already has. . . . It is the efficacy of the means we are already in possession of to protect [him] against farther personal annoyance, that ought to make us doubly cautious of embarking in any offensive proceeding, except upon the clearest grounds of practical expediency.'[56]

But how to tell the Prince that divorce was out of the question? Satisfied that Ompteda's researches and certain other information had made the case against his wife complete, he had explicitly demanded the Cabinet's opinion on this point as early as July 1816. The reply had been a masterpiece of noncommitment, of the evasiveness which characterised the government's strategy for some time to come. Since a state of separation was no bar to a divorce suit, a proceeding in Doctors' Commons had been found to be feasible. So also, an indictment for high treason. But any British court, the ministers had argued, whether ecclesiastical or secular, would be wary of a prosecution case founded on the testimony of foreigners, especially foreigners of low station; and, even more damaging, Ompteda had gone about his business 'making promises and paying beforehand', which, if discovered, would destroy the credibility of his witnesses immediately, however convincing their evidence.[57] Nor had the ministers recommended further inquiry 'into the nature of the Evidence, as well as into the Characters and Circumstances of the Witnesses'. They had maintained that Caroline's legal advisers were by now on the alert for spies and detectives, and that there was no sense in the Prince Regent risking 'the advantageous ground', which 'in the eyes of this

[56] Ibid.
[57] Lord Stewart to Lord Castlereagh, 9 January 1816, Londonderry MSS.

Country and of Europe' he at present held, by provoking a premature proceeding. Thus the sum of their advice had been that unless 'fresh information or other circumstances' changed the situation dramatically, he would do best to bide his time. There had been little comfort here for a cuckolded husband. 'I hope the Prince will continue to be satisfied' had been Harrowby's dubious comment when Lord Bathurst had sent him the gist of the minute.[58]

As it happened, he had accepted the rebuff with good grace. Castlereagh, who had conveyed to him the Cabinet's impressions, had reported a 'great disposition to abide by the Advice which might be offer'd' and the Prime Minister had found him 'equally accommodating the next Morning'.[59] Not for long, however, would he play the waiting game his ministers recommended. His agents had kept up a close pursuit of the Princess and her entourage as they had continued their bizarre odyssey from Sicily to Jerusalem. In June 1817 the Cabinet had again perused the latest intelligence, only to provide the same advice as before.[60] Rebuffed a second time, the Prince had ordered Leach, his first law officer, but in his individual capacity, to amass all the available evidence and report his opinion of the case. When he too had concluded that 'considering the great importance of the subject' impeccable testimony was essential, a commission with no official attachments, the famous Milan Commission, had been sent at once to Italy to make 'proper researches'.[61] Particularly with regard to this last step the government had been hurried forward much further than it had liked. They had noticed an increasing obsession with divorce and had variously attributed it to Leach's interference and the death of Princess Charlotte, which the Prince Regent himself had admitted had removed 'much difficulty in point of delicacy'.[62] In their minute of 1816 the ministers had vehemently opposed the idea of 'authorising any Person or Persons . . . to

---

[58] *Bathurst*, p. 423. For the Cabinet minute see HO 126/3 and Add. MSS. 38368, ff. 312–18. Lord Bathurst summarised its contents in a letter to Lord Harrowby dated 21 August 1816. Harrowby MSS. 14, ff. 78–80.

[59] Ibid.

[60] Lord Liverpool to the Prince Regent, 26 June 1817, Add. MSS. 38267, f. 203.

[61] *George IV*, ii. 410–14; *Liverpool*, iii. 11 n.1.

[62] *Eldon*, ii. 305.

make further Inquiries into the Validity of the Testimony already had', and only on the strict understanding that 'the question of the expediency of any proceeding must always be considered as an open question' and that the government would provide nothing other than money and letters of introduction had they now acquiesced in the Milan Commission.[63]

Perhaps fortunately for the ministers, before the commissioners could report, and before the Prince Regent could force the Cabinet to a definite decision, Brougham, who had been handling the Princess's case, had taken an initiative which opened an entirely new prospect. From his brother James staying with her at Pesaro he had received word that she was strongly disposed to come to some kind of arrangement, and without further ado he had written to Lord Hutchinson, a stout Whig and personal friend of the Prince Regent, suggesting a formal separation to be ratified by act of parliament, a renunciation of her right to be crowned and to use the royal appellation, and the retention of her annuity for the term of her natural life.[64] As was to be expected, the Prince had immediately interpreted Brougham's move as an acknowledgement of his wife's guilt, as an admission that the Milan Commission would find irrefutable proof of criminal misconduct. To him the chance of divorce by amicable arrangement, without the 'adverse Proceedings' his ministers were so chary of, had clearly beckoned. Needless to say, the government's assessment of the situation had been altogether different. While they, too, had heartily welcomed Brougham's overture as a step towards avoiding the public nuisance of a proceeding at law, they had been forced to point out to the Prince that separation not divorce was being offered, inasmuch as the latter could never 'be accomplished by arrangement nor obtained except upon proof of adultery to be substantiated by evidence before some tribunal in this country'.[65] On Brougham's terms, of course, the only practical difference between the two was that remarriage was impossible for either party; but since the Prince Regent had no intention of remarrying,[66] and a judicial contest to enable it

[63] *Liverpool*, iii. 11 n.1.
[64] *George IV*, ii. 280–5; *Liverpool*, iii. 15–16.
[65] Prince Regent to Lord Liverpool, 16 June 1819, Add. MSS. 38190, f. 31; *Liverpool*, iii. 17–19. [66] *Hobhouse*, p. 4.

was hazardous in the extreme as far as the government was concerned, such a proposition, in principle, had been perfectly acceptable. However, the questions which had over-shadowed all others had been whether the Prince would come to his senses and whether the Princess would endorse a settlement along the lines her legal adviser had proposed. Having been repeatedly balked, he was obviously counting on the Milan Commission to provide incontrovertible proof. She for her part was unpredictable. At the same time that she had been telling James Brougham and personal friends of her desire for deliverance, bold letters—the atrocious spelling was a personal hallmark—were being written to Canning and Liverpool announcing her return to England, 'her injured character having been once again attaqued by fals Witnesses'.[67] In the circumstances the ministers had done the best they could. Brougham had been encouraged but politely told that negotiation required the Princess's authority,[68] and when the report of the Milan Commission had been laid before them they had again played for time by arguing the insufficiency of the evidence and difficulties over the mode of proceeding.[69]

The King's death at the end of January 1820 did not so much change the ministers' policy as hasten its fulfilment. As long as Caroline remained Princess of Wales, all that the Cabinet had to decide concerning her was whether the nation could afford the price of her husband's private comfort. Once he ascended the throne, however, the question became pressing whether or not a woman of her repute should be accorded the usual honours and privileges of Queen Consort. By custom, perhaps by right, she had legitimate claims to be crowned, to reside in a royal palace, to have her name included in the liturgy; and

[67] Princess of Wales to Lord Liverpool, 1 June 1819, Add. MSS. 38277, ff. 202–3; Canning's diary, 1 August 1819, Canning MSS.
[68] Brougham to Lord Hutchinson, 24 June 1819, Lord Eldon and Lord Liverpool to Lord Hutchinson, 26 June 1819, Add. MSS. 38565, ff. 22, 24. The government first replied to Brougham through Lord Hutchinson sometime between 17 and 24 June. The substance of the communication was that 'there would be no indisposition, at the proper time, to entertain the principle on which the proposal was grounded, if it should turn out that it met with the approbation and concurrence of the princess'. *Hansard*, 2nd ser., iv. 489.
[69] Minute of Cabinet, 24 July 1819, Add. MSS. 38368, ff. 306–11. The document printed in *Liverpool*, iii. 19–22 which purports to be this minute, though mistakenly dated 1820, is actually that of August 1816.

because the annuity granted her in 1814 lapsed with George III's demise, if the ministers shrank from defining her prerogatives parliament was certain to do it for them. As it happened, almost the first act of the new king forced them to a decision. The day after his father's death happening to be a Sunday, George suddenly remembered that the prayers for the royal family required revision and sent word to that effect to the Archbishop of Canterbury. According to the precedents and the Act of Uniformity, which established the liturgy's original form, the alteration was confined to a phrase, but when the Primate proposed to substitute 'our gracious Queen Caroline' for 'Their Royal Highnesses George Prince of Wales, the Princess of Wales'[70] the King flatly refused to allow any public mention of his wife's new dignity. Such an attitude placed the government in an immediate quandary. In view of his notable tenacity on personal points, if the Cabinet defied him they would perhaps dare him to dismiss them. If, on the other hand, they indulged him they would not only sanction an act of uncertain legality but also run the risk—since exclusion implied misconduct—of provoking the Queen into the very proceeding they were desperate to avoid. By a stroke of good fortune, no sooner had the King disclosed his wishes than he was laid low with chronic pleurisy, and for the ten days he was incommunicado his ministers had ample opportunity to decide their best course, marshal their arguments and garb their conclusions in careful prose. A formula for unanimity did not come easily, partly because, as the debates in parliament later showed, the rights and wrongs of the case could be argued indefinitely. Canning was wholly hostile to omission, and, if Croker is to be believed, there were others as well.[71] Only by ignoring the legalities and weighing the political pros and cons was agreement eventually reached. The King, it was decided, was the chief enemy of a settlement short of divorce and in this instance the party most likely to take offence. Where his mood was obdurate the Queen's was conciliatory, or from Brougham's overture six months earlier appeared so at least, and where he invariably made a fetish of personal honour and the royal *metier*, she

---

[70] Archbishop of Canterbury to the King, n.d., Add. MSS. 38282, f. 341.
[71] *Croker*, i. 160.

appeared to live her life with singular disregard for both. Obliged once, there was always a chance he would return the favour when 'greater & more essential sacrifices' were demanded. Thwarted, no one could answer for the consequences. A crumb thrown, it seemed to the ministers, might easily do a whole world of good.[72]

The Order in Council announcing the alterations in the liturgy appeared in the *Gazette* of 12 February. Because a deprival of privilege was in effect an allegation of misconduct before matters were put in legal train, the proclamation gave or was meant to give public notice that no penal proceeding was in contemplation. Far from prejudging the question, the ministers saw themselves as acting on the public notoriety of her conduct and taking the first step towards an arrangement which would strip her of her royal distinctions while taking full account of her private comfort. Canning was the first to plot this course. He saw at once that the particular question of the liturgy was inextricably related to the Queen's situation in general, that the moment she was deprived of one privilege the government was committed to remove the rest, and that unless positive action was taken in favour of compromise her advisers might easily be frightened into the only alternative left them— redress at law. Partly by refusing to be a party to any penal proceeding, partly by arguing that after Brougham's offer public opinion would throw the responsibility for further negotiation on the government, he had within five days brought the entire Cabinet round to his way of thinking.[73] But Canning's was not the only influence. Other circumstances equally compelled the ministers to decide exactly where they stood regarding divorce. In the previous four or five months important supplementary evidence had come to hand and English members of the Princess's suite had been sounded with discouraging results, which made the prosecution's case as complete as it would ever be.[74] Furthermore, following the advice of an earlier minute, crucial questions of legal procedure had been referred to the Crown lawyers, and their report had just become available. This statement, along

---

[72] Canning to Mrs Canning, 9 February 1820, Canning MSS.
[73] Canning to Mrs Canning, 6 February 1820, ibid; *Hobhouse*, p. 7.
[74] Ibid., p. 6; *Castlereagh*, xii. 211.

with Canning's strictures, probably had a decisive effect in the discussions which ensued, for it made it quite clear that any one of a number of options—a divorce bill, a bill of attainder, an arraignment for high treason or a suit in Doctors' Commons—were all open to serious if not insuperable objections.[75] When legal difficulties made it doubtful that a formal prosecution could succeed, there seemed little point in the ministers risking either their reputations or their sovereign's at the cost of certain public mischief. And perhaps more than this was at stake. A triumphant Queen might assume leadership of the popular party, sedition might again rear its ugly head, and the monarchy might succumb even as the Bourbons did in 1789. An arrangement guaranteed by act of parliament commended itself by the very horror which the alternative inspired.

If a proceeding was going to be avoided either now or in the future, the terms of settlement were all-important. Since deprival of any kind would immediately impute misconduct, a subtle distinction had to be drawn between privileges which were the sovereign's gift and rights peculiar to the Queen Consort herself. The former, which the government asserted included coronation and mention in the liturgy, could safely be withheld without any disparagement of her constitutional character. The latter could not. Because the abrogation of a right is essentially penal, the ministers could insist only that their exercise be voluntarily suspended. Niceties such as these had to be observed if parliament was to condone a separation without involving itself in 'hostile discussions'. The moment the Queen was stripped of what few legal rights she possessed, especially the royal title, the question immediately followed whether the deprivation was deserved, whether in fact the allegations of misconduct were true or false. Only honours and privileges conferred by grace and favour, never rights, could be revoked without recourse to judicial process, which meant that any impairment of the Queen's dignity that parliament did impose resulted purely and simply from the common fame of her indecency and out of regard for the long subsisting separation between her and her husband. An arrangement regulated;

[75] 'Opinion of King's Advocate and Attorney and Solicitor General on the case of the Princess of Wales', 17 January 1820, HO 126/3.

it did not condemn. Here, though, a further problem arose. No matter how ingeniously contrived a settlement was, the possibility of repudiation always remained, and of course the awful consequences attending it. As long as the Queen continued to live abroad, the government's terms made very little difference to her personal comfort, but in the event of her return, merely to refuse her coronation or use of the royal appellation would give lasting cause for offence possibly leading to direct legal challenge. At all costs a deterrent against her reappearance had to be erected. The obvious way to do this, the Cabinet decided, was to make residence outside the British dominions a condition for the continued payment of her annuity. On her husband's death the marriage treaty entitled her to a jointure of £50,000 a year, but until then she was wholly dependent on whatever parliament or the King on its behalf saw fit to give her. By replacing this dower with an annuity of equal amount payable for the term of her natural life on condition that she stayed abroad, not only would the exclusion appear a public rather than personal act but the alternatives of private comfort and possible ruin would lie clearly before her. The chief recommendation of the arrangement the government had in mind was that parliament was certain to prefer it to 'discussions and disclosures offensive to public decency and likely to disturb the peace of the country'. Once carried through, if a proceeding did eventuate, the evil would be the Queen's doing and no other's, and sitting in judgement upon her or simply deliberating on her concerns, parliament was hardly likely to forget it.

Having concluded that divorce was too dangerous and that a compromise was possible, the ministers had only to communicate their decision to the cuckolded husband. No one among them anticipated an immediate capitulation. Some indeed dreaded outright defiance. As Canning told his wife: 'there is one much greater than we still to be reconciled to our decision— & whom it will be a task of no small difficulty to reconcile to it. I *am sure* that the decision is right for him, for his honour, for his happiness: but I am by no means sure that he will not send us about our business for coming to it.' Even so, except for Lord Liverpool, who was his usual jittery self, everyone counted 'the greater probability' a royal tantrum, followed by royal sulks, followed by abject submission.[76] After daily Cabinets for a week or more, the Prime Minister had his first audience on 9 February. Because his colleagues were hard at work rendering their advice both unambiguous and inoffensive, he took no minute with him, though there can be no question that the King was given a full account of all they had been about. Certainly Leach, now Vice-Chancellor, was round at Eldon's early next morning frightening the government with stories that divorce was a *sine qua non* which the King would even retire to Hanover to achieve.[77] Needless to say, at this late stage retreat was unthinkable. Canning and Liverpool put the finishing touches to what must have been a minute of record deliberation, and the latter delivered it to Carlton House on Friday, 11 February.[78] Though the provisions of a bill of separation were already roughly drafted,[79] the ministers were anxious above all to get the principle of conciliation accepted. Argued with compelling clarity, their minute began by pointing out that decisions regarding the Queen were now 'not matters of choice, but of necessity' and went on to discuss the manifold difficulties attending any conceivable proceeding, concluding with a firm avowal that a separation ratified by act of parliament would save the public morals, 'the peace of the country', and 'your Majesty's dignity and peace of mind'.[80]

A reply came on Saturday afternoon when Eldon, Sidmouth and Liverpool were all summoned to the King's presence after a meeting of the Privy Council.[81] Probably Leach had drawn up the memorandum which was handed them, for every argument which the Cabinet had invoked was carefully refuted; the remarkable coincidence of the testimony would overcome the prejudice against its origins, recrimination was disallowable where the plaint was public mischief, the Queen could repudiate an arrangement when she chose, and so on.[82] Determined to

[76] Canning to Mrs Canning, 6–9 February 1820, Canning MSS.

[77] *Liverpool*, iii. 24 n.1. Canning's diary makes it clear that the date was 10 February. Canning MSS.

[78] Lord Liverpool to Canning, 10 February 1820, Canning's diary, 10–11 February 1820, ibid.

[79] See memorandum in Canning's hand, 6 February 1820, ibid.

[80] *Liverpool*, iii. 25–32.   [81] *Hobhouse*, p. 8.

[82] *Liverpool*, iii. 34–8.

refuse divorce, however, the ministers were less impressed with Leach's ingenuity than the King's obvious displeasure. According to rumour, and there is no reason to disbelieve it, Eldon and Liverpool met with a brusque reception in the Closet, the King breathing fire, brimstone and dismissal if his wishes were thwarted.[83] Such a threat had to be taken seriously. Most men living could remember at least one occasion when George III had parted with ministers over a difference of policy, and, if divorce really was an irrevocable point of conscience and personal honour, it was by no means unlikely that his son would follow suit, gambling on Tory restraint and Whig ambition to see himself through.[84] Castlereagh, for one, was so sure that he would try the experiment that he considered the government 'as virtually dissolved' and anticipated receiving Metternich, who was contemplating a visit, not as a minister but 'as a *Kentish farmer*'.[85] Not that the mood of despair lasted very long, for word soon came that the King's discretion was gradually getting the better of his valour. A day or two after the unpleasantness at Carlton House his private secretary secretly advised delay and a soothing reply, at the same time encouraging Castlereagh to warn him of unfavourable foreign reactions.[86] Thus emboldened the ministers took firm hold of the trailing lead and eventually brought him to heel. Though the second minute was mild and conciliatory without the Cabinet yielding an inch,[87] it was in fact Castlereagh's intervention which finally proved decisive. The Prime Minister, interestingly enough, after the outburst against him in the Closet was never again in the King's good graces. A few days later George was complaining of his deficiencies 'both in manner and temper', and henceforward it was remarkable that Sidmouth, Wellington or Castlereagh, each urbane and imperturbable, where Liverpool was sometimes gauche and excitable, handled the royal huffs and pets.[88] The latter saw the King on Monday, 14 February

---

[83] *The Greville Memoirs, 1814–60* (ed. Lytton Strachey and Roger Fulford), i. 89. According to *Hobhouse*, p. 8, the King 'expressed himself with a particular warmth of affection towards Lord Sidmouth'.

[84] Canning to Mrs Canning, 15 February 1820, Canning MSS. In 1783, 1801 and 1807 George III dismissed his ministers or forced them to resign.

[85] *Castlereagh*, xii. 213–14.

[86] *Hobhouse*, pp. 8–9; *Mrs Arbuthnot*, i. 2–3.

[87] *Liverpool*, iii. 38–44.   [88] *Hobhouse*, p. 9.

and again two days later, just before the interment of George
III's remains at Windsor Castle. According to Canning, the
first interview, which lasted five hours, 'began with threats but
ended with remonstrance & supplication'. Castlereagh certainly came back with the impression that his resumé of the
recriminatory matter the defence might urge had left the King
thoroughly chastened. The second audience revealed a definite
change of heart. A request that Castlereagh discover whether
the government would pledge itself to divorce should the Queen
'force enquiry' was a last desperate attempt to hobble if not
halter the ministers. Turned down on this as on everything else,
the King reconciled himself to unconditional surrender.[89] On
Thursday morning (17 February), the day on which parliament
reassembled, he announced, 'for the sake of public decorum and
the public interest', 'this great and painful sacrifice of his
personal feelings'.[90]

One great question remained outstanding. The King had
made his peace with his government, but would the Queen
with him? All that the ministers really knew of her disposition
was what Brougham deigned to tell them, and though he
readily assured Lord Liverpool that he would do his utmost to
carry an arrangement, the fact remained 'that there was a
difference between proposing to her to give up advantages which
she now enjoyed, but which did not belong to her when the
former proposition was made'.[91] If the Queen, wilful and
irresponsible as she was, took it into her head to return to
Great Britain, the government could never, without being
inconsistent with itself, acknowledge her reginal dignity, and an
inquiry then became necessary either to vindicate or refute the
proscription whatever the calamitous consequences. And
calamitous they seemed likely to be. In the first place, Canning
was committed to resignation in the event of a 'trial', and his
going, at the very least, would produce a serious weakness in the
administration's parliamentary array. Secondly, and worse,
there was the possibility that the King's private character
would be blasted for ever, and that he would attempt to salvage

---

[89] Canning to Mrs Canning, 15 February 1820, Canning MSS.; *Hobhouse*,
p. 9; *Croker*, i. 161; *Mrs Arbuthnot*, i. 3.
[90] *Liverpool*, iii. 44–5.   [91] Ibid., pp. 54–5.

an iota of popularity by blaming all on the ministers. The Cabinet had no firm idea of the power which the Crown still wielded in the constitution, but by and large they were inclined to overestimate it. Most of them did not find it inconceivable that George, to save his reputation, would dismiss them and call on the Whigs, who would be able to make a secure capture of parliament by invoking the goodwill of the Court and the favour of public opinion. This in turn drew attention to a further and more terrible danger. Recent happenings had made it clear that the 'revolutionists' could marshal the crude political feelings of the 'lower sort' for their own wicked purposes, and a barrage of insults directed at the sovereign was an obvious means by which a way could be prepared for the degradation of the monarchy and a full-scale attack on the constitution. None of the ministers had much confidence that parliament or a Whig administration would stand up to the people as they ought. Parliament had already shown itself lacking the government's staunchness, and the Whigs, placed in office by an indignant populace, were unlikely to sunder the alliance which was appropriate both to their situation and their traditions. In short, the danger was that the Radicals would emerge as the real power in the land, and that this would merely be the prelude to a 'convulsion', the total destruction of a social order whose excellence was beyond dispute. Once in command of a public of low political intelligence, the Radicals could hardly be checked, it seemed; they could freely menace parliament and, when it suited them, they could break the Whigs at a stroke. Much, too much depended on a woman's whim.

Chapter Five

THE QUEEN'S BUSINESS

I. 'THE TONE OF ENGLAND'

For the moment the Queen was forgotten. By the Act of Succession of 1707, parliament could continue in session six months after the sovereign's demise. But in view of the improving economic situation and the fact that the Radical threat was fast waning—both of which would redound to the government's credit—the Cabinet decided instead on an immediate general election. A new reign brought a mass of business in its train anyway, notably the settlement of the civil list, and with the estimates unvoted, the House of Commons difficult on financial questions and members 'thinking of cockades, and hustings, and returning officers', it seemed wisest to sit for a week or so, pass a short-term Mutiny Act and then proclaim the dissolution. The result of the excursion into the country was sobering, to say the least. Though the government regained a lot of ground lost in 1818, particularly in Devonshire, Leicestershire and London, in point of numbers the opposition again finished with a slight edge. Duncannon, who managed the election for the Whigs, calculated a gain of four or five, and, meeting to decide a bet of Lord Anglesea's, Tierney and Holmes, the latter a government whip, gave the opposition five in England less minimal losses in Scotland and Ireland.[1] Of course, with allegiances blurred by anti-party professions and the like, the figures could be juggled indefinitely. When party managers had seen nearly three hundred new faces come and go in the last two years,[2] what mattered more was the spirit of the return, the apparent leaning of public opinion. In this sky Huskisson read many storms; and he was not the only one who

[1] Mitchell, p. 140; Charles Williams-Wynn to Lord Grenville, 3 April 1820, Coed-y-maen MSS.
[2] According to Judd, p. 28 n. 4, 247 members without previous parliamentary experience entered the House in the elections of 1818 and 1820, and 36 in intervening by-elections.

had forebodings. As he told Arbuthnot, besides depriving the government of its 'best & steadiest props', which would encourage fresh parliamentary unruliness, the election had shown only too clearly 'not dislike to the late measures, nor disaffection ... but ... a soreness on every subject connected with expence, a clamour for economy, a feeling growing out of the present straightened circumstances of the Yeomanry contrasted with the ease which they enjoyed during the War'. Assuming this protest was given increasing political direction, he continued, 'the Period may not be remote, in which we may find it necessary to do something to secure the affection & more cordial goodwill of some great Class in the State.'[3] As he saw it, to run before every wind gave a passage to nowhere. It was time for the government to display more resourceful seamanship, to keep the public confidence by drawing up fresh sailing orders. Almost to the day Peel was writing in much the same vein to Croker.[4]

The behaviour of the new parliament did nothing to bely these gloomy expectations. Throughout the session, until the Queen's coming captured the headlines, the government grappled constantly with recalcitrant 'country gentlemen'. 'You will see hardly any addition of names to the Opposition, or any increased numbers, but the *feature* is the want of attendance of the Government friends,' one member observed.[5] As always, financial questions were the most troublesome, 'parliament men' continuing to see frugality in the public expenditure as the best way of restoring the nation's faith in aristocratic government. Parsimony had been preached in and out of the House for so long that it had become almost second nature for the government to pare down every departmental estimate that came before it. In view of past skirmishes over the cost of the monarchy, in 1820 'the fightable matter' promised to be the civil list, customarily settled at the start of the reign. While Huskisson was fearful lest the government offend parliament, and therefore the country, with too generous a proposal, his superiors were afraid of the King to whom the subject was 'of a sort to worry

---

[3] Huskisson to Arbuthnot, 24 March 1820, Add. MSS. 38742, ff. 6–8.
[4] *Croker*, i. 170.
[5] Buckingham, *George IV*, i. 19.

& agitate him excessively'.[6] Liverpool, indeed, wanted the matter to be decided as quickly as possible. '*Time*', he explained to Arbuthnot, 'will be requisite to reconcile the King's mind to the arrangement, and we must not put this off, as we were obliged to do in the case of the Princess to the last moment.'[7] Some time in March the Treasury sent out letters to the Lord Steward, the Lord Chamberlain and the Master of the Horse requesting estimates for their departments, and the informal committee which settled financial business—consisting of Huskisson, Long, Vansittart and the Prime Minister—arranged to meet immediately after Easter.[8] Probably, before the consultations began, there was general agreement that there could be no going back on the 1816 arrangement.[9] From the point of view of both economy and good government, though the Treasury had had to keep a sharp eye on things, this had given little cause for complaint, the expenditure generally keeping within the estimates then decided.[10] Unfortunately the Household officers, and George himself, chose to think differently. When the new estimates were returned to the Treasury they were found to exceed the old by £65,000, and no sooner had the Cabinet reduced them to an acceptable amount than the King made a protest of his own. At first he contented himself with submitting ungraciously, but when the Speech for the opening of parliament was sent to him he proposed alterations in the paragraph relating to the civil list so provoking that Lord Liverpool believed the government's days were numbered. Frantically, he spent a Sunday sending high and low for ministers, and at a meeting the following day they emphatically reasserted that the income intended was 'fully sufficient' to maintain the

[6] Huskisson to Arbuthnot, 24 March 1820, Add. MSS. 38742, ff. 8–9; Canning to Mrs Canning, 15 February 1820, Canning MSS.
[7] *Arbuthnot*, p. 19.
[8] Ibid.; *Hobhouse*, p. 18.
[9] e.g. See Huskisson to Arbuthnot, 24 March 1820, Add. MSS. 38742, f. 9: '. . . sanguine indeed must be the turn of that Mind, which (if the Enquiry is to be transferred from Fife House to the House of Commons) can indulge even the faintest hope of doing better for the Crown than we did in 1816. . . . I am sure, if *we ask for more*, that like the Dog in the Fable, we shall drown ourselves by gnashing at a shadow; & that instead of getting that *more*, we shall see the Crown hampered & curtailed in some of the Powers & facilities which it possesses over the Revenue now at its disposal.'
[10] Memoranda on the civil list, n.d., ibid., 38369, ff. 140–6, 147–155.

Crown 'in as ample a manner as . . . any Sovereign for more than a century'. Once again, confronted by an intransigent Cabinet the King yielded, though not without his usual spitefulness. A few days afterwards he was asking Sidmouth whether he and his colleagues regarded themselves as his servants or Lord Liverpool's.[11]

As was usual where 'topicks of money' were concerned, an exemplary stinginess paid off handsomely when the civil list came up for parliamentary discussion. The opposition took the view that the arrangement of 1816 had been wildly overgenerous and that parliament should become the accountant for the 'casual' revenues of the Crown; but by pointing out the recency of inquiry, the Crown's solvency since then and the habit of regular information which had grown up, this was easily quashed. A motion of Brougham's to incorporate 'the Droits of the Crown and Admiralty, Four-and-half per cent West India duties, and other funds not usually deemed hitherto to be within the immediate control of Parliament' into the civil list failed by over a hundred votes, and Lord John Russell's attempt to force inquiry met a similar fate. Content as the ministers were with their work of four years before, it was left to a new reign and new men, the same who now argued it, to take the logical step of finally separating the charge of government from that of the Crown's dignity and comfort.

This early success did not long go unavenged. If the ministers congratulated themselves that they had correctly gauged the mood of the House, they were soon given a rude reminder that economy was an issue which one debate could never lay low. To convince the country that a policy of cheap government was being followed, the ministers had to prevail on a number of trifling questions. One such now came to parliament's attention. As far back as 1814, commissioners had been appointed to prepare for the economical reform of the Scottish law courts, and in their sixth report, tabled in 1819, they had recommended four judges in the Court of Exchequer, including the Chief Baron, in place of the customary five. Doubting whether the Act of Union or the constitution of the court

---

[11] *Hobhouse*, pp. 18–20; *Bathurst*, p. 483; *George IV*, ii. 324–6; *Mrs. Arbuthnot*, i. 14, 15; *Eldon*, ii. 362–3.

allowed the change, the government had sought the opinion of the superior judges, who had unequivocally disapproved.[12] Their authority had been taken as conclusive, and, a puisne baron having announced his resignation, the vacancy had been immediately filled up by the promotion of the court's remembrancer. Though the saving would have been 'some paltry thousand pounds', a little more since the remembrancer's office lapsed with the expiration of the existing interest, the Whigs raised an outcry as soon as parliament reassembled. They complained loudly that a job had been done and that commissions of this nature formed a smokescreen behind which the government carefully cultivated the canker of corruption. Much to the ministers' chagrin, many 'country gentlemen' appeared to be willing believers. When Lord Archibald Hamilton asked the House to endorse the commissioners' recommendation, well over thirty joined the opposition despite Castlereagh's promise of a committee, and the government counted itself fortunate to carry the division with a majority of twelve.[13] In this way, by occasional rebuke, by an occasional twist on the rack of parliament's displeasure, the ministers were reminded that the legislature was acutely anxious not to lose the country. Economical government was an obsession which parliament shared with the nation; and because of it, other issues, like commercial reform or the revision of the corn laws, were of much less importance politically. A day after the near defeat the Prime Minister and Arbuthnot casually wondered whether an infusion of new blood was needed, as if to deplete the opposition would solve all. Mrs. Arbuthnot could have set both of them right. 'A junction . . . wd only add a few individuals', she mused in her private journal, '& wd not give . . . the least more hold on the mind & opinion of the nation generally, which is in fact what the present Government wants the most.'[14] An unwavering attention to economy continued to be the best guarantee of popularity and parliamentary quiet.

The attacks on the corn laws and the old commercial system, which were a feature of the same session, were mainly

[12] *PP*, 1819, xi. 183; 1820, vii. 261–4.
[13] For the debate see *Hansard*, 2nd ser., i. 347–86.
[14] *Mrs. Arbuthnot*, i. 18–19.

distinguished by the ministers' determination to uphold the
executive as the real location of political decision. On the one
hand they made a resistance to a vigorous, highly organised
protest from the immensely powerful landed interest, while on
the other they boldly led the equally powerful commercial
interest into courses it was viewing with caution and some
uncertainty. Of course, these policies were not at all contradic-
tory. The government, convinced of the mutual dependence of
land and trade and having an interest in the country's prosperity, always professed to act out of concern for the whole
economy. The demands of the agriculturists for a revision of the
corn laws were rejected because greater protection would serve
neither them nor the nation. Similarly, commercial reform was
advocated because the particular benefits which would accrue
to the mercantile and manufacturing community would also
percolate to the rest of society. Again the Cabinet demonstrated
its awareness that an aristocracy could not afford to consult
merely the wishes of one interest or class in the state. Government had to be in accordance with national needs, and at the
same time had to be a search for solutions which would find
national acceptance. There was no other way in which an
oligarchy could justify its custodianship of power when public
affairs were becoming the concern of an ever expanding public.

Though the act prohibiting the import of corn until a 'remunerative price' had been reached was largely their handiwork,
the agriculturists had been protesting against its imperfection
and unfairness almost from the day of its first enforcement. As
early as 1816 'Squire' Western had criticised the warehousing
clause for allowing the stockpiling of foreign grain,[15] and this
and other shortcomings had become the main bone of contention between the landed interest and the government thereafter.
Increasingly, irrespective of the fact that many farmers were
not corngrowers, petitions which had touched on every agricultural subject, from the distillery laws to the duties on rape
seed, had become diatribes on a single injustice. From 1819–
1821 no fewer than 1,200 petitions, 'all of them complaining
of the principle and operation of the law of 1815', were brought
up to Westminster, 'the greatest number of petitions', it

[15] *Hansard*, 1st ser., xxxiii. 48–9.

was later said, 'ever presented to parliament upon one subject'.[16]

For the next two years the irony of the situation was that the
government, supposedly dependent on the votes of the 'country
gentlemen', paid less attention to the 'clamour' set up by
agriculturists than the tepid agitation of the commercial interest. The fact was that the demands of the landed interest
were rejected because they rested on the false premises that
the legislation of 1815 was the chief cause of its distress and
that greater protection would afford the best relief. Except for
one or two trifles, mainly the method of calculating the averages,
the ministers could fairly claim that the corn law had worked,
which was both a presumption in favour of its continued working
and a cogent reason for non-interference now. The great object
of the act had been to secure the farmer a fair price and a
degree of protection against cheaper foreign produce. With the
price of wheat averaging out at over 78s. a quarter and importations no heavier than before, this had surely been
achieved.[17] As the government realised, and as it was to realise
more and more after 1820, the agriculturists had to learn to
adjust to permanently lower prices—prices which were partly
a consequence of their own production—by greater diversifica-
tion and greater efficiency. Whatever the farmers' champions
said, they already had a protection comparable to the manufacturing interest, and to expect the ministers to continue 'the
unnatural prosperity' of the war period for their exclusive
benefit was asking the government to forsake its essential
arbitral role. The danger of a stronger measure against foreign
corn was obvious; it would increase the possibility of starvation
prices in the event of a bad harvest, which in their turn would
invite widespread disorder and vehement representations from
manufacturers who feared for their profits and property. In the
circumstances, even to tamper ever so slightly with the act of
1815 might do irreparable harm. Few men could forget the
ugly scenes in the metropolis at the time of the bill's passing,
nor the parliamentary wrangles and mass meetings. No
administration in its right mind would invite a repetition when

16 Ibid., 2nd ser., xvii. 988.
17 Ibid., 2nd ser., i. 580-1, 643-6.

the common people were at last beginning to settle down into their usual complaisance, especially when the means of protest were limited by unpopular laws. 'Surely common prudence', Castlereagh thundered in the House of Commons, 'would suggest that every topic of discontent ought to be avoided at a moment when general distress pressed upon every class of society'.[18] The warning did not pass unheeded, even in a parliament of landlords. Though Holme-Sumner, the member for Surrey, carried a committee to consider the agricultural petitions, the government succeeded in quashing a 'broad inquiry' the day following. Robinson had already suggested confining the terms of reference to the method of taking the averages and legal deficiencies, but on the main question a procedural technicality had prevented this amendment from being put. By now carrying an instruction along these lines, which it was mandatory for the committee to observe, the ministers made good the mischance and gained for the corn laws a wholesome respite.

The landed interest had to be bullied out of uncompromising ways: merchants and manufacturers had to be encouraged into better. The first petition in favour of 'freer' trade came as late as 1820, and even then Tooke's attempt to rally the City nearly ended in dismal failure. Until Samuel Thornton, one of its leading figures, lent his support, signatures came very slowly indeed, a disappointment which prompted the sponsor to jibe in after years that the ministers were 'more sincere and resolute Free Traders than the Merchants of London'.[19] In part, Tooke's Radical associations explained the coolness, but there were many deeper reasons which were as pertinent elsewhere as in the metropolis. The most important was that where the landed interest was questioning the workability of a particular law, the mercantile was being asked to make a declaration of principle. While there is no reason to think that Smith's ideas had not achieved a wide currency among commercial men, the attention of such men, naturally enough, focused on their practical application. Their own salvation mattered more than

---

[18] Ibid., 727.
[19] Thomas Tooke and William Newmarch, *A History of Prices*, vi. 335–40, 342.

the theology which might explain it in general terms. The economic instability which had afflicted the country since the peace heightened this feeling, and indeed had the effect of recommending minimal disturbance of the existing system. In the midst of distress and foreign measures against British trade, the protection of home production by the state appeared more of a blessing than a disaster. What has to be particularly remembered is that in 1820 no one could be certain that the sharp and vicious alternation of boom and depression had come to an end, that a long period of prosperity was in prospect. But basically 'freer' trade was bound to arouse as much opposition as support among the commercial classes. A whole host of examples showed that profit was the god of commercial men and self-interest their creed. As Robinson, the President of the Board of Trade, once pointed out: 'In all the communications which he had had with persons engaged in trade, he had never heard the general principle [of greater freedom] denied, but he never could get the individual to allow that the general principle ought to be applied in his case.'[20] The wool grower wanted a heavier duty on foreign wool and a bounty on export; the manufacturer wanted neither. The farmer wanted rape seed in quantity; the whaling industry did not. Propose to reduce the duty on exported coal and the glass manufacturers complained. Tamper with that on foreign linen and the President of the Board of Trade was burnt in effigy over half of Northern Ireland.[21] In 1820 the government was not swept away on a tide of merchant enthusiasm, but rather acted deliberately and with due circumspection. Once it began bringing forward concrete proposals for 'freer' trade, cross-eddies made any current in the country barely perceptible. Furthermore, where the agriculturists had their Agricultural Association and so able a propagandist as George Webb Hall, the commercial interest had nothing. Fewer than a dozen towns had time to follow the metropolis's lead before parliament took up their grievances.

The government, therefore, was not merely abreast of commercial opinion but some distance ahead. Certainly, as far as a

[20] *Hansard*, 1st ser., xxxv. 1046.
[21] Robinson pointed these examples at the House in 1816 and 1817. Ibid. xxxiii. 697–8, xxxv. 1050–1.

declaration of principle went, the commercial classes were beaten easily. In March 1816, a full four years before the City's famous petition, Robinson asserted that the 'system of prohibitions' had gone far enough, 'if not indeed too far', and twelve months later, on a motion of Brougham's on the state of the economy, he stated that his policy was founded on 'wishing that we had never entered the restrictive system, and thinking that it would be advantageous if we could break through it'.[22] Nor was his a voice in the wilderness. The Prime Minister and the rest of the 'economic Cabinet' held similar views, it seems, though without it being so generally known. Thornton, in sounding out the government at Tooke's request, found that there was no objection to a petition, and when a small deputation of City merchants called at Fife House in April 1820, Lord Liverpool somewhat surprised them by acknowledging that their principles were in complete accordance with his own.[23]

But granted that the economic attitudes of the government were 'liberal', the significant question is why these received increasing expression through a 'freer' trade policy after 1820. Although the economic situation had brightened and was still brightening in 1820, it is difficult to imagine that this was the factor which commended such an expedition. True, distress had made substantial reform impossible in the immediate post-war period; to convince the mercantile community that 'freer' trade was in its best interests was a task beyond any administration when war in South America had upset one valuable market and the protectionist policies of foreign powers had threatened others. The most that was managed in these years was the repeal of a handful of obsolete statutes and the modification and reduction of duties on a small scale.[24] But the point to be emphasised is that in 1820 the ministers, like everybody else,

<hr />

[22] Ibid., xxxiii. 698, xxxv. 1051.

[23] Tooke and Newmarch, vi. 337–41.

[24] *Hansard*, 2nd ser., i. 183. The government may have achieved more than is commonly thought in the period 1815–20. Robinson on 8 May 1820 claimed that 'a considerable alteration had been made, and a considerable relaxation had taken place, in our commercial regulations, within a few years'. He made a particular reference to a 'report from the Lords' which recorded 'the repeal of duties on 300 articles, upon some of which large duties existed, and upon others there was a total prohibition'. What report this was is not known. But if what he said was indeed true, commercial reform must have been well under way before 1820.

could not be certain that the country was out of the economic
doldrums. While there was evidence of improvement in the
trade figures and the revenue returns, there was no saying that
it would continue, especially when world trading conditions
had changed little and the state of agriculture was giving cause
for concern. The fluctuations of the economy over the previous
five years had bemused and dismayed so many that prophets
and optimists, if they existed, preferred to keep their own counsel. Two other developments explain the administration's
sterner pursuit of 'freer' trade. The first was the appearance,
in spite of economic uncertainty, of a body of support in the
trading and industrial community. Undoubtedly the petitions
which came in at the beginning of 1820, few though they were,
provided the ministers with valuable leverage when way had
to be made against particular interests. The second change was
in the financial circumstances of the government. There was
no real hope that expenditure could be reduced by any significant amount, but the plan of borrowing from the sinking
fund adopted in 1819 made it possible to realise surpluses without increasing the debt. No one, of course, could know how
large these surpluses would be. The difference merely was that
a surplus could be budgeted for and that a reduction of indirect
taxation—the customs and excise contributed two-thirds of the
revenue—could therefore be contemplated.

In all likelihood a single decision to commence a more
ambitious reform of the commercial system was never taken.
The Cabinet, alive to fiscal considerations and convinced of the
importance of acting with a measure of parliamentary and
popular support, regulated its effort in strict accordance with
the circumstances. Initially it seemed that little would be done
at all. When Tooke and other 'free-traders' saw Lord Liverpool
before the City petition was presented on 8 May, the Prime
Minister stressed the need for the 'utmost caution' and saw no
prospect of 'any great or immediate alteration'.[25] But the
situation changed considerably with the reception accorded the
petition in the House of Commons. A remarkably full attendance, and warm applause for Baring, who made the actual
presentation,[26] showed clearly that parliament as well as much

[25] Tooke and Newmarch, vi. 340.   [11] Buckingham, *George IV*, i. 20, 21.

influential opinion was favourably disposed to reform, indeed
that not to pursue the subject would place the government in a
position of some embarrassment. This does not mean that the
ministers were coerced into 'freer' trade or, more correctly,
into its more vigorous pursuit. As usual, their approach to
reform was practical rather than doctrinaire. They required no
instruction in the disadvantages and imperfections of the
existing system, but reform also had to be responsible in the
sense that it had to accomplish as much as was desirable without
creating dangerous divisions in the government, in the legislature, or in the country at large. To have the administration go
through the motions of responding to a definite public demand
was not necessarily to be abhorred. It was dangerous only when,
as happened in 1832, the governing class and a large populace
appeared to hold conflicting views of the national interest, and
the latter seemed to prevail. On the issue of 'freer' trade,
governors and governed were seen to be largely in agreement.
The implementation of policy was likely to be facilitated because any opposition would feel inhibited, while at the same
time the ministers could safely advertise their responsiveness to
representations emanating from the people. Even so, in 1820
it was important that the executive show itself not only responsive but assertive. Lord Liverpool and his colleagues knew that
they had to keep the goodwill and confidence of 'respectable'
opinion, but they also knew that that could only be kept by
appearing sympathetic rather than subservient. The role of the
public, when it wanted one, was to indicate the broad lines of
political action; the role of the government was to shape these
'desires into perfect forms'. Huskisson and Peel were seriously
concerned at the beginning of the year at the administration's
unpopularity, and their feeling was that the situation called
for a deliberate effort on the part of the Cabinet.[27] In all
probability the ministers shared their anxiety. But what was to
be done was the problem which baffled. It was not unreasonable
to assume that economic uncertainty and distress were the main
causes of popular discontent; but here the only possible policy
was parsimonious government, one which had been sedulously

[27] Huskisson to Arbuthnot, 24 March 1820, Add. MSS. 38742, f. 7;
Croker, i. 170.

followed with meagre economic and political returns—in particular, the lower orders apparently refused to be convinced that authority, as it was at present constituted, could ever be sufficiently frugal. The commercial petitions, therefore, appeared at a most appropriate moment. They provided the government with an opportunity to cultivate in a new way the impression of a concerned and diligent administration. From the point of view of principle the ministers could feel no embarrassment, for their 'freer' trade convictions were as deep as any that could be found elsewhere. From the point of view of expediency no time could be better than the present: the public having displayed an interest in reform, the government could pursue the matter further, making a proper exertion of its power to ensure that the 'improvement' was well-ordered. At a time when the aristocracy was fearful of the country's growing alienation, the best it could do was to demonstrate in no uncertain terms the quality of its government.[28]

The favourable reception of the petitions, both in and out of parliament, thus cleared the ground for a concerted and open attack on the old commercial system. Even so, it was not until the following session that battle was actually joined between the government and those interests which had a stake in its survival. That the ministers decided to do something in 1820 seems more than likely. They certainly assured Tooke that the petition he had drawn up had their approbation; and Robinson told the House of Commons on the day it was received that he had already decided to propose the revision of the timber duties sometime during the session—significantly, when the Lords' committee on foreign trade was appointed it devoted most of its time to this very question.[29] However, there is no evidence that the government planned to proceed to legislation or bring other tariffs under review. It is difficult to believe that the threat of foreign retaliation—justified to the extent that much of the protectionist system was the product of recent war—became

[28] In this connection it is worth noting that before the City petition was presented to parliament the ministers were not at all in favour of a select committee. Afterwards they changed their mind. Tooke and Newmarch, vi. 341, 342.

[29] Ibid., p. 338; *Hansard*, 2nd ser., i. 183. For the committee's report see *LJ*, liii. 188–9. Some shipping interests were alarmed enough to make representations on the subject.

any more explicit at this juncture. Nor could the deteriorating condition of agriculture have been influential; to regard 'freer' trade as an attempt by the ministers to neutralise the resentment of the landed interest with the goodwill of the commercial classes is to ignore the fact of—in Lord Liverpool's words—'so many vested interests . . . so connected and complicated with the existing commercial system'.[30] Also there was of course the financial situation, the question of whether the government could afford a possible loss of revenue through the reduction of the indirect taxes. Doubtless the feeling was that it could not. Vansittart, in his 'budget speech' delivered on 19 June, predicted a surplus of about £3,500,000, which, as he himself was quick to point out, was the result of a sluggish economy and well below the £5,000,000 which had been considered desirable the previous year.[31] But though the situation in general was not such to encourage a full-scale effort in favour of reform, and almost certainly ensured that none was planned, the immediate reason why nothing substantial was achieved was Queen Caroline's sudden return from the Continent at the beginning of June. This event made an investigation into her conduct or the negotiation of a settlement short of a 'trial' unavoidable, and it was her concerns which commanded the government's whole attention for the remainder of the year. From July onwards even the legislature was forced to lay the subject to rest. The Lords was fully involved in the process against the Queen by bill of pains and penalties, and as long as it continued it was arranged that the Commons should meet only intermittently. The select committees appointed unanimously in both houses presented reports within six weeks of their inception, on 3 and 18 July, but once this small advance had been completed a halt was necessarily called.

II. The Trial

The feature of Caroline's return at the beginning of June was its very unexpectedness. Though she muttered every sort of imprecation and threat in letters to friends, even trying to

[30] Tooke and Newmarch, vi. 340.
[31] *Hansard*, 2nd ser., i. 1166–7.

frighten Lord Liverpool with an ungrammatical 'ultimatum',[32] not for a moment did anyone take her seriously, a point of view more than verified by her continued sojourn at Rome throughout February, March and most of April. Nor did Brougham's attitude lead the government to suspect any mischief afoot. In an interview with the Prime Minister on 18 February he promised to do his utmost to avert a proceeding, a few days afterwards in parliament he called the omission from the liturgy a 'trifle light as air', and all along he made it perfectly plain that when speaking of 'some convenient place' for negotiation he meant one near at hand just across the Channel.[33] So much reliance on Brougham was, it turned out, the ministers' great mistake. As the Queen's legal adviser, and after April her first law officer, he was bound to consult his client's interest before any other. Also, as a leading light among the Whigs, he could not be blamed for having an eye to political advantage. But the greatest calamity of all was that he was too clever by half, a politician who was always something of a free spirit and who in one move thought he could advance himself, serve the Queen and save the nation. From the start he played a deep and difficult game, on the one hand trying to frighten the government into generous concessions, on the other warning the Queen against the folly of a contest at law. In February he reminded Lord Liverpool that the Queen 'was a woman of such strong passions, he cod. not answer for her following his advice', the same day writing to a lady-in-waiting: 'If she arrives plump on you at Paris make her either stay there or at Calais till I can come out to her.'[34] In March, in the sure knowledge that every word would be passed on to the Pavilion and Fife House, he hinted the Queen's growing popularity, and soundly abused the ministers for encouraging her to drive a hard bargain by letting their newspapers 'praise them on account ... of their constitutional firmness in resisting the King'.[35] In April and May he was assiduous in arranging a Continental rendezvous, meanwhile lashing the government for forcing Denman and

[32] *Liverpool*, iii. 46–7.
[33] Ibid., pp. 54–5; *Hansard*, 1st ser., xli. 1626.
[34] *Hobhouse*, p. 10; New, p. 232.
[35] *Mrs. Arbuthnot*, i. 72–3. The letter, which is also found in Add. MSS. 38284, ff. 27–8, was probably written on 30 March 1820.

him to present their credentials as the Queen's law officers, a degree of recognition, he warned, which would make her more intractable than ever.[36] The tragedy was that there was no one else but Brougham. Of her former champions, Perceval and Whitbread were dead, and Canning's intimacy had faded with the years, which led the government to conclude that 'Mr. Harry' was her truest friend and the one whose influence was paramount.

The belief that everything depended on his good offices was only too apparent in the famous squabble over his taking silk. Eldon had refused him the honour, to which his standing at the Bar alone entitled him, on two occasions, but in March 1820, about a month before the courts opened for their Easter term, he renewed the application to avoid the embarrassment of his taking precedence as Attorney-General of the Queen. When the Lord Chancellor again turned him down, Canning and Lord Liverpool immediately intervened, not to prevent the assertion of the right, 'a miserable point of Etiquette' they were already prepared to concede, but simply to keep Brougham and have his good offices. 'I am satisfied that Brougham for his own interest will be sincere in this Business if he does not consider himself as ill used,' the Prime Minister entreated Eldon; to which Canning added: 'you can only get [an admission from the Queen] by *consent*—& if Br's consent is thrown away, you will have to fight for it, uphill.'[37] Even the King realised the importance of the gesture and sent Leach with a peremptory order, though in the end no one could budge the Chancellor from his attitude of arrant professionalism.[38] Brougham, therefore, despite his political animosity and a certain reputation for slippery conduct, was given sole charge of a brief to save the government and the nation. He, it was felt, was under no illusions concerning Caroline's infidelity and would soon impress her with the precariousness of her present situation.

---

[36] Brougham to the Queen, 29 April 1820, Brougham to Lady Charlotte Lindsay [29 April 1820], the Queen to Brougham, 7 May 1820, Brougham to the Queen, 13 May [1820], Add. MSS. 38284, f. 302, 38565, ff. 101, 102, 115–16; *Mrs. Arbuthnot*, i. 73.

[37] Lord Liverpool to Lord Eldon, 3 April 1820, Canning to Lord Liverpool, 2 April 1820, Add. MSS. 38193, ff. 113–17, 38284, ff. 25–6.

[38] *Hobhouse*, p. 20. A good account of the episode is in New, pp. 235–7.

Too late both parties discovered that the Queen had a mind of her own.

To the country at large the Queen's homecoming was a drama from beginning to end. For two months after receiving news of her husband's accession she dallied at Rome, finally setting out for her rendezvous with Brougham about the middle of April. Detained nearly a week in Milan with a rheumatic complaint, lingering over a fortnight in Geneva until Brougham prodded her forward, she did not reach St. Omer until the beginning of June, by which time huge wagers for and against her coming were being laid in all the gaming clubs of fashionable London. Only the government remained relatively unperturbed. From the start Brougham had insisted that she come close to England, and if negotiating was to be done the request seemed not unreasonable.[39] Nevertheless, the news of her coming did force the ministers to deliver a formal statement of their terms and also a warning of what would ensue should they be absolutely rejected. Brougham arrived back from Westmorland on 30 March to find a letter from the Queen announcing her imminent departure, and out of common courtesy he immediately sent word to the government through Hutchinson and Bloomfield.[40] Having the same day received what now appeared to be a similar intimation,[41] Lord Liverpool at once decided that the time to talk business could no longer be postponed. Most of the Cabinet still being on holiday, he, on his own initiative, summoned Brougham and Hutchinson to Fife House for a verbal summary of the government's conditions. A further briefing and the handing over of a precise memorandum took place a week or so later.[42] Unbeknown to all of them the Queen had scarcely begun her journey northward.

The significant development which emerged out of these discussions was an unqualified commitment on the part of the Cabinet that some proceeding—no one knew what sort—

[39] *Liverpool*, iii. 55, 59.
[40] Brougham to Lord Hutchinson [30 March 1820], Add. MSS. 38284, ff. 27-8; *George IV*, ii. 318-19.
[41] *Liverpool*, iii. 46-7. Since the courier to Brougham left the Queen on 16 March, the letters presumably arrived together.
[42] Ibid., pp. 56-7.

would be instituted the moment the Queen set foot in Great
Britain.[43] The proposition handed Brougham was identical to
what the ministers had already proposed in their February minutes, indeed almost identical to what he himself had suggested the
previous year. Provided Caroline engaged to stay abroad, forego
her royal title and leave her other rights, except her legal
patronage and judicial privileges, in abeyance, the Crown was
willing to recommend to parliament that she have an annuity of
£50,000 for the rest of her natural life.[44] With respect to what
would follow should this arrangement fall through, the ministers
up to now had stoutly refused to have their hands tied. In view
of the risks to be run, whether to take legal cognizance of
Caroline's misconduct was a problem they preferred to leave
until circumstances forced an answer. To the King at least, the
pledge presently given must have seemed a surprising retreat,
but it was in fact quite consistent with the Cabinet's desire to
avoid a 'trial' until every other expedient had failed. In February
the great need had been to reconcile George to separation as a
preferable and sensible alternative. In April it was to frighten
his wife into a similar state of mind. Since the government had
reopened the door to an arrangement, the ministers had become
increasingly conscious of their meagre bargaining strength, of
just how much there was to tempt the Queen into a judicial
contest with all its attendant perils. Merely to invite negotiation,
as they had done, could be interpreted as a marked reluctance
to proceed to extremes, or worse as an absolute refusal to seek
legal satisfaction. Furthermore, once accepted by the Queen,
any derogation of right constituted an admission of guilt which
a prosecution would otherwise have to prove, and an adverse
vote in parliament could deprive her of an income as surely as
an adverse verdict in a court of law. Somehow she had to be
told that the case against her was overwhelming and that the
government had stomach enough to produce it. Not for nothing
did Lord Liverpool warn Brougham that an imputation of
forgery hung over her as a result of a suit in the Court of

[43] Ibid., pp. 56, 58; Lord Liverpool to Lord Hutchinson, 20 April 1820,
Brougham MSS.
[44] 'Memorandum for a proposed Arrangement with the Queen', 15 April
1820, PP, 1820, xii. 533.

Chancery.[45] Not for nothing were the consequences of her coming placed squarely before her.

Caroline reached St. Omer on 1 June, two days before Brougham and Lord Hutchinson arrived to bring to fruition a policy which had gradually shaped itself over most of five years. Yet the negotiation which followed lasted a bare twenty-four hours. It failed not because Brougham played the government false, though the ministers never ceased to think it, but because his cleverness in the end proved a two-edged weapon. His game was too deep for her, their acquaintance too shallow. Where he came with an innocent determination to wring the best possible terms from a government he knew to be on the defensive, she came inherently suspicious of being double-crossed by an artful lawyer and a political adventurer.[46] In his first interview with her he learnt the limitations of his influence, not even daring to mention the proposition he was authorised to present lest she order post horses for Calais there and then.[47] From the moment it dawned on him he tried his utmost, quite un-availingly, to win back her confidence and gain time any way he could. It was here that Lord Hutchinson was called in to play his part. Because Brougham himself could hardly tell his client that she had reason to fear inquiry, Hutchinson was at St. Omer to enforce the government's warning of the consequences of her landing, actually carrying a letter to that effect from the Prime Minister.[48] Of this the Queen knew nothing. She

[45] In a bill filed in Chancery in 1818, Caroline demanded payment of a considerable sum from her brother's, the late Duke of Brunswick's estate. Two promissory notes drawn up in August 1814 were the basis of the claim, but the executors had serious doubts concerning their authenticity. When the plaintiffs failed to produce one of them, according to the order of the court, the bill was dismissed with costs. See Clement Tudway Swanston, *Reports of Cases argued and determined in the High Court of Chancery*, i. 114–27, 580, iii. 567–72.

[46] Lord Hutchinson, who accompanied Brougham to St. Omer, was only too aware of the Queen's mistrust. 'In the whole of this disagreeable discussion', he wrote to Sir Benjamin Bloomfield, 'I have had one uniform impression on my mind to endeavour to screen Brougham from the imputation that he was acting in concert with us and that he was a negotiator as much employed by the Government as by the Queen. From what you know this was a task not quite so easy to perform: some suspicions might with some little degree of apparent truth attach to him and I am led to imagine, from a variety of circumstances, that the Queen did not place implicit confidence in him.' *George IV*, ii. 341.   [47] *Liverpool*, iii. 65–7.

[48] Ibid., pp. 56–9; Lord Liverpool to Lord Hutchinson, 20 April 1820, Brougham MSS.

assumed, naturally enough, that he was the bearer of the government's proposition, and when Brougham saw her mood he subtly encouraged her mistake in order to gain what seemed likely to be immensely precious hours. Before the misunderstanding was sorted out, he calculated, London might have sent a reply to his demand for recognition of the Queen abroad, and a courier might have arrived from Paris, enabling Lord Hutchinson to make contact and prolong the negotiation even further. Fortunately, when Brougham requested the conditions of settlement, Hutchinson kept his head, pleading for 'a short delay' to draw up a proposition which 'has not been conveyed to him in any specific form of words'.[49] 'I thought that his object was to gain time,' he wrote later. 'I answered it under that impression, he has since acknowledged to me that my impressions were correct, and that in the answer I gave, I had entered into his views.'[50]

It was the Queen herself who spoilt all. Headstrong and impulsive, her suspicions heightened by finding a negotiator unready to negotiate, she gave Hutchinson a bare three hours to state the government's terms, made preparations for her departure meanwhile, and petulantly demanded an answer before her ultimatum had even expired.[51] Not knowing that Brougham's brother had surreptitiously left him Lord Liverpool's memorandum, Hutchinson did his best to paraphrase it from memory while faithfully passing on the warning that a proceeding would be the inevitable outcome of a landing in England. The errors he made—he said nothing of rights the Queen might retain and declared that no royal title would be allowed her—were of no significance. Caroline had already made up her mind to go if her innocence was not acknowledged, and this the government would never have conceded. Five minutes after Hutchinson had made the offer of the ministers, she was on her way to Calais.[52] Even then Brougham refused to admit defeat. On his advice Hutchinson offered to convey her terms to the ministers, and this he followed up by recommending an arrangement whereby she would have full

---

[49] *Brougham*, ii. 357–8.
[50] *George IV*, ii. 340.
[51] *Brougham*, ii. 359; *Liverpool*, iii. 73.
[52] *Brougham*, ii. 359–61; *George IV*, ii. 341; *Liverpool*, iii. 68.

recognition abroad in return for a voluntary exile.[53] But both letters, which reached her in the early hours aboard a packet lying off Calais pier, were scarcely given a glance. The afternoon of the same day (5 June) she was stepping ashore on Dover beach. Hutchinson, mulling over the utter failure of the government's plans, caught its essence in a couple of sentences: '. . . in the whole of this negotiation, Mr. Brougham . . . does not appear to have possessed the smallest degree of power, weight or authority over the mind of the Queen. . . . I believe she took counsel from her own rashness, presumption, and obstinacy alone.'[54]

According to their pledge the ministers presented both houses of parliament with 'certain Papers respecting the conduct of Her Majesty' while Caroline's carriage was yet rattling through the London suburbs. Though the few precedents relevant to the case seemed to indicate this course, the production of the infamous 'Green Bag', with its harvest of scandalous report, still left a trial in the proper sense of the word very much in the air. Eldon likened the secret committees, which were to examine the papers, to a grand jury having to decide whether or not a true bill existed,[55] and even if the comparison was a little unfortunate, the inquiry being *ex parte* and subject to government influence, the fact remained that as soon as parliament took cognizance of the case it could interrupt the preliminaries at a hundred different points. There can be no doubt that the government hoped this would happen. To be sure, the ministers had promised 'an end to all Negotiation or Compromise' should the Queen made an appearance; but if parliament ordered a renewed search for an amicable adjustment neither party could afford to stand on its dignity. Whether Queen's men or King's men secretly encouraged such intervention is impossible to say, though in the circumstances more than likely. Certainly on 7 June, when Castlereagh moved a secret committee, Brougham made an eloquent appeal for further negotiations. Canning endorsed it by refusing to be a party to penal proceedings and, as if on cue, Wilberforce, followed by five county members,

[53] *Brougham*, ii. 361–5; *Liverpool*, iii. 73.
[54] Ibid. See also *George IV*, ii. 343.
[55] *Hansard*, 2nd ser., i. 898.

rose to request a two day adjournment.[56] 'I endeavoured to interpose a pause,' Wilberforce explained, 'during which the two parties might have an opportunity of contemplating coolly the prospect before them.'[57] If the thunderous applause of the House were anything to go by, parliament supported him almost to a man. Gratefully, the government grasped the straw thrown out. Wilberforce's proposal was carried unanimously, while in the Lords, at Liverpool's suggestion, the first meeting of the secret committee was put off five days.

At the outset Wilberforce's intervention had more than a remote chance of success. The negotiation at St. Omer was hardly worthy of the name; the Queen had yet to receive a proper explanation of the government's terms, since Hutchinson had inadvertently misrepresented them; and an overture on British soil would in itself constitute a major triumph which might induce her to see reason however belatedly. The real difficulty was found to be the resumption of negotiations. The Queen did not want to make the first move because her strength lay in the government's abhorrence of the ultimate step. The ministers, feeling that they had already made an offer and seen it rejected, were equally hesitant, afraid to appear too conciliatory. Thus Wilberforce's adjournment was carried on Wednesday evening and no note was exchanged until late on Friday afternoon. However, after this cautious beginning, progress was auspiciously rapid. Anxious to gratify parliament and contradict aspersions of her complete irresponsibility, the Queen announced herself ready to attempt a compromise. The ministers, for their part, agreed to consider 'suggestions' modifying their April memorandum, and each party appointed two plenipotentiaries for the purpose of 'unreserved personal discussion'.[58] At this stage it was the King who became the chief obstacle in the way of further negotiations. Canning had already offended him by paying the Queen some profuse compliments in the House,[59] and the rest of the Cabinet were probably in his eyes guilty of double-dealing in their undisguised eagerness to evade inquiry. No sooner had negotia-

---

[56] For the debate see ibid., 906–85.   [57] *Wilberforce*, v. 55–6.
[58] See the correspondence between Brougham and Lord Liverpool, *PP*, 1820, xii. 531–3.   [59] *Hansard*, 2nd ser., i. 962.

tions with Brougham been resumed than the King secretly sounded the opposition to see if they would do his will. Hutchinson, his brother Lord Donoughmore, Bloomfield and Leach separately approached Tierney, Landsdowne, Buckingham and Holland, while George himself saw Wellesley. In every quarter the response was wholly discouraging. The Whigs were conscious that they needed more than the King's goodwill to succeed, and Buckingham called it 'complete ruin' if application were made to Holland House. To come to power pledged to a proceeding when parliament was so obviously against one was totally unrealistic anyway.[60] The episode, in effect, reminded the King once again that much more was involved in the case than the satisfaction of his personal wishes.

Characteristically, his frustration at finding that he could advise but not enforce expressed itself in petulance and petty-mindedness. As soon as Canning's remarks of 'unabated esteem and respect' for the Queen came to his knowledge, he began pressing Lord Liverpool for an explanation, and when none was forthcoming he bluntly refused, at a crucial point in the negotiations, to discuss any other subject until the matter was settled.[61] The crisis which threatened was very real indeed. It was a Saturday (10 June) and on Monday, if the ministers could not report progress or offer anything substantial, the Queen might easily throw caution to the winds, forcing parliament to resign itself to the inevitable. 'The whole question will be out of our hands ... if we have not taken our line and got upon good ground,' Lord Liverpool warned the King's private secretary, in pleading for an audience on Sunday morning.[62] His appeal was made in vain. Even a further note, asserting that Canning's speech 'however misrepresented in the Daily Prints, was honourable to himself and substantially useful to Your My. & Your Govt.', failed to budge the King, and, desperate to resolve the deadlock, Castlereagh and the Prime Minister spent most of Sunday afternoon at Carlton House on the off-chance of seeing him. Only towards evening did he simmer down, probably on a promise that Canning would be

[60] Mitchell, pp. 144–5; *Lord Holland, Further Memoirs of the Whig Party, 1807–21*, pp. 400–3; *George IV*, ii. 391–3 which, according to Mitchell, is wrongly dated November 1820.   [61] *George IV*, ii. 344.   [62] Ibid.

informed of his displeasure and also because the lukewarmness of the opposition was now fully known.[63] He was still 'much irritated' the next morning, half-heartedly trying to persuade Sidmouth into a Cabinet *putsch*,[64] but at least the negotiations with the Queen had been saved and in the nick of time. The ministers were able to deny that any renunciation of her royal title would be sought, Wellington and Castlereagh made arrangements to meet Brougham and Denman, and both houses carried adjournments to the end of the week.

So far so good. It had been the government's fervent prayer that the Queen would see reason and talk, and, mainly thanks to Brougham's continuing goodwill, this had been achieved. The ground of agreement, of course, was as yet hardly explored. In the negotiation to begin negotiation all that the government stipulated was that the Queen should reside abroad, accompanying this condition with an assurance that 'whatever appertains to Her Majesty by law . . . must continue to appertain to her so long as it is not abrogated by law'. Brougham in reply alleged that 'the basis of her recognition as Queen' was admitted, and, 'Her Majesty's dignity and honour being secured', the particulars of residence, patronage and income were 'of comparatively little importance'.[65] However, when serious talking began, the inadequacy of such a formula was soon obvious. If the Queen was refused the customary marks of grace and favour, if she voluntarily left part of her prerogative in abeyance, if a sentence of banishment was pronounced against her, the world could not but regard her as a woman in disgrace. Thus to comply with the government's terms became an admission of misconduct, something to which Caroline could never reconcile herself. A deadlock, indeed, portended after the very first conference. Though both parties agreed that 'the Queen must not be understood to *admit*, or the King to *retract* anything', Brougham and Denman at once asked for 'certain steps' to be taken to dispel the inferences which were sure to arise from her self-imposed exile; in other words, for a tacit rebuttal of the insinuations already made. They suggested either that her name

---

[63] Lord Liverpool to the King [11 June 1820], Add. MSS. 38285, ff. 218–219; *Hobhouse*, p. 27; *Mrs. Arbuthnot*, i. 22–3.
[64] Ibid., p. 23; *Hobhouse*, p. 27.   [65] *PP*, 1820, xii. 532.

should be restored to the liturgy or that British representatives abroad should formally introduce her to foreign courts. Each was anathema to the government because it was impossible to ignore the imputation of misconduct whether a charge was formally laid or not. The ministers had seen the evidence relating to the case, and it had been enough to persuade them to advise the Crown to show a signal disapprobation. So it would be until the Queen could prove herself innocent. An impasse had been reached, and there was no way out of it for the ministers except the way of dishonour, undoing all they had done, unsaying all they had previously said. In Castlereagh's words, Caroline could be a queen of right, never a queen of grace and favour. Nonetheless, so anxious was the government for an amicable adjustment that the interpretation was strained to the utmost. While the Queen was still refused a palace, she was offered a royal yacht or a ship of war to take her to Europe, a privilege usually allowed royalty and one which had been denied her a fortnight earlier.[66] Furthermore, without agreeing to her introduction to foreign courts, which was hardly possible when she had none to her husband's, Wellington and Castlereagh did go so far as to propose notice of her legal entitlements to a court of her choice. But it was all to no avail. When pressed, Brougham admitted that the liturgy or recognition abroad or some equivalent was a *sine qua non*, and, both sides having agreed to reach a decision by 19 June, a stalemate was the sole reward of parliament's patience. Between a queen wanting vindication, a king wanting condemnation and a government anxious to protect its own consistency there was very little room for manoeuvre.[67]

One last chance beckoned. If parliament lent its mighty influence to open a way of gracious retreat, a compromise could yet be attained, for an address that nothing derogatory attached

---

[66] Regarding the liturgy, Lord Grenville could not understand why one 'mere mark of ostensible respect should be withheld when others of the same description are yielded up to her'. Lord Grenville to Thomas Grenville [20 June 1820], Add. MSS. 41853, f. 389. The fact of the matter was that mention in the liturgy was an explicit recognition of Caroline as Queen, where a palace, had it been granted, or use of a king's ship were privileges given to royalty generally.
[67] See the protocols of the conferences, 15–19 June 1820, *PP*, 1820, xii. 534–9.

to acceptance of the government's terms would place the responsibility for any proceeding squarely on the Queen's shoulders. That the 'country gentlemen', on the breakdown of direct negotiations, would favour this sort of pressure was never in doubt. As Williams-Wynn reported: '. . . the disposition of the House of Commons, even to compel if necessary attention to its wishes seems to manifest itself more strongly from hour to hour. The language of the Ministerial Country Gentlemen is that the opening of the bag *must* be prevented & that terms must be imposed on either of the Parties who refuse to consent to reasonable offers.'[68] It was to Wilberforce, the most notable of the 'Saints', that everyone looked. He, of course, had been instrumental in securing a breathing space for negotiations immediately after the Queen's arrival, and though he was at odds with the ministers over the liturgy, even making a personal representation to the King against the omission, he willingly undertook to propose an address which would not only be an acceptable equivalent but also take the Queen at her word when she declared herself ready to submit to parliament 'with the gratitude due to the protection she has always received from it'.[69] Acland and Stuart-Wortley, the members for Devonshire and Yorkshire respectively, were his closest collaborators. The extent of the government's connivance is impossible to say, but since the act had to have an essential spontaneity, Williams-Wynn's contention that Wilberforce was the cat's-paw of ministers was undoubtedly an exaggeration which Wilberforce himself indignantly denied.[70] The last thing anybody wanted was a head-on legal collision, and the spokesman of moral England was surrounded with good advice from Brougham, ministers of the Crown and the 'country gentlemen' who were his nearest political neighbours.[71]

[68] Williams-Wynn to Lord Grenville [10 June 1820], Coed-y-maen MSS. See also Thomas Grenville to Lord Grenville, 12 June 1820, Grenville MSS.
[69] *Wilberforce*, v. 58–9.
[70] Williams-Wynn to Lord Grenville [20 June 1820], Coed-y-maen MSS.; *Hansard*, 2nd ser., i. 1312.
[71] *Wilberforce*, v. 57–8. It is interesting to note that during this time Castlereagh asked Williams-Wynn to see him and handed him the protocols of the late negotiation just before they were given to parliament. 'The evident intention of the communication', Williams-Wynn told his uncle, 'indeed almost declared, was to procure a recommendation from the House

Among government men Canning was the most forward, understandably so when his remaining in office depended on the outcome. Fully aware that the card was the last up his sleeve, he called on Wilberforce by appointment the same day that the negotiators returned to parliament to report failure, and won from him what he described as 'a half-consent'. The two days following he also saw him, 'from fear of his vacillations'.[72] Despite these honest endeavours, it was the knowledge that Brougham's hold over the Queen left much to be desired which made Wilberforce wary of rushing in to no purpose. Indeed, his caution in this direction was amply justified, for no sooner had he announced his motion than the Queen sent 'a warm, expostulatory letter—her own ebullition', adamant on the point of the liturgy. On the eve of the debate he and his friends had to choose between retiring, putting on as brave a face as possible, or recasting their proposal entirely. Luckily, Brougham and the government refused to give in. The Queen was cajoled into writing a second 'more moderate' letter which gave Wilberforce hopes anew; and Castlereagh obligingly arranged a twenty-four hour adjournment, though the Lords was becoming restless at the delay and the King was still waiting for parliament to take his message into 'immediate consideration'.[73]

The attempt to force a compromise was finally made on 22 June when Wilberforce's address entreating the Queen to yield to 'the earnest solicitude of the House of Commons' was carried by 391 votes to 124 at five in the morning. Most of the marathon was devoted not to the question of intervention—the result showed overwhelming approval—but to the rights and wrongs of exclusion from the liturgy, a contest in which the Whigs for the first time openly took the side of the Queen. There was never any suggestion that the Commons in taking the initiative had embarked on a hopeless errand. After so decisive a division, Brougham was supremely confident that the Queen would accede,[74] and certainly, while she could count on the opposition and the fairly general disapprobation of the govern-

---

to the Queen. . . .' Williams-Wynn to Lord Grenville [19 June 1820], Coed-y-maen MSS.
[72] Canning's diary, 19–21 June 1820, Canning MSS.
[73] *Wilberforce*, v. 59.   [74] Ibid., p. 65.

ment's uncompromising attitude on what seemed a point of no
consequence, the ministers by resolutely staking their all on
exclusion, raising the larger issue of their continuance in office,
made a compelling appeal to the instinctive loyalty of every
'country gentleman'.[75] The people might be on her side: more
likely than not, parliament would be against. The news, then,
that still she spurned conciliation stunned the political world,
if not the whole nation. To her enemies it seemed the act of a
madwoman, to her admirers a sure sign that Brunswick blood
ran thick in her veins. To those who knew her best it was one
more example of the unseemliness which she carried to the
point of self-destruction. A 'trial' could not now be more certain.

While fully alive to the dangers and difficulties ahead, the
ministers, on looking back, had few regrets. In retrospect, of
course, the omission from the liturgy was an unfortunate
mistake, but it was easy to be wise after the event when reinsertion had only become a *sine qua non* at the last moment and
one which could not be conceded without admitting that an
injustice had been perpetrated. As it was, the ministers had
been both true to themselves and careful of the King's honour.
They had retracted nothing of their original allegation, they
had painstakingly explored every avenue leading to possible
conciliation, and they had placed the Crown on 'high and safe
grounds' where a proceeding commenced by the Queen's own
invitation. 'Upon the whole,' Castlereagh wrote, 'I do not think
matters, up to the present point, could have worked more
favourably. . . . His Majesty has had all the forbearance without
conceding anything; and the mind of Parliament has been
gradually brought to settle to the calamity of a public trial of
the Queen as an inevitable evil, from which no prudential effort
could relieve them.'[76] Now that the die was cast it was the
prospect of Canning's resignation which was most worrying.
Such was his reputation that not one of his colleagues could be

[75] The ministers held a meeting of official men on 20 June to tell them
that they stuck to their original decision and would resign if defeated. At
the same time Arbuthnot passed the news on to several of the most prominent
'country gentlemen'. Aspinall, 'English Party Organization in the Early
Nineteenth Century', *English Historical Review*, xli (1926), 394, 395 n. 2.
Castlereagh explained the government's stand in the House when Wilberforce made his motion. *Hansard*, 2nd ser., i. 1258–9.

[76] Alison, iii. 122 n.

sure of his game. As early as February he had refused to be a
party to omission from the liturgy if a proceeding had been in
contemplation, and now that one was in the offing it seemed that
he could not, with honour, postpone his departure. But might
he not have arranged matters thus in order to have an escape
route if the government found itself facing the embarrassment
and danger of a trial? And now that he was at odds with the
rest of the Cabinet, might he not see a quick road to greater
power in a carefully contrived act of treachery? Certainly, his
going was the last the ministers could afford. With the limited
talent of the front bench, to have Canning in opposition
championing the Queen would double the government's agony;
it was preferable by far that he stay on, even as a spectator. In
fact, these suspicions and speculations did him less than justice.
After twice jeopardising his career Canning had outlived the
ways of a political buccaneer, and to him the Queen's affair was
a savage kick of fortune which left him, much to his regret,
no option but resignation. The reasons which made him unable
to act the part of her accuser or judge were without doubt
strictly personal. Perhaps he feared, as he had feared at the time
of the Delicate Investigation,[77] that an indiscretion or amourette
of the past would be revealed to do his career irreparable
injury. The King himself was convinced that this was his real
reason, even believing after one tête-à-tête that he had won from
him a near confession of 'his former extreme intimacy'. Castlereagh, among others, gave similar credence to these stories.[78]
But more probably Canning was embarrassed because he had
been forward in advising Caroline to go abroad in 1814, a
sojourn which now seemed likely to have dire consequences for
her. Certainly the excuse he gave to the world was along these
lines. When he went to the King to discuss his situation, he
opened the conversation by insisting that 'his former habits of
intimacy' and 'the confidence . . . reposed in him . . . by unreserved communications' made it impossible for him to act
with complete impartiality.[79]

[77] *Lord Granville Leveson Gower: Private Correspondence, 1781–1821* (ed.
Castalia, Countess Granville), ii. 202, 204, 206.
[78] *Mrs. Arbuthnot*, i. 25, Alison, iii. 122 n.
[79] Canning to Mrs Canning, 30 June 1820, Canning MSS. Canning, of
course, was convinced of the public mischief of a proceeding, but there is

With the Queen's arrival in early June, Canning had to keep his word and proffer his resignation at least, and this he did with becoming reluctance at a Cabinet meeting on the night of her landing. Almost immediately he received a token of his indispensability, for, when he called at Fife House the next morning, Liverpool begged him most earnestly to consult his closest friends before taking the final, irrevocable step. He was, he said, 'strongly impressed with the Conviction that such an Event would be productive of the most serious Evils & Inconveniences . . . if it did not lead to the immediate Dissolution of the Govt,' a plea which probably had less weight with Canning than the fact that a proceeding was still avertible.[80] Stay he decided he would, for the meantime anyway, though in a fit of pique a week later he actually tendered his resignation after the King had taken exception to his parliamentary eulogy of Caroline. Fortunately, George appreciated the embarrassment of his position, and, having been lectured by the Prime Minister on Canning's indispensability, he refused to hear another word until a proceeding was certain.[81] When that moment arrived, with the abject failure of Wilberforce's mediation, probably his retention in office was already decided. On his renewing his offer to retire, the King requested a day to think over a matter 'full of difficulty'. All that he in fact did was to send for Liverpool to convey his commands that he stay on, with perfect liberty to take whatever course he pleased.[82] Such an arrangement suited Canning admirably. He remained faithful to his pledge of neutrality, he had the King's express permission to act as he did, he could never be accused of deserting his colleagues in an hour of need and his political worth received frank recognition.[83] The last was especially

no evidence to suggest that this was the cause of his refusal to be a party. If it had been, to have stayed in office and withdrawn from parliament would have completely destroyed his political character, regardless of Liverpool's or the King's approval. When he saw the King on 25 June, he told him that he 'had now put himself completely in the right, and ought not . . . to make any further concession'—which hardly suggests any serious disagreement with his colleagues. *Canning*, p. 290.

[80] Canning's diary, 5–6 June 1820, Canning MSS.; Lord Liverpool to the King [11 June 1820], Add. MSS. 38285, ff. 218–19.

[81] Canning's diary, 14 June 1820, Canning MSS.

[82] Canning's diary, 25–26 June 1820, ibid.; *Canning*, pp. 290–2.

[83] On hearing that he had offered his resignation to the King, Bathurst

gratifying. For four years he had been an exemplary colleague, more than pulling his weight in general debate, labouring without complaint in a minor Cabinet office. But ambition was beginning to demand some reward. His importance plainly acknowledged, perhaps he would not have to wait much longer.

With a settlement short of legal action no longer in question—though the Queen in a melancholy moment did seek a last minute reconciliation through Canning's good offices[84]—the government turned its attention to the procedure which would best minimise the case's inherent difficulties. Needless to say, the precedents were utterly unreliable. The adultery of Sophia Dorothea, George I's consort, had not even a remote relevance because her conviction had been secured under Hanoverian law; and to go back as far as Anne Boleyn was to invoke an example from the bad old days of Tudor England when an all-powerful sovereign had simply commanded his servants to do his royal bidding. Instead, the ministers had to feel their way through the legal jungle as best they could, accepting the assistance of the law officers whenever necessary. Some sort of legislative proceeding perforce commended itself, partly because the government would have a measure of control throughout, partly because only parliament could deprive the Queen of her title and legal rights. Beyond this, however, there were any number of dubieties. Had Bergami, the alleged lover, been a British subject owing allegiance to the British crown, Caroline could have been arraigned on a charge of high treason, for her adultery could have been construed as abetting an offence described in Edward III's Statute of 1351–2.[85] As it was, her crime was neither a felony nor a misdemeanour, and this ruled

---

was most anxious to prevent its acceptance. Lord Bathurst to Lord Liverpool, 26 June 1820, Add. MSS. 38285, f. 321.

[84] Sir Robert Wilson contacted Canning through J. H. Frere, and told him that the Queen seemed ready to comply with the government's terms. Knowing well the Cabinet's aversion to further delay, Canning advised her to 'throw herself frankly upon the generosity of the King'. When Sir William Grant asked him to arrange an audience, however, he demurred on the grounds that it would compromise his neutrality. Canning's diary, 30 June, 2 July 1820, J. H. Frere to Canning, 1 July [1820], Canning MSS.; *Hobhouse*, pp. 30–1; *Brougham*, ii. 369.

[85] Opinion of the law officers on the case of the Princess of Wales, 17 January 1820, HO 126/3; *Hansard*, 2nd ser., ii. 17–18, 24.

out a bill of attainder as too severe and an impeachment as
totally without precedent according to the doctrine that the
only impeachable offences were those indictable at common
law.[86]

The alternatives, the government concluded, were a bill of
divorce and a bill of pains and penalties. The first had the
insuperable disadvantage that it would relieve the King without
relieving the nation. Everyone knew that George's infidelities
made a divorce next to impossible in the ordinary course of law.
Because parliament was unlikely to make an exception even in
his case, the ministers were forced to proceed on the presumption that the greater offence was the disparagement of the state
and the lesser the dishonour of the husband. Public necessity was
to come before private injury. The chief merit of a bill of pains
and penalties was that it recognised this principle implicitly.
One clause might pronounce a sentence of degradation and
deprivation, which was the punishment appropriate to the crime
in a public view, while a second could order divorce incidentally,
or as Lord Liverpool put it, as a 'corollary' being 'the least
important part'.[87] The Cabinet's first instinct was to drop
divorce altogether from fear of recrimination and religious
objections, but on reflection this seemed pusillanimous and
scarcely logical.[88] In a case where the state and no one individual
was seeking redress, the right of the defendant to show the
complaining party's conduct did not entitle him to relief was
assumed to be inapplicable. Even if it was admitted, and then
only in defiance of the maxim that the king can do no wrong,
the ministers thought that the Crown could claim special
treatment inasmuch as every divorce bill was, strictly speaking,
a dispensation of the law in a particular case. Surely, their
argument ran, it was the public interest that a woman in
disgrace should not remain the sovereign's wife. Surely,
therefore, 'a comparison of the claims and respective conduct of
the individuals concerned' had no relevance whatever. The
question left a-begging was whether parliament would willingly
swallow the fiction that no personal relief was involved. After
all, degradation might well be a proper pain and penalty if the

[86] Ibid., 18, 207.   [87] Ibid., 724.
[88] *Hobhouse*, pp. 29–30, 31–2.

Queen had offended the state, but divorce on the same grounds still gave an erring husband a freedom he little deserved.[89]

When parliament acted in its judicial capacity, either by bill or impeachment, more often than not the proceeding was initiated in the House of Commons, it being generally recognised that its susceptibility to public opinion and its powers of inquiry made it ill-suited to be the court of ultimate decision. This occasion, however, was remarkable for a contrary procedure, one which in great measure looked to the relative position of Commons and Lords in the constitution. In the eighteenth century the Lords was mainly regarded as 'an occasionally useful long-stop' to throw out legislation which an administration found it impossible or embarrassing to oppose in the Commons.[90] By the early nineteenth century, the often manifested reluctance of the lower house to oppose a strong current of public feeling had encouraged the notion that the upper was more insulated and therefore had better preserved its deliberative character. Certainly most of the peers believed this, which was not without importance. The Queen's 'trial', in view of the party squabbles which had distinguished the Commons' attempt to establish the Duke of York's guilt in 1809, was precisely the sort of question where its sense of detachment from public opinion could be of service. In letting the bill originate with the peers the government was in fact being both sagacious and just. Where the Commons because of its numbers and procedural rules could drag out a proceeding interminably, the Lords had legal equipment equal to, if not surpassing, any other court of justice; a wealth of judicial talent sat on its benches, reference might be had to the judges to settle controversial points of law, and, most important of all, witnesses could be sworn at the bar before their examination by counsel or the House. In the Commons, as when the articles of an impeachment were voted, the bill would have to run the gauntlet of popular impression rather than any serious judicial test, and, with the people stout for the Queen and the Whigs manoeuvring for party advantage, there was no saying that that house would behave as it ought. The Lords,

[89] *Liverpool*, iii. 104–6. For Canning's argument that a divorce clause would 'change the nature of the proceeding from national to personal', see *Canning*, pp. 293–4.

[90] Richard Pares, *King George III and the Politicians*, p. 40.

on the other hand, could be relied on to do the job decently and well. Not all men would have demurred when the Prime Minister averred 'that if there existed in the world a tribunal whose character for strict justice and rigid impartiality was unimpeached, that tribunal was the House of Lords of this Kingdom'.[91] Practised in sitting as a court of law, less partisan by habit and tradition, the peers would send down a verdict of authority which the Commons could not easily discard. Unlike her brother-in-law, Caroline at least had the consolation of being tried with dignity.

The decision to bring in a bill of pains and penalties did not quite clear the stage for the major performance. Most of the precedents directed some form of preliminary inquiry to establish the charges, and, anxious to observe the conventions as much as possible, the ministers had already announced a secret committee for the Commons and had actually appointed one in the Lords, suspending its sitting, though, while negotiations were in progress. Partly, of course, the committees were intended to exhibit parliament as the Queen's accuser, and the difficulty which now arose was the noticeable reluctance of the lower house to cast the first stone. Some members, mainly from the opposition, objected to a report from above stairs on the ground that it would have to be hostile to justify the ministers: an impression of guilt would be fixed which would give the prosecution an unfair advantage. Others, from the tenor of the Queen's reply to Wilberforce, understood her to have invited a proceeding, and they argued that the Commons might wash its hands of the affair, for the meantime anyway, and leave an uncongenial task wholly to the Lords. Impressing everyone, however, was the feeling that the country was inching its way along the brink of a precipice over which at any moment it might plunge to revolution and civil war. Ever since the Queen had arrived there had been mounting public excitement; addresses had flowed in from plebeian admirers, the popular press, little deterred by the 'gagging' acts of the previous year, had renewed its expletives against authority in general, and even the troops had displayed the first symptoms of outright disobedience. The last was particularly unnerving, as the

[91] *Hansard,* 2nd ser., ii. 17.

prompt removal of an offending regiment showed.[92] Throughout the emergencies of 1817 and 1819 the soldiery had never once been suspect, and yet now the King's guards were openly drinking the health of the Queen.[93] Already the crowd was roaming the streets mostly unmolested—the authorities 'wait till the windows are broken when they send for the H. Guards instead of sending for the Glaziers', Thomas Grenville complained[94]— and the Duke of Wellington was not alone in thinking the country was lost if the troops joined them.[95] Little wonder that the government, and almost everyone else, agreed that in the circumstances the 'gravity and decorum' of the Lords was much to be preferred.[96] Although it meant publicly confessing a change of plan, the Commons was stood easy on 26 June without getting further than an adjourned debate on the King's message of three weeks before. Castlereagh tried gamely to smooth away some of the government's embarrassment by promising a proceeding if the peers did nothing within ten days. When that time elapsed the bill of course had been introduced, and the House could do nothing except put off the question until the middle of August. The Lords held the stage from this moment on.

The secret committee, under Harrowby's chairmanship, convened for its first meeting on 28 June. Six days later, in plenty of time to stop any independent initiative in the Commons, it presented its report, and a bill of pains and penalties followed almost immediately. In letting the green bag be opened at last, the government, in effect, passed the point of no return. An inquiry above stairs under the auspices of ministers was bound to make out a convincing *prima facie* case, if only to bear out the insinuations of the King's original message, and once the trial had begun it was but just to let it reach its own conclusion. Indeed, as it turned out, with Erskine's and

---

[92] On 15 June there was a mutiny in the 3rd regiment of Foot Guards, which the London crowd did its best to encourage. The next day the troops were ordered to Portsmouth. *Hobhouse*, pp. 25–6; *Mrs. Arbuthnot*, i. 23–4; *Croker*, i. 175–6; *Courier*, 16, 17 June 1820.

[93] *Mrs. Arbuthnot*, i. 26.

[94] Thomas Grenville to Lord Grenville, 10 June 1820, Grenville MSS.

[95] Duke of Wellington to Lord Liverpool, 28 June 1820, Add. MSS. 38196, f. 92.

[96] *Hobhouse*, p. 29; *Mrs. Arbuthnot*, i. 25.

Lansdowne's withdrawal, the report was unanimous and worded even more strongly than the government thought necessary.[97] A proceeding being unavoidable, the ministers' great concern was to press forward in haste and be done at the earliest possible moment. Unfortunately for them, they were not able to order it so. Before the secret committee began its sittings, Brougham and Denman applied at the bar for a postponement of 'two short months', in order, so they said, to prepare the Queen's defence, but really to frighten parliament out of a proceeding with the full blast of public indignation. Needless to say, the Cabinet gave them scant satisfaction. Briefly the ministers toyed with the idea of an even longer delay, presumably to let the country quieten down, but in the end they decided in favour of an adjournment between the first reading and the hearing of evidence on the second.[98] After consulting the precedents, it was discovered that the period of grace usually allowed the lawyers was a fortnight, and at first the government had no objections to adhering to this rule.

Both sides, however, were constantly seeking the advantage. As soon as the secret committee reported, Brougham and Denman again appeared at the bar, this time to demand that the trial proceed *de die in diem* without any adjournment whatever. Ostensibly, they used the excuse that, an accusation having been laid, an immediate reply was essential to counter its impression, though, as Lord Liverpool pointed out, every accused person suffered the same disadvantage.[99] In actual fact what they were trying to do was force the government to prosecute before it was fully ready. Defence by recrimination was out of the question as long as parliament preferred the responsible course of ignoring the case as a private injury. Grey himself condemned it by declaring that 'it would have been equally improper to have allowed Thistlewood to defend himself by saying that his treason was directed against tyrants and oppressors'.[100] It

[97] Lord Liverpool to Lord Harrowby, 3 July 1820, Harrowby MSS. 15, f. 253; *Hobhouse*, p. 31. After sitting in the committee a day, Buckingham was convinced that some inquiry was justified, and Lauderdale, another member, described the evidence as 'complete and to the last degree disgusting'. Lord Buckingham to Thomas Grenville, 29 June 1820, Add. MSS. 41854, ff. 68–70; G. M. Trevelyan, *Lord Grey of the Reform Bill*, p. 194.
[98] *Mrs. Arbuthnot*, i. 26; *Hobhouse*, p. 30.
[99] *Hansard*, 2nd ser., ii. 209–10.   [100] *Ibid.*, 5.

was also impossible to hope to contradict the prosecution in detail point by point because the King's agents had been amassing evidence to sustain their case since the beginning of 1816; Brougham could hardly have done the necessary detective work in a year let alone a month. The Queen's best chance, her lawyers realised, lay in demolishing the witnesses brought against her. Since many of them would be foreigners, mainly Italians, of low class, it was fair to assume that the court would regard them with a jaundiced eye and also that they would be particularly vulnerable to cross-examination, which meant the less prepared they were the better. The ministers, naturally enough, were not unsuspecting of Brougham's strategy. Possibly his show of confidence unnerved them a little, no doubt just as he intended, for Castlereagh was pressing Vienna for more information about the middle of July.[101] But other than the danger of exposing their witnesses prematurely, they had to bear in mind that until August most of the judges were away on circuit, and that the peers themselves needed time to settle their affairs before the long sitting. The ideal, then, of instant justice proved totally unacceptable in practice. The best the government was able to arrange for itself was a delay of five weeks, which the Lords obliged with on 10 July. Typically, Brougham continued to play the gad-fly. Though he had professed himself ready to undertake the Queen's defence at a moment's notice, he now had her petition against the vagueness of the bill's preamble, demanding first a list of witnesses from the Attorney-General, as a compensating advantage, and then a precise delineation of the charge of 'licentious, disgraceful and adulterous intercourse'.[102] Anything which made his client appear the underdog struggling against ministerial omnipotence was not to her disadvantage.

The Lords adjourned itself until 15 August, two days before the second reading was due to be proposed, on 26 July. The interval, despite processions and a prurient press, passed off

[101] Alison, iii. 122 n.
[102] By 7 Anne c. 21 persons indicted for high treason were allowed a list of witnesses, and Brougham rested his claim on the argument that the Queen's case was roughly equivalent. Motions to secure this point and to let counsel be heard on the other were brought forward by Lord Erskine, but easily defeated.

much better than the government expected. Among drawing-room society, it was true, there was talk of Caroline being 'the D. of Orleans in petticoats' and a second Catherine II.[103] But in the main, though they were dismayed at the King's chronic unpopularity, the ministers firmly believed that the situation was under control. To their way of thinking it was the troops on which the Queen 'principally relied', and once Wellington was able to report that the army was sound, 'excepting the loose conversation of some in Publick Houses', the worst horror thankfully receded.[104] Of more immediate concern was a renewed attempt on the part of 'the Saints' to avert a proceeding, regardless of how this would embarrass the government. As soon as direct mediation with the Queen failed, Wilberforce declared that he 'would embrace any creditable way of stopping it', and a few weeks later he began suggesting, in private, county meetings to place Crown and parliament in a stranglehold of 'respectable' opinion. Apart from the lateness of the hour, which all but made it impracticable, the great weakness of the plan was the only too palpable fact that the nobility and gentry no longer commanded these sort of assemblies. In the words of William Lamb, himself a leading Whig, at most 'other counsels and other feelings would prevail' which made them more likely 'to inflame and excite, rather than to tranquillise. . . .'[105] Rebuffed here, Wilberforce prepared to strike out in an alto-gether different direction. His plan this time was the rather naive one of persuading the King to go down to the Lords in person and withdraw the bill for 'the gratifying of his people'. Oddly enough, it was not a fear of taking too much upon him-self which made him draw back, but an open letter of Lord John Russell's published in *The Times* urging him to intervene; in his view such advice coming from 'one of the strongest partisans of the opposition' made any move on his part at once seem a contrivance of the Whigs. To return to London, he decided, ready to clutch at any opportunity that presented

---

[103] Lord Buckingham to Thomas Grenville, 23 July 1820, Add. MSS. 41854, ff. 71–3; *Plumer Ward*, ii. 56.

[104] Duke of Wellington to Lord Liverpool, 30 July 1820, Add. MSS. 38196, ff. 93–4; *Wellington Desp.* (new series), i. 141; *Hobhouse*, pp. 33–4; Alison, iii. 122n.

[105] *Wilberforce*, v. 67; *The Correspondence of William Wilberforce* (ed. Robert Isaac Wilberforce and Samuel Wilberforce), ii. 433–5.

itself, was the only course left open to him, and he moved up from Weymouth accordingly about 12 August.[106]

The government had meanwhile watched these manoeuvres with the utmost suspicion and dismay. What the Cabinet most feared was an open declaration against the bill by the 'country gentlemen' should Wilberforce feel that his last chance; for under those circumstances neither the Crown, which had thought the Queen's conduct worthy of investigation in the first place, nor the Lords, which had seen fit to prosecute her, could retreat unharmed with honour intact. The resignation of the ministers would almost certainly follow because the House of Commons would have shown itself in total disagreement with a policy of their recommendation. The peers, for their part, would have the unenviable alternatives of either surrendering their dignity by obeying a remonstrance issuing from below or pressing on with the bill in the full realisation that it would never pass into law, the monarchy all the while being dragged through the mire to no purpose. Not surprisingly, in government circles Wilberforce's intervention was bitterly resented, Castlereagh even going so far as to accuse him outright of intriguing political change.[107] In the last resort, however, there was nothing to fear simply because nothing could be done. The day before the second reading was moved, Wilberforce determined to leave no stone unturned, requested an interview of Lord Liverpool, and though he gave no promise that he would stay quiet when the Commons met, the ministers came away with the impression that, bankrupt of ideas, he was at last prepared to accept the inevitable.[108] The final test, of course, took place on 21 August when that house reassembled briefly to adjourn itself for a further month. A handful of Whigs tried to inaugurate a rebellion by asking the King to prorogue parliament, but Wilberforce himself admonished them to silence by describing it 'just neither to the Queen nor to the country to leave her majesty in her present condition'.[109] The saint had truly laboured and retired to his rest.

With a cordon of troops holding back a milling throng outside

---

[106] *Wilberforce*, v. 74–7; *The Times*, 5 August 1820.
[107] *Mrs. Arbuthnot*, i. 31–2. See also *Hobhouse*, pp. 35–6.
[108] *Mrs. Arbuthnot*, i. 32.   [109] *Hansard*, 2nd ser., ii. 835.

—the government reverted to the security precautions which had been applied during Hastings' impeachment—the Prime Minister moved the order of the day for the second reading on 17 August. Out of a total membership of over 340, and brought there on pain of a fine if no reasonable excuse could be offered for absence, 256 peers attended to hear him, roughly twice as many as the major debate of a session would draw. This last fact was of a prime importance. The peculiar property of a bill of pains and penalties, its endearing characteristic as far as the government was concerned, was that it required parliament to declare the offence and administer punishment in one and the same act. Thus where an ordinary court of law simply resolved the judicial issue of guilty or not guilty, in this instance Lords and Commons had to tackle a legislative issue besides, whether or not the bill should pass. Here considerations of expediency loomed quite as large as those of justice. No matter what legal expertise the government could command, in other words, the skills and techniques of parliamentary management would be equally important if the prosecution against the Queen was going to succeed.

As far as the bill's passage went, despite Grey's grandiose declaration that he would act the judge and not the party man, the ministers fully expected the temptations of power and popularity to be too much for the Whigs to sit idly by. Perhaps some government men, along with Thomas Grenville, thought that the opposition crossed their Rubicon when Lord John Russell published his letter,[110] but the real test came when the Lords resumed its sitting. Lord Liverpool correctly anticipated that Grey's side of the House would give 'all the Trouble they can upon Collateral Points', without trying to change the course of proceedings to which the peers were already committed.[111] When the Duke of Leinster moved to discharge the order for the second reading, only forty 'thick and thin' Whigs responded, while Grey and Lord King collected over sixty in support of

[110] Thomas Grenville to Lord Grenville, 8 August 1820, Grenville MSS. Actually, Russell's initiative was much criticised by the 'big wigs who think our party ought to stand by, profess no principles, and hazard no opinions'. *Early Correspondence of Lord John Russell, 1805-40* (ed. Rollo Russell), i. 213.

[111] Lord Liverpool to Lord Harrowby, 11 August 1820, Harrowby MSS. 15, ff. 251-2.

motions declaring the bill to be unnecessary and inexpedient.[112] On these grounds the whole of the opposition could safely muster, whatever the weight of evidence against the Queen, whatever verdict the peers might return. No one included in these minorities voted with the government on either the second or third readings. This put the ministers at a serious disadvantage from the beginning. While the House of Lords undoubtedly had an established Tory bias, mainly thanks to Pitt's rash of creations, an occasion such as this brought out a considerable number of peers with no close association with either party; so that, instead of having two little knots of regular attenders, the situation became somewhat analogous to the Commons where a vast mass of lackadaisical supporters filled the hindmost benches. Moreover, in this instance what loyalties there were were weakened by the nature of the case, for divorce was abhorrent to many on religious grounds and in the high and mighty matter of judging the Queen Consort it seemed singularly inappropriate to make Caroline a political hare to be hallooed after and hunted down by partisans of the King. The Whigs, if they were going to gain anything, could afford to take sides. The ministers dared not appear to do so. And the more the opposition showed themselves ready to combine against the bill the more the government had to pander to the instincts and inhibitions of the backwoodsmen.

Quite early on in the proceedings the Cabinet found it necessary to challenge the obvious disquiet of a majority of the House concerning divorce. In his opening address, Brougham had strenuously argued that the government was submitting to the sovereign's personal caprice under pretence of a state necessity, refusing to deny himself in these circumstances the right of recrimination, and the Prime Minister, after 'extensive personal communication' with peers and other persons 'acquainted with publick opinion', had to admit that this feeling was general.[113] The trouble was that parliament was anxious to abide by the rules even where the sovereign was concerned. It had no objections to degrading the Queen because it knew it had an indubitable right to bestow the crown as it pleased. But

[112] *Creevey*, p. 308; *Hansard*, 2nd ser., ii. 612, 710–41.
[113] Ibid., 644–8; *George IV*, ii. 361–2.

it had abundant objections to divorcing her because the bill
spoke indefinitely of an 'adulterous intercourse', because the
husband was not prepared to appear and defend his own purity
and because there was no judgement from an inferior court to
support his application. From the government's point of view,
divorce was the consequence of degradation, inasmuch as a
woman in disgrace could not remain the king's wife without
disparagement of the Crown's honour and dignity. In the eyes
of almost everyone else, divorce only followed if the Queen's
adultery could be sufficiently proved and if the offence was great
enough to overlook the notorious infidelity of her husband. To
reconcile the two was clearly impossible. Since Liverpool was
sure in his own mind that the clause was past saving, he decided
that the best the government could do was bow out gracefully
by getting the King to declare it dispensable and by dropping it
at the first opportune moment. Then recrimination would more
than likely be scotched, the King would flatly deny his personal
interest in the bill, and the House of Lords would be correspondingly friendlier. Fortunately George, who was enjoying
his latest dalliance at his cottage retreat at Windsor, saw the
wisdom of keeping his name out of the proceeding as much as
possible. In his reply to Lord Liverpool he requested time to
think it over. A few days later he summoned him, Wellington,
Castlereagh and Sidmouth down for an evening when, 'with
no common feelings of regret', he signified his acquiescence.
Because only the prosecution had been heard on the case, it was
impossible at this stage to remove or alter any clause until the
bill went into committee. In the meantime, in reply to a pre-
arranged question, the Prime Minister repeated that divorce
was to be regarded as inessential, also assuring the House 'that
the illustrious individual alluded to had no wish whatever that
the bill should operate as a measure of personal relief'. This way
the King was protected, the government conceded of its own
free will and the peers could go on in a far happier frame of
mind.[114]

The comparative strength of the forces for and against the
bill was not really tested until a vote was taken upon the second

[114] Ibid., pp. 361–3, 366; *Hobhouse*, pp. 36–7; *Hansard*, 2nd ser., ii.
1383–5.

reading. By then, the Crown lawyers certainly had the better of the legal case. The foreign witnesses, whom Brougham had hoped to terrify into contradiction or silence, went through the ordeal with amazing aplomb, producing between them a remarkably extensive and corroborative testimony of Bergami's promotion from courier to chamberlain, his admittance to the Princess's table, his constant attendance on her person as well as the strange sleeping arrangements that were sometimes made. Under cross-examination only two witnesses, admittedly two of the most material, obviously succumbed. As a result, Brougham was left in no doubt about his best course. Everything depended on his bringing forward foreigners to contradict the detail, and English persons to back them up wherever possible.[115] On both counts he failed miserably. His most important foreign witnesses —Bergami's sister, who had lived with Caroline for years, and a Swiss servant girl—were found too unreliable to be risked on the stand, and their non-appearance inevitably aroused suspicion. Worse still, while the English ladies and gentlemen who were called to the bar performed encouragingly well, the two naval officers who had accompanied the Queen on a voyage around the Levant in 1816 both broke down under relentless cross-examination. Lieutenant Flynn, who had navigated the by now notorious polacca, was shown to have lied on one point, which immediately threw the rest of his evidence into doubt; and Lieutenant Hownam, a protégé of the Queen's, did his patroness even greater harm by eventually confessing that during the voyage she had slept with Bergami under a deck awning. Coming when it did, when Brougham had only Italians to call, this last admission made the prosecution's victory almost a certainty, for an impropriety, to call it nothing worse, in one place suggested the same in countless others. For the first time during the trial it really did seem that the foreign riff-raff had been speaking the truth when they had mentioned snatched kisses, secret caresses and tumbled bedclothes. Gifford and Copley's splendid closing perorations gave nothing of this advantage away.

[115] George IV, ii. 361; Liverpool, iii. 107; Huskisson to Canning, 14 September 1820, Canning MSS.; Lord Liverpool to Huskisson, 29 September 1820, Add. MSS. 38742, f. 27.

The vote on the second reading, however, was more than a verdict on the legal case. Insofar as a bill of pains and penalties created the crime, the peers had to ask themselves not only whether the accused was guilty but also whether it was wise to punish her if she was. The further the trial proceeded the less expedient the latter seemed. Though the government had nursed great hopes that the prosecution's evidence would sober the Queen's partisans,[116] public opinion persisted in its error throughout the whole of the proceeding. As Canning clearly saw, the question of guilt or innocence was of little or no account to both 'the mass of mankind' and 'the better sort'.[117] To the first the trial was the climax of the Queen's abominable persecution over the years, the final chapter of a foul conspiracy which underlined the perfidy of the King and of Authority in general. For them, or for those who claimed to speak for them, it was enough that she was a victim of the same tyranny which ground them down. 'Here,' wrote Lord Eldon from the country, 'they have settled all matters, because they say, sweepingly, Italians are not to be believed.'[118] The feeling of 'the better sort', or 'the sober minded people', was a compound of fear and moral outrage. As always, the sight of an excited populace alarmed them; and on this occasion their alarm was the greater because of the events of the previous year. The nature of the case was such as to give impetus to the Radical attack on traditional institutions. If parliament condemned the Queen, that would be taken to be a testimony of its corruption by the Crown; if in the end it acquitted her, evil would be done nonetheless because the monarchy could not avoid being thrown into disrepute by the scandalous disclosures emanating from a trial. What was even more certain was the imperilling of the country's morals by the publication of royal indecency. The common people had all the vulnerability of limited understanding, and for this reason anything which challenged the existing social order and the values it enshrined was to be condemned out of hand. These were deep fears, and, generally speaking, they were faithfully

[116] Lord Bathurst to Lord Liverpool, 8 August 1820, Add. MSS. 38286, ff. 365–6; Lord Liverpool to Lord Harrowby, 11 August 1820, Harrowby MSS. 15, ff. 251–2.
[117] *Canning*, p. 297.
[118] *Eldon*, ii. 386.

reflected in the House of Lords. The 'respectable' classes cared relatively little whether the Queen or the ministers were to blame for the calamity of a proceeding. Of greater consequence was how it could be speedily terminated or its dangers minimised as much as possible. After the vote on the second reading, it was clear that many of the peers had the same priorities.

But though 'the better sort' preferred considerations of expediency to the needs of justice, they also felt strongly that a moral principle was involved in the case. In their eyes the King little deserved the relief which it was proposed to grant him because his own conduct was such as to extenuate, to a greater or lesser degree, the offence of his wife. The Queen was more sinned against than sinning, for however great her 'propensity for evil', however badly she had conducted herself, a husband who had put away his wife and repeatedly flouted his marriage vows had no cause to complain. This was no peculiar sympathy for a woman of royal rank or for one whose treatment had been harsh enough to gain an exceptional notoriety. The law of England normally required in such cases that a comparison be made of the conduct of the respective parties, and not many men, notwithstanding the ministers' argument of the interest of the state, would see a vital difference in the situation of the king and queen.[119] In this regard, 'respectable' opinion did not allow Caroline's political misdemeanours, her unscrupulous flirtation with 'the Revolutionists', to detract from the cardinal moral issue. Indeed, in their reluctance to see her hunted down to ruin and disgrace, 'the better sort' shared the sentiments of the common people, though they did not express them as enthusiastically or as obviously. Lord Granville rightly assessed the overwhelming feeling as against the King rather than for the Queen,[120] and here it was that Cruikshank's famous caricatures of the middle-aged, pot-bellied debauchee struck a particularly vibrant note. 'Honest hatred to hypocrisy— generous resistance to power unjustly used—and sympathy with persecuted innocence' was how one observer analysed the public opinion which was being brought to bear on the House

[119] See *Canning*, p. 281.
[120] Lord Granville to Canning, 3 September 1820, Canning MSS. See also Lord Castlereagh to Lord Stewart, 1 September 1820. Castlereagh MSS. xxxvi. 355–6.

of Lords.[121] When a whole nation was moved by them, these were emotions to be neither lightly disregarded nor easily appeased.

Perhaps as was to be expected, suggestions that the peers should murder the bill of their own accord were now heard for the first time. The reasoning of the defeatists was that the lower house would be fully exposed to the disconcertment and reservations of the 'respectable' classes, that it would never allow the bill to pass, and that its refusal to condemn the Queen would place the administration in jeopardy and do the House of Lords inestimable damage. They were only too well aware that the procedure of the Commons afforded numberless opportunities for mischief. There the defence might spring a surprise attack on an altogether different front with new witnesses uninhibited by any oath; at every stage, with no judges to guide the House, questions of evidence or procedure could be exploited to waste precious hours in trivial debate; and the longer the proceeding dragged out, the more acrimonious the discussions became, the greater the pressure of public opinion to have an end to the whole unsavoury business. In these circumstances, the reluctance which the House of Commons had displayed at the outset would only intensify. The bill of pains and penalties would never become law, and therefore to send it on from the Lords would prolong the evil unnecessarily. Moreover, defeat in the Commons was likely to have worse consequences than defeat in the Lords. The lower house, as the representative body in the constitution, would certify the country's disapprobation of the ministers, and in view of the obvious disagreement over what constituted the interest of the state, their resignation, and their replacement by the Whigs, would be almost inevitable. At the same time, the peers, having refused to do the people's work, would find themselves with the diminished affection of the country and derided as the servile instruments of the executive.

In the search for an honourable retreat, Huskisson and Granville, also a close friend of Canning's, led the way, wholly, it must be said, on their own initiative. Both allowed themselves to believe that an address moved by an independent peer justify-

[121] *Letters of the Earl of Dudley to the Bishop of Llandaff*, p. 264.

ing the government and condemning the Queen would cover the bill's withdrawal to the satisfaction of all parties, if only because a legal acquittal accompanied by a moral lecture and approbation of the prosecution was an everyday occurrence in courts of inferior jurisdiction.[122] Certainly at first sight the move had much to commend it, for the government would receive a certificate of good conduct, which could possibly save it from the full consequences of defeat, while the censure pronounced on the Queen would form a sufficient excuse to withhold the several marks of grace and favour already refused her. The difficulty was that in the long run such an escape created more problems than it solved. Having begun an inquiry into the Queen's conduct and pursued it over a period of months, the House of Lords could hardly bring matters to a close by shirking a pronouncement on the evidence, which meant that the proceeding had to be carried as far as the second reading at least, if not to the voting of the preamble in the committee. Come what may, therefore, the government had once to run the risk of outright defeat before withdrawal was even thinkable. To do otherwise would satisfy nobody. The peers would feel themselves to have been needlessly exploited, the Crown would be left with nothing except a chastening thought of its own incredible folly, and the Queen would be tempted to complete her half success numberless times when opportunity offered in the Commons. 'A legal process must have a legal issue', Canning instructed Huskisson. 'Else the whole question would be liable, and likely to be entered upon anew, starting only from the ground conceded to the accused, but not resting while an inch of ground remains to be gained to her.'[123] With this, Liverpool was in substantial agreement. Some of his fellow ministers, in defiance of the accepted procedure, were inclined to favour a vote on the preamble before the second reading, which would, if retirement of the bill followed, fix a moral taint on the Queen while securing her full legal acquittal. But he for his part was determined to 'press upon the House that it was their duty, and the necessary consequence of what they had

---

[122] Huskisson to Canning, 20 October 1820, Canning MSS. For a draft copy of the address see Add. MSS. 38760, ff. 251–2.
[123] *Canning*, pp. 308–10.

already done, to come to a Result'. On 22 October he more or less told Huskisson that the government would persist until a vote could be taken, and the Cabinet actually made a decision to this effect the following day.[124] Granville and those who had supported his intervention were forced to resign themselves to the inevitable.[125]

As it was, immediately the decision to press on to the second reading was made, the less courageous it seemed. On the same day Brougham abruptly closed the defence, ostensibly because foreign governments were preventing the procurement of witnesses; but among the peers the impression remained that his ingenuity was exhausted, and the prosecution was careful to appear correspondingly confident by calling back only one witness. Moreover, Denman's summing-up, even apart from the unlucky *faux pas* at the end—'go and sin no more'—was reckoned 'lame', attacking the government as much as the evidence, while the Attorney-General's performance was the talk of the town.[126] Not surprisingly, the ministers began to predict a fairly sizeable majority. Eldon spoke of one between forty-five and fifty, Wellesley-Pole of fifty at least and others ventured as high as sixty.[127] The actual result, then, a majority of twenty-eight, was immensely disappointing, a staggering blow which encouraged the more apprehensive within the Cabinet to speak up boldly and demand an immediate end. Of ninety-five votes against the bill, they could point out, over fifty had been cast by an unrepentant opposition and almost forty by backbench supporters of the administration.[128] Remarkably few admitted the Queen to be 'as white as the unsunned Snows', the overwhelming impression in fact being that adultery had been proved;[129] but this only emphasised that a substantial

[124] Huskisson to Lord Granville, 23 October 1820, Granville MSS., PRO. 30/29; Arbuthnot to Huskisson, 24 October [1820], Add. MSS. 38742, ff. 77–8.

[125] Lord Ellenborough made an attempt to secure a *mezzo termine* along the lines Grenville and Huskisson had suggested, but after the Cabinet's decision to press forward, further effort in this direction was bound to be fruitless. *Mrs. Arbuthnot*, i. 44; *Hobhouse*, p. 37; *Plumer Ward*, ii. 68.

[126] Arbuthnot to Huskisson, [23], 24, [25], [27], [28] October 1820, Add. MSS. 38742, ff. 58–9, 77–9, 81, 99–101, 103–4.

[127] *Plumer Ward*, ii. 69, 70, 77.   [128] Alison, iii. 220 n.

[129] Arbuthnot to Huskisson, [6 November 1820], Add. MSS. 38742, ff. 117–18; *Arbuthnot*, p. 20. Only eighteen peers signed protests to the effect that adultery had not been proved.

minority was more concerned with realities than rights. Nor were its numbers likely to dwindle. Many peers had conceivably followed Eldon's advice and simply voted on the legal facts. Hereafter, their duty as judges done, they could justifiably ignore them to save the country and appease public opinion; and the nearer the bill progressed towards the Commons the greater the temptation. When the margin in the division had been so narrow, only a handful needed to move.

As could be expected, it was the House of Commons ministers in the Cabinet who were most impressed by these considerations and most forward in urging an immediate capitulation. Castlereagh, especially, dreaded the thought of having the bill his responsibility,[130] and certainly, since no one could imagine it ever passing, to rest content with a general expression of guilt, which would excuse the Crown in the future paying the Queen the conventional marks of respect, seemed a satisfactory enough conclusion. 'She *is blasted*, & that is sufficient,' in Arbuthnot's words.[131] An equally strong party, however, was staunchly opposed to getting rid of the bill 'by any trick'.[132] These bolder spirits argued, with greater appreciation of the legal proprieties, that, the original allegation having been sustained, the ministers were not only justified in promoting inquiry in the first place but pledged to pursue the consequences until they were manifestly unattainable. To surrender from a position of strength, which was what a majority of twenty-eight could be said to represent, would seriously impair the impression of guilt, betray the course of justice for no other reason than the appeasement of public opinion, and doubtless encourage the Queen to follow up her success at the bar of the lower house. By persevering a little longer, the peers could pronounce a formal judgement on the case when the preamble came to be voted, and the divorce clause could be discarded to render the bill less objectionable. The essential difference was over what moment all the parties concerned—parliament, public opinion, the King and the Queen—would consider the case finally closed. A letter from Lord Grenville, advising withdrawal and reminding the ministers of the Queen's opportunity

---

[130] Ibid.; Arbuthnot to Huskisson, [5 November 1820], Add. MSS. 38742, ff. 113–14.   [131] *Arbuthnot*, p. 20.   [132] Ibid.

to recriminate in person before the bill went into committee, proved to be an insufficient reinforcement for Castlereagh.[133] In the end, the stout-hearted, who included Liverpool himself, prevailed, though not before there was an appeal to numbers which showed how evenly the Cabinet was divided.[134]

That the government could make up much lost ground before the vote on the third reading was by no means inconceivable. Had the Queen told her scandalous tales as she at one time intended, had the preamble been altered to satisfy the scruples of the greatest possible number and had divorce been decided purely on the merits of the case, the bill might have emerged from the committee both more desirable and eminently more acceptable. In the event rather the contrary happened. Instead of doing some muck-raking of her own, the Queen took Brougham's advice and made a show of moderation, contenting herself with a sharply worded remonstrance passed on second-hand. Then the preamble went through unamended and virtually unchallenged, which, though it advertised the prosecution's triumph yet further, was still to disturb some because of the inexplicitness of a charge of 'licentious, disgraceful and adulterous intercourse' in 'various places and countries'. Worst of all, the divorce clause, in spite of the scruples of possibly half the peers, was never jettisoned, mainly thanks to a shameless exhibition of political roughriding by the Whigs.

This last setback was fatal to the bill's chances. The government, of course, wanted to drop the clause to save the bill, and had already prepared for this eventuality by declaring it a 'collateral' part from the beginning. Originally, divorce had been included because the Crown would demean itself by having an affinity with a proven adulteress, but Lord Liverpool had defended a withdrawal as possible if the religious objections were sufficiently strong.[135] It so happened that many peers did see the bill, partly at least, as the King's personal application for relief. Thus the moment the government prepared to retreat the House could not avoid embarking on an *exposé* of the King's own conduct, Eldon applying immediately to the episcopal

---

[133] Lord Grenville to Lord Liverpool, 6 November 1820, Add. MSS. 38288, ff. 76–7.
[134] *Hobhouse*, p. 38.   [135] *Hansard*, 2nd ser., ii. 1384–5.

bench for guidance regarding the Scriptural justification for divorce contained in the passage 'whosoever shall put away his wife, saving for the cause of fornication, causeth her to commit adultery'. Those for the clause argued that Christ's words had never implied that the husband's adultery was an extenuation for the wife's, and, accordingly, that the public necessity of the case should have explicit recognition. Those against either held that matrimony was an inviolable contract in the eyes of God or that George had put away his wife a year after the marriage, divesting himself thereby of his rights under English law and entitled to no more than a legal separation in consequence.[136] With the bishops divided in their opinion—York and Canterbury on different sides—the lay peers had no certain authority to follow, though the number in favour of retaining the clause probably astonished the government. Not counting the ministers and the peers in regular opposition, all of whom had strong political motives for acting as they did, roughly sixty ayes confronted forty noes. On this occasion, therefore, the Whigs dished the Tories with rare accomplishment. Determined to murder the bill at all costs, Grey unashamedly threw sixty votes in support of divorce, and the Cabinet found itself in a minority half the size of the majority.[137] 'This may so reduce our former Majority as to make it absurd to send the Bill down to us' was Arbuthnot's hopeful comment.[138]

The slick triumph of the opposition—they 'have made the defeating of the whole a complete party question', Castlereagh complained[139]—made the decision whether to continue more difficult than ever. Much the same considerations still held good, but now with greater urgency. According to Arbuthnot, three-quarters of the Cabinet wanted to keep the bill from the

[136] Ibid., iii. 1709–26.
[137] The clause was carried 129–62 with three bishops in the majority and ten in the minority. Since Castlereagh (Alison, iii. 220 n.) calculated that the Whigs rallied 60 votes for the occasion and there were 9 ministers in the House, the rest of the lay peers divided in the proportion of approximately three to two. Of course, this does not mean that they were all conscientious votes. But, because most who voted in favour of divorce rejoined the government for the third reading, it is a fair assumption that the weight of 'independent' opinion was against the ministers.
[138] Arbuthnot to Huskisson, [8 November 1820], Add. MSS. 38742, ff. 125–6.
[139] Alison, iii. 220 n.

lower house and professed satisfaction with the affirmation of guilt gained when the preamble was passed and the report brought up without a division.[140] Even those ministers who sat in the House of Lords had no desire to see the peers condemn the Queen and the Commons acquit her; for, besides encouraging her to press her claims whenever it suited her, it was likely to give rise to an invidious distinction between the House shackled by the influence of the Crown and that responsive to popular aspirations and feeling. Lord Liverpool, nevertheless, would not be moved. It was not a sense of obligation to the King which explained his stubbornness: George, hypersentitive to public criticism, was already in a panic lest the bill reach the Commons.[141] Rather it was a carefully pondered decision, perhaps stiffened by a genuine moral repugnance which Huskisson for one fancied he detected.[142] As Liverpool saw it, the question of the Queen's conduct could not be kept from the Commons in any case; firstly, because no matter what happened an allowance had to be voted her sooner or later, and secondly, because the opposition could reopen the subject whenever they chose over the liturgy, the coronation or a demand for a palace. The wisest course was to let parliament exhaust the subject of its own accord, for then the Queen's capacity for making trouble would be severely limited and it would be difficult to argue that the government had been forced into submission by the 'Revolutionists' who had whipped up the popular frenzy. The only terms on which he was prepared to concede the bill were if the majority on the third reading was small enough to make defeat in the Commons a foregone conclusion, and after some unpleasant scenes in the Cabinet, when he completely lost command of himself, these were accepted. As had been usual throughout the trial however, the actual decision was left to him alone.[143]

More by good luck than management, since the government

---

[140] *Mrs. Arbuthnot*, i. 52.
[141] Ibid., p. 51.
[142] Huskisson to Canning, 23 October 1820, Canning MSS.
[143] *Hobhouse*, pp. 39–40; *Mrs. Arbuthnot*, i. 52; Arbuthnot to Huskisson, [9 November 1820], Add. MSS. 38742, f. 127. 'I walked to the House with Ld. L. & he was not prepared to give It up if the Majority had not come very near to the number of the Cabinet.' Same to same, [10 November 1820], ibid., f. 129.

to obtain a conscientious vote refused to divulge what had been decided,[144] the margin on the third reading was just sufficient to justify withdrawal, specifically on the ground that measures of importance were never passed on from either House if the majority was exceedingly small. Significantly enough, it was the retention of the divorce clause which made all the difference. Of the fifteen who crossed the floor or abstained after supporting the government on the second reading, twelve had opposed divorce in the committee. With this assistance the opposition vote rose to 99 and the majority slipped to nine. Only Eldon, as usual apt to see everything through legal spectacles, disdained to retreat when the Prime Minister gave the word. On the carrying of a motion putting off further consideration of the bill for six months—a way of disposing of embarrassing legislation short of outright defeat—the rest of the Cabinet could not have been more pleased. Wellington came back from the House in 'high good humour', the nervous Pole remained 'in great spirits' throughout an evening of riotous celebration, and Castlereagh heaved a sigh of relief that he did not have to superintend a measure 'in every stage of which questions spring up that shake not only the Administration, but the throne itself to its foundation'.[145] Such joy was not undeserved. The ministers had insisted that Caroline's conduct required investigation before she could be allowed the usual privileges of Queen Consort, and the accusations they had brought against her had been upheld by the House of Lords after judicial inquiry. Furthermore, they had succeeded in killing the penalising bill without appearing to have been overwhelmed by public opinion or to have totally ignored it. By persevering to the third reading, in spite of the disquiet of the 'respectable' classes and the ugly showing of the 'inferior sort', they had advertised their powers of resistance. By yielding before being actually defeated, they had made clear that they were not so oblivious of political realities as to set no limit to their defiance. It was the only possible *via media* for an executive which had a belief in its own rightness and yet a strong awareness of how the 'rise of public opinion' had altered the conditions on which power was held.

[144] *Mrs. Arbuthnot*, i. 51, 52.
[145] *Eldon*, ii. 399–400; *Plumer Ward*, ii. 93–4; Alison, iii. 220 n.

Even so, the day of rejoicing also had a sober morrow. In the first place, the 'trial', and all that had happened in consequence, had perhaps destroyed the goodwill of the King. Though he in this most personal of matters had behaved with his usual propriety, occasionally challenging but never completely rejecting the counsel his Cabinet offered, the ministers appreciated only too well the temptations which beset him in the agony of defeat. By now, pathetically conscious of his subjects' dislike, he was not unlikely to turn to the Whigs, both to ingratiate himself with the nation and to obtain revenge against those who had brought him so low at the commencement of his reign. What could not be forgotten was his great weakness, as one involved in politics, for seeing too much in terms of his personal interest. Not that public arguments to support a change of administration were lacking. George could easily attempt the experiment of 'popular rule' on the grounds of protecting the monarchy from further damage. He could even claim that by replacing the provocative boldness of the Whigs with the more diffident opposition of the Tories he was cooling party passions which were doing the country unaccountable mischief. Out of office the Whigs were driven to excite public opinion because of their meagre prospects; in it their popularity would have the effect of relieving the pressure on authority. It was too much to hope that no one around the King would whisper these things. To close the gap between people and government, which many feared was widening, would, from his point of view, indeed be a worthy enterprise.

Of course, the ministers had more valuable resources than the favour of the Court to lose. Whether the King would act against them at all, perhaps, certainly whether they would have a long tenure of the opposition benches, mostly depended on the degree of unity they maintained among themselves and the extent to which parliament and public opinion, especially 'respectable' opinion, turned against them. There was little reason for apprehension on the first count. It was true that Canning had refused to take a part against the Queen in June, but now that the 'trial' had been satisfactorily concluded the last anyone expected was his resignation. No serious differences had appeared among the other ministers. Indeed, they had been content to follow Lord Liverpool as long as the bill of pains and penalties was before the Lords. He alone had managed the proceeding in conference with the Attorney-General, and on two occasions, when the dropping of the divorce clause and passing the bill to the Commons were discussed, his opinion had prevailed against the Cabinet majority. As Wellington complained, he 'never consulted with or spoke to any of them, never wd. listen to any argument or remonstrance and took the most important steps without consulting with them'.[146] Liverpool's authority as premier, therefore, was as firm as ever, if not firmer than before. In part, no one would resist 'this tyrannical and fractious spirit' because if he went there was no obvious successor. Also his expertise on economic and financial questions seemed particularly appropriate for the times. But a toughness and fortitude in the man had also become apparent. Though this combined oddly with his social awkwardness and his highly strung temperament, it was to receive ample and increasing expression with Canning's return in 1822.

If the administration itself was well braced, parliament was a not altogether reliable foundation. That the House of Commons would take up the issue of the Queen's future situation was never really in doubt, both because an allowance had still to be voted her and because it was possible to argue her entitlement to the customary privileges on the grounds of her legal acquittal. The clash between government and opposition was most likely to occur over the second point. After failing to secure a legal condemnation, the ministers could hardly reduce the amount of the annuity they had held out to her before her 'trial'. On the other hand, they had been willing to argue that her moral guilt had been established by the Lords, and it was only consistent to have her omission from the liturgy accompanied by the withdrawal of other privileges which it was within the prerogative of the Crown to bestow. The degree of success the Whigs would enjoy, however, depended on more than their ability to convince the Commons that it was just to treat the Queen as innocent. 'Parliament men' also had to consider whether the ministers had been careless of the national interest in promoting a proceeding, and what the effect of further

[146] *Mrs. Arbuthnot*, i. 45–6. See also *Plumer Ward*, ii. 80 n.

proscription would be. Here the government was most vulnerable to the charge that it had antagonised and would continue
to antagonise the country, thereby devaluing aristocratic rule
and disturbing the whole social order. The obvious conclusion
to be drawn from such an argument was that control of the state
was better placed in the hands of the Whigs, who as the champions of popular causes in the past, could be expected to have
a greater measure of the nation's confidence.

It could not be denied that the 'trial' of the Queen had
excited public opinion and given the Radicals a renewed opportunity to work their mischief. But the question was, as it had
been all along, to what extent the old oligarchy could afford to
resist the demands of a politically interested public. Concerning
the government itself, it is probably true to say that with the
proceeding against Caroline Lord Liverpool and his colleagues
finally came to terms with the 'rise of public opinion'. The
tumultuous post-war years, when the 'lower sort' displayed their
political muscle as never before, forced on them the realisation
that they had neither the resources nor the sanction to coerce
alien opinion into silence, however much it seemed to threaten
all that they held dear. As late as 1819 their attempt in the Six
Acts to achieve a permanent regulation of public expression
showed that they were still not fully aware of the limitations of
their power. The next year it was obvious they were. 'Every
Wednesday,' wrote Creevey in the midst of the Queen's 'trial',
referring to the processions of her supporters through the
metropolis, 'the scene which caused such alarm at Manchester
is repeated under the very nose of Parliament and all the constituted authorities, and in a tenfold degree more alarming.'[147]
In addition, he might have mentioned the broadsides, squibs
and cartoons which had subjected King and ministers to constant ridicule. Never again did a Tory administration try
coercion. It was left to the Whigs to learn the same lesson in
the 1830s when they battled unavailingly against the unstamped
press. Of course, the greater the political activity of the 'lower
sort' the stronger perhaps the incentive to reach some compromise with their desires. 'Respectable' opinion was really of two
minds as soon as it encountered the phenomenon of a politically

[147] *Creevey*, p. 332.

aware populace. On the one hand, as the 'rational part of the community', it was loath to make any submission to the ignorant and prejudiced majority. On the other, it recognised the danger of resisting these demands until a point was reached where the mass of men had exhausted their satisfaction with the existing system of government. In 1820 the most the administration could do was hope that popular support for the Queen would subside and that in parliament and among the 'intelligent portion', which could influence the legislature so strongly, the necessity of proceeding against her and penalising her would have full recognition. The more disturbed the situation in the country the greater the danger that the ministers would appear a liability. As it happened, the events of 1830 were not anticipated in 1821.

Chapter Six

THE KEEPING OF THE COMMONS

I. The Closing of the Case

Not only the politicians, but the King as well, recognised
the importance of public opinion in the struggle which
loomed. Appropriately, since he had felt its lash more than
anyone, the latter betrayed the greatest concern and also the most
exaggerated notions of its influence and strength. Even before
Liverpool and Sidmouth arrived at Carlton House with news
of the bill's withdrawal, George had made up his mind that 'the
Radicals [would] work double tides to keep treason and tumult
afloat', and that the best the government could do was vote the
Queen's allowance without further delay. In his view, which his
ministers would not have disputed, the 'public opinion' that the
Radicals referred to was a commodity manufactured by the
press and other 'collateral engines' to be forced on a gullible
people. Since it could not be resisted, it had to be endured; and
he went on to argue, the shorter the agony the less the evil
which could be inflicted. Hence his haste to be done with the
Queen before the Radicals were properly organised for their
'most wicked purposes'. The sooner parliament laid the subject
to rest, the sooner, he was persuaded, the Queen would go,
securing his 'tranquillity' and the nation's.[1]

In contrast, the Cabinet did not take long to come to the conclusion that it was more advantageous to take the matter out of
parliament's hands for a time. It was never in doubt that the
Whigs would attempt to raise the country during an adjournment, because in that lay their only hope of parliamentary
success. But, as always, the danger they faced in such a course
was that they would be accused of appealing to popular passions,
making common cause with the villainous Radicals and disturbing the nation for their own selfish purposes. 'Respectable'
opinion was especially likely to turn against them if the interest

[1] *George IV*, ii. 377–8.

of the 'lower sort' in defending the honour of the Queen clearly
showed signs of abatement. It was in this respect that the
ministers' optimism far exceeded the King's. While they agreed
that opinion was artificial in the sense that it was very largely
the manufacture of a designing few, they also believed that the
efforts of these miscreants to work their wicked will mostly
depended for their success on the circumstances prevailing at
the time. In the past the periods of particular menace, when the
lower orders seemed to be mobilising against the rest of society,
had been relatively short lived. This is not to say that the
ministers would have denied that during the previous five or
six years the Radicals had acquired a hold on the public mind
which threatened more frequent and more serious trouble in the
future. But at the same time the economic causes of the post-
war disturbances were well understood. An improvement in the
economic situation, and it was manifestly improving by the end
of 1820, would make it difficult for the Radicals to repeat their
triumphs of the past; and the fact that the proceeding against
the Queen, which had created much political excitement, had
ended would frustrate them even further. They still could
summon up a power which could shudder the very foundations
of the state, but for the moment, in all likelihood, the elements
of it were lacking.

The possibility of a calmer populace after the lapse of a few
months was the primary consideration with the government. It
was not difficult for the ministers to imagine how a House of
Commons under hot siege from public opinion would eventually
conclude that the Whigs could deal more effectively with the
enemy without than they ever could. Already there were
disturbing reports that Peel's friends were hostile and Canning's
as well.[2] If the loyalties of the politicians had crumbled to this
extent with what had passed, the 'country gentlemen' could
hardly be expected to withstand a renewed assault by Radicals
out-of-doors in alliance with the Whigs. Indeed, because of the
damage that the 'trial' had inflicted, the government desperately
needed time to look to its parliamentary defences. A sitting over
the Christmas period was out of the question, for the simple
reason that attendances were certain to be adversely affected.

[2] *Croker*, i. 174; *Arbuthnot*, p. 21; *Mrs. Arbuthnot*, i. 52–3.

But in addition a concerted effort to inform backbenchers of the government's views and another to prepare for the Milan Commission and other 'collateral questions connected with the recent inquiries', questions which could be raised inasmuch as the bill of pains and penalties had not been passed or positively rejected, were obvious ways in which the ministers could make ready for what Castlereagh, only half jocularly, called 'our trial'.[3]

The Cabinet decided in favour of an immediate prorogation the day after the bill was withdrawn (11 November). Nonetheless, the King took some convincing that a continuation of the session would be of little service. Since his feelings were already known, Eldon, who was one of his favourites, was delegated the task of bringing him round at his usual Sunday audience the following morning. But much to Lord Liverpool's consternation the Lord Chancellor was able to make no impression.[4] Nor did his colleagues, who trooped in regular succession to Carlton House throughout the rest of the week, fare any better, Wellington even resorting to a confidential memorandum 'that I neither have communicated . . . nor will communicate . . . to anybody'.[5] It was Sidmouth, according to Hobhouse, the Home Office under-secretary, who eventually broke the King's resistance; but this is almost certainly an exaggeration.[6] Probably the action of the Queen herself was decisive. On the Monday of the same week (13 November) Keppel-Craven, her chamberlain, made application for a palace and establishment 'suited to the rank which she holds in the country',[7] and at once the King was warned that she intended to stay and also fight, a warning which was given additional force when Lauderdale

[3] Alison, iii. 220 n.

[4] *Arbuthnot*, p. 21; *Hobhouse*, p. 4 1.

[5] *Wellington Desp.* (new series), i. 150–3. The date of this memorandum is actually 16 November 1820. See *George IV*, ii. 380. Arbuthnot saw the King several times, Sidmouth had at least one audience, as did Liverpool and Castlereagh. *Mrs. Arbuthnot*, i. 53; *Hobhouse*, p. 41; *Courier*, 16 November 1820.

[6] *Hobhouse*, p. 41.

[7] *George IV*, ii. 380. The claim of a palace was resisted on the grounds that the Queen's guilt had been acknowledged by the House of Lords, but at the same time the government offered to assist her in finding a suitable residence. For the rest of the correspondence see Lord Liverpool to R. Keppel Craven, [15 November 1820], Add. MSS. 38288, f. 127; *George IV*, ii. 381–3.

reported 'that the violent Party in the House of Commons earnestly desire the meeting of Parliament on the 23rd'.[8] Convinced now that parliament would never do his business as quickly as he wanted, he gave the necessary authority for a prorogation early on Friday morning (17 November).[9]

However, this was not the full extent of the King's submission to his ministers. On the very day that he relented he almost sent a letter of dismissal as well,[10] and in the course of the next fortnight he was to learn that he could make an administration much less easily than he could break one. It must be supposed that thoughts of a change had been crossing his mind from the time that the government had first appeared in difficulties, but only during the trying week which followed the bill's defeat did he give the matter serious consideration. In this connection, Sir William Knighton, one of the King's physicians, was reputed by the politicians to be the *eminence grise*; the greater likelihood is that he was nothing more than a willing confidant. Among the papers at Windsor there are two memoranda in George's hand obviously written for Knighton's perusal, one on the 'Advantages supposed to be gained by a new Govt', the other on 'The Evils'. In these, the arguments for and against a change are clearly stated. As the ministers themselves realised, the greatest temptation facing the King was that the Whigs would form a popular government which would settle with the Queen as quickly as possible and also remove the grievance and disillusionment of the nation in general. 'Human nature', he observed, 'is . . . fond of change, and the difficulties attendant upon our domestick policy might perhaps for a time be lessen'd.' On the other hand, a new government would mean new measures quite as much as new men; a more liberal foreign policy in the sense of support for popular movements abroad, retrenchment perhaps carried to excess and attempts to force Catholic emancipation against the Crown's traditional Protestantism. Perhaps even worse, it would drive the King out of politics altogether, for if the Whigs proved unacceptable and the Tories refused to forgive and

[8] Ibid., p. 378.
[9] Ibid., pp. 388-9; Arbuthnot to Huskisson, 17 November [1820], Add. MSS. 38742, ff. 135-6.   [10] *George IV*, ii. 380.

forget he could not escape 'the horror and inconvenience of being shut out on all sides from any set of men'.[11] Probably George never made up his mind one way or the other. As Knighton seems to have pointed out, the first thing to find out was who among the opposition was game to try and on what terms.

Curiously, because it gave them an importance they little deserved, the Grenvilles were approached before the Whigs, most likely in the belief that such a coalition would keep the Radicals out, which was a prime consideration. About Friday, 17 November, Bloomfield had an interview with Buckingham, but the result when reported back to Carlton House left the King 'sadly puzzled'.[12] Why it is not difficult to imagine. No record of the meeting apparently exists, but if George had hopes of matching the Grenvilles and moderate Whigs, Buckingham would doubtless have dashed them with an absolute refusal of co-operation. Nothing else could be expected from one who had accused 'our Constitutional Whigs' of aiding and abetting 'the spirit of Military Revolution which now prevails all over Europe' and who saw an almost sacred duty to save the country from the Radicals.[13] This rebuff, however, by no means sent the King back to where he had started. Everyone knew Buckingham as an underling who could best be managed through his uncle, and, if application there failed, the Whigs might yet be found to be fully confident in their own resources. Personal communication with Grey proved out of the question. As soon as inquiries were made as to his whereabouts, it was discovered that he had slipped out of Town on 12 November and was on his way home to Howick.[14] Instead, the King consulted his Whig friend Donoughmore for an impression of his party's views, and had his worst fears confirmed that they would restore the Queen to the liturgy, make drastic reductions in the army and fulfil their pledge of concessions to the Catholics. Nor was the result any more encouraging when Tierney was approached for

---

[11] George IV, ii. 390–1.
[12] Lord Buckingham to Lord Grenville, 26 November 1820, Grenville MSS.; George IV, ii. 389.
[13] Lord Buckingham to Thomas Grenville, 23 July 1820, Add. MSS. 41854, ff. 71–3; same to Charles Williams-Wynn, 5 November 1820, Coed-y-maen MSS.   [14] George IV, ii. 389.

information first hand, for he simply referred all inquiries to Grey.[15]

Having found the Whigs unenthusiastic and unaccommodating, George had no other course but to heed Knighton's advice and apply to Lord Grenville at Dropmore, though it would make public his displeasure with the government and lead to speculation that a change was imminent. The pretence for the meeting, the same used to excuse the overture to Tierney, was to show Grenville, as an elder statesman, papers relating to the Captain Hesse affair in 1813 when Caroline had allegedly tried to arrange her daughter's seduction.[16] Considering that the point could never be satisfactorily proved and that the country was likely to regard the attempt more as an insult to Princess Charlotte's memory than a justification of himself,[17] the King cannot have been serious in his suggestion of a parliamentary inquiry, rather using it as a cloak to conceal his real purpose. At the same time his obvious anxiety to avoid discrediting his ministers by openly seeking their removal, showed that his object was limited to sounding the opposition. Exactly what passed at the five hour conference with Grenville remains obscure, for the King's lips were sealed and Grenville's version was that he had been summoned to advise as a disinterested party in a great public exigency.[18] Nevertheless, it is almost certain that Grenville was asked whether he would undertake to form an administration should the government collapse. Equally certain, he declined to commit himself, maintaining that he had retired from active politics though disapproving the Whig alliance with the Radicals and the government's foolhardiness where the honour and dignity of the Crown was concerned.[19] The hint here was only too apparent. Indeed, Donoughmore's caution and Tierney's reluctance amounted to the same advice. No government could be formed on the

[15] Ibid.; Mitchell, pp. 148-9.
[16] See *George IV*, i. 515-23.
[17] *Hobhouse*, p. 43; Lord Buckingham to Lord Grenville, 26 November 1820, Grenville MSS.
[18] Buckingham, *George IV*, i. 80-1.
[19] This much can be deduced from Lord Buckingham to Lord Grenville, 26 November 1820, Grenville MSS.; Lord Grenville to Charles Williams-Wynn, 27 November 1820, Coed-y-maen MSS.; *Bathurst*, p. 490; Buckingham, *George IV*, i. 80-1.

strength of Court favour alone, only on the presumption of an assured majority in the House of Commons, which in turn could be reckoned an expression of confidence from the country at large. The Whigs did not palpably have such confidence. Neither did the Grenvilles nor any combination of which they might form the nucleus. Parliament was the great decider, and until the government was brought to its knees there or collapsed of its own accord, a discussion to settle the succession was of no point whatever. 'My sense of duty to Him', wrote Grenville of the King, 'must prevent [me doing it] under circumstances in which I know with certainty that my efforts could be of no use to Him'.[20]

As was to be expected, the ministers regarded these rustlings behind the curtain with some alarm, though Lord Liverpool knew of Grenville's tête-à-tête before it occurred and no one thought anything serious would come of it.[21] The King, of course, considered that he could consult whom he pleased, and to the extent that Leach, Knighton and others were allowed to be his confidants the government did not disagree. But with Grenville the case was vastly different both from the point of view of his standing in the world and the administration's situation. As Arbuthnot bluntly put it to Sir Benjamin Bloomfield: 'the King is breaking down the strength of his Government by sending at this moment for men of great political consequence who do not belong to it'.[22] He may have had the right, but he was exercising it in a manner which suggested that the ministers had been deprived of his full confidence. Still, this much was hardly worth worrying about. What the government really had to guard against was a situation where the expression of public opinion in the Queen's favour became strong enough to lead to defeat in parliament, when the King could not be stopped from sending for either Grenville or Grey. Already there was plenty afoot to show that this was the strategy the Whigs intended to follow. Indeed, they could storm the Closet no other way. By the beginning of December Grey was heart and soul behind the

[20] Lord Grenville to Williams-Wynn, 27 November 1820, Coed-y-maen MSS.
[21] Canning to Mrs Canning, 28 November 1820, Canning MSS.; Arbuthnot to Herries, [28 November 1820], Herries MSS.
[22] *Bathurst*, p. 490.

idea of county meetings; Tierney and Holland were busy giving encouragement and advice from London; and an address voted by the City's Common Council had set an example for the rest of the nation. If parliament was not going to be overawed by the sheer magnitude of the protest, somehow a counter-opinion had to be organised.

The administration itself could do little to create expressions in its favour, and in fact even that little was hampered by its reluctance to make any appeal to the people because, however necessary it was politically, it violated the notion of an executive above the people. With the press, its main means of educating opinion, an obvious difficulty was lack of money. As one historian has pointed out, the whole of the secret service fund, out of which subsidies to the press were paid, could not have bought a second-class London newspaper.[23] Moreover, the little money that was made available went to papers which supported the government less from interest than inclination, and every Treasury Secretary, whose duty it was to disburse the largesse, had to learn to cope with the occasional spasms of independence which were the inevitable result. The irresolvable problem was that those papers which would have gladly prostituted themselves had no value because they had no circulation, and, conversely, successful papers were profitable enough to do without these payments. 'The truth is', Lord Liverpool once said, 'they look only to their sale. They make their way like sycophants with the public, by finding out the prejudices and prepossessions of the moment, and then flattering them; and the number of *soi-disant* Government or Opposition papers abound just as the Government is generally popular or unpopular.'[24] Friendly editors, then, were what the ministers relied on most, and in 1820 in this respect they were able to count themselves fortunate. Both the *Courier*, which once or twice before had wavered, and the more virulent *New Times* remained loyal, but of greater service than either was the weekly *John Bull* established 'without aid or patronage' by Theodore Hook in December 1820. Gossipy, at times downright abusive, this paper met the Radicals on their own ground of public

[23] Aspinall, *Politics and the Press, 1780–1850*, p. 373.
[24] *Castlereagh*, xi. 17.

house journalism, so much so that by the April following it had a circulation of 9,000, 'more than any Sunday paper that ever was known'. Mrs. Arbuthnot's mixed reaction of approbation and censure cannot have been untypical: 'It is a most ably written paper, has done more towards putting down the Queen than anything, but certainly has been wrong in attacking the characters of women.'[25] Significant above all else, the achievement was Hook's alone. True, the government made some effort to influence opinion, producing pamphlets under the eye of the law officers, printing and publishing notable speeches in the Lords and recommending articles in the London dailies to friendly provincial editors.[26] But this by itself could do little to overcome the superiority of 'the Old Times and other wicked journals'. Newspapers had to be fought with newspapers, as Harrison of the Treasury realised when he suggested a weekly or twice weekly 'Collectanea' comprising 'a judicious selection of the best-written papers which have appeared in the daily journals'.[27] The very measure of Hook's services was the government's inability to do the like.

If the ministers relied on friends in the press world, they also relied on friends in the country, for declarations of support could no more be organised from Whitehall than could a newspaper offensive. Here the government's weakness was simply its unpopularity. To be sure, the 'rational part of the community' continued loyal in the main, but at meetings where 'respectability' was overwhelmed by sheer weight of numbers this could never find a proper expression. Rather than be outvoted, giving their opponents even greater cause for triumph, the Tory gentry were happier staying away. Plumer Ward's strictures on the subject bespoke their feelings exactly:

> I told him [Wellesley-Pole] that as to addresses they had lost all their force, and as a mode of expressing the real public opinion had become even ridiculous. They were carried by force, by the introduction of mobs and people who were not what the titles of the addresses called them; that the majority of people staid

[25] *Mrs Arbuthnot*, i. 89. Note also Lord Lowther's comment that *John Bull* was read in all the public houses. Aspinall, *Politics and the Press, 1780–1850*, p. 29.   [26] *Bathurst*, p. 489.
[27] George Harrison to Lord Liverpool, 30 November 1820, Add. MSS. 38288, f. 221.

at home from fear of turbulence, so that it had now become a contest between meetings usurping a corporate name and the opinions of individuals. We were not bound literally or morally to consider such addresses, under leaders, whether Whigs or Radicals, whose arts and sometimes whose downright false-hoods were well known.[28]

Nevertheless, to say that 'those meetings in which clamour and confusion prevailed . . . did not convey a correct expression of public opinion' was to resort to a platitude which had less and less relevance.[29] The Whigs knew and the ministers knew that numbers as well as 'respectability' had become a weight in the political balance; that if the Queen's friends and the govern-ment's enemies were allowed to conquer the country un-opposed, parliament itself might shortly succumb. Harrowby, for one, admitted as much when he prayed for a quiet recess in order 'that Parliament, meeting under the influence of no exter-nal intimidation, will freely & indifferently exercise its own judgement'.[30] For the Whigs this meant meetings wherever possible, and before long Brougham was up to his old tricks circularising the boroughs.[31] For the ministers it meant demon-strations of support elsewhere than on the platform, or rather elsewhere whenever there was there a definite risk of defeat. Of course, their role was necessarily limited. The persons who could best assess the local situation were obviously those on the spot, and, apart from publicising successes in the *Gazette* and other friendly newspapers, there was little that the government could do beyond giving advice when advice was asked for. Certainly, there were a number of moves which could be played. A Whig requisition could be met by a counter-requisition of even greater 'respectability'; a 'loyal' address could be circulated exclusively among the government's friends; a body like the grand jury could claim to speak on the county's behalf or a signed protest could take the sting out of defeat at a public meeting. The importance of these stratagems to let property have a proper influence cannot be over-estimated. Of

[28] *Plumer Ward*, ii. 72–3.
[29] Lord Liverpool in the House of Lords, 25 January 1821, *Hansard*, 2nd ser., iv. 113.
[30] Lord Harrowby to [Thomas Lister], 14 December 1820, Harrowby MSS. 17, ff. 76–9.   [31] *George IV*, ii. 400.

the sixteen county meetings which were held, not all with the leave of the sheriff, the government's friends managed to carry only two, and then only because the chairmen showed a notorious partiality for their side.[32] Notwithstanding, by the time that parliament reassembled at the end of January the Home Office had acknowledged receiving almost 450 addresses, over 300 of which had been acceptable enough to be printed in the *Gazette* in weekly instalments.[33] Virtually every town of any size had sent a declaration of loyalty bewailing the licentiousness of the times, and most of the counties where the Whigs had been successful sooner or later returned counter-addresses. An important task had been done. It had been demonstrated that public opinion was divided, and that, if anything, the government's following more than made up in 'respectability' whatever it lacked in numbers. With such a testimony of support from the country, Harrowby's prayer that parliament would exercise its judgement 'freely and indifferently' was closer to being answered.

However successful this skirmishing in the provinces, it was, after all, a pitched battle at Westminster which was going to decide the government's fate, and quite early on, much earlier than usual, Castlereagh and the Treasury began their recruiting by sending out the customary circular and some private letters, where the importance of the individual demanded it. All were much alike, a summary of what the government intended to propose in the forthcoming session, and an invitation to the recipient, and any friends he cared to consult, to tender an opinion. The Queen, they were told, was to have a provision 'Suitable to Her Rank & Station' with no conditions attached, but neither 'a Royal Residence' nor mention in the liturgy, her guilt having been irrevocably established in the House of Lords.[34] That the government had guessed the feelings of the

---

[32] At the Cheshire meeting on 11 January 1821 Lord Grosvenor moved an amendment, but the sheriff ruled that it could not be put and declared the Tory address carried on a show of hands. Much the same had happened at Shropshire the day before, where the meeting was also evenly divided and the sheriff's decision disputed. *Courier*, 12, 13 January 1821; *The Times*, 13, 15, 16 January 1821.

[33] See HO 43/30; *London Gazette*, 18 November 1820–23 January 1821.

[34] Castlereagh's circular, 5 December 1820, Sidmouth MSS.; *Liverpool*, iii. 111–14.

'country gentlemen' aright was shown by the replies. Everyone
agreed, except Wilberforce—no opinion could be extracted
from him—that the nation's moral character required some such
reproach as the ministers suggested, at the same time conceding
to the Queen full and free possession of her legal rights. What
dissent there was came from those who viewed her allowance
as a subsidy for revolution, which matter the Cabinet was quite
prepared to leave to parliament's discretion anyway.[35] After
these promises of support, Liverpool was sure that the liturgy
question would be less troublesome than he had anticipated,[36]
and Arbuthnot's joy was completely undisguised:

> ... the letters from our Chief County Members [he told Herries]
> are without exception so stout & so friendly that I defy the
> Whigs to hurt us. Greatly shall I be mistaken if we don't triumph.
> For the letters to me & to others come from opposite parts of the
> Country. The Irish are all right as Grant informs Ld Cast[le-
> reagh], Ld Melville hears from Scotland that the *Scotch blood
> is up* for us. Acland writes that we deserve to be kicked if we do
> more than we announce as intended—Admiral Sotheron—
> Wodehouse—Gooch—Wortley—Cartwright—Lord Clive—and
> several others (for we only wrote to the leading) have expressed
> themselves breast high with us. ... I do assure you that I never
> was in so high Spirits during the whole Course of the Proceed-
> ings as I am at this present.[37]

At last a way beckoned out of the *mêlée* which would finally settle
the issue. In the past it could have been argued that in dispatching
the Milan Commission and in omitting the Queen's name from
the liturgy, the government had taken too much account of the
King's sensibilities and too little of the people's.[38] Now those
mistakes could be conveniently overlooked. No longer was the
Queen being refused marks of honour on the ill-fame of common report but on the fact of her adultery as proved by the
House of Lords. Therefore there could be a minimum of awkwardness in any 'country gentleman' voting with the government and against his former misgivings.[39] In stating their terms

[35] Ibid., pp. 114–19.   [36] *Arbuthnot*, p. 22.
[37] Arbuthnot to Herries, [?27 December 1820], Herries MSS.
[38] See Stuart-Wortley's letter, *Liverpool*, iii. 114–19.
[39] Lord Harrowby to Lord Sandon, 10 January 1821, Harrowby MSS.
59, ff. 111–12.

the ministers planted a banner around which they could only fight or fall, but it was a banner which a majority of the House of Commons apparently still held dear. With the Queen's popularity seemingly on the wane, the partialities of parliament could have preference over those of the people, and the blunders of the ministers could be overlooked by the greater evil perpetrated by the Whigs in making common cause with the Radicals.

When all was said and done, probably the government's greatest weakness was itself. The common people might be losing interest in the Queen, Arbuthnot might dance with glee when he opened his post-bag, and yet it had to be remembered that parliament only helped those ministers who also helped themselves. As Croker said: 'though good speeches do not perhaps get many votes, they prevent many shy votes going away . . . a Government cannot go on without the gift of the gab'.[40] Any administration which appeared to drift helplessly, unable to make effective reply to the broadsides of the opposition, could keep no one's confidence. In this respect Canning's return in 1816 had been crucial. Whatever the qualities of Castlereagh's oratory, which was pedestrian most of the time, and whatever the talent of the up and coming young men, without Canning the government in the Commons would have been poorly served indeed: Vansittart had no power of general debate, Robinson spoke no more than he had to, and Pole and Bragge-Bathurst were quite unable to command an audience. Almost invariably, Castlereagh led off with a speech of solid sense, a few others dutifully delivered their lines and at 'the pinching time' Canning arrived with a flurry of words to restore the balance of debate. Plumer Ward's comment, made during the Queen's trial, that while he was away the ministerial bench 'seemed like victims', said everything.[41] When the opposition was preparing a massive parliamentary offensive, his resignation was one which the government could least afford.

That he did not mean to resign when he arrived back from his enforced Continental vacation passes without question. The day after his return he went out to Coombe Wood to stay with

[40] *Croker*, i. 184.
[41] *Plumer Ward*, ii. 63.

Liverpool, and it was only then that he learnt that his colleagues intended to declare the Queen guilty and act out the consequences by refusing her a palace and inclusion in the liturgy. This he never had condoned and never would. From the start he had faithfully abided by the principle that the Queen was innocent until proved guilty. The previous February his public reasons for supporting her exclusion from the liturgy were not that she stood accused but that such exclusion would form a necessary part of any amicable arrangement. In October, when he saw the bill against her creeping to inevitable defeat, he was equally insistent that 'a public inquiry once instituted, the result must be, if not condemnation, acquittal, and acquittal with all its benefits'.[42] To his way of thinking, what the government was now trying to do was 'act upon the *impression* of guilt, independently of actual conviction'. That this was unjust followed from the bill's withdrawal, for a legal acquittal, which was what withdrawal amounted to, entitled the Queen to be treated as innocent. Or in another sense, inasmuch as parliament had been trying her and not the House of Lords, only part of the court had delivered its verdict. Because the Commons, by the very act of government, had been deprived of the opportunity of passing judgement on the case, it was there that the assertion of guilt would naturally be challenged. Thus, instead of peace and quiet, the ministers had obligingly provided the Whigs with a rod for their own chastisement. 'It would but have been one gulp more, after withdrawing the Bill', Canning told his wife, 'to give to that withdrawal all its legitimate consequences. If they had restored her to the Liturgy in the next Gazette & offered her Hampton Court for a residence, & declared their willingness to propose an Establishment for her on the meeting of Parlt, I will answer for it that by this time She would have been packing-up for Pesaro. As it is, they have just broken off the thorn at the skin, and left the little point of it rankling in the wound.'[43]

Here then, on the question of the Queen's continued proscription, he parted company with the rest of the Cabinet. As soon

[42] *Canning*, pp. 274, 305.
[43] Canning to Mrs Canning, 28 November 1820, Canning MSS. See also same to same, 21, 24 November 1820, ibid.; Canning to Lord Liverpool, 14–16 January 1821, Add. MSS. 38193, ff. 143–151.

as he learned the decision made in his absence, he was convinced that the difference was irreconcilable, wholly because
his parliamentary position became altogether untenable. Having
once refused to penalise the Queen whilst she was incurring
moral censure, he could hardly sanction it now when she had
won legal acquittal. Even worse, the government's decision
made it incumbent on him to discuss the question of guilt and
innocence, which past events and his pledge of neutrality would
never allow. Much to his dismay, he saw himself as a minister
who could serve no one, speechless when his colleagues came
under attack and encouraging the onslaught by his very silence.

Nevertheless, he did not tender his resignation immediately.
Three weeks in fact were to pass before his abdication was
finally decided, three weeks during which his own strict notions
of what was right combatted the Prime Minister's reproaches
and an unashamed liking for prominence and power. Perhaps,
more brutally, it was a matter of money and a matter of principle. Because he could not make a show of agreement with the
rest of the Cabinet, he felt bound to resign; but for him politics
was more than an occupation, and being out of office was a
luxury he could less and less afford. Except for a small sinecure
in the Alienation Office and an unreliable income from two
trifling estates, he had nothing, and in the political world,
though nowhere else, the fact was notorious that ministers often
left office much poorer than when they came in.[44] Until now,
it was true, his wife's fortune had largely financed his career,
but, with children and old-age to provide for, Canning was
increasingly loath to live off this capital. More than anything
else, it was his pecuniary embarrassment which attracted him
to India where he fancied he could clear fifteen thousand a
year, endow his family with the proceeds and live in comfort to
the end of his days. From about the end of 1819, impatient to
make up the ground lost seven years before, he had been carefully weighing the alternatives of office and oriental retreat. In
January 1820 he had actually told Liverpool that promotion and
the lead in the House of Commons were the price of his staying

[44] See his letter to his wife, [November 1821], Canning MSS., where he
estimates his net income as £1,500 per annum. A note on Canning's financial
position throughout his career is to be found in Arthur Aspinall, *The
Formation of Canning's Ministry*, pp. lv–lvii.

on in a new parliament.[45] As it happened, George III's death a few days later had made this ultimatum unenforceable; there was no time to arrange Hastings' recall, Castlereagh's attitude remained unknown and Sidmouth, whose office was designated for Canning, could hardly have been shifted on pure speculation. Throughout the year Canning's position had remained uncertain in the extreme. Hastings had seemed content to stay on at Calcutta indefinitely and, mindful of Portland's monumental blunder in 1809, Liverpool had not dared to say a word to Castlereagh of reshuffles and retirement. As Canning had soon realised, the best he could do was stay quiet until an opportunity arose when he could use the natural influence of his office to secure the Indian succession.[46] The alternative was so unlikely as to be not worth bargaining on. Though Lord Liverpool had obligingly arranged his retention in office in June, and, true to his word, had offered Canning first refusal of the Home Office if Sidmouth quitted,[47] the awkwardness remained that he would still be Castlereagh's lieutenant, that the job was not to his taste and that his Liverpool friends would be subjected to their fifth contest in eight or nine years. Either way, to leave the Board of Control was to invite 'total and permanent exclusion from power'. If, by some remote chance, Castlereagh was removed from the scene, letting him take 'the full inheritance' or a near equivalent, there could be no guarantee that his erstwhile colleagues would have him back; and, when Hastings at last ventured home, if he were in an unofficial situation he could not so easily pull the strings that would assist him to secure appointment in his stead. On this occasion, it seemed, honour and ambition could never be reconciled. Canning had to choose which of two gods to serve.

In the dilemma which faced him, perhaps Canning's only consolation was the constancy of Liverpool's friendship; for if anyone could shift Hastings or arrange another comeback for him, like that of 1816, it was the Prime Minister. Needless to say, the prospect of Canning's resignation, when the government could soon be fighting for its life in the Commons, filled

[45] Canning to Mrs Canning, 28 January 1820, Canning MSS.
[46] Canning to Mrs Canning, 6, 15, 20 February, 6 April 1820, ibid.
[47] *Canning*, pp. 294-5.

Liverpool with dismay, and it was not long before entreaties to
ponder the matter carefully materialised into an invitation to
Walmer for 'a long & thorough talk'. This took place on 7
December, after Canning and his friend, Charles Ellis, who also
happened to be Liverpool's nephew, had spent three days
waiting for their nervous host to summon up sufficient courage
to broach the subject.[48] Even before the tête-à-tête, Canning
had made up his mind that he would withdraw abroad rather
than affirm the Queen's guilt by participating in the parliamentary discussions. The only question, therefore, on which he was
open to conviction was whether or not resignation should
accompany his neutral stand.[49] Naturally enough, the Prime
Minister thought it quite unnecessary. He indeed came to
Walmer with a strong suspicion that Canning was looking 'to
his private advantage', so sure was he that he was using his
personal difficulties as an excuse to 'gain a certain degree of
popularity as a friend to the Queen & . . . turn up in a new
Government something higher than a President of the Board
of Control'.[50] As Canning wrote to his wife, referring to the
expected motion on the liturgy: 'L. hopes it will be the only
one—& on that ground has persuaded himself to believe that
I might very well take part with the Govt for that once—&
there an end. But I cannot & will not, *if* it were the only motion
—for the argument against it can only be sustained by affirming
guilt, which I will not do. But further—he is quite mistaken as
to the *onliness*. There will be a dozen field-days—& if I were in
the H[ouse], a Minister, there would be fifty.'[51] At Walmer
Canning was at least successful in convincing his chief that his
intentions were honourable, that if he did go he went from 'the
awkwardness of his own situation, personally' and not 'from any
difference of opinion'.[52] 'Absence either abroad or at home is
acknowledged to be my course till this sad business is over' was
how he summed up a two hour deliberation on the beach. As
for his resignation, that was left undecided, for the moment
anyway. Liverpool had fond hopes that he might continue a

[48] Canning to Mrs Canning, 1, 7 December 1820, Canning MSS.
[49] Canning to Mrs Canning, 28 November 1820, ibid.
[50] *Mrs Arbuthnot*, i. 55.
[51] Canning to Mrs Canning, 1 December 1820, Canning MSS.
[52] *Arbuthnot*, pp. 21–2.

minister *in absentia*, and Canning, anxious to be as accom-modating as possible, agreed to hold his hand. No sooner had this been settled, however, than Charles Ellis persuaded his uncle to think again before sounding the King. As Canning was well aware, and no doubt it was one reason why he brought him along, Ellis could say things he never could, and a few words behind closed doors after the morning beach walk more or less convinced Liverpool that Canning's going was unavoidable.[53] Certainly, on his return to London, the Prime Minister told Arbuthnot that the matter was virtually decided, and Canning came away with the distinct impression that he was 'acquiescent' as well.[54]

Now, if never before, the full measure of Liverpool's partiality for Canning became plainly apparent. As soon as he realised that he and the Cabinet were in hopeless disagreement, Canning's first concern was to avoid the mistake he had made in 1812 when he had been forced into the wilderness with no prospect of succour except from the mercy of those he had offended. 'No purpose,' he told Lord Binning, defending his resignation, 'is more fixed in my mind than that of not getting again into the difficulties & responsibilities which attended my last retirement from office. I will have no connexion or con-federacy. I will bind myself to nobody; & will on no account allow any one to bind themselves avowedly or implicitly to me. . . .'[55] Lord Titchfield, his wife's brother-in-law, gave him great offence by speaking 'the language of 1809'—open opposi-tion, the overthrow of the government, '& coming in again with things all my own way'.[56] Convinced that as usual the 'country gentlemen' would come to the government's rescue, he would have none of it.[57] Indeed, the probability that the Whigs would be beaten off encouraged his going out, for then his colleagues would have no cause to complain, and to keep on amicable terms with them was the crux of his future position. Long before he went to Walmer, he determined that his ostensible reasons for resigning would refer only to the personal difficulties in the

[53] Canning to Mrs Canning, 7, 12 December 1820, Canning MSS.
[54] *Arbuthnot*, p. 22; Canning's diary, 7 December 1820, Canning MSS.
[55] Canning to Lord Binning, 28 December 1820, ibid.
[56] Canning to Mrs Canning, 12 December 1820, ibid.
[57] Canning to Mrs Canning, 1 December 1820, ibid.

way of his staying on; there would be no mention of the difference over policy. Ideally, of course, and he had done it before, he would have brought the whole Cabinet round; but there was little chance of that this time when the ministers had already acknowledged the Queen as guilty in refusing her a palace. In these circumstances the less he said the better. Six days before he set off for Walmer he told his wife: '. . . it is better to say no more of my difference of opinion than may be necessary (& that is already done) to make it plain to the K[ing] & to my Colleagues:—but to assign it as a ground of separation would be to impose upon myself the duty of maintaining it afterwards in P[arliamen]t and *that* would be an unnecessary, & I am satisfied, a most unwise deviation from the line of neutrality which I adopted & declared in the first instance, & to which I have hitherto strictly adhered.'[58]

The Prime Minister's great fairness in Canning's eyes was his readiness to assist in this course once resignation had been decided. It was Liverpool himself who suggested a circular letter to his colleagues comprising 'a simple statement of motive and declaration of goodwill', and he too who scrutinised the drafts of both this and the communication to the King.[59] Together the two letters made an apt summary of Canning's position. Lest his fellow ministers should misinterpret his motives as hostile, there was a strong reassurance that he acted 'solely from a sense of the increased difficulty of his personal position, and of the inconveniences which his continuance in office under that increased difficulty must entail upon his colleagues. . . .' Lest they should regard him as a political misfit who could never be safely readmitted to office, there was a neat reminder of their agreement upon 'general principles of policy, internal and external'.[60] Whether he was believed was something he could never know until his political worth was again put to the test. Sidmouth, who had no reason to love him, replied with a brief note of 'extreme regret', but the rest of the Cabinet seemed coldly indifferent, only Wellington mentioning the matter at the last meeting he attended. Castlereagh, to all

[58] Canning to Mrs Canning, 28 November 1820, ibid.
[59] Canning to Mrs Canning, 12 December 1820, ibid.; *Canning*, p. 315.
[60] See ibid., pp. 315–18.

appearances, had to be prompted by Arbuthnot into writing an acknowledgment a week after the box had been round.[61] Still, Canning had no illusions about what he had done. 'The step, therefore, is taken,' he wrote, forwarding his letters of resignation to his wife. 'It is an unavoidable one: but it is a fearful one—for I take it purely to avoid evil—not in the hope of good. My position in the H of C would have been intolerable: but what will be the result of my moving from it unless total and permanent exclusion from power, I do not know. However my judgment & conscience are alike convinced that I have done right—the rest must follow as it may....'[62]

To fill the vacancy created by Canning's departure, the government obviously had to turn to Peel. Of all the promising young men on the Tory side, no one else could match his administrative capability and experience or his talent in the House of Commons, though in the latter respect he fell far short of Canning's 'glittering' eloquence and the drubbing Brougham had given him over the charities inquiry was still a parliamentary memory. In addition, only he had the beginnings of a political retinue, which meant that his accession to high office would also cement the allegiance of an impressive body of ministerial supporters, in his case the Irish members and 'Protestants' in general. 'It is perfectly true,' wrote Williams-Wynn, probably speaking for those not Peel's immediate acquaintances, 'that his irritability & a certain degree of arrogance which the want of family & connection renders less tolerable, have during the last two years rendered the House (particularly the ministerial men) less favourably disposed to him, but still he combines advantages of general character in the country, of talents & habits of business which altogether place him higher than any other man in the House.'[63] Since he was the obvious choice, why Liverpool, Wellington and Bathurst went off to Stratfield Saye two days after Canning's resignation remains something of a mystery. Possibly it was an innocent house party—the Bathursts for certain had invited themselves

[61] Ibid., p. 318; Canning to Huskisson, 12 December 1820, Add. MSS. 38742, f. 145; Canning to Mrs. Canning, 15, 20 December 1820, Canning MSS.   [62] Canning to Mrs. Canning, 12 December 1820, ibid.

[63] Charles Williams-Wynn to Lord Grenville, 26 December 1820, Coedy-maen MSS. See also Buckingham, *George IV*, i. 102–3.

there sometime before.[64] Possibly Vansittart's offer to exchange the Exchequer for the Board of Control was causing some reflection.[65] Possibly the Prime Minister had wind of Peel's disapproval of the government's proceedings, and therefore thought had to be given to the alternatives.[66] It is even conceivable that he did not mean to replace Canning at all, but ride out the storm, which to his mind would be brief, with reduced numbers and bring him back immediately.

Certainly, when he did make Peel an offer on his return from Stratfield Saye, he never acted like a premier at his wit's end for parliamentary assistance, merely sympathising with him that his disapproval of the Queen's original proscription made it impossible for him to take an active part on the government's behalf. Sidmouth remained convinced that Liverpool might have tried harder, presumably because Peel refused to take 'a hostile part' and hinted that another offer of office might not be unacceptable in the near future.[67] Moreover, after this first rebuff, Liverpool appeared to show even less enthusiasm for seeking a replacement. No doubt the main explanation for his attitude was that assurances of support had begun to come in from the 'country gentlemen', which made the government's first fears seem greatly exaggerated. At the same time it must have dawned on every member of the Cabinet that no outsider would take office to defend measures not of his advice nor of his responsibility. But there was still a notable reluctance to lock the door on Canning altogether. After Peel had politely demurred, Castlereagh favoured an approach to the Grenvilles short of a definite offer, but the Prime Minister countered the suggestion immediately with a proposal that Bragge-Bathurst should take over the India Board on a *pro tempore* basis in anticipation of a general reshuffle.[68] As he explained to Bragge-Bathurst, trying to cajole him into acceptance: '. . . the best

[64] *Bathurst*, p. 489.   [65] *Hobhouse*, p. 45.

[66] Canning knew of Peel's reservations, having discussed the subject with him in Paris during the Queen's trial. 'He is clearly against the Bill', he wrote in his diary, '& thinks as I do that there is no alternative but acquittal. Surely he cannot take Office, if I should go out.' Canning's diary, 31 October 1820, Canning MSS. Whether he told Liverpool this is a moot point.

[67] *Hobhouse*, p. 45. Accounts of the interview on 18 December 1820 are in Add. MSS. 40304, ff. 4–5 and *Bathurst*, pp. 490–1. The version of Peel's memorandum printed in *Peel*, i. 298 contains some slight verbal errors.

[68] *Bathurst*, p. 491.

course appeared to be to make a temporary Arrangement which would give an opportunity of strengthening the Govt after the Conflict was over, for I need not impress upon you what the Difficulties of the Government will be, if in addition to the Whigs & the Radicals, they are occasionally to be exposed to a cross-fire from Mr Canning, Mr Peel, & the Grenville Connexion.' 'If the Government is to remain,' he went on, 'something must be done sooner or later to strengthen it, & it appeared to be inexpedient to put out of our Power so important an Office as that which is now Vacant.'[69] Almost certainly, the place he looked to Canning to fill was Sidmouth's, which was one step towards the inheritance he had claimed at the beginning of 1820. From time to time the Home Secretary had hazily mentioned his retirement as soon as 'a happy change in the internal state of the country' occurred, and Liverpool probably now saw the Coronation in July 1821 as good an opportunity as any.[70] What made it even more desirable to delay matters was the possibility that Castlereagh would not be unwilling to retire to the Lords when his fast-ailing father died and he succeeded to the marquisate, for then Canning could be ideally provided for.[71] A patch now could allow a complete refit in the space of a few months. Little wonder that Bragge-Bathurst was bullied into compliance despite his pleas that he knew nothing of India, that a temporary President was needless and that the cry for 'reform & consolidation' would only be strengthened by having two offices in one minister.[72]

[69] Lord Liverpool to Charles Bragge-Bathurst, 29 December 1820, Add. MSS. 38288, ff. 386–7.

[70] *Sidmouth*, iii. 353. In March 1820 Liverpool told Canning that Sidmouth might vacate his office after the Coronation in August. Canning to Mrs Canning, 6 April 1820, Canning MSS. However, in July 1820 the ceremony was postponed for another year.

[71] Liverpool and Canning discussed this possibility in January 1820. Canning to Mrs Canning, 28 January 1820, ibid. Only a few days after Bragge-Bathurst accepted the India Board there came news that Castlereagh's father had suffered a severe lapse which eventually led to his death in April 1821. Canning to Mrs Canning, 5 January 1821, ibid.; *The Times*, 9 January 1821. Irish peers did not sit in the Commons for Irish constituencies.

[72] For the wrangle over Bragge-Bathurst's appointment see Sidmouth to Bragge-Bathurst, 20 December 1820, Bragge-Bathurst to Sidmouth, 22 December 1820, Sidmouth to Bragge-Bathurst, 25 December 1820, Liverpool to Sidmouth, 25 December 1820, Sidmouth to Bragge-Bathurst, 26, 27 December 1820, Bragge-Bathurst to Sidmouth, 28 December 1820, Sidmouth to Bragge-Bathurst, 2 January 1821, Sidmouth MSS.; Liverpool

The loss of Canning and the failure to recruit Peel did little
to shake the government's confidence that it would survive the
parliamentary ordeal which awaited it. Arbuthnot, who had
been particularly gloomy about its chances, was soon reporting
that Canning's defection had made 'little sensation', and though
Croker's claim that the Treasury Bench had 'not one man in the
house who can speak so as to command attention' had an element of truth, the stout assurances of 'country gentlemen' less
and less inhibited by a popular outcry more than made up for
this weakness on the floor.[73] One observer saw the coming
struggle as a contest between the influence of the Crown aided
by 'the old tory feeling' and public opinion with 'a most decided
superiority of parliamentary talent'—which was probably an
accurate enough generalisation.[74] The Whig's great weakness
was that their public opinion never looked like overawing the
House of Commons. Eldon, soon after the proceeding in the
Lords had concluded, had prophesied that 'this thing . . . will
probably die away like all other nine days' wonders'.[75] So it
turned out. Though nearly every town in the kingdom had
celebrated the Queen's triumph, though she continued to hold
mock court at Brandenburgh House throughout the recess, by
the time parliament reassembled neither her concerns nor her
consortings won the same attention that they had done a few
weeks earlier. Even before the New Year Arbuthnot found the
subject 'become very stale' in the country, noticing a difference
after a mere fortnight's absence, and in the City Hobhouse was
pleased to note the white cockades disappearing from the
streets and hurrahs for the King at the state opening of parliament.[76] In these circumstances, that the 'country gentlemen'
would hold stout seemed a foregone conclusion. By making
party with the Radicals, the Whigs were again guilty of abetting
the destruction of the settled order of things, and, since there
was little fear of reprisals from the country at large, they could
expect scant mercy at the hands of the Commons. 'When the

---

to Bragge-Bathurst, 29 December 1820, Add. MSS. 38288, ff. 386–8;
George IV, ii. 400–1.
    [73] *Mrs Arbuthnot*, i. 56–7, 60; *Croker*, i. 184.
    [74] *Letters of the Earl of Dudley*, p. 272.   [75] *Eldon*, ii. 400.
    [76] Arbuthnot to Lord Liverpool, 26 December 1820, Add. MSS. 38574,
f. 233; *Hobhouse*, p. 47 and n. 2.

House sees clearly that the option must be taken between these united powers and us,' wrote Harrowby hopefully, 'I am inclined to think they will not desert us, even upon a point where they may think we erred.'[77]

This test of continuing confidence soon took place. When the King went down to Westminster in person and mentioned the Queen's name and 'new arrangements' regarding her annuity, it was a sign to the world that the ministers intended no further incrimination and full acknowledgement of her legal position. Once this much was known the opposition's scope was limited to urging conferment of the usual privileges and harking back to the mistakes of the past. In each case the debate promised to centre on the liturgy question. The granting of a palace was no dubious royal prerogative: the discretionary authority of the King-in-Council to alter the prayer for the royal family distinctly was. The Milan Commission, as an act of ministerial vindictiveness, could be explored only by raking through the evidence already heard before the Lords: to make the omission from the liturgy appear the root cause of present discontents, there was no need to go beyond the failure of the negotiations in June 1820. Even the ministers helped shape the strategy of their opponents. By letting it be known, from the moment that parliament was prorogued, that they would stand or fall on this one question, they encouraged the Whigs, and indeed everyone, to look here for the culmination of the struggle. What Brougham twelve months before had dismissed as a 'trifle light as air' now became an issue which would decide the government's existence. On the first day of the session, Lord Archibald Hamilton gave notice of a motion on the subject and a dissident Tory lawyer moved for the relevant papers.

Up to the first real trial of strength nothing occurred to upset the portents of success, which government men interpreted rather moderately in terms of a seventy or eighty majority.[78] Before the Speech had even been read, Castlereagh was forced to oppose the production of papers on procedural grounds, and

[77] Lord Harrowby to Lord Sandon, 10 January 1821, Harrowby MSS., 59, ff. 111–12.
[78] Buckingham, *George IV*, i. 112; Broughton, *Recollections of a Long Life*, ii. 140; Charles Williams-Wynn to Lord Grenville, 23 January 1821, Coed-y-maen MSS.

the discussion and division which ensued were said to have shown immediately that the government would survive.[79] In succeeding days this impression was confirmed to a point where complete exculpation became scarcely matter of doubt. By declaring that the Queen's conduct was a closed book, by refusing all inquiry into the Milan Commission, Castlereagh at once removed apprehensions that the ministers would attempt self-justification at the nation's expense,[80] More and more the 'country gentlemen' realised that the greater the government's triumph the sooner the Whigs would refrain from raking a dying fire. In this connection, a speech on the second day by Heygate, a London alderman, was particularly heartening. A ministerial supporter who had grave reservations about the omission from the liturgy and subsequent events, he welcomed the news that there would be no further action against the Queen and looked forward to the time when 'the permanent and great interests of the country would occupy the attention of parliament', strongly reprobating Caroline's conduct during and since her trial as worthy of continued proscription.[81] Not surprisingly, the cheers from the ministerial benches which greeted these remarks led the government to assume that these views were the views of the rest of his kind. The Whigs, certainly, were left much 'disconcerted'. Already 'the Mountain', as the more 'advanced' part of the opposition was called, had been at odds with the leadership over an amendment to the Speech, and Lord Archibald Hamilton's motion for naming the Queen in the liturgy, tabled the first day in defiance of the party's decision, showed that bad feeling still existed. By making it clear that the House would never support Hamilton, Heygate's speech only led to new recriminations. While a hastily summoned meeting at Burlington House agreed to attack the original omission instead, the rebels again refused to give way to the motion of no confidence which the party intended. The result was that a mild and somewhat irrelevant censure that the Order-in-Council of February 1820 had been 'ill-advised and inexpedient' became the opening

[79] Buckingham, *George IV*, i. 111-12. The motion by Wetherell, whom Tierney described as 'a uniform supporter of ministers', was defeated 260-169.
[80] *Hansard*, 2nd ser., iv. 67, 68, 69, 76-7, 77-8.
[81] Ibid., 82-5, 88-90.

move of the opposition's offensive. As the government quickly realised, this put the Whigs on weak ground from the start. When Wilberforce had sought the mediation of the House the previous June, a similar proposition had been overwhelmingly defeated. To try afresh, after all the bold language and petitions in favour of the Queen's reinsertion, seemed a pathetic attempt to catch votes and eat words. The description which the ministers thought most apt was 'milk and water'. Not only did the motion rehash a question already decided and superseded by events, but it also led to no practical result, for to condemn the government on 'an insulated point in the whole mass of misconduct' could secure neither the Queen's innocence nor new advisers for the Crown. 'There are two notices before the House,' ran Lord Harrowby's brief of the situation, 'one for an address to reinstate the Q. in the liturgy, the other for a direct censure upon the whole conduct of government respecting the Q. Why therefore decide separately an abstract question. . . . The decision, both as it respects the Q. & as it respects the government, can be pronounced by the House much more fairly, fully & effectively upon either of those. . . .'[82]

Of course, the essence of the Whig plan was to attract sufficient votes on the least offensive motion to begin a momentum which would carry both the general censure and the Queen's restoration to the liturgy. Where it failed was the unswerving distrust of the 'country gentlemen' for the Whigs as the guileless tools of Radical revolution; as political undesirables who had sought power too eagerly, joined in an unholy alliance and dragged the country on a rack of popular commotion. For Hamilton's motion, Castlereagh made no avowal that the government would stand or fall by the result, but it would have made little difference if he had. The mass of ministerial 'country gentlemen' refused to give the opposition even a cheap success. On Robinson's motion of adjournment, which technically evaded the issue of censure, the government collected 310 votes to their opponents' 209; and this success came at half past six in the morning, after the lawyers had exhausted their part of

---

[82] Lord Harrowby to Lord Sandon, 26 January [1821], Harrowby MSS., 59, ff. 48–9. See also Huskisson to Canning, 30 January 1821, Canning MSS.; *Mrs Arbuthnot*, i. 65–6; *Hobhouse*, p. 48.

the subject and the rest of the House in the process.[83] Huskisson,
who all along had been sceptical of the government's chances,[84]
was astonished at the victory. 'I did not make sufficient allowance for the dread of the Whigs among the Country Gentlemen', he explained to Canning. 'Their alarm has been much
increased by the recent conduct of the Whigs at County Meetings; whilst, on the other hand, the tone of the Speech, the
declaration that nothing further was or had been in contemplation agst the Q. and that after making a liberal provision for
Her the question would be for ever at rest, as far as the Ministers
were concerned, has greatly conciliated our Friends.'[85] The
Whigs had some comfort that the minority was their largest
vote since the defeat of the property tax. But at the same time
the government had anticipated desertions from among the
'weak-hearted', and, of the thirty who crossed the floor,
Castlereagh expected fully twenty to return.[86] He knew, as
everyone knew, that the omission from the liturgy had been the
weakest part of the ministers' case, if only because the motions
to come placed the question of confidence squarely before the
'country gentlemen'. Next time there would be no opportunity
for nice distinctions. 'This division will probably decide the
fate of the Session,' said Hobhouse of the government's
success.[87]

The Whigs, for their part, were quite aware that they had
encountered an inveterate hostility which they had no hope of
overcoming. If Mrs. Arbuthnot is to be believed, their fury was
commensurate. Some of the wilder spirits, including the Duke
of Bedford, wanted 'to give up all further efforts in the House
and make their way out of doors', hoping to bludgeon parliament
into submission by the sheer weight of public opinion. The more
timid members preferred 'the good old plan of making speeches
and motions' to keep the government under constant pressure,

---

[83] For accounts of the debate see Huskisson to Canning, 30 January 1821,
Canning MSS.; *George IV*, ii. 406–9; *Mrs Arbuthnot*, i. 66.
[84] Huskisson to Canning, 17 December 1820, Add. MSS. 38742, ff. 156–8.
[85] Huskisson to Canning, 30 January 1821, Canning MSS. See also
J. W. Ward's comment in *Letters of the Earl of Dudley*, p. 275: 'I regard
the majority as a majority against the Foxites, rather than as an expression
of an opinion upon the particular question. And in that view the House of
Commons is perhaps not so unfaithful a representative of the public will
as some persons pretend.'   [86] *George IV*, ii. 406.   [87] *Hobhouse*, p. 48.

though even they were tempted by the daring and probably illegal project of raising a subscription for the Queen by public appeal.[88] In the end, the whole party came to accept a parliamentary course. No move was made to withdraw the motion of general censure which Hamilton had obstinately forestalled, and notice of another to restore the Queen to the liturgy, the logical conclusion of all the Whigs' efforts, was given shortly after the House resumed. Both motions, of course, were, in effect, motions of no confidence, and in pushing them now the party could only appear faithful to its principles. In the words of one member, to out-argue the government and yet be outvoted was their fate for the session.[89] The 'Tory feeling', which mainly brought them to defeat, was perhaps best exemplified in Bankes, a government supporter who in the manner of his kind was often independent but in the last resort always loyal. To him the country stood in obvious peril from the Radicals. There was 'a dangerous faction', he warned the House, 'endeavouring to extend itself by all the means it could command, and catching hold of every principle of ruin, by which it might succeed in involving the Kingdom in a general conflagration'. Not only had the Whigs given it 'vastly too great a countenance' by organising and attending meetings in concert, but they had pledged themselves to the repeal of the Six Acts, parliamentary reform and Catholic relief, to 'a complete change of the system of government' which could open the floodgates of revolution. In contrast, their adversaries united safe principles with 'great talents', 'a large share of practical knowledge' and 'a coincidence of public opinion'. Not to be forgotten was that 'under their auspices a most brilliant war had been put an end to by a peace more glorious than any which the country had enjoyed for four centuries'. Past and present then, according to Bankes, the Whigs had failed the nation.[90] Theirs was a marriage of convenience with the people, which, while it might bring them to power, could end in the worst of social catastrophes. As a ministerial majority of 146 on the motion of censure and one of 120 on the liturgy showed, these fears were the fears of many others.

---

[88] *Mrs. Arbuthnot*, i. 66, 67–8; Huskisson to Canning, 30 January 1821, Canning MSS.   [89] *Letters to the Earl of Dudley*, pp. 274–5.
[90] *Hansard*, 2nd ser., iv. 392–4.

These two drubbings, the last of which occurred in only the
third week of the session, finally laid the subject of the Queen
to rest. The inquiry into the Milan Commission, which for
months the opposition had been threatening, was quietly
dropped, and though some 'country gentlemen' objected to the
amount of the annuity, the money was quickly forthcoming
once it was realised that nothing was better calculated to drive
the Queen into obscurity. Nor was the government any less
circumspect; soon after the triumph in parliament, the Treasury
requested friendly editors to let her alone, and Sidmouth
quickly quashed the latest notion of the King that divorce was
yet possible.[91] Except for threats to gatecrash a Carlton House
levee and the Coronation itself, the latter which she actually had
the temerity to attempt, Caroline was no longer a nuisance, much
less a serious menace. Radicals and Whigs alike put her aside as
a forgotten plaything. On the last day of the session, with the
Black Rod knocking on the door, Hume tried to get the House
to address the Crown on her right of coronation, but this was
the last parliament heard of her. A month later she had been
hurried into the even greater obscurity of the grave.

II. A Sense of Weakness

The ministers did not make their victory a cause for complacency. The issue of the Queen, in all its episodes, served to
emphasise parliament's vulnerability to a forthright expression
of public feeling; and, with the disillusionment of the post-war
period far from being dispelled, it was obvious that the administration had to continue to distinguish itself by its activity and
enterprise. Sound government, of course, had come to mean,
above all, economical government. By the beginning of March,
Vansittart was able to promise a reduction of over £1,000,000
on the estimates, and in the end a saving of £1,650,000 was
claimed. This left the total considerably below the figure set by
the finance committee three years before.[92] Strictly speaking, it

---

[91] Huskisson to Canning, 20 February 1821, Canning MSS.; *Hobhouse*,
p. 48.
[92] *Hansard*, 2nd ser., iv. 1112–13, v. 1075. The finance committee in 1818
estimated the army, navy, ordnance and miscellaneous services to cost
£18,672,000. Vansittart's budget in 1821 put them at £18,021,800.

is true, comparison should have been made with 1819, for the army had had to be substantially increased during the 'state of emergency' of that year.[93] Even so, the 'country gentlemen' remained agreeably surprised. From them, Hume and the rest of the 'economical monomaniacs' received no comfort whatever; a running fire kept up in the committee of supply left the ministers completely unscathed, and a final barrage, in the shape of an address to the throne pledging the Crown to economy, made far more noise than damage.

Progress towards the rationalisation of the commercial system was equally auspicious. In 1820 the House of Commons committee on foreign trade had produced a comprehensive report on the navigation laws, which is perhaps best described as a statement of general intent. Barely one practical recommendation was contained in it, but the harsh strictures on the 'vast and confused mass of legislation' which made up 'a policy of useless severity' and the idealistic flourish at the end—that commerce ought to be 'a source of reciprocal amity between nations, and an interchange of productions to promote the industry, the wealth and happiness of mankind'—showed along what lines, though with 'the utmost circumspection and caution', the government intended to advance.[94] Because of the Queen's trial, nothing further could be done in the meantime. Nevertheless, the ministers did not delay matters unnecessarily. Parliament's interest in the subject, indeed the existence of a 'party' in favour of reform, had been clearly attested by the reception of the 'freer' trade petitions and the appointment of committees in both houses. Early in February 1821, Wallace, the Vice-President of the Board of Trade, asked the House of Commons to reappoint a select committee, and the Lords followed suit a week or so later. Between them these two committees produced five reports on the timber trade, East India shipping regulations and silk and wine imports, paving the way for legislative redress as soon as parliamentary time became available.[95] Though towards the end of the session Wallace gave

[93] According to a memorandum in Add. MSS. 48436, pp. 114–16, the British and Irish establishments were increased by 11,950 in 1820. The difference between the total estimates of 1819 and 1821 was less than £500,000. [94] *PP*, 1820, ii. 365–503.
[95] Ibid., 1821, vi. 1–433; *LJ*, liv. 189–320, 472–503.

notice of a general revision of the navigation system, it so happened that a bill reducing the preference enjoyed by Canadian timber was the sum of the government's achievement. Still, even this little was of some significance and distinction. As was expected, the opposition from powerful colonial and shipping interests was strongly felt inside and outside the legislature, and the Board of Trade's perseverance in spite of it made good Wallace's boast that the government had taken up the subject neither grudgingly nor against its better judgment.[96] One blow had been successfully aimed at the venerable edifice of protectionism, and the way was set for its further demolition.

In contrast, concerning legal reform, the ministers appeared indolent if not openly obstructive. In 1819 Mackintosh's committee on the criminal law had tabled a report recommending three major improvements; the repeal or amendment of obsolete capital statutes, the abolition of the death penalty in certain cases of larceny and a considerable mitigation of the punishments for forgery.[97] Attempts to implement these during the following two years, however, met with very little success. Indeed, to many reformers it must have seemed that the government represented the essence of the reactionary spirit against which they were contending. Mainly at Eldon's instigation, many obsolete offences were saved from extinction, and the two bills dealing with these anachronisms passed into law very severely mutilated. When the law officers threatened opposition to Mackintosh's larceny bills, two had to be withdrawn and the third was allowed through with the death penalty still intact. Finally, and perhaps worst of all, the forgery bill was done to death at Castlereagh's orders, after its supporters had conducted it past the third reading and believed it safe to the Lords.

Of course, the ministers were not the ogres of reaction which some imagined them to be. Admittedly, as long as Sidmouth remained, the Home Office was unlikely to step far outside its administrative routine, for his conservatism was instinctive without the saving grace of being imaginative. On the other hand, something was done, and, even if it was very little, there was more than one extenuating circumstance. The most obvious was that the Home Office was overworked. Sidmouth may have

---

[96] *Hansard*, 2nd ser., iv. 425.   [97] *PP*, 1819, viii. 1–273.

been hidebound by the tradition of his department, but throughout a year and a half of unrest his under-secretaries and a handful of clerks were kept fully occupied operating the machinery of order, which, not unnaturally, was taken to be their foremost responsibility. Nor did he have much respite supervising their work. 'This is my second *week* day at Richmond Park since the 12th of August,' he complained to Bragge-Bathurst in the middle of December.[98] True, with things in this state, it is arguable that the ministers should have helped, not hindered Mackintosh. The difficulty here, apart from a dislike that the opposition should have the initiative on such an important question, was that they firmly believed the Whigs were tackling reform from the wrong point of view that uncertainty of punishment was the chief cause of crime and that the fear of death was the only deterrent that was presently effective. Theirs was an approach more influenced by practicalities than ideology, though the penalty they paid was that prison reform as an issue inspired less interest and less emotion than capital punishment. Nonetheless, the ministers stuck faithfully to what as a relatively thankless task. While the committee appointed in 1819 'to inquire into the State and Description of Gaols' made few practical suggestions, the evidence it collected from a number of expert witnesses provided the groundwork for a reforming and consolidating bill which was introduced in the following session.[99] As it happened, this was purely a reminder that the government had the matter in hand, for the Queen's trial prevented any progress beyond the first reading. The next session, however, everything went more smoothly. A select committee with a generous sprinkling of reformers was again appointed, the discarded bill was reintroduced for their comment and the way was set for 'the first measure of general prison reform to be framed and enacted on the responsibility of the national executive'.[100] Only in 1823 did the bill finally become law, but it is enough to show that the Whigs' share of glory was more than they deserved. Behind the scenes in the committee rooms, the

[98] *Sidmouth*, iii. 338. On his retirement Sidmouth complained that 'the whole strength of the establishment has been insufficient to carry on the current business of the office'. Gash, p. 298. [99] *PP*, 1819, vii. 1–560.
[100] Sidney and Beatrice Webb, *English Prisons under Local Government*, p. 73.

government was quietly cultivating the subject of legal reform,
until under Peel it yielded up a rich harvest of achievement.

Whatever their importance in the long term, as parliamentary
issues, commercial and legal reform were, comparatively speaking, fairly innocuous. Certainly, in the 1821 session, agricultural
distress and parliamentary reform, forgetting the annual or near
annual scrimmage over Catholic emancipation, aroused much
greater passions and constantly obtruded into other business.
That there would be trouble from the 'country gentlemen' over
the state of agriculture was never in question. In 1820 an
exceptionally good harvest again demonstrated that the farmer
had ample protection against a glut of foreign-grown corn but
none against his own over-production; and as prices plummeted
in anticipation of an excess supply yet another fresh wave of
petitions inevitably began. Initially, the ministers tried to turn
the wrath from their door by carrying into effect the one
substantive recommendation of the previous year's committee.
The mode of calculating the price which determined the opening and closing of the ports had always caused complaints that
unscrupulous middlemen could exploit it to their own advantage. A bill changing the units, from which an average price
was obtained, from twelve specially defined maritime districts
to a hundred or so towns was an obvious improvement. But this
slight amendment was not nearly enough to satisfy impatient
and irate 'country gentlemen' who saw the corn laws as a whole
at fault, and taxation and the gold standard as well. When
Gooch, the member for Suffolk, moved to refer the petitions
to a select committee, the government did not demur but only
pointed out that 'the country should understand that there did
not exist any reasonable expectation of being able to provide a
remedy for evils which were dependent on causes beyond the
control of the legislature'.[101] Fortunately, after a hard struggle,
which Huskisson bore the brunt of for the government, the
committee came to agree that the agricultural community could
be offered no greater consolation. As a result, the corn laws
were saved for yet another year.[102] But the ministers did not
quite get off scot-free. While the inquiry was in progress, the

---

[101] *Hansard*, 2nd ser., iv. 361, 1139–61.
[102] Charles Ellis to Canning, 29 May 1821, Canning MSS; *PP*, 1821,
ix. 1–479. According to Huskisson's own statement in the House of Commons

repeal of 'an unjust and oppressive' tax on farm horses was
secured by a joyous coalition of Whigs and agriculturists; and
the additional duties on malt imposed in 1819 almost met a
similar fate, in spite of Castlereagh's pleas that the sinking fund
could not operate without a surplus of revenue.

By this time the ministers could not be blamed for regarding
disgruntled agriculturists as a more or less established hazard
to be negotiated every session. Much of the opposition in 1821,
in fact, came from predictable quarters: from Joseph Hume
who led the usual chorus against extravagant government, from
the squirearchy who feared for their rents, from shipping
interests against a reforming Board of Trade, and from legal
reformers who continued to see only the scaffold. But the most
remarkable, and for the administration the most worrying
development, was the 'country gentlemen's' seeming inclination
for a 'temperate' reform of the representation. Though motions
by Lambton and Lord John Russell on the general principle
were defeated, they were by no means the resounding victories
of previous years when the reformers had been silenced by
majorities of a hundred or hundred and fifty. Suspicions
naturally arose that the Tory backbenchers, like many of the
Whigs, were having serious second thoughts on the subject.
What really gave these fears substance was their attitude towards the disfranchisement of Grampound, a rotten borough
which had been condemned for corruption in 1818–19 after
inquiry by the Commons and the conviction of the patron and
several electors for bribery. There was no difference of opinion
over what penalty was appropriate, for the House had decided
that with similar cases in the past. Instead, disagreement
occurred over what place should be enfranchised, again the
usual practice, to supply the vacancy created by Grampound's
removal. Hitherto, the offending borough had been invariably
thrown into the adjoining hundred; but in this instance the
hundred already contained four other parliamentary boroughs,
which, with the county, would give some freeholders an

---

on 18 February 1822 (*Hansard*, 2nd ser., vi. 506), he had presented a series
of resolutions to the committee and drawn up a report founded on them.
But his draft had been discussed paragraph by paragraph, 'and many
alterations were made in the propriety of which he did not concur', alterations affecting 'not only the wording but the principle. . . .'

excessive electoral privilege. The reforming party led by Lord John Russell wanted Leeds to have the benefit, others preferred Yorkshire, and the government had to make up its mind which was the lesser evil, all the while strenuously contending that the remedy was peculiar and that no principle of representation by population was involved or conceded.

The disconcerting feature was that the 'country gentlemen' appeared to come round in favour of Leeds, despite ministerial protests that, as in Westminster, 'it would subject the population to a perpetual factious canvass . . . and keep alive a permanent spirit of turbulence and disaffection amongst them'.[103] In December 1819, when Lord John Russell had tried to establish the principle that towns like Leeds ought to be represented, Castlereagh had meekly put him off by suggesting that where Grampound was concerned the House should only consider the merits of the particular case. The following year a bill had been brought in tacitly stating the reformers' proposition, and his attitude had hardened into a distinct preference for enfranchising the hundred. The proceeding against the Queen had prevented parliament from making any definite decision but enough had been done to show that a strong party was emerging among the county members in opposition to the government's plan. This became obvious with the reintroduction of the bill in February 1821. A proposal to save the seat for Cornwall was negatived without a division, and the second best alternative of adding to Yorkshire's county representation was defeated by sixty votes. Thereupon Stuart Wortley, himself the member for Yorkshire and by now the guardian of the bill in place of Lord John Russell, immediately secured in triumph the insertion of Leeds. According to Huskisson, the Prime Minister was struck with dismay. He saw the whole question launched 'into the sea of speculation' by 'the idle conceit of the Country Gentlemen that a temperate Reform would put an end to grievances and distress'. The fact that in this instance the House of Lords could, and did, make amends was of little comfort, for the peers could not be expected to resist the lower house indefinitely.[104] With the Whigs closing

[103] See Lord Liverpool's memorandum on the subject, *Liverpool*, iii. 137-9.   [104] Huskisson to Canning, 20 February 1821, Canning MSS.

their ranks on reform and with some ministerial supporters apparently beginning to agree with them that public opinion was too formidable to resist absolutely, the possibility that in the not too distant future the government would find itself forsaken on a point which it had always regarded as fundamental had at least to be considered. Doubtless there were optimists who played down the incident as some passing spasm of irritation or as an attempt to appease the country without imperilling the existing order. Nevertheless, no one could be certain that a movement of parliamentary opinion, scarcely perceptible as yet, was not taking place similar to that which was to occur in 1830–1. After the triple disappointment on the Grampound bill and Lambton's and Lord John Russell's motions, what the ministers looked for most was an unequivocal endorsement of the constitution's excellence.

Dissatisfaction out-of-doors, and the concerted demands which now more than ever seemed to spring from it, was the main explanation for parliament's restiveness. Though a period of despondency and hardship, such as the nation had experienced after 1815, would have visited any administration with parliament's displeasure, the efforts the ministers had made to establish credit with the country had never been conspicuously successful. But there was another aspect of the problem of the executive's authority in the Commons which could be more easily dealt with. This concerned its bearing in the House itself. The three most obvious sources of the ministers' strength in the legislature—the fact that they were the King's ministers, that they were the government, and that they were against the Whigs—were not totally sufficient to ensure the government's survival. An administration which in the opinion of a majority of the Commons had misgoverned the country was killed instantly. One which could not govern the House in appearance as well as in fact met a slower death as the impression of weakness was increasingly mistaken for the reality. Parliament had to be managed in all its moods firmly and decisively by a proper command of its procedure and with a proper concern for its dignity. More important still, the Treasury bench had to have, in Croker's words, 'the gift of the gab' to give the legislature the information and argument which was its entitlement. It was this latter quality which the administration seemed to be lacking most in 1821. Though the government emerged triumphant from the debates on the Queen, the showing of its leadership was such as to raise doubts whether it commanded a reasonable proportion of 'speechifying' talent. On Lord Archibald Hamilton's motion, only Castlereagh and Robinson spoke, the latter losing himself and sitting down abruptly after barely quarter of an hour.[105] On the next, Bragge-Bathurst's rising was greeted with loud jeers and a mass exodus from the chamber.[106] On the last, not one minister or official man spoke at all. Not surprisingly, soon after they had expressed their confidence, the 'country gentlemen' were 'loud in their representations to Ministers of the necessity of their strengthening themselves, if they wish for a continuance of support'.[107] Already painfully aware of the government's weakness, the Cabinet did not need to be goaded further. With Canning and Peel out of office, it was obvious that the administration had less than sufficient talent to keep the Whigs in their place. Indeed, following the embarrassing defeat on the Grampound question, Lord Liverpool was driven to distraction lest Canning fail to turn up for Lambton's motion on the general principle of reform.[108]

Nevertheless, an arrangement which had to take into account any number of conflicting aspirations could not be settled overnight, however anxious everyone was to remove the patch resulting from Canning's resignation and make a lasting repair. The Prime Minister's first plan was to give Vansittart the India Board, Peel the Exchequer, Canning the Admiralty—for which he had always had a preference and in which he would transact a minimal amount of business with the King—and Melville the Home Office. On the face of things such an arrangement seemed easily attainable: when asked, Sidmouth had no compunctions about retiring; and Vansittart, having offered to take the India Board the previous December, was unlikely to put up a vigorous

---

[105] For accounts of the debate see Huskisson to Canning, 30 January 1821, Canning MSS; *George IV*, ii. 407–9.

[106] Charles Ellis to Canning, 8 February 1821, Canning MSS. See Creevey's cutting comment: 'Brother Bragge could scarcely be heard, in which he was highly judicious'. *Creevey*, p. 354.

[107] Buckingham, *George IV*, i. 118.

[108] Charles Ellis to Canning, 16 February 1821, Canning MSS.

resistance to his demotion. What Liverpool under-estimated was Castlereagh's (now Lord Londonderry) wariness of possible rivals and Canning's strong determination to make up the ground he had lost in 1812. Curiously enough, Londonderry saw Peel as more of a threat to his primacy than Canning, which shows how carefully the latter, mindful of the past, was conducting himself. When Peel's promotion to the Exchequer was first mooted in ministerial circles, Londonderry immediately interposed a number of fatuous objections; that the balance of power between 'Catholics' and 'Protestants' would be destroyed, that bad blood would be created between Vansittart and the rest of the Cabinet, and that Peel as yet lacked the necessary qualifications for high office.[109] The kindest explanation for his conduct is either that he wished to bring one of his own men forward, probably Robinson, or that, after Plunket's success in getting a committee on the Catholic claims and two relief bills through the Commons, he thought the front bench should become rather more 'Catholic'. Unlike Vansittart, Peel was not simply a 'Protestant' but the 'Protestant' leader; and since the Chancellor of the Exchequer 'from the nature of his office, *ought* in time of peace to be the most powerful member of the Government', Londonderry may have feared that a competition for power would aggravate the difference of opinion on the Catholic issue, which Plunket had succeeded in exciting, and make neutrality less and less practicable. Even so, many of his objections seemed to have a personal venom. To say that Peel was 'decidedly a bad debater' was to ignore the fact that he was easily the best of the other young aspirants and possibly a match for Londonderry himself. To suggest that he was unfitted for high office after six years as Irish Secretary was equally absurd, if only because he who now complained had served exactly the same apprenticeship. Somewhere in Londonderry's makeup there was a weakness or lack of confidence which led him to resent able or abler men. It seems that the more he was

[109] *Mrs Arbuthnot*, i. 82, 89–90. Castlereagh repeated these arguments some months later when the government was negotiating with the Grenvilles. See memorandum of a conversation between Lord Liverpool and Lord Buckingham, 30 November, memorandum of a conversation between Londonderry, Buckingham and Williams-Wynn, 5 December 1821, Grenville MSS.

vilified before the public the more this weakness revealed itself. He had achieved outstanding success as a diplomatist and he was a popular leader of the Commons; but he was also being flayed constantly in parliament and the press for his clumsy oratory, his ignorance of finance and his European sympathies. A nature as proud and sensitive as his found these attacks increasingly difficult to bear. By using the utmost discretion Canning had avoided the accusations of making a party against him which Peel now suffered. But as long as he remained Leader of the House it was difficult to see how the talents of either could receive a proper recognition.

It was Londonderry's hostility which made Canning hesitate between accepting a certain offer of office at home and trusting to luck that the governor-generalship of India would shortly become his. On one point his mind was quite made up, and that was that he would never accept a permanent appointment as Londonderry's 'lieutenant-General'. 'If there was any high-way making hereabouts (upon Mr Mac Adam's new principles),' he wrote half jocularly, half seriously to his wife, 'I would rather work upon it, for my subsistence.'[110] Sometimes his despair almost got the better of him. A letter written after a series of brilliant speeches in support of the relief measures for Catholics was full of bitter reflection:

> . . . in truth I am sick of the whole thing. I have nothing now to gain in Parlty reputation—The last three weeks have placed that at the pinnacle. All to come is risk, rather than gain. And what does the reputation of being the First Speaker in the H of C do for me? Nothing. It only leads people to believe that *first speaking* is not necessary for carrying on the affairs of the Government —that it is very well to have—very delightful to witness—but that business can go on very well without it. And so it can. And the more it goes on without me the better. I am weary—& at 51 or thereabouts I cannot afford, either in the common or in the moral sense of that word, to hazard new experiments, & new combinations, as I could with the probability of 20 years before me. The next step—whatever it be—must be decisive for life— & if it be as barren of advantage as all former steps have been— I shall have done little for the comfort of old age, & for that of

[110] Canning to Mrs Canning, 16 April 1821, Canning MSS.

those whom I ought to have thought of long ago rather than of my own etiquettes & points of honour.[111]

The alternatives facing him became clearer when the Prime Minister saw him twice towards the end of April. Though most of the Cabinet thought his resignation in December 1820 was of a piece with his former conduct,[112] it was readily admitted on all sides that he was an invaluable friend and a dangerous enemy, and Liverpool accordingly was able to intimate that he might have the option of the Admiralty and the Home Office. This, of course, fell far short of what he wanted. Indeed, unaccompanied by any assurances that Londonderry would move upstairs, it appeared quite unacceptable. The only terms on which it could be agreeable were if, ignoring the inconvenience to his Liverpool friends, he could take a temporary lease of office on the clear understanding that the government would secure his nomination to India. Yet the retreat to the East seemed as far away as ever. The Chairs at East India House favoured his candidature certainly; but Hastings had given no hint of leaving Calcutta, the government was loath to recall him, and the most that Canning could wring out of Liverpool was a non-committal mutter that his claims to the governor-generalship were 'fully admitted'. To all intents and purposes, his choice had narrowed down to accepting office once again as Londonderry's subordinate, staying out and hoping against hope that India would not elude him, or complete retirement from public life. Fortunately for him, with so much pending on the outcome of other negotiations, Liverpool did not require an immediate answer. At the end of April Canning returned to the Continent to await developments and ponder his position.[113]

By this time, or very soon afterwards, Vansittart's replacement by Peel was no longer in question. Londonderry made another furious protest at the beginning of May, which

[111] Canning to Mrs Canning, 3 April 1821, ibid.
[112] Lord Sidmouth to Bragge-Bathurst, 15 December 1820, Sidmouth MSS.; Lord Harrowby to Lord Sandon, 21 December 1820, Harrowby MSS. 59, f. 97.
[113] The result of Canning's interviews with Liverpool on 20 and 23 April and his meditations on the subject of his political future can be traced in his letters to his wife, 27 March, 3, 6, 13, 16, 24 April 1821, Canning MSS.

Wellington appeared to support; and the amiable Melville finally persuaded the Prime Minister 'that at best it wd be an experiment' when 'he could go on perfectly well with Van'. The changes now intended were for Peel to take the India Board, Canning the Admiralty and Melville the Home Office, with an approach also to Wellesley Pole to see whether he would vacate the Mint, probably, though the point remains uncertain, in favour of one of the Grenvilles.[114] Hobhouse guessed exactly what was afoot: 'Ld. Lpool.,' he wrote in his diary, 'now considers that the first object is to recal Canning, the second to introduce Peel, and the third to take in some of the Grenvilles.'[115] For all that, within a fortnight it looked much as if he would achieve none of them. When Wellington, at Liverpool's behest, called on his elder brother he was roughly received, Pole indignantly refusing to quit and regarding the mere suggestion as an insult.[116] An even greater blow was Peel's polite but firm rejection of the India Board or, what some ministers feared, of office in general. Liverpool asked to see him on 30 May, and, wary that in the event of Canning's refusal he might have something better to offer, he put the proposition 'in a strange, shuffling, hesitating sort of way', offering nothing specific but hinting all the while that the India Board was the least he would have. Not surprisingly, Peel retired more puzzled than enlightened. To clear the air he sought a further interview a few days later. Though he continually complained of his poor state of health, there can be little doubt that the office was not to his liking, and once he ascertained that the Prime Minister had indeed meant the India Board he was quick to return a flat negative. 'And anything else I should offer?' Liverpool inquired hastily, anxious to know whether Peel was to be put completely out of his calculations. 'When anything else should be offered, it would be time enough to decide on it' was the frosty reply, which really left the government none the wiser. The Prime Minister had only himself to blame for the misunderstanding. Had he begun at the beginning and settled with Sidmouth and Canning beforehand, or, failing that, given Peel his full confidence, much

[114] *Mrs Arbuthnot*, i. 89–90, 92, 94–5.
[115] *Hobhouse*, p. 58.   [116] *Mrs Arbuthnot*, i. 96, 99.

of the embarrassment would have been avoided. Talking in generalities and making half propositions aroused everyone's suspicions.[117]

The decisive setback to the whole arrangement, however, was the King's reluctance to part with Sidmouth and his determination never again to have Canning as his confidential and responsible adviser. The day after his first interview with Peel, Lord Liverpool went to Carlton House, and, on his broaching the subject, George at once let it be known that Canning's readmission would be regarded as a personal affront. To make matters worse, there was also a difference over whether Sidmouth should have a pension in addition to his Clerkship of the Pells, which the next day, with the Lord Chancellor's connivance, deepened into a contest whether or not he should keep a place in the Cabinet.[118] At the outset it is hard to imagine that Liverpool was unduly alarmed. The King often swore defiance to the last against his ministers, but among them it was well known that his deeds never measured up to his words. What really brought the premier to the verge of resignation was the way in which the rest of the Cabinet gathered against him in order to effect Canning's permanent exclusion. Theirs was a surprising change of heart, since for weeks those who knew of the proposals for recasting the government had appeared to take Canning's promotion for granted. The only possible explanation is that a whisper of his Indian ambitions had at last got around—the Arbuthnots and Hobhouse at least knew the secret[119]—and, encouraged by the King's opposition, his enemies seized the opportunity finally to be rid of him. Londonderry and Lord Bathurst both began to urge that Sidmouth should not stir for the time being, which would have left Canning only the India Board; and the Home Secretary succumbed to their entreaties sufficiently to warn Liverpool that he would obey the King's commands to stay on until an inferior Cabinet office became available if he (Sidmouth) felt this to be necessary. Facing such incorrigible opposition, the

[117] For the approach to Peel see ibid., p. 97; *Croker*, i. 186–191; *Bathurst*, pp. 497–8.
[118] *Hobhouse*, pp. 58–61; the King to Lord Liverpool, 1 June 1821, Add. MSS. 38190, f. 43; *George IV*, ii. 436.
[119] *Hobhouse*, p. 58; *Mrs. Arbuthnot*, i. 90.

Prime Minister played his master card, a scarcely veiled threat that if Sidmouth did not shift to make room for Canning his own resignation would shortly follow. As he had calculated, at this everyone came to their senses. Sidmouth told the King that he was absolutely resolved to quit the Home Office, Liverpool was given permission to explain himself in writing and Londonderry tacitly admitted that any negotiation should proceed 'upon a broad Intelligible Publick Principle'.[120]

Even so, having regained the initiative, the Prime Minister soon lost it again through a domestic tragedy which destroyed his already drooping spirits and temporarily removed him from the scene altogether. His letter to the King, expounding his proposals on Londonderry's 'broad Intelligible Publick Principle', suggested an arrangement between the government and 'those individuals and interests' with whom 'there exists a general coincidence of opinion on the great principles of domestic and foreign policy', regard being had 'to all the considerations of talents, standing in political life, and former connexion with the existing Government';[121] in practical terms, the India Board for Charles Williams-Wynn, the Home Office for Melville and the Admiralty for Canning. The King's reply to this was cold and uncompromising, hostile enough to snap the last strings of self-control in the highly strung Liverpool. 'The King', he was told, 'can see no necessity, and consequently has no wish, or intention of changing the present frame of his Government'. Further, that since Sidmouth could be better employed than as a minister without portfolio, 'surely some arrangement with his colleagues might be satisfactorily made, to effect this desireable object'.[122] Though, as Lord Londonderry remarked, 'the ostensible objection' was that Sidmouth should have an office he had already declined, the implication of the rest was sufficient to provoke a paroxysm of rage in which the letter and its author were equally abused.[123] Still, all was not yet lost. Simmering down, Liverpool realised

[120] *Hobhouse*, pp. 61–3; Lord Liverpool to Lord Londonderry, Lord Londonderry to Lord Liverpool, 10 June 1821, Add. MSS. 38289, f. 204.
[121] *Liverpool*, iii. 142–4.
[122] *George IV*, ii. 437.
[123] Lord Londonderry to Lord Liverpool, [11 June 1821], Add. MSS. 38289, f. 208; *Mrs Arbuthnot*, i. 100.

that until Canning was positively forbidden office there was room for negotiation. Accordingly, he at once sent off a note requesting to know 'your Majesty's determination as to what he has most humbly proposed whenever your Majesty shall have fully consider'd it'.[124]

At precisely this moment fate intervened. A few hours after the letter had been sent, Lady Liverpool, who had been near death for weeks, finally expired, and in the agony of his anguish her devoted husband came very near to total physical collapse. Unable to spare a thought for public concerns, indeed ordered by his doctors to take a complete rest, he remained incommunicado for three or four days. Only on learning from Arbuthnot that the King was as obdurate as ever and his colleagues wavering did he rouse himself, and then only to say that 'a secret scheme' for weakening the government was in evidence, that Canning's admission was a test of the sovereign's goodwill and that he for his part would resign rather than submit.[125] Obviously, this new ultimatum, which, it is not too much to say, threatened the existence of the government, left the next move to his colleagues. Nor did they fail to take advantage of the opportunity to impose their own compromise. While they appreciated the need for an infusion of talent, while they realised that Canning could attract both fame and an opposition as a proscribed person, forever impressing itself on their minds was the chance that in a few months' time he might be safely consigned to an Indian exile. Time was what they wanted and what they sought, time during which the issue would be suspended, Canning removed and the government secured. At a meeting held at Londonderry's house, Wellington, Bathurst, Sidmouth and Melville agreed unanimously 'that there was no reason for readmitting Canning into the Cabinet, except to prevent his becoming a rallying point for the dissatisfied friends of the Govt'. This led to further declarations that they would stay on if Liverpool saw fit to resign, and refuse to force Canning on the King if his proscription was made a matter of time, not principle.[126]

[124] George IV, ii. 437.
[125] Liverpool, iii. 146–7; Lord Liverpool to Arbuthnot, 15 June 1821, Add. MSS. 38289, f. 209; Hobhouse, p. 64.
[126] Arbuthnot, pp. 23–4; Hobhouse, pp. 64–5.

By the time that the Prime Minister returned from Gloucestershire, whence he had gone to attend his wife's funeral, he had no hope at all of bringing the Cabinet to heel. Even before he left Town, Melville and Sidmouth intimated that they would never be parties to an arrangement which foisted Canning on the King, and, while he was away, Harrowby added his voice to the rest of the rebels. Still more provoking, having kept possession of the royal ear, they persuaded the King to assist their plans by wholly disclaiming 'the idea of absolute and interminable exclusion', which immediately nullified Liverpool's argument of a Court plot to keep the government permanently debilitated.[127] In these circumstances, the best the Prime Minister could do was submit with good grace. Already Canning had written him a handsome letter absolving him from any obligation that he may have felt on his account,[128] and, since the contest was beginning to cause speculation in the wider political world, it seemed most sensible to let the matter drop before the government's weakness at Court became too apparent to be denied. The one point which he insisted on making clear, however, was that the King, except perhaps where offices connected with his 'personal service' were concerned, should always select his ministers on public grounds and public grounds alone. Canning's exclusion, therefore, was to be regarded as temporary, with the government reserving a full right to renew the subject before the next session of parliament. Moreover, to emphasise that 'personal pique and resentment' were not the cause of the suspension, the Grenvilles were also to wait, and Sidmouth was to stay on merely to accompany the King on the forthcoming royal visit to Ireland. None of the parties concerned could really object to these terms; Canning still disliked the thought of office at home; Sidmouth, who a fortnight before had spoken of his absolute determination to quit, was ready to stay; and the rest of the Cabinet sat back satisfied that much could happen in six months. Only the King appeared to take exception to Liverpool's interpretation of his constitutional role. While he stoutly denied that he was a 'proscriber of persons', he continued to

---

[127] Ibid., pp. 65, 66, 67.
[128] Canning to Lord Liverpool, 22 June 1821, Add. MSS. 38193, ff. 156-7.

insist that his personal honour was the real issue at stake, and from him there came no certain promise that he would drop his opposition when the negotiations recommenced.[129]

Of course, the constitutional issue was what the struggle fundamentally was all about. As the Prime Minister put it: 'it is not *Mr. Canning out of office*, but Mr. Canning *out of office by the personal exclusion of the King, agreed to by his Government*, which is the question'. Alone, he clung to the notion that the King's right to choose his own ministers had to be limited by the advice of the Cabinet where that advice did not recommend a man of low character, of dubious loyalty or of 'strong discordance of opinion on political events actually depending'. George, in contrast, insisted that account should be taken of his personal feelings whether or not the office was one of constant personal intercourse; and the other ministers and Canning himself, in refusing to be a party to any arrangement which would force his wishes, seemingly agreed. Nevertheless, by giving way to them, Liverpool did not yield his principles. He saw the issue as merely postponed. There is no reason to think that the claims of friendship were given preference over other considerations. Like the rest of the Cabinet, his foremost object was to keep the Whigs out for the good of the nation. He differed from his colleagues in that he regarded Canning's readmission as a political necessity for which he was quite prepared to resign. It was necessary in the first place because the government had great need of Canning's talents in the Commons. In a negative sense he was wanted too because he might otherwise be within reach of the opposition, though this fear of him as a renegade was greatest with those who believed him capable of such treachery. Liverpool did not think that Canning was an adventurer, but it suited his purpose to point to the danger of antagonising him and so forcing him to seek his fortune elsewhere. Canning's return was necessary secondly because the King, having made an opposition, had to be disciplined into showing more restraint in the future. In the early nineteenth century, when the power of the Cabinet was obviously increasing at the expense of the Crown, the former had the difficult task of playing a double role as servant and

[129] *Liverpool*, iii. 147-9; *George IV*, ii. 441.

master of the sovereign. Always the weight of the past was felt, but also the opportunity of the present. To oblige the King to some extent, which in practice was the course the ministers followed, led to complaints of ministerial disrespect in some quarters and of ministerial cowardice in others. During George III's descent into total incapacity and during the Regency itself, these clashes between a Crown, which was the traditional centre of government, and a Cabinet, which could summon party feeling and public opinion to its aid, were virtually unknown. But with George IV in unfettered possession of the royal power they definitely became more frequent. Liverpool in 1821, in effect, was protesting against the appearance of a politically active monarch who was challenging the authority that the ministers had taken to themselves and to which they had become accustomed. If George were difficult over the details of patronage and policy, which interested him more than great questions of state, it mattered because the impression was bound to go forth that he was on bad terms with his ministers when the constitution supposed communication and close cooperation between them. If he refused to allow the government to strengthen itself according to the advice of the Cabinet, it mattered even more because the supposition would be that the relationship had broken down entirely. Though the influence of the Crown in the form of the favours it could dispense was declining, the King was still a political force to be reckoned with, because of his resources of sentiment and tradition. A refractory monarch was a liability for any administration. George IV's petulance and obstinacy on little matters had been the source of all 'past errors and calamities', as far as Lord Liverpool was concerned. 'A further stock of humiliations', he was convinced, awaited the government if the proprieties governing the prerogative of appointment were not distinctly stated and recognised. In his book, the rule of proper conduct for a king was to be seen and not heard.

The Prime Minister, therefore, was 'modern' in his constitutional views, at least to the extent that he spoke for royal impotence and ministerial omnipotence. Proudly he remembered that it had been he who had induced George III to bring in Fox in 1806. But whether he could do the like again in

1821 was truly in the balance. The King had taken a pronounced dislike to what he regarded as his unfeeling and dictatorial ways, and George was a man whose personal grudges coloured his politics more than faintly. As he well knew from what had passed a few months earlier, to effect a complete change of government was an undertaking full of hazard. The problem for him was to retain Liverpool's administration without Liverpool, which presumed a hopelessly divided Cabinet. Here the fact most in his favour was the reservations against forcing the King expressed by the most influential members of the government other than the premier himself, reservations partly founded on a Tory feeling for the dignity and custom of the Crown but mainly on personal dislike of Canning or, to be more specific, on a conviction that his talents were no compensation for his intrigue and trickery. This animosity was at the root of their insinuations that the administration could do without Canning in the House of Commons, or even survive his active hostility, and that the King's ill-will imperilled it more than the loss of Liverpool. It was ignored that to strengthen the government in the lower house it was better to bring in both Canning and Peel, and that the King had already discovered its resilience in the events of the session and in sounding out the opposition before that. However, this was their frame of mind; and as long as it remained thus, Liverpool could hardly hope to blackmail them into compliance by a threat of resignation and George could cherish thoughts of having a set of ministers more to his personal liking. Perhaps, unlikely though it appeared at the moment, the King would relent, for it was common knowledge that his powers of endurance under the strain of high politics were not very great. Failing that, everything depended on Liverpool and Canning. If the latter could be persuaded to give up, or of his own accord gave up the idea of office at home in return for assistance in procuring India, all would yet be well. If he refused, both he and the Prime Minister were almost certain political casualties.[130]

[130] For the difference of opinion between the Prime Minister and his Cabinet colleagues over Canning's readmission see *Liverpool*, iii. 146–7; *Arbuthnot*, pp. 23–4, 24 n. 2; *Wellington Desp.* (new series), i. 176–7; *Bathurst*, pp. 499–501.

Chapter Seven

NEW MEN

I. THE REJECTION OF CANNING

In the three months which followed the truce of July, it seemed more and more likely that the Prime Minister would be the main victim if the war was ever renewed. By the time that the Coronation was over and the royal visit to Ireland about to begin, the King was seething with fury at what he represented were yet further attempts to encroach on his prerogative, and, true to his usual form, he began a brisk trade in slurs and insults to demonstrate his displeasure. The trouble began over promotions among the Irish peerage on the occasion of the Coronation. With the King's permission, the Lord Lieutenant and the Prime Minister drew up a list between them; but, showing in the circumstances an unpardonable lack of tact, Liverpool sent the warrants to Carlton House without consulting him further, and in a passion he refused to sign any. To mark the lesson, 'Green Ribands' were promised to Lauderdale, Melville and Cassillis before the Prime Minister could object, notwithstanding that the honour was highly coveted and the number of knights hitherto had been limited to twelve.[1] These were pinpricks at most, however. The battle royal threatened to be over an appointment to supply the Marquis of Hertford's place as Lord Chamberlain in the Household, an office which combined considerable patronage with personal attendance on the sovereign, and therefore one of some political significance. From the start the King took offence because Hertford sent his letter of resignation to Lord Liverpool, which at once implied that the position was at the government's and not his disposal. When the Prime Minister sought to reassure him that his personal feelings would be fully taken into account, the angry reply came back that he should distinctly understand 'that whatever appointments the King

[1] *Hobhouse*, pp. 68, 69–70; *Mrs Arbuthnot*, i. 105.

may think proper to make in his own family, they are to be considered as quite independent of the controul of any Minister whatever'. Even the King's word that he would choose a friend of the government did little to ease matters in the circumstances. The obvious favourite for the post was the Marquis of Conyngham, the husband of George's latest conquest; determined at all costs to avoid aspersions of petticoat influence which would benefit neither them nor the King, the ministers lost no time in agreeing that the most he should be at Court was an ornament—and the darker the recess the better. Though the advice was only commonsense, the King still insisted on showing himself master in his own house. Whether Conyngham was actually offered Hertford's place and refused it is not clear, but within a day or two he was being proposed as Master of the Horse, a position hardly less objectionable insofar as the incumbent was allowed unrestricted use of the royal liveries. In the end it took a lecture from Sidmouth, on the need to keep up a facade of decency at least, to persuade the King to take stock of his true situation. Even this had a limited effect because all that he would promise was that no appointment would take place until he returned from Ireland.[2]

At the beginning of August, then, the Cabinet were not sorry to wish the King godspeed and a lengthy sojourn on the other side of the Irish Sea. These quarrels and other occurrences —among them the prominence of the Whigs in posts of honour at the Coronation—forced them to observe, in Wellington's words, that 'His M[ajest]y has in several recent instances shown to His Ministers & to the World that they do not possess His Confidence'.[3] Since Lord Liverpool bore the brunt of the humiliations, there was also a growing apprehension that his exasperation would become great enough to produce his resignation. Croker, indeed, after listening to a long revilement of

---

[2] *Hobhouse*, pp. 68–9, 70–1; *George IV*, ii. 446–7, 448–9; Arbuthnot to Lord Liverpool, 22, [23] July 1821, Add. MSS. 38289, ff. 267–8, 38290, ff. 229–32; *Arbuthnot*, p. 25; *Bathurst*, pp. 502–3, 504, 506, 507.

[3] See 'Substance of a Conversation between the Duke of Wellington, Sir B. Bloomfield, & Mr. Arbuthnot', 21 July 1821, Add. MSS. 38370, ff. 25–31, in which Wellington also warns the King's private secretary that the government must be allowed to strengthen itself or it would be destroyed with all the baneful consequences of a Radical accession to power. His colleagues fully approved what he said. *Arbuthnot*, p. 25; *Bathurst*, pp. 502–3.

the Prime Minister in the Closet, could not see how he could possibly stay, the King finding him 'captious, jealous, and impracticable', always objecting and never indulging.[4] But whether his going would bring down the government was by no means certain. As had been amply attested in June, the loyalty of many in the Cabinet to him was less than their dread of a Whig assumption of power, so that in all probability if the administration was sorely wounded in its head and members the trunk would attempt to maintain life notwithstanding. Its chances of survival were definitely less inasmuch as Liverpool had no obvious successor. Sidmouth was out of the running because he was preparing to superannuate himself. Wellington, in appearing, and posturing to some extent, as a professional soldier rather than a professional politician, could expect limited support from party men and public opinion. Londonderry's accession was certain to arouse fears that the Cabinet had become too 'Catholic' for comfort, the government's dealings with Ireland inevitably being affected.[5] As for the others, Melville was also a 'Catholic', and Bathurst, while a perceptive and intelligent politician, was at his strongest behind the scenes. It was not difficult, in these circumstances, to imagine Liverpool as the administration's linchpin. He was the man who could best hold together a reconstruction of Pitt's old party. He was the one man perhaps who stood between the Radicals and the national calamity of popular government.

Seen in this light, the riot with which the City paid its last respects to the Queen was the worst that could have happened while the King was away. As Lord Bathurst put it: 'as we have been for some time at single anchor, I think the storm may most probably take us out to sea'.[6] The immediate arrangements consequent on the Queen's death caused little upset. Apart from being annoyed that almost the first he knew of her illness was word of its fatal termination, the King readily agreed with Lord Liverpool 'that nothing should be omitted which Decency & Decorum require'. Orders for his private entry into Dublin, a period of Court mourning and removal of the body to Brunswick were issued as early as communications between Ireland

[4] *Croker*, i. 198–9.   [5] e.g. See *Eldon*, ii. 434–5.
[6] *Bathurst*, p. 512.

and London permitted.[7] Alas, where the Queen was concerned, decency and decorum could not last for very long. When her funeral cortege with its escort of Life Guards attempted to skirt the City *en route* for Harwich, the 'inferior sort' who had been her staunchest supporters made one final sally for old times' sake, barricading the streets and forcing the procession past Temple Bar and out along the Essex road. Needless to say, the King was furious. Bloomfield confided to Croker that he had sat up most of the night brooding over the incident, and throughout the rest of his progress he was constantly comparing the enthusiastic loyalty of his Irish subjects with the violence and perfidy of London.[8]

Even worse, as Sidmouth, the minister in attendance, quickly noticed, his anger began to turn in Lord Liverpool's direction. Originally, it had been decided to move the body by water down the Thames, and the King made up his mind that the contrary decision and all that ensued was the Prime Minister's folly and his alone. Before he left Ireland, Sidmouth sent an urgent warning that there would be 'Difficulties to meet, not inferior, as far as the Government is concerned, to any which we have yet encountered'. 'The King', he explained a few days later, 'is in a very uncomfortable State of Mind. The Circumstances attending the Queen's Funeral, He is perpetually recurring to, in a Manner which shews a Degree of Chagrin, & Irritation, beyond what I have ever observed in Him.'[9] His advice was that the government should put itself right with the King by prosecuting and punishing those responsible for the outrage. Forewarned of what was in the wind, the ministers gathering in London lost no time in taking appropriate action. As soon as George disembarked, he was confronted with proposals that Sir Robert Wilson and Sir Robert Baker should be dismissed, the one from the army for inciting the crowd, the

[7] The King *en route* for Ireland in the royal yacht arrived at Holyhead late on 6 August and the Queen died the following night. News reached the King of her serious condition on the morning of the 9th and of her death later the same day. For the correspondence which ensued see *George IV*, ii. 452-3, 453-5; Lord Londonderry to Lord Liverpool, [10 August 1821], Add. MSS. 38191, ff. 63-4; *Liverpool*, iii. 132-3; Lord Sidmouth to Lord Liverpool, 15 August 1821, Sidmouth MSS.   [8] *Croker*, i. 202-3.
[9] Lord Sidmouth to Lord Liverpool, 27, 29 August 1821, Sidmouth MSS.

other from the magistracy for grievous neglect of duty. 'It is a great object to us', Lord Liverpool observed, 'to place ourselves in a situation of attack rather than in one of defence. This should be done even at some risk of ultimate failure, for, amongst other advantages, it will make the course of the King far more difficult, if he is, as I still believe, meditating hostilities . . . against his Government.'[10]

In the event, the King's return passed off better than anyone, most of all Liverpool, expected. Though Lord Londonderry came back with warnings of a 'complete breach' and though the whole Cabinet assembled to learn their fate,[11] politics turned out to be a forbidden subject at Carlton House, all attention being given to an autumn visit to Hanover now suddenly decided. In the nine days which elapsed before the King's departure, the most that Lord Liverpool could do was make a fumbling apology for keeping him in ignorance of the Queen's illness and submit a memorandum explaining why movement of the body by water had been out of the question.[12] The very refusal to talk, however, looked ominous because usually the King, who hated unpleasantness, was the last person to gnaw a political bone for some months. Certainly, the Prime Minister cherished no illusions that he had been pardoned for his misdeeds. Apart from Lord Londonderry's disclosure that the King while in Ireland had tried to tempt him and also Sidmouth with the premiership, Liverpool suffered the indignity of seeing the Lord Chancellor, Bathurst and Londonderry pass into the Closet before him, only gaining an audience on the second day of the King's return. This slight he took as conclusive evidence that 'a *personal* change' was intended.[13] 'L[iverpool] seems fully aware of the K's undissembled, unqualified dislike of him', Canning commented after paying a call to Fife House.[14] With Conyngham a conspicuous member of the royal party to

[10] *Bathurst*, p. 512. See also Lord Bathurst to Lord Sidmouth, 5 September 1821, Sidmouth MSS.: 'I am sure you will agree with me in thinking that everything depends upon our shewing the King immediately that we are prepared with our Measures—particularly as Liverpool is to be the object of attack from the King.'   [11] *Mrs Arbuthnot*, i. 116; *Croker*, i. 211.
[12] *Bathurst*, p. 517; Memorandum, [September 1821], Add. MSS. 38289, ff. 368–9; *George IV*, ii. 458–64.
[13] *Mrs Arbuthnot*, i. 116–17; *Croker*, i. 211–12; *Bathurst*, p. 517.
[14] Canning to Huskisson, 22 September 1821, Add. MSS. 38742, f. 277.

Hanover, with Canning as despised and rejected as ever, it still remained to be seen who commanded the Cabinet's first loyalty—the King or his Prime Minister.

Had the difference ever come to a head, Liverpool, in all likelihood, would have succumbed. While it is accurate enough to speak of a Tory party at this time, 'Toryism' was less the creed of a party than an ideology which overrode what were often called 'mere party considerations'. As Arbuthnot and Wellington told Liverpool in no uncertain terms, the government had to save the country from the Radicals, and if the choice lay between having him out and them in, they believed that official men and parliament would not hesitate in knowing where to stand. Canning, they said, was not indispensable. To be sure, any administration would have found his talents precious, while out of office 'he would immediately be surrounded by the discontented of all descriptions & by the Young Philosophers'. But he was not worth the country's irretrievable ruin. Without him, without Liverpool even, the government still had a chance of survival, especially if the 'intermediate' parties were persuaded to join. Indeed, the feeling was that, as always where Canning was concerned, the Prime Minister's political vision was being sadly distorted by his personal preferences.[15] What might have happened in 1821 was what eventually did happen in 1827, when, with Liverpool removed from the political scene, the government split into two irreconcilable factions, though on this occasion the so-called 'high Tories' would have stayed in power while the rest joined Canning in uneasy co-operation with the Whigs.

That nothing of the sort occurred was due to the King. His attitude towards Canning mellowed remarkably during his not particularly pleasant sojourn in his German dominions. At his departure from England the government had been left in no doubt that the old sore still rankled, Croker being treated to a philippic almost on the steps of Carlton House.[16] But within

[15] *Mrs Arbuthnot*, i. 123–4; *Wellington Desp.* (new series), i. 192–6; *Arbuthnot*, p. 24 n. 2. See also 'Substance of a Conversation between the Duke of Wellington, Sir B. Bloomfield & Mr. Arbuthnot', 21 July 1821, Add. MSS. 38370, ff. 25–31.
[16] *Croker*, i. 213–14; *Mrs Arbuthnot*, i. 119; Lord Sidmouth to Charles Bragge-Bathurst, 24 September 1821, Sidmouth MSS.

three weeks he was telling Londonderry, who had accompanied him to the Continent, that, while he would not submit to 'a continuance of a system which renders my life full of inquietude and vexation', he would neither change his government nor insist further on Canning's exclusion. With regard to the latter he did add two important conditions: on no account was Canning to have an office of 'personal communication' and at the first opportunity he was to be sent off to India.[17] Since Londonderry thought it wisest to avoid a discussion by letter, the Prime Minister was only given a hint of the King's friendlier disposition, and then only indirectly through Arbuthnot.[18] Still, reading between the lines, Liverpool learnt enough to cease his gloomy meditations. Where he had convinced himself that the negotiation would assume 'a Shape in which continuance will be scarcely practicable', he now appeared 'in a Temper, the most favourable to useful Discussion & the best calculated to smooth Difficulties'.[19]

The event which made the King adopt a more conciliatory tone was, almost certainly, news that Hastings was definitely contemplating retirement. From about May 1821, the Court of Directors, the King's private secretary and the Governor-General's friends had been receiving letters complaining of an intrigue to displace him; but while these had shown a readiness to quit Calcutta, there had been no word of resignation or demand for recall.[20] In these circumstances, no one knew whether a successor should be nominated or not. After having Hastings tell him that 'our political relation will probably be soon at an end', Canning concluded it was necessary,[21] and, mindful of the year which elapsed between sending a letter and receiving a reply, many at East India House were inclined to agree. Possibly two years would pass before the new governor-general even set foot in India. On the other hand, until Hastings' intentions were clearly known, many felt with Lord Liverpool

[17] *George IV*, ii. 466–7.
[18] Ibid., p. 465; Lord Londonderry to Arbuthnot, 12 October [1821], Add. MSS. 38566, ff. 71–2.
[19] Lord Liverpool to Lord Sidmouth, 4 October 1821, Lord Sidmouth to Lord Londonderry, 30 October 1821, Sidmouth MSS.
[20] e.g. *George IV*, ii. 375–7, 405–6, 409.
[21] Lord Hastings to Canning, 2 February 1821, Canning to Lord Liverpool, 12, 13 August 1821, Canning MSS.

that there was indecency and perhaps illegality in appointing a replacement. Hastings' real game, of course, was to obtain a recall not at the Company's but at the sovereign's behest; for this, if accompanied by a mark of honour, like an embassy or dukedom, would thoroughly vindicate his somewhat controversial period of office. When yet another bundle of remonstrant letters arrived towards the end of September, the King in a flash saw the solution to all his difficulties.[22] Hastings was indebted to him for his appointment in the first place, and if he could be persuaded to return the favour by now retiring—there were rumours that his resignation was already in England—Canning could be accommodated and his own honour and comfort secured. For this much, even Canning's temporary presence in the Cabinet was not intolerable, if it happened at all.

Probably his eagerness to spring the trap explained his premature homecoming, almost a fortnight earlier than he had originally planned. Certainly, he arrived back more his old amicable self. 'Such a Changed Man as the King you never saw,' Londonderry reported to his half-brother in Vienna. 'He is in the highest Spirits and says he, L[iverpool], is again entitled to all his Confidence.'[23] Over the Household there was never a glimmer of further trouble. Londonderry, who returned ahead of the King, went to see Liverpool at Walmer,

[22] Precisely what intelligence the King received in Hanover is not clear. Letters from Lord Hastings certainly arrived while he was there, but, according to Lord Liverpool's information, they gave no indication that he intended to leave India. Lord Liverpool to Canning, 23 October 1821, ibid. On the other hand, Liverpool may well have been misinformed. About the same time that the King received his letters, the Chairman of the East India Company also had word from Hastings that his return was imminent, and it is hardly likely that the Governor-General would have openly contradicted himself. Canning's diary, 28 September 1821, ibid. A further intriguing possibility is that the King learnt that Colonel Doyle was holding a letter of resignation to be tendered at his discretion. Though on his arrival back in England he professed to know nothing about it, there were some who thought otherwise. Hobhouse concluded that he 'must have been playing a double part for a good while past', having known about Doyle's authority for five or six months. Canning to Lord Liverpool, 29 September 1821, Add. MSS. 38568, ff. 96-7; Lord Liverpool to Canning, 7 November 1821, Canning MSS.; Hobhouse, pp. 79-80. Certainly, on 3 October Doyle told the Chairman of the East India Company that he was holding Hastings' resignation, and word may have reached the King this way. Thomas Reid to Canning, 4 October 1821, Add. MSS. 38411, ff. 67-9.

[23] Lord Londonderry to Lord Stewart, 14 November [1821], Castlereagh MSS.

and divulged that, though Conyngham was still wanted in the
Household, the King was now prepared to have him in the
lesser post of Lord Steward. At first the Prime Minister
hesitated, for even this office was efficient rather than honorary;
but no doubt remembering Wellington's advice, that the
question was a triviality which should not be allowed to
obscure the larger issue, when he next saw the King he gave
his entire concurrence. Montrose was promoted to Chamberlain, Dorset replaced him as Master of the Horse and
Cholomondeley, who had been Lord Steward, was consoled
with a promise of the Garter and a seat in the Lords for his
son and heir.[24]

Concerning India, to which the whole question of new-
modelling the Cabinet was related, things did not go nearly as
smoothly. A few days after his return from Hanover the King
sent for Colonel Doyle, who as Hastings' confidant in England
had been holding a letter of resignation since November 1820
to be presented at his discretion. As Canning realised, the
initiative to open India lay wholly with the man who despised
him.[25] The East India directors would never recall the governor-
general unless the government gave the word: the government
would not act 'without the Knowledge & Sanction of his Royal
Friend & Patron'.[26] Only the King could stop the flow of
expostulation and allusion issuing from Calcutta and bring
Hastings scurrying home. The purpose of an interview with
Doyle was to find out whether that advantage could be acted
upon immediately. Bearing in mind that Doyle's authority was
now a year old, Liverpool did not for a moment think that it
could. Great then was his surprise to learn that, lured by a
promise of the Paris embassy (which Londonderry incidentally
may have arranged), Doyle had agreed to submit the resignation.[27] Nor was his astonishment unaccompanied by dismay,
for this development tumbled every hope of Canning's and

---

[24] *Wellington Desp.* (new series), i. 194; *Mrs Arbuthnot*, i. 124, 125–6;
Lord Liverpool to Canning, 7 November 1821, Canning MSS.; Lord
Liverpool to Lord Sidmouth, 8 November 1821, Sidmouth MSS.; Lord
Londonderry to Lord Stewart, 21 November 1821, Castlereagh MSS.
[25] Canning to Lord Liverpool, 3, 4 October 1821, Add. MSS. 38568,
ff. 100–103, 104–105.
[26] Lord Sidmouth to Lord Liverpool, 1 November 1821, Sidmouth MSS
[27] Canning to Mrs Canning, 16, [19] November 1821, Canning MSS.

indeed his. Both had already agreed that immediate acceptance
of India was out of the question, mainly because Hastings had
made no clear statement of his intentions and to appoint
Canning as governor-general designate would look much like
the consummation of the intrigue he had been complaining
about. Each had his separate reasons as well. The Prime
Minister was convinced that once Canning was safely installed
at the Admiralty he would probably never leave the Cabinet,
even if there was an understanding that he would eventually
retire to India. As for Canning, while the pecuniary temptation
was as strong as ever, his wife could not bear the thought of
years away from Europe, especially when their daughter was
ready to make her social debut, and he yet hoped for time to
reconcile her to the sacrifice.[28]

Thanks to the King, and probably his enemies in the Cabinet,
these plans now came to naught. Instead of having office for at
least a year and the offer of India when the vacancy had been
definitely established, he seemed about to lose both. On hearing
that Doyle was ready to oblige the King, Lord Melville hastened
to do likewise. By refusing to vacate the Admiralty when India
was Canning's for the asking, he upset Liverpool's calculations
entirely,[29] for this left open only the Home Office and the
India Board; the King would never have Canning in the one
and Canning would never go back to the other. Equally frus-
trating for Canning and Liverpool was the risk that if India
were refused on this occasion, King, government and Company
would feel acquitted of any future obligation and no further
offer would be forthcoming. Someone else would be appointed
to take Hastings' place, and all that Canning would be able to
look forward to was another long period as a political outcast.
Yet after Liverpool with his usual consideration had arranged
a temporary respite for him and he had retired to Welbeck to
ponder the matter carefully, there did seem no alternative to
outright refusal. The King was bent on getting him away, and
many ministers, he could not help suspecting, were similarly
inclined. Since he had made it quite clear to the Prime Minister

---

[28] Canning to Lord Liverpool, 8 October, 10, 11 November 1821, Lord
Liverpool to Canning, 7 November 1821, Canning to Mrs. Canning, 15,
16, [19] November 1821, ibid.   [29] *Mrs Arbuthnot*, i. 126; *Hobhouse*, p. 79.

that he should not jeopardise his own office for his sake or have his name put forward and rejected a second time,[30] every avenue of escape, to all appearances, was closed.

Returning to London, he at once set to work on a justificatory letter which Liverpool was to forward to the King. Naturally he made no mention of his domestic difficulties, only saying that he could not accept India when the Governor-General appeared to be in a quandary whether to stay or quit and, worse, when some would be ready to interpret his appointment as a cunning usurpation. Nor did he pledge himself to accept nomination when the way had been cleared, for the simple reason, though he did not state it, that it would lessen his chances of office at home and destroy his freedom of action. The most that he wanted the King to understand was that refusal now did not necessarily mean refusal later on. From communication with the 'Chairs' of the East India Company he knew that pretexts could be invented to delay the proposal of Hastings' successor, and also that the Prime Minister was seriously considering the idea of a locum tenens appointment. He still wanted the governor-generalship, indeed still regarded it as preferable to a permanent subordination in parliament and the government. But, hamstrung by financial embarrassment, he could not afford to wait too long; two sessions without remuneration were the most that his purse could stand. Since the King aided by others was fighting to deny him a Cabinet position *pro tempore*, since it was doubtful whether Liverpool could have forced the issue had he allowed him to try, India was the only possibility left to him. If that failed, so it seemed would his life as a public man.[31]

Luckily for him, the knife wielded by his enemies was never allowed this last cruel twist. To be sure, not two days after he had declined India, Peel accepted with alacrity Liverpool's offer of the Home Office.[32] Liverpool and Londonderry had discovered when they had gone down to Brighton to consult

[30] Canning to Lord Liverpool, 8 October, 10 November 1821, Canning MSS.
[31] Canning to Huskisson, 16 November 1821, Add. MSS. 38743, ff. 21–2; Canning to Mrs Canning, 16, [19], 23, 24, 27, 29 November 1821, Canning to Lord Liverpool, 20 November 1821, Canning MSS.; Huskisson to Lord Grenville, 29 November [1821], PRO 30/29.   [32] *Peel*, i. 300–1.

the King on the government reshuffle that Canning was to go to India or make his own way in the world, and the former, whose hopes can never have been high, reluctantly retired in despair against this inveterate prejudice.[33] The next day Liverpool had written to Peel, inviting him to take the seals. Locked out in such a peremptory manner, Canning could not help feeling aggrieved. He understood the King, correctly it must be added, to have agreed that if India were not immediately available he should hold a Cabinet position in the meantime. Yet before the first point had been definitely ascertained the alternative had been put wholly out of his reach. Bitterly he began to reflect that Liverpool must have either misunderstood or tricked him or been the dupe of others more cunning than himself. The Prime Minister knew well that his preference for India was qualified by the circumstances of his appointment, that he wanted to succeed through 'a voluntary vacancy' or not at all. If he took the governor-generalship after exclusion from the Cabinet he would appear as a pawn in a larger arrangement. Worse still, he had been willing enough to forego his claims to ministerial office provided they endangered the government itself; but no sooner had Lord Liverpool expressed his confidence in this respect and admitted that India was not available on his terms than the door had been locked, barred and bolted without a breath of an offer.[34]

Actually, in musing like this, Canning did the Prime Minister less than justice. For close on two years he had been reminding him of his aspirations for the 'Mogulship' if primacy in the Commons was denied him, and an arrangement which left him a chance of their being realised, a good chance since no one in the government wanted him free-lance in parliament for very long, should not have had him casting reproaches. The fact of the matter was that Liverpool, much to his regret, had gradually come to see that an opening at home was impossible to achieve, which he was the first to admit left Canning in a limbo of uncertainty. Before Colonel Doyle had announced himself ready to tender Hastings' resignation, he had been confident

[33] *George IV*, ii. 470–1; Canning's diary, 26, 28 November 1821, Canning MSS.
[34] Canning to Huskisson, 24 December 1821, Add. MSS. 38743, ff. 86–93.

that he could secure him a temporary place at the Admiralty. Afterwards, he 'manifestly apprehended that the question of Office was gone by', and the eagerness of the King and his colleagues to get rid of Canning, exemplified by Melville's refusal to budge, must have finally convinced him.[35] Fortunately for Liverpool's peace of mind, Canning's sourness was fairly shortlived, for by the end of December he occupied the position that had been his before Doyle had sprung his surprise; that is, 'the option of the appointment when the contingency shall arise'.[36] When Hastings' resignation, according to the usual form, was referred to the East India Company, Canning's supporters in the Court of Directors vehemently disputed its validity; and, though the point remained in doubt, the nomination of a successor was indefinitely postponed. As a result, even if Hastings left India the following day, Canning gained the breathing space he desired so desperately.[37] The government was no less pleased. 'I must say,' wrote Lord Liverpool, discussing arrangements for the government of Bengal should Hastings leave, 'that I hold the keeping the situation of Governor General open for Canning as a question of *vital importance*. We shall find the greatest inconvenience in his being here for any time out of office, and yet his return to office now is rendered nearly impracticable, even if the King's objections could be over-ruled.'[38] With little further ado, the governor-generalship dropped neatly into his lap just three months later, when Doyle urgently represented that Hastings wanted to leave India for personal reasons but would not do so until his successor had been appointed.[39]

[35] Canning to Mrs Canning, 16, [19] November 1821, Canning MSS.
[36] Canning to Lord Liverpool, 11 November 1821, ibid.; Canning to Huskisson, 5 January 1822, Add. MSS. 38743, ff. 112–13.
[37] Court of Directors to Lord Hastings, 12 December 1821, Canning MSS.; Bragge-Bathurst to Lord Liverpool, 7 December 1821; Canning to Huskisson, 20, 24 December 1821, Add. MSS. 38411, ff. 77–8, 38743, ff. 80, 86–7.   [38] *Bathurst*, p. 527.
[39] Thomas Reid to Canning, 14 March 1822, Canning to Colonel Doyle, 17 March 1822, Doyle to Canning, 18 March 1822, Canning to Reid, 19 March 1822, Add. MSS. 38411, ff. 86–94. Of course, after Peel had accepted the Home Office, Canning's great concern was how long he would have to wait before India became his. Shortly before Peel actually received the seals he badgered the Prime Minister to re-cast the arrangement so that he could have the Home Office, and it is a measure of his desperation that he was even prepared to relinquish the governor-generalship to get it. Canning to Lord Liverpool, 10 January 1822, ibid., 38568, ff. 112–14.

As far as Canning was concerned, had a position in the Cabinet not eluded him, the office in which he would have found himself would have been either the Admiralty—his and Liverpool's preference—or the Home Office. Not for a moment was it suggested that he might return to the Board of Control, and indeed it was hardly likely that he would have accepted to serve as Peel's inferior even on a professedly temporary basis. But the post was never offered simply because it was never offerable. In July the Cabinet had decided that an approach to the Grenvilles was an essential item in any negotiations to rearrange the government, and, since it was understood on all sides that Bragge-Bathurst's office had been exclusively reserved for their first refusal, there was never a doubt in the ministers' minds that in this respect their hands were well tied.[40] This part of the negotiation, then, could and did proceed quite independently of the other. That it would lead to a conclusion satisfying to both parties was almost taken for granted. From the time that they had deserted the main body of the opposition, the Grenvilles had given fairly reliable support to the government side. But seemingly the real fuel which drove their political engine was an insatiable appetite, an indecent avidity for the lucre of office. The reputation, which was a standing joke among politicians, like most concocted by old enemies and erstwhile friends, was not a little exaggerated. Williams-Wynn, it is certain, had more faith in an administration of moderate Whigs than in one which retained Addingtonian mediocrities like Vansittart and Bragge-Bathurst and left out Canning and Peel; Buckingham, in consequence, was constantly bemoaning his posture of neutrality. Moreover, he took the Grenville pledge of concessions to the Catholics immensely seriously. 'If there appeared any reasonable chance of our carrying the Catholic question,' he once declared, 'I should myself feel that a paramount motive to accede to the government.' His conduct throughout the, for him, trying negotiations of December 1821 make it difficult not to believe him.[41]

[40] *Liverpool*, iii. 142; Buckingham, *George IV*, i. 174–5; Huskisson to Canning, 21 November 1821; Canning to Huskisson, 23 November 1821, Add. MSS. 38743, ff. 30, 36.
[41] Buckingham, *George IV*, i. 77–8, 198, 201; Williams-Wynn to Lord Grenville, 23 June 1821, Coed-y-maen MSS.

Nevertheless, a rather colourless personality, remembered best for an encyclopaedic knowledge of standing orders and a voice of peculiar timbre which earned him the nickname 'Mr. Squeaker', he lived perpetually in the shadow of the head of the connexion, the thrusting, self-important, much less scrupulous Marquis of Buckingham. Where Williams-Wynn viewed the question of coalition with the government as largely a question of expediency, the ambitious Buckingham tried to make it a matter of principle. The administration, he argued, was horrifyingly weak, and a ready prey for the Radicals as long as it so continued. The Grenvilles should not wait until the opportunity arrived to form a government 'strong enough to carry on the public business advantageously and creditably', but infuse strength into the ailing article without further delay. To avoid the 'calamity' which would follow surrender of power to the Radicals, he knew of 'no sacrifice too great to be made, no duty so imperious to be followed. . .'.[42] By the spring of 1821, when rumours of a government reshuffle were prevalent, this insistence of his that the Grenvilles should force themselves on the administration could no longer be controlled by a nature so impulsive. After the Queen's 'trial', with the government believed to be near the point of collapse, Buckingham's cousins had been annoyed to find in him 'so much disposition to accept office . . . that . . . he will scarcely be persuaded to reject it'.[43] But now he appeared to discard propriety altogether by openly angling for some political reward. Towards the end of March he announced to Wellington that the prize he coveted was the Lord Lieutenancy of Ireland, to which the tactful reply was made 'that there is no man more desirous than I am of strengthening the connexion between your family and the government'. Six weeks later, irked by the fact that no offer was forthcoming, he tried a more dubious form of pressure. Fremantle, his confidant and middleman in such matters, called at Apsley House with a message 'that the encreased acknowledged weakness of the Govt made more extensive communications necessary', and that unless the ministers took positive steps to

---

[42] Lord Buckingham to Williams-Wynn, 5 November, 24 December 1820, 22 June 1821, ibid.
[43] Williams-Wynn to Lord Grenville, 2 December 1820, ibid.

strengthen themselves they 'must not expect assistance as before from me'.[44] Of course, duly informed of the suspension of the negotiations, Buckingham had to forgo blackmail and bear his impatience as best he could.[45] But after this the ministers could not be blamed for thinking that buying would be easy at the sale of the Grenville stud.

Acting by Liverpool's instructions, Wellington renewed his contact with Fremantle on 21 November. This was some days before the ministers informed the King of their plans for reconstructing the administration, which shows how far they felt themselves committed.[46] As the government hoped, the offer, as outlined to Fremantle the following week, met with Buckingham's hearty concurrence, though it only gave him a dukedom and office to Williams-Wynn and one other. In addition, Plunket, who was an ally rather than a dependent, was to be Attorney-General in Ireland with a proviso that he take an active part in the House of Commons. 'Now my dear Charles,' Buckingham wrote to his cousin full of enthusiasm, 'I agree fully to this offer. I have a right to speak strongly upon it, because I am not to have Office. I therefore say that you will be *mad* if you do not accept the offer yourself.'[47] Lord Grenville, to whom he hastened after receiving Fremantle's report, was not nearly so impressed. He thought that the Prime Minister in his plans to recast the administration was being too soft-hearted to do much good, Vansittart especially deserving no mercy for his incompetence and unpopularity. When he learnt that Sidmouth was to continue in the Cabinet, while Wellesley as a 'Catholic' Lord Lieutenant was to be checked by Peel in London and Goulburn in Dublin, he also began to argue vehemently that the government would be too 'Protestant' in complexion for a Grenville to give it countenance. This latter objection he never renounced, and in fact, consti-

---

[44] Buckingham, *George IV*, i. 114, 148–9, 150–1, 162–3; Lord Buckingham to Williams-Wynn, 12 June 1821, Coed-y-maen MSS.
[45] *Wellington Desp.* (new series) i. 177; Buckingham, *George IV*, i. 174–5.
[46] Ibid., p. 231. Wellington was at Teddesley, E. J. Littleton's place in Staffordshire, and Arbuthnot probably brought the message down. Huskisson to Canning, 21 November 1821, Add. MSS. 38743, ff. 30–3.
[47] Buckingham, *George IV*, i. 232–5; Lord Buckingham to Williams-Wynn, 28 November 1821, Coed-y-maen MSS.

tuted the main difficulty in the transaction, for, as Buckingham snidely remarked, Williams-Wynn's 'fears always keep pace with his Uncle's'.[48] The government's reply naturally referred back to the principle adopted in 1812, which gave every minister and official man a freedom to pursue or oppose concessions to the Catholics in parliament as a private member. Londonderry, who took over the negotiations when Liverpool departed to Bath for a recuperative holiday, also defended the Dublin appointments as contributing to the pacification of Ireland which was again experiencing a rising tide of disorder and violence. At the Home Office Peel's understanding of the Irish problem would be invaluable, no one could deny Goulburn's talents as a man of business, and between them Wellesley and Plunket would prevent any preponderance of 'Protestant' feeling at Dublin Castle. Indeed, he even went so far as to argue that if the Grenvilles spurned the government's offer 'the Catholics naturally would take the alarm and conclude that [they] did so from finding the Catholic Question in so hopeless a state as to make it impossible for [them] to take office, that this would have the worst effect upon the public mind there and make the pacification of that country a most distant and doubtful measure'.[49]

Partly by threatening to withdraw from politics altogether, Buckingham gradually broke down his cousin's resistance. Whatever Lord Grenville said, the public arguments in favour of a junction easily outweighed those against. Not only would the Grenvilles strengthen the 'Catholic' element in the government, with complete freedom to pursue their opinions on the subject which mattered most to them, but Wellesley was confident that he could defeat any 'Protestant' cabals against his authority and Plunket would become Attorney-General regardless of what they did. In addition, Canning was believed

[48] Buckingham, *George IV*, i. 235–6; Lord Grenville to Williams-Wynn, 7 December 1821, Coed-y-maen MSS.; Lord Buckingham to Lord Wellesley, 3 December 1821, Lord Sidmouth to Lord Liverpool, 9 December 1821, Add. MSS. 37310, ff. 189–92, 38290, ff. 137–8.

[49] Memorandum of Lord Liverpool's conference with Lord Buckingham, 30 November 1821, Lord Buckingham to Lord Grenville, 1 December [1821], memorandum of conference between Lord Londonderry, Lord Buckingham and Williams-Wynn, 5 December 1821, Grenville MSS.; *Liverpool*, iii. 160–1.

to have pledged himself not to go into opposition. In other words, if they turned down the administration's offer they would be in grave danger of ceasing to exist as an effective political force, for some would join and the rest would stay out while the government would have become stronger than ever.[50] Things came to a head between Buckingham and Williams-Wynn on 7 December. On that day a letter arrived from Lord Grenville repeating the argument that the 'Protestant' bias of the arrangements was too strong to be ignored and warning the second that all he had heard from Londonderry of his freedom of action on the Catholic Question was a 'beautiful metaphor' and 'not one word of explanation'. Buckingham replied immediately complaining that his cousin would now be 'guided entirely by considerations hostile to mine', the hereditary honour sought by his father lost for ever and the family's political greatness brought to an untimely end. Clearly, the final decision rested with Williams-Wynn, and, already impressed with his cousin's 'vehemence & eagerness almost dictation' which could lead 'not only to Political but Personal disunion', he at length agreed to accept.[51] The only stipulations he insisted upon, partly out of deference to Lord Grenville, partly to show that his action was principled, were full permission to press emancipation even to the point of resignation and liberty to criticise Goulburn's appointment as encouraging 'apprehension in the public mind of counter action and opposition between the Lord Lieutenant and his secretary'. These, of course, the Prime Minister had no difficulty in accepting.[52] Hereafter the only delay resulted from the government's and the Grenvilles' mutual desire to make Plunket's appointment coincide with the others. By letting it appear that the entire plan

[50] Lord Buckingham to Lord Grenville, 30 November, [3], 6 December 1821, memorandum of Lord Liverpool's conference with Lord Buckingham, 30 November 1821, Williams-Wynn to Lord Grenville, [4], [5 December 1821], Grenville MSS.; Lord Buckingham to Lord Wellesley, 3 December 1821, Add. MSS. 37310, ff. 189–92; Buckingham, *George IV*, i. 238–40; *The Life, Letters and Speeches of Lord Plunket*, ii. 86–9.

[51] Lord Buckingham to Williams-Wynn, 3, 8 December 1821, Lord Grenville to Williams-Wynn, 7 December 1821, Coed-y-maen MSS.; Williams-Wynn to Lord Grenville, [5 December 1821], Lord Buckingham to Lord Grenville, 7 December 1821, Grenville MSS.; *Liverpool*, iii. 163.

[52] Buckingham, *George IV*, i. 249–53; Williams-Wynn to Lord Liverpool, 13 December 1821, Add. MSS. 38290, f. 199.

of reconstruction depended on Plunket's procurement, a vacancy for him was soon created, though it did mean two retirements, a new Chief Justice and a new Solicitor-General.[53] On 17 January 1822 Peel and Williams-Wynn performed the ritual kissing of hands and the transaction was complete.

The great object of the negotiations with Peel and the Grenvilles was the strengthening of the government in the House of Commons. The Prime Minister, in fact, said that they were 'grounded on this consideration alone' when he saw Fremantle in the interview which opened proceedings with the Grenvilles. His insistence that Williams-Wynn and not Buckingham should have a place in the Cabinet and that Plunket as Attorney-General in Ireland should take his fair share of debate must seemingly have driven the point home.[54] Yet if the ministers wanted numbers their new allies brought them very few. Probably Buckingham and Wellesley together could muster no more than twenty certain votes, and when it is remembered that in the past these had usually been employed in support of the government, the balance of parties was barely disturbed. The changes made more sense when the 'speechifying' capabilities of the Treasury Bench were considered. Even so, the session of 1822 must have been an acute disappointment, since the new men did little to improve its articulateness: Peel tended to wrap himself up in the specialities of his own department; Williams-Wynn's treble and his longwindedness on points of parliamentary procedure often rendered him ludicrous; and Plunket did not pull his weight in general debate as much as the Cabinet had bargained on. The sorry tale was that Londonderry still bore the brunt of the opposition's attacks while there was no absolute guarantee that Canning's brilliant eloquence would be for ever at the government's service. If ever he did cross over, the administration would end up weaker instead of stronger, as Lord Grenville realised. 'What is called *strengthening* Government in the House of Commons,' he observed to his nephew, 'consists in driving Canning into

---

[53] Lord Liverpool to Lord Sidmouth, 10 December 1821, Lord Sidmouth to Lord Manners, 12 December 1821, Lord Sidmouth to Bragge-Bathurst, 6 January 1822, Sidmouth MSS.; Lord Buckingham to Lord Liverpool, 14 December 1821, Add. MSS. 38290, ff. 155–7; Buckingham, *George IV*, i. 255–6.   [54] Ibid., pp. 232–3.

opposition, who was before the best speaker on the Government side, and having Peel in Government, who was before a speaker also on their side.'[55]

The real advantage of the changes was that they, in the full sense of the eighteenth century phrase, broadened the bottom of the administration. This the ministers were quite deliberate about. Before 1822 it was never inconceivable that, if Liverpool and his colleagues went out, a moderate Whig, like Lansdowne, would join with Wellesley and Buckingham to establish a viable government independent of the Radicals. By absorbing these 'intermediate' parties, the likeliest alternative to the Tories would be a purely Whig administration, which, many believed, would soon be reduced into an auxiliary of the Radicals and end with a republic and civil chaos. Parliament, therefore, would have more reason than ever to ponder the consequences of discarding the present set of ministers. 'Let him have his explanation,' Londonderry wrote, advising the Prime Minister to accept Williams-Wynn's stipulations, 'and consider his comments as constituting no difficulty to our union. In this way you will be sure of taking this connection out of that central position in the House of Commons which invites intrigue, and might facilitate an intermediate arrangement. I regard this as constituting the preponderating motive for forming this connection.'[56] Needless to say, most politicians regarded the new arrangements as a reunion of Pitt's old party split asunder since 1801, an accession, in Liverpool's words, of 'those individuals and interests . . . between which and the Government there exists a general coincidence of opinion on the great principles of domestic and foreign policy'.[57] Much of this was undeniably true. Wellesley and the Grenvilles had both held office in Pitt's first administration, and, except for their aversion for Sidmouth, they might have joined Liverpool in 1812 instead of in 1821. With their accession, all who were left in declared opposition were the lineal descendants of Fox. But to say that a sentimental desire for reconciliation was the driving force of the

---

[55] Ibid., p. 244.
[56] *Liverpool*, iii. 163. See also *Mrs Arbuthnot*, i. 133.
[57] Huskisson to Lord Granville, 3 December 1821, PRO 30/29; Huskisson to Lord Binning, 6 December 1821, Lord Liverpool to Huskisson, 8 January 1822; Add. MSS. 38743, ff. 59, 115; *Liverpool*, iii. 142.

negotiations is obviously an overstatement. The Grenvilles were invited to share office because it was feared that they might otherwise share it with the Whigs. Wellesley was dangerous because he was able, and when the Irish troubles made a change at Dublin necessary, his appointment served the double purpose of providing for Ireland and attaching him to the government.

II. 'NEITHER CREDITABLE NOR SAFE'

Whether increased political dimensions would give the administration the increased confidence of parliament remained to be seen. Certainly, with yet another good harvest in 1821 hastening the decline of corn prices, the government expected the 'country gentlemen' to arrive back in bad humour. The New Year signalled a fresh round of protest meetings, and these produced an abundance of fiercely-worded petitions complaining of everything from the system of representation to exorbitant government spending and the gigantic confidence trick perpetrated on the country by 'Peel's Act' of 1819. Of course, the well-embedded idea that the wielders of power should look to the nation first ensured that, no matter how hard the landed interest pressed the government, the ministers would only go so far to meet its demands. They continued to insist that the prevailing distress was an evil which legislation could do little to relieve; they refused to tamper anew with the currency, while acknowledging the deflation which had accompanied the return to gold; and they remained intransigent on the subject of parliamentary reform, though the petitions showed that the notion was making way among the yeomanry to an alarming degree. Yet, even within these limits, there was ample that the government felt obliged to do. The agriculturists cried out against extravagance, so the government scrimped and scraped to reduce the estimates. They complained of 'overwhelming and all-devouring taxation', so ways and means were pondered to alleviate the burden. They libelled the corn laws and compared the prosperity of the manufacturing interest, so direct assistance and more effective protection for agriculture were items placed on the legislative agenda. At once the issue of their distress became the central issue of the session, ground fought over by an opposition scenting blood, a government anxious to conciliate, Ricardian economists and the representatives of the distressed themselves.

The work of retrenchment began when the old session had barely concluded. One of the last acts of the House of Commons had been to pass an address to the Crown demanding 'a minute inquiry into the several departments of the Civil Government' and 'every possible saving . . . more especially in the Military expenditure'.[58] Charged in this manner, the ministers regarded economising as one of their first priorities. Sometime during July 1821 'the *paring* committee' produced a plan for reducing the army by 12,000; a cut equal to any since the post-war disbandments, and urged in spite of past warnings from the Horse Guards that the peace establishment had already reached its absolute minimum. Notwithstanding, the Commander-in-Chief did not flinch and, with his usual good sense, announced himself ready to take drastic action if the politicians deemed it necessary. As it happened, he even improved on their work, proposing a reduction of 15,000 by demolishing completely ten infantry and two cavalry regiments, the consequence of which was that the discussion was confined to the advisability of keeping reduced battalions or a lesser number at full strength. Eventually the decision was made in favour of the former. Two cavalry regiments were broken, but throughout the rest of the army, in accordance with Wellington's view that 'weak regiments, for internal service, are nearly as efficient as strong ones', the reductions were made in troops and companies. Altogether, more than 12,000 officers and men were to be taken from the establishment at an estimated saving, when commissariat, barracks and so on were taken into account, of just over £1,000,000. With the navy undergoing a similar survey, the government in August 1821 found itself able to promise economies totalling close on £1,600,000, the sort of amount, the ministers explained to the King, which 'the most reasonable and moderate of their supporters look to'.[59]

---

[58] *CJ*, lxxvi. 478–9.
[59] *Bathurst*, pp. 504, 505, 506; Goulburn to Lord Bathurst, 27 July 1821, Bathurst MSS.; *George IV*, ii. 449–52.

Even so, these imposing plans did not pass without further
scrutiny. The outbreak of disorder in Ireland, amounting to
near rebellion in the west, caught the imperial government
largely unawares, mainly because Grant, the Chief Secretary,
failed to apply the civil power that Peel had built up for precisely such an emergency. The result was that, in response to
repeated calls for military assistance from Dublin, Great
Britain had to ship over more troops than she could safely spare.
As the Duke of York was soon pointing out, all that the country
had left were four cavalry regiments 'dispersed from the Trent
to the North of Scotland' and four of infantry, 'scarcely
sufficient to protect the Public Stores'. This warning led on to
a demand for an augmentation of five or six thousand and a
fierce attack on the whole policy of imperial defence: 'The fair
Question,' he wrote in a memorandum submitted to the
government, 'and that which should be boldly put and faced is,
whether the present times and the general state of The Country,
viewed either in its Domestic or its Foreign Policy and Con-
tingencies, are such as to admit of this Country continuing
with a Military Establishment which proves wholly inadequate
to the common Exigencies of The State, which affords no
Resource applicable to extraordinary Exigencies, and which so
often as it has been resorted to, has been productive of disappointment, and has sooner or later forced into use, arrangements of a temporary Character, entailing more Expence than
permanent Establishments. . . .'[60]

Despite this outburst, the ministers refused to concede to
the panic of the moment. Both Liverpool and Londonderry
'agreed that it would not do to tread back our steps as to any of
the *permanent* reductions', and Lord Talbot, the Lord Lieutenant, anticipated their views nicely by calling out three battalions
of out-pensioners. In vain Wellington urged his colleagues to
reform the two cavalry regiments recently disbanded. 'Our
Parliamentary Campaign,' Londonderry explained, 'perhaps
our moral Influence to carry the Country thro' Its difficulties,
depends on having good ground to stand on in our Military
reductions. It can afford any Temporary Effort, which Internal

[60] Memorandum by the Duke of York, 15 November 1821, Add. MSS.
38370, ff. 39–49.

safety and Tranquility may require, if you take it on grounds
of Temporary Policy & upon a Case made out. . . . Were we
upon the present Irish Alarm . . . to rescind our decision of
July . . . We should shake all Confidence and be supposed to
have been looking out for an Excuse to Mobilize a feeling
which is already imputed to the Horse Guards, of wishing to
Keep up Cavalry beyond the Wants of the Country at least
beyond its Means. . . .'[61] As a result, when the estimates were
presented, the legislature still found them remarkably pleasant
reading. The charge for the land forces and the navy afloat—
that is, the cost of troops and seamen actively employed—was
down £584,000. The ordinaries of the three services, which
included 'the dead expense' of half pay and pensions which
always mounted with reductions, showed a saving of £146,000.
Most gratifying of all, the extraordinaries, in spite of the Irish
emergency, had been cut back over £1,000,000. Conscious of
work well done, Londonderry did not hesitate to announce that
the estimates had been pruned by little short of two millions.[62]

Nevertheless, the ministers fully realised that to the public's
way of thinking this was only tackling half the problem. While
a large army, even a large navy, represented a system of
extravagance only sustained by feeding the huge maw of the
Exchequer, thereby hung another tale of the increasing influence
of the Crown of which parliament at all times ought to have a
constitutional jealousy. Probably every 'parliament man'
accepted the desirability of the executive's representation in

[61] Duke of Wellington to Lord Sidmouth, 4 December 1821, Lord
Liverpool to Lord Sidmouth, 10 December 1821, Lord Sidmouth to Lord
Londonderry, 18 December 1821, Lord Londonderry to Lord Sidmouth,
19 December [1821], Sidmouth MSS.; Lord Sidmouth to Lord Liverpool,
9 December 1821, Add. MSS. 38290, ff. 135–8.
[62] *Hansard*, 2nd ser., vi. 365–6. It is interesting to compare the 'proposed
reductions' of July 1821 with the estimates finally presented. The increase
in the barracks estimate can be attributed to the reinforcement of the Irish
garrison.

	Proposed reductions £	1822 estimates £	
Navy	500,000	576,730	reduction
Army	450,000	540,900	reduction
Commissariat	77,000	57,511	reduction
Barracks	53,000	18,052	increase
Extraordinaries	200,000	300,000	reduction
Ordnance	60,000	83,000	reduction
Miscellaneous	250,000	190,000	reduction

the legislature, and there must have been very few who genu-
inely believed that it was excessive as that a situation existed
which cried out for another Dunning. But as long as the
country remained morbidly preoccupied with the expense of
government, and indeed with the danger of corruption, the
House of Commons felt it expedient to investigate the position
once in a while at least. Hence the report on sinecures from a
select committee in 1817. Hence also the insistence on 'a minute
inquiry into the several departments of the Civil Government'
in June 1821. Naturally, in matters of this sort, it was up to the
Treasury to take the initiative and set an example which the rest
of the administration might follow, though some departmental
obstruction was always to be expected. On this occasion a
minute of 10 August 1821 set the pace. The implication of the
Commons' address of June was that the number and expense
of the establishments should be reduced as nearly as possible
to the pre-war totals, or to be precise, to what they had been
in 1797. Having revised the offices under their control according
to this principle, the Lords of the Treasury instructed forty-
four other heads of departments to show the same willing
spirit.[63] Together with a plan of compulsory superannuation
and new salary regulations, these economies were expected to
save between £250,000 and £300,000, not less than £150,000
accruing from the reductions themselves.[64]

The demand for frugal government, in enhancing the
Treasury's importance, always had the counter effect of
arousing departmental jealousies. On this occasion, the Marquis
of Camden, one of the Tellers of the Exchequer, claimed that
his office was exempt from Treasury regulation, and Sidmouth
declared his independence to the extent of reporting his reductions to the King-in-Council.[65] But these resentments and
formalities really made little difference. In the final analysis it
was impossible to mislead or trifle with parliament, because
since 1810 the government had had a statutory obligation to
provide annual returns of the increase and decrease of establishments and emoluments. Indeed, the figures show that where
Pitt had paddled delicately the administrations of the early

[63] *PP*, 1822, xvii. 3–9.   [64] *Hansard*, 2nd ser., vi. 1025–6, vii. 1305.
[65] *PP*, 1822, xvii. 91, xviii. 145–55.

nineteenth century took a headlong plunge. In June 1822 Arbuthnot drew up a memorandum for Londonderry in which he handily summarised the achievements of forty years of 'economical reform'. Since 1782, he claimed, relying on George Rose's *Observations respecting the Public Expenditure* for the earlier period, over two thousand offices had been abolished or consolidated; eighteen hundred since 1810 alone, including 94 sinecures, half of which were tenable with a seat in parliament. Furthermore, he estimated the total saving to the public in the last dozen years at £580,000, almost three times as much as in the previous thirty.[66] And now in one sweep the government was arranging a reduction probably equal to, if not surpassing, the reductions of a whole first generation of reform. Little wonder, then, that the Radical picture of ministerial influence as a hydra against which reformer heroes battled in vain was never taken for genuine by the 'country gentlemen' or anyone else acquainted with the facts. When a report was laid on the table in July 1822, probably only Hume and his fellow 'Democrats' were surprised to find that roughly two-thirds of the placemen in the House of Commons held efficient offices.[67]

The logical consequence of 'economical reform', one which the petitions of irate agriculturists never ceased to point out, was the remission of taxes; and because the expectation existed so strongly it was quite impossible for the government to refuse the country completely. Nevertheless, Vansittart and Liverpool were no more generous than they had to be. The 'economic Cabinet's' thinking was still ruled by an obsession for the

[66] Memorandum of the Reductions made in the Public Departments, 13 June 1822, Add. MSS. 38761, ff. 24–35, 37–8. The copy in Castlereagh MSS. xxxvii. 631–56 is endorsed: 'Prepared for Lord Londonderry's use upon Mr. Brougham's Motion on the Influence of the Crown—Arbuthnot.'

[67] On 8 June 1821 the House of Commons ordered a return of members who were placemen and pensioners, and a select committee made a report thereon in 1822. *PP*, 1822, iv. 41–59. The appendix listed 89 names, but as some of the offices were honorary rather than remunerative (aides-de-camp and K.C's were included), the actual number of 'ministerial dependents' was nearer 80, less than 70 if appointments for life are disregarded. Of these, probably little over 50 could be described as 'efficient'. Londonderry himself said that 'he could not find more than seven or eight and forty persons sitting in that House who held offices under the Crown, in a sense to which influence could be fairly attached'. *Hansard*, 2nd ser., vii. 1303. It is interesting to note how a list in the Herries Papers endorses these figures; 50 'efficient' placemen, and 81 army and naval officers as against 79 given in the parliamentary return.

sinking fund as the bastion of financial confidence. Inasmuch as a surplus of £5,000,000 had never once been achieved in the three years since 1819, to succumb to the panic of the moment and throw away revenue indiscriminately was dismissed as cowardly and foolhardy to the first degree. Of all the ministers, only Williams-Wynn, who had had no share in the decision of 1819, was ready to defy the monied interest to the extent of suspending or slowing redemption of the public debt.[68] The rest clung stubbornly to the old notion that the sinking fund was workable and that it must be made to work. 'In endeavouring to perpetuate the system of an adequate sinking fund . . . I feel that I have had a sacred cause to defend—I feel that I have been treading on consecrated ground', one of their number was soon to declare.[69] In their view, if the essential surplus was ever going to be obtained, any reduction in the revenue would have to be matched by a compensating reduction in the expenditure, the underlying assumption being that the increasing yield of the taxes, as indicated by the excise returns—'the great barometer of consumption'—would wholly make good the disappointing performances of previous years.

At first, an arrangement along these lines seemed barely feasible. Mainly the problem was to find something which would help quieten the clamouring agriculturists and also contribute effectively to their relief. Every minister knew in his own heart that were the government to remove £4,000,000 of taxes, as some Whigs wanted, it would make little difference simply because agricultural distress was the result of circumstances largely beyond any government's control. The most anybody could do, they believed, and then without a firm guarantee of success, was to improvise some form of mild economic stimulant. Londonderry spoke for all of his colleagues when he saw 'the true source of the farmer's hope' in 'the hand of Providence', 'the due course of nature', 'the uncontrollable operation of all those great laws and principles which govern the markets of the world'.[70] For a time the ministers toyed with the idea of reducing the window tax to a bare

---

[68] Buckingham, *George IV*, i. 283; Williams-Wynn to Lord Grenville, [31 January], 4 February 1822, Coed-y-maen MSS.
[69] *Hansard*, 2nd ser., vi. 397.   [70] Ibid., 363–4.

minimum to give 'an immediate & general Relief ... particularly to Country Gentlemen of Small Incomes & to Ireland'.
But, as Williams-Wynn pointed out, even this 'would apply
more efficaciously to the towns than to the country', and, half
despairing, the government was tempted to turn to the scheme
that Bathurst favoured, which was for direct assistance by way
of loans to landed proprietors.[71] In the end several expedients
were adopted. The tax on malt, which had been reduced in
1816 and increased in 1819, was again put aside for reduction;
the corn laws were to be subjected to hitherto resisted parliamentary inquiry; and to uphold the government's reflationary
plans, 'an extension of the currency' Vansittart called them,
four millions were to be borrowed from the Bank and a portion
used for advances to parish vestries on security of the rates.

Of course, there was method in the government's madness,
if madness it was to increase the unfunded debt and throw
away £1,400,000 in taxation. On the one hand, the need to keep
somewhat in step with the fallacies of public opinion could not
be denied. Because the belief persisted that fewer taxes would
bring material relief and that politicians were rapacious and
corrupt, there was some sense in removing a much detested
impost and in announcing a ten per cent cut in official salaries.
On the other hand, it made much greater sense to regard both
as sauce for the pudding proper. As the ministers realised only
too well, the farmers would have been able to tide over a difficult period more easily had they been facing a different
monetary situation. It was not that finance was unavailable.
Idle capital was actually in great abundance: the government's
demands on the money market had been minimal for many
years; canals, enclosures and foreign trade formed a limited
field for investment; and a sharp decline in prices meant that a
smaller circulation sufficed to finance a given turnover of goods
and services. The great problem was to get this capital moving,
particularly to give relief to the land. When year after year the
farmer faced the prospect of low prices, he often had no inducement to borrow except to make ends meet; and then his bank

[71] Memorandum (probably in Vansittart's hand), January 1822, Vansittart
to Lord Liverpool, 22 January 1822, Castlereagh MSS., xxxvii. 301-10,
335-49; Buckingham, *George IV*, i. 279-80, 283.

had no great inducement to lend. To make matters worse, coincidental with the agricultural depression, the country banks were pursuing a deliberate policy of credit contraction for other reasons. Ever since 'Peel's Act' had been passed, the financial world had become hypnotised by the quantity theory of money which lay behind it. Some deflation, by curtailing the Bank of England's advances to the government and by steadily reducing note issues, was regarded as an essential precondition for getting the exchanges back to par and gold back to mint price, and, if anything, the law's stated intention to replace small notes with gold after the completion of resumption only added to the misery. Even a rough guess as to how much the circulation was affected is well nigh impossible, mainly because no one can tell to what extent cheques and other substitutes for 'money' were coming into use. But the government suspected the truth and sought to take appropriate action. Londonderry, for instance, was quite positive that 'the country bankers are not acting even up to the natural scale of the credit to which the property they possess entitles them', and Liverpool described his financial measures in the Lords as being designed 'to extend and quicken the general circulation'.[72]

Cheaper credit, then, was the government's prescription for effective agricultural relief. How to provide it was its pre-occupation throughout the fortnight of Cabinet deliberation which always preceded the meeting of parliament. From the outset Vansittart was keen to find some way of converting the five per cents into four per cents. Since this would have achieved two desirable ends, it was all along the most favoured plan; not only would the charge of the debt be reduced, thus permitting an equivalent remission of revenue, but interest rates in general would be encouraged to fall by reducing the stock bearing the highest interest. The great difficulty was to engineer a rise in the already high funds to make it a feasible operation. Vansittart was confident that this could be done by inflating a little; borrowing £3,000,000 from the Bank for the

---

[72] *Hansard*, 2nd ser., vi. 716, vii. 158. See also Vansittart's statement 'that the best relief which could be afforded to the distresses complained of would be, an extension of the currency of the country' and 'that one of the most efficient means of relieving the landed interest was the facility of borrowing money at a moderate rate of interest'. Ibid., vi. 71, 74.

year's supply and advancing £4,000,000 or £5,000,000 to the
landed interest in Exchequer bills to provide relief where it
was most wanted.[73] Indeed, provided the latter plan made
money available at a reasonable rate, there would be a further
incentive for mortgages and other long-term loans to continue
their downward trend. There were hitches however, hitches
which always existed whenever the government launched full-
scale expeditions out of the realm of *laissez-faire* economics.
The Bank directors, despite their concern for laying up treasure
in preparation for resuming cash payments, were willing
enough to lend, though only on condition that the money could
be called back at short notice; but, as Williams-Wynn observed,
'with the present superabundance of capital in the market', a
few millions by themselves could scarcely make a sufficient
impression.[74] A worthwhile inflation really depended on whether
the loan to the landed interest also went through. Here lay the
rub. In the first place, the whole Cabinet, with the exception of
Harrowby and Bathurst, were by now stout adherents of the
quantity theory and automatically looked askance at a substantial issue of paper which to their mind would bring down the
exchanges and put off yet again the golden day of actual
resumption. In the second, there were the inevitable legal and
administrative intricacies involved in giving aid to private concerns. To whom was the money to be advanced? If to the
occupiers, the plan was bedevilled by the 'multiplicity and
complexity of transactions'. If to the proprietors, the government had the option of becoming mortgagee for most of the
private property in the kingdom or making invidious distinctions between one case and the other. Further, how was security
to be arranged? With the commercial and manufacturing
interest there was a 'great tangible property to be pledged'.
More often than not, the landed proprietor could offer only an
estate loaded with encumbrances and settlements and the
occupier the produce off his fields. Who was to disburse the
loans? Crown commissioners might, as in the past, have a
'general superintendence', but if assistance was to be given
safely and profitably some degree of local knowledge was

[73] Vansittart to Lord Liverpool, 21 January 1822, Castlereagh MSS.,
xxxvii. 335–49.　　　[74] Buckingham, *George IV*, i. 282.

essential. Who had that information and also the necessary disinterestedness?[75]

All these considerations greatly cramped the government's initiative. Indeed, at one stage the whole plan of issuing Exchequer bills to succour agriculture was nearly dropped, which left the inflationists nothing except the Bank loan to fall back on.[76] When an approach to the country bankers was tried, it met with a stinging rebuff, from 'the impossibility on the part of the farmers to offer sufficient security'.[77] By this time, with parliament impatient to hear from the government, the most that could be managed was a scheme of parochial loans to be provided out of £4,000,000 advanced by the Bank. On application to commissioners appointed by the Crown, parish vestries could receive an amount not exceeding one year's assessment of the parochial rates, to be employed for 'corporate purposes' and repaid in instalments over a period of four or five years. This was relief administered in a very indirect way. Possibly Vansittart, and those who thought like him, hoped that where the government left off others would carry on, that with this little lubricant the wheels of the economy would gradually pick up speed to create a momentum. Certainly, in deliberately trying to induce an expansion of credit, the ministers displayed a peculiarly modern grasp of the situation. It is also interesting that Vansittart, whom it has always been fashionable to deride, may have done the most to direct the Cabinet's thinking. The oft-heard accusation that Liverpool's administration wandered aimlessly in a torpor of financial unimaginativeness at least deserves serious reappraisal.

Once their financial preparations were complete, the ministers had reason to feel that they had done their utmost to be true to both popular expectations and their own convictions: they had shaved the estimates as far as they dared and they were

[75] Vansittart to Lord Liverpool, 21 January 1822, Castlereagh MSS., xxxvii. 335–49 is an interesting résumé of the difficulties.

[76] Buckingham, *George IV*, i. 283; Williams-Wynn to Lord Grenville, [31 January 1822], Coed-y-maen MSS.

[77] Liverpool and Vansittart met several London bankers, including the Governor and Deputy Governor of the Bank of England, on 4 February 1822. *The Times*, 5 February 1822. Though the next day in the Lords the Prime Minister denied that he had proposed to issue Exchequer bills through the country banks, it is obvious that he was sounding out opinion in the financial world. *Hansard*, 2nd ser., vi. 16.

ready to deliver up a million and a half of revenue; at the same time they continued to maintain the principle of a sinking fund nourished on an annual surplus, and engaged themselves to relieve the country by a considerable addition to the unfunded debt. It remained to be seen whether parliament would support or oppose these seeming contradictions. According to Williams-Wynn, the only measure of relief that would be 'comprehensible' to the Commons was a much greater reduction of taxation than the government was inclined to propose.[78] In the event, the first fortnight of the session proved that his fellow ministers had not been amiss in judging the mood of the legislature. On the opening day (5 February) Brougham and Londonderry both promised to discuss the problem of distress either that week or the one following, and though Hume, in default of a party amendment, at once raised the issue of 'excessive taxation', the House preferred to look forward to these two motions as the acid test of parliamentary confidence. Even so, Hume's brief sortie left the government none too confident of the outcome, for a handful of 'country gentlemen', notably including Lethbridge of Somersetshire, had hastened to join him despite Londonderry's pleas that the ministers should be allowed a fair hearing before judgement was passed. Arbuthnot's impression was that 'the country gentlemen seem all very much for taking off taxes & putting an end to the sinking fund',[79] and the Prime Minister, whose habitual pessimism already led him to expect the worst, quickly made up his mind to stake all on the attempt to save the public credit. 'L[iverpoo]l,' Huskisson reported, 'appears quite determined to stand or fall with that Fund, & told me yesterday that it was the measure of all others in the defence of which He should be best satisfied to close his political existence; only reserving the discretion to retire if defeated in the first onset or to continue the fight with greater tenacity, according to circumstances.'[80] As it turned out, there was never a need to deliver any such ultimatum. 'The Boodle Cabinet', the nickname given to a number of leading 'country

[78] Buckingham, *George IV*, i. 283; Williams-Wynn to Lord Grenville, [31 January], 4 February 1822, Coed-y-maen MSS.
[79] *Mrs Arbuthnot*, i. 140.
[80] Huskisson to Canning, [2], [8 February 1822], Canning MSS. Lord Londonderry was of a like disposition. *Mrs Arbuthnot*, i. 140.

gentlemen' who were consulting together, decided to oppose Brougham's motion, which was to come on first, to give the government an opportunity to state its case. Learning this, the ministers agreed to enter into their feelings as much as possible by preferring the previous question to a direct negative.[81] These tactics appeared to pay off handsomely. Londonderry countered a masterly speech of Brougham's, which had ended in a demand for 'such a reduction of the Taxes as may be suited to the change in the value of money, and may afford an immediate relief', with a vehement charge that he had attempted to 'entrap the House into a premature decision' before the subject was fully before it, and, much to his relief, the government gained a comfortable hundred majority.[82] As an expression of confidence, of course, it was far from being unambiguous. But it at least showed that the 'country gentlemen' were keeping their own counsel and would not go every length with the Whigs.

The opposition found the level of parliamentary discontent too high to renounce a contest at this early stage. They continued to believe that the government's financial policy was where its chief vulnerability lay; that inasmuch as public opinion imagined taxation to be the principal cause of distress, sooner or later parliament would have to pretend that it knew no better. The 'country gentlemen', for certain, were anything but stouthearted. Londonderry admitted that every once in a while they voted 'to make a figure in the columns of the opposition papers & please their constituents'.[83] On this occasion a few deft strokes aimed at the sinking fund or particularly obnoxious taxes could do the government serious harm with always a chance of mortal injury. No sooner, therefore, had Londonderry made his résumé of the government's relief programme than Althorp brought forward a motion to the effect 'that the Reduction in the amount of Taxation proposed by His Majesty's Ministers is not sufficient to satisfy the just expectations of the people'. Each side invoked the same old arguments. The Whigs insisted that Vansittart had made a mockery of Pitt's sinking fund and that it would be better to

---

[81] Huskisson to Canning, [11 February 1822], Canning MSS.
[82] *Hansard*, 2nd ser., vi. 220–78.   [83] *Mrs Arbuthnot*, i. 147.

abandon the idea of a surplus in order to give an immediate and wide-ranging relief: Tierney, in particular, accused the ministers of having an eye for the fundholder's interest when nothing stood between the country and a prosperity which would content all parties except ruinous taxation. In reply the government derided the opposition's ingenuousness: they were prepared to retrench; they were prepared to give away taxes when they could properly afford it; but nothing could detract from their awesome responsibility to maintain the public credit of which the sinking fund, however imperfect hitherto, was the great bastion.[84] There can be no doubt that this was the decisive debate on the issue of whether the repayment of the debt ought to be suspended because of the present exigency. Already the 'country gentlemen' had been agreeably impressed by the proposals set forth by Londonderry,[85] and a further majority in excess of a hundred, which included some who had voted with Brougham, drove the point home that they had been convinced and bowed to the government's greater wisdom. Four days later Vansittart expounded his plan for the conversion of the five per cents to an amiable House,[86] and the ministers sat back to congratulate themselves that the worst was behind them. Little did they know that their troubles were only beginning.

The first signs that all was not well came later in the same week when Calcraft renewed his efforts to obtain a repeal, this time a gradual repeal, of the duties on salt. Inevitably the government argued that since the House had already pledged itself to a £5,000,000 surplus[87] the opposition was beguiling it into a dangerous inconsistency. But the 'country gentlemen' were strongly tempted to forget their good resolutions by the hatefulness of the tax—a select committee in 1818 found that its removal 'would be productive of the greatest and most important advantages to all descriptions of persons'[88]—and also by what the Treasury bench called a crooked notion that the ministers could be coerced through attacks on particular taxes into further economies. These considerations and others—

---

[84] *Hansard*, 2nd ser., vi. 558–609.
[85] *Mrs Arbuthnot*, i. 144.   [86] *George IV*, ii. 502.
[87] As an alternative to Lord Althorp's resolution on 21 February, the government had moved that a surplus of £5,260,000 was estimated for the current financial year.   [88] *PP*, 1818, v. 346.

some no doubt were out to curry favour with their constituents
or impress upon the government the seriousness of the situation—prevailed over Vansittart's protest that the loss of
£500,000 from the revenue would jeopardise his conversion
operation and Londonderry's that the sinking fund was being
staked for 'premature or speculative retrenchments'. Well over
thirty ministeralists and independents converged on the opposition side to give the government a meagre majority of four.[89]
'All this lowers the Government in public estimation & gives
an idea of weakness which we do not deserve,' Mrs. Arbuthnot
complained.[90] Worse, it revived the flagging spirits of the
Whigs and seemed to give them fresh inspiration. During
Calcraft's debate, many 'country gentlemen' had declaimed
along with Knatchbull, the member for Kent, that 'ministers
could effect further retrenchments to meet their diminished
income', and their adversaries smartly perceived in this loss of
faith the opportunity to open a new line of attack. On the
following day, Ridley, in the committee of supply, moved for
the third time since 1817 the reduction of two commissioners
from the Admiralty Board, and this time his persistence was
rewarded with a majority of fifty-four, the largest winning
margin that the opposition had enjoyed for some years. Not
surprisingly, the order book was filled with similar 'economical'
motions in a matter of days. Lord Normanby gave notice that
he would bring the postmaster-general's office under attack,
and Creevey the Board of Control, while Althorp made preparations for a general censure of ministerial extravagance. Most of
the agricultural taxes were down for discussion as well.[91]

Even so, the ministers were too inured to the caprices of the
'country gentlemen' to lose their nerve or to be anything but
philosophical. Buckingham, who was more often wrong than
right when it came to politics, got it into his head that the
government ought to resign to give the country a taste of the
villainous Whigs,[92] but those in the Cabinet found such a
drastic step as unnecessary as it was undesirable. Londonderry

[89] *Hansard*, 2nd ser., vi. 837–62.
[90] *Mrs Arbuthnot*, i. 146.
[91] Buckingham, *George IV*, i. 295.
[92] Duke of Buckingham to Thomas Grenville, 5 March 1822, Grenville
MSS.; *Mrs Arbuthnot*, i. 150.

regarded the behaviour of the 'country gentlemen' as a nuisance rather than a threat: he, and no doubt his colleagues, professed to believe that no principle of the influence allowable to an administration in the Commons had been impugned by the successful attack on the Admiralty Board and that an occasional embarrassment on a point of detail was something to which every government had to accustom itself.[93] A real danger developed only when the 'moral influence' of government was weakened by a string of consecutive or near consecutive defeats, forcing in the end a crucial test of confidence. Wellington, to be sure, was inclined to believe that this moment was not too far away. While he dismissed recent setbacks as the result of the 'country gentlemen' finding themselves 'obliged to follow the torrent rather than stem it', he also feared that they were learning a habit of constant opposition which could bring the government to its knees before the session closed.[94] But only he, it seems, felt that the rot had set in to this extent. Not once, even while the opposition was applying maximum pressure, did the ministers apply to the House for a new lease of confidence. Instead, the most that the Treasury felt called upon to do was send out notes urging attendance on certain members to defend 'the just and necessary influence of the Crown' against an opposition 'determined to break down the means of administering the affairs of the country'.[95] The wisdom of withholding the ultimate deterrent was amply borne out in the contest which followed. Normanby's proposal to vest the postmaster-generalship in one man rather than two was lost by twenty-five votes; and Creevey's the next day for a select committee to investigate the Board of Control was crushed by little short of two hundred. Since it was obvious that no profit could come of further discussion the remaining motions were tactfully dropped. Thereafter, even the estimates sped through the House with little molestation. One member spoke of them getting through 'with fewer delays and remarks of Hume than was expected' and Londonderry, who had hoped to have all but the miscellaneous services provided for before Easter, was

[93] Ibid., pp. 146–7.
[94] *Wellington Desp.* (new series), i. 219–20.
[95] *Mrs Arbuthnot*, ii. 449.

gratified to find that this deadline was very nearly achieved.[96] Once again the government had successfully endured a passing spasm of displeasure on the part of the 'country gentlemen', this time without conceding a moral victory to the Whigs by making the issue a question of confidence.

Unbeknown to the ministers, there were even greater tribulations ahead, though it is hard not to believe that some of them, at least, suspected that the House of Commons had not been permanently settled. A further display of bad temper from peevish 'country gentlemen' after the Easter holidays was only to be expected because of the price of corn. All parties measured the distress of agriculture by the price calculated by the Receiver of Corn Returns, and this, thanks to a 'genial spring', showed a continuing downward trend—the wheat average from March to May was 45s. 2d. compared with 49s. od. for the previous quarter.[97] Furthermore, it was becoming increasingly clear that there existed a hard core of recalcitrants to deal with among the country members. Earlier on, Wellington had accused 'the Boodle set' of acting in concert; but only now, after constant battles in the agricultural committee and on the floor of the House, were the consistent opposers on questions of taxation and 'economical reform' earning a notoriety of their own. Undoubtedly the chief culprit in the government's eyes was Sir Thomas Lethbridge. Backing him there may have been twenty or even thirty others, many of whom represented agricultural counties like Lethbridge himself. With irregulars like this ready to take the ministerial army in the rear, ready too to urge others on to join them, Londonderry and his colleagues fully appreciated the need for further appeasement. The problem was that there was little left to try. After seven years of rigorous economy, it was difficult to see that much more could be gleaned from the establishments; the sinking fund was inviolable and so therefore the revenue which supported it; and that the corn laws were a hornets' nest which did not bear disturbance was obvious from the heated discussions already distinguishing the agricultural committee. The search for expedients would have to be carried far and wide, over ground

---

[96] *Colchester*, iii. 250; *George IV*, ii. 520.
[97] *PP*, 1825, xx. 231.

which had been traversed earlier when plans for the session were under discussion, and perhaps over territory which the government had not yet ventured upon.

As was expected, it was soon found that the pitiless economies planned during the prorogation did not allow another penny to be squeezed from the estimates in the immediate future. A few weeks previously Londonderry and the Prime Minister had gone down to Brighton to deprive the civil list of £30,000, and having accomplished this—the King, referring to the agreed reduction in official salaries, said that 'as a gentleman he could not do less himself than he had imposed upon his servants'[98]—the government had exhausted all that it seemed sane to attempt. Fortunately, once again a little financial ingenuity saved the day. Since the committee sitting on agricultural distress had looked askance at the Cabinet's plan of parochial loans, a decision was taken to make £1,000,000 available to farmers warehousing their corn under the king's lock as an alternative. To assist the inflation still further, another £1,000,000, also part of the sum that the Bank had promised earlier, was assigned for poor relief in Ireland, and the country banks, which had been steadily contracting their issues in anticipation of the expiry of their note-issuing authority, were given an extended term to circulate paper of £1 denomination. There was a measure of boldness in the first and last of these decisions. While public money for public works had a firm precedent in the crisis of 1817, a few weeks earlier Londonderry had complained that 'lending money on the produce of the land' involved 'so great a multiplicity and complexity of transactions, that the execution of it would become impracticable';[99] and to encourage five hundred different banks to increase their issues of legal tender was enough to give any believer in the quantity theory nightmares of falling exchanges and a rush towards gold.

However, this was by no means the limit of the government's daring, for one other expedient, in a very unobtrusive way, contradicted much that had already been heard in defence of keeping a sinking fund. This measure concerned the annual

[98] *Arbuthnot*, pp. 29–30; *Bathurst*, p. 529; *Wellington and his Friends* (ed. Duke of Wellington), pp. 20–1; *Mrs Arbuthnot*, 149–50.
[99] *Hansard*, 2nd ser., vii. 385–6.

charge of roughly £5,000,000 for military and naval half-pay—
'the dead expense' as Londonderry called it, 'the Deadweight' as
Cobbett named it for posterity. After discussion on the constitutional points arising—the Crown had to be kept as paymaster
though parliament lost its power of annual surveillance—the
government proposed to convert this portion of the estimates
into a fixed annuity of £2,800,000, selling it to contractors who
throughout a forty-five year period would be obliged to provide
the whole but a steadily diminishing sum as death overtook the
beneficiaries. Since this, in effect, was a form of loan to be
repaid a generation later, a loan moreover which disguised the
real extent of the annual surplus, it was fair to argue, as many
on the opposition side did, that the ministers had departed from
the sinking fund's basic premise of public credit sustained by
continuing redemption of the national debt.[100] Still, the particular sin was, as far as the sinners were concerned, a misdemeanour
in aid of the good work of further tax reductions. With between
£1,800,000 and £1,900,000 to spare, so the Cabinet calculated
after some complicated arithmetic on the statistics of survival,
the government could safely prepare for the repeal of the salt
duty and the diminution of the window tax sometime during
the next session. These reductions were promised in general
terms immediately after the Easter recess.[101]

Financial measures such as the ministers were willing to propose sprang largely from a feeling of impotence before the
inexorable laws of the economic universe; a little good might be
done, a little palliative might be administered, without getting
to the root of the disorder or effecting a lasting cure. Exactly
the same attitude prevailed concerning the corn laws. Just as
fiscal relief could never set agriculture to rights, so recasting
the act of 1815 could offer nothing for the 'country gentlemen's'

[100] See Williams-Wynn's comment, Buckingham, *George IV*, i. 290:
'. . . I must say for those who support [the sinking fund] it is somewhat
ridiculous with one hand to expend five millions in relief of the burthens
of posterity, and with the other to transpose a burthen from our own
shoulders upon theirs.' According to an opposition member, for the first
sixteen years the state would contribute £42,000,000 and the contractors
£63,000,000, while for the remaining twenty-nine the respective payments
would total £84,000,000 and £39,000,000. *Hansard*, 2nd ser., vii. 285.
[101] Towards the end of February Vansittart confided to Williams-Wynn
that salt and windows were on his list of priorities for taxation relief.
Williams-Wynn to Lord Grenville, 25 February 1822, Coed-y-maen MSS.

present satisfaction. Indeed, it was not extravagant to argue that
reducing the tax bill according to the demands of 'the agri-
culturasses' had more purpose than enforcing the absolute
prohibition of foreign corn which they also demanded, for the
one at least went some way towards stimulating consumer
spending while the other simply legislated what was already an
existing fact—since 1820 the ports had been closed, and yet the
condition of agriculture had worsened rather than improved.
Two committees of the House of Commons sat on the corn
laws in 1821 and 1822, but both frankly admitted that extending
the eighty shilling prohibition was a futile amendment. The
only consolation that the first had been able to offer the landed
interest was that 'there is a natural tendency in the distribution
of capital and labour to remedy the disorders which may
casually arise', and the second bluntly drew the obvious conclusion that 'little prospect of immediate relief can be held
out'.[102] It is more than likely that by 1822 public opinion was
coming to realise as much. Londonderry certainly thought so,
and probably to emphasise that the government had been right
all along, he attributed the enlightenment of the agriculturists
to the report of the previous year, which had been largely
written by Huskisson. That report, he claimed in parliament,
had 'had a most important and salutary effect on the public
mind, by leading it to take more just and temperate views. I
believe,' he went on, 'that the period of delusion has now, in a
great measure, passed by. I believe that sounder doctrines than
those which were last year promulgated, have become generally
prevalent.'[103] Whether or not the government was indulging in
self praise, this disposal of the champions of absolute monopoly
did mean that there was one less reason for tampering with the
act of 1815. There was some point in surrendering something
to the popular misconception that the removal of taxes would
cure the country's economic ills: where the people did not pretend to know any better than the government, there was none.

Why then did the ministers propose a radical reconstruction
of the corn law in 1822? For years they had refused to alter
what the agriculturists themselves had originally pronounced
acceptable, and which had in fact worked, assuming protection

[102] *PP*, 1821, ix. 7; 1822, v. 5.   [103] *Hansard*, 2nd ser., vi. 389.

from foreign competition in years of plenty to have been the bill's great object. Admittedly, one serious defect stood out, inasmuch as absolute prohibition could be translated overnight into unlimited importation by the opening of the ports. But this defect had always existed, and it was obvious that its correction would do nothing to help the farmer out of his present difficulties. There can be no doubt that the ministers were impelled towards the undesirable—the undesirable because no one wanted to arouse the 'lower sort' or have the commercial interest range itself against the landed interest—mainly by the whiplash of the 'country gentlemen's' growing displeasure. To bring in a bill to control the flow of foreign corn more precisely was a tactic intended to reassure the agriculturists that the government had not forsaken them. All the evidence indicates that the Cabinet was contemplating sweeping changes well before the commencement of the parliamentary session. A memorandum among the Castlereagh papers, possibly in Vansittart's hand, of 'measures to be considered' includes a proposal to reduce the foreign import price to 67s. a quarter with a duty of 20s. gradually decreasing to 10s. over a ten-year period. In the discussion on this measure, the Cabinet apparently resolved to recommend free importation above 95s. or 100s. and prohibition at 60s. or 70s. with a sliding scale of duties to regulate the transition in between.[104]

However, this decision was not mentioned to the Commons immediately. Londonderry chose instead, despite insinuations that the government was again throwing dust in the eyes of the legislature, to give a hint of the way his colleagues were thinking and lay the whole question before another select committee.[105] The main object now became to achieve something substantial, to avoid accusations which one prominent county member had made of producing 'a piece of mystification'.[106] If any incentive were needed, the deteriorating situation in parliament most surely provided it. Londonderry himself became chairman of the inquiry, no doubt intentionally, for the government's con-

---

[104] [Memorandum], January 1822, Castlereagh MSS., xxxvii. 301–10; Williams-Wynn to Lord Grenville, 4 February 1822, Coed-y-maen MSS.

[105] See *Hansard*, 2nd ser., vi. 388–97.

[106] T. S. Gooch, the member for Suffolk, who had been chairman of the agricultural committee in 1821. Ibid., 463.

trol of proceedings was thereby strengthened. Apart from him, in a committee eventually numbering thirty-eight, there were half a dozen government men, almost as many Whigs, and nineteen who could best be described as stalwart agriculturists. This hardly gave the ministers a commanding position. Nevertheless, on only two points did they succumb, and neither concerned the corn laws directly; the loans to parishes on security of the parochial rates were thrown out and a plan to advance money for warehoused corn was brought forward as an alternative. As for the suggestion earlier propounded by Londonderry, of 'a moderate scale of duty . . . to render the supply not sudden, inordinate and overwhelming', that won triumphant acceptance, though it offered nothing in the way of relief and prepared for a contingency—wheat at 8os. a quarter—which many were wont to believe would never again occur.[107] But the government had won some applause and it was therefore encouraged to persevere. Londonderry spoke later of 'my having received many pretty strong hints in the committee . . . that it would be considered an extraordinary dereliction of public duty, if his majesty's government were to suffer such a report as the agricultural report to lie on the table of the House of Commons, without proposing to parliament the adoption of some measure founded upon it.'[108] To keep the initiative the ministers themselves drafted the resolutions embodying the report's recommendations, when the normal practice was for this to be done by the committee. By the time that parliament had straggled back after the Easter recess, then, the ministers had firm plans for dealing with troublesome agriculturists and those who would make alliance with them. Whether their house was proof against all weathers, however, depended on whether a breeze or a hurricane lay in the offing.

The first ruffles came very quickly indeed. Scarcely a week after the House resumed, Lord John Russell moved, as a preliminary to a reform bill along moderate lines, that the state of the representation required 'the most serious consideration'. Though Canning was widely expected to 'take the labouring oar' on the question, the government following the smarting humiliation over Grampound, could never rest certain that it

[107] For the report see *PP*, 1822, v. 3–8. [108] *Hansard*, 2nd ser., vii. 176.

could gather a majority sufficiently hostile to reform to put up an uncompromising resistance. Thomas Grenville, presumably, was not the only one who noticed the baleful effects of Radical propaganda which was continually blaming distress on parliament's unresponsiveness: 'some who were steady anti-reformers', he reported of the yeomanry, 'have suffered themselves to be gulled by Cobbett into attributing the pressure of their rents to an inadequate representation in Parliament, though it has no more to do with their rents than with those of the Cham of Tartary'.[109] The division on Russell's motion partly confirmed fears that the legislature was not immune or would give way in time to public opinion as a *force majeure*. The minority of 164 in support of him read much like a roll-call of the opposition side; but it was at the same time the largest reform vote since Pitt's airing of the question in 1785.[110] Inasmuch as the necessity of some change was gaining wider acceptance, if only among the Whigs, the result did little for the government's sagging morale. More than ever, the opposition was encouraged to set their house in order by making it their stated policy to extend the representation of the counties and large towns at the expense of the rotten boroughs. Thereby they could consolidate their reputation as champions of the people against Tory interest and indifference. Thereby too they had some chance of making inroads among 'respectable' opinion, in which direction lay their best chance of ultimate parliamentary success.

The worst setback of the spring sitting, however, befell the government exactly a week later when Lord Normanby renewed his attack on the jointly-held postmaster-generalship. This time Normanby tried the more direct tactic of an address to the Crown and this time the ministers acted with less astuteness and with less decision. Instead of arguing the constitutional function of ministerial influence, which was the most effective defence that they could put up, they tried to sidle round the issue by suggesting, but not definitely offering, a parliamentary commission to investigate the office, and in disgust at this temporising with public opinion over fifty independents and ministerial supporters, led by the member for Yorkshire,

---

[109] Buckingham, *George IV*, i. 291.   [110] *Mrs Arbuthnot*, i. 159–60.

crossed over to the opposition side. Though the difference between a government majority of twenty-five in March and a Whig majority of fifteen in May was not, as Mrs Arbuthnot liked to imagine, the result of deliberate treachery on the part of the 'country gentlemen',[111] there was naught for the government's comfort in such a signal embarrassment. When the causes of defeat came to be examined, the assumption had to be that the least reliable part of the House was under increasing pressure from outside and the opposition fully alive to the advantage which beckoned. While only four had voted against Normanby and then for him, about thirty Tory backbenchers and almost sixty Whigs who had not previously declared themselves had seized the opportunity to take the side of the public. In these circumstances, it was difficult not to accept that the 'country gentlemen's' exasperation was increasing with that of the nation's. Certainly, Henry Bankes' comment that 'these occasional defeats neither shake nor endanger the Ministers' missed the whole point of the adverse moral effect.[112] Peel was not the only one who was beginning to think that the government could no longer afford to distinguish between 'vital and indifferent' questions.[113]

The sequence of events which finally brought about a vote of confidence developed during the discussions in committee of the government's plans for agricultural relief. Three days before Normanby's motion had come on, Lord Londonderry had announced these to the House, but resolutions bringing them into actual consideration had been introduced more than a week after this. From the start it was obvious that the administration had sailed into troubled waters. No less than four sets of counter-resolutions were placed on the table, two from agriculturists seeking a virtual monopoly and two from 'abominable' political economists—Huskisson was one, Ricardo the other—anticipating what Londonderry called 'a more natural state of things'.[114] Many also kept up a sniping fire to add to

---

[111] Ibid., p. 161.   [112] *Colchester*, iii. 253.
[113] Buckingham, *George IV*, i. 326.
[114] *Hansard*, 2nd ser., vii. 400. The main difference between Huskisson and Ricardo's and the government's proposals was that they favoured a fixed duty according to price where the ministers preferred an additional duty for the first three months to guard against excessive importations.

the government's discomfiture. In spite of the ground won
earlier in the session, the old complaint of 'all-devouring
taxation' was again heard, the currency faddists continued to
see Peel's Act as the original great iniquity and opposition stalwarts propounded the line that to remove present discontents
one had only to remove the Crown's present advisers. Though
in the end but two of the government's thirteen resolutions
failed,[115] this harassment had the effect of driving the ministers
to a point where they felt compelled to ask for a further affirmation of the 'country gentlemen's' allegiance. It was not so
much that the administration stood in mortal danger, as that its
strength needed to be demonstrated anew. By bringing forward
propositions in defiance of the King's ministers and by forcing
them to withdraw propositions of their own, Lethbridge and
his collaborators were ostensibly taking the part of the official
opposition, which their return to the fallacy that distress was
not due to 'natural causes' did nothing to belie. On 9 May,
therefore, the same day that the agricultural resolutions were
voted, the Cabinet decided in favour of a meeting of official
men, through whom the 'country gentlemen' could be informed
that the administration staked its existence on the next two votes
of the House. That nothing could obscure the issue of confidence followed from the nature of the questions themselves,
for one concerned the rank of Great Britain's representation at
Berne and the other the diplomatic expense in general, in both
of which matters the ministers had fully obeyed or gone
beyond parliament's express injunctions.[116]

As it turned out, the decision to make the ultimate test of
parliament's loyalty left the government with no regrets.
Common report had it, so Williams-Wynn heard, that 'all the
loose fish come into our net',[117] but, notwithstanding, consecutive majorities of 127 and 106 must have been particularly

[115] That providing for loans on security of warehoused corn and that
permitting the grinding of foreign corn already under bond to help off-load
the country's surplus. Londonderry was particularly annoyed at having to
withdraw the first, accusing the 'country gentlemen' 'who ought to regard it
with parental feelings' of leaving him in the lurch. Ibid., 363–4. See also
Mrs Arbuthnot, i. 161–2.
[116] Williams-Wynn to Lord Grenville, 11 May 1822, Coed-y-maen MSS.;
Buckingham, *George IV*, i. 324–5; *Mrs Arbuthnot*, i. 162–3.
[117] Buckingham, *George IV*, i. 326.

gratifying on what were after all points of economical government. Certainly, the remainder of the session, which dragged
on for another seven weeks, petered out into a series of unexcit-
ing skirmishes. At one time the salt duties and window tax
were each threatened with immediate elimination; twice
Western, who by now was blaming the state of agriculture
wholly on the state of the currency, demanded inquiry into the
deflationary effect of Peel's Act; Brougham made a forlorn
attempt to establish the fact of the Crown's increasing influence;
and, in a fitting end to the session, Hume rang down the curtain
with a brave and fruitless onslaught on the entire sinking fund
rationale. All, of course, was much travelled terrain and not
surprisingly the number of passengers got fewer and fewer.
Throughout the early part of July the Irish members left in
droves, and the Englishmen were not slow to follow them. As
one of their number remarked a fortnight before the House
rose: 'Everybody but Hume and Bennett are sick to death of
it, and literally every other Opposition man gone out of town.'[118]
Nevertheless, the final government ascendancy was not enough
to prevent much uncomfortable reflection. The Prime Minister
treated Huskisson to a long tale of woe shortly before each went
their separate ways, 'fully admitting that much valuable ground
had been lost . . . and that to concede every thing and propose
nothing was a course of Administration neither creditable for
the Govt, nor safe for the Country'.[119] Liverpool knew well
that the executive had failed miserably in the task of producing
measures which were as acceptable to the legislature as they
were necessary for the good ordering of the polity. Though the
ministers had not come to parliament unprepared, it was perhaps
worse that many of their original plans had come unstuck and
that much of their patching had been no better. In the circumstances of the time, an incompetent administration was one
which was uncomfortable in the legislature, inasmuch as its
flounderings there were public, stimulating opposition, creating
the impression of a weak executive and generally devaluing
the existing political system. Likewise the long and arduous
session had taken a heavy toll of reputations and bodily

[118] Ibid., pp. 340, 354.
[119] Huskisson to Canning, 11 August, 1822, Canning MSS.

constitutions. Vansittart's inarticulateness at a time when finance was the dominant parliamentary topic, the failure of the 'dead-weight' scheme to attract private contractors, the general air of deviousness which was now constantly surrounding him, had seriously depleted his political worth; and Bragge-Bathurst, broken in body and spirit by his own ill-health and domestic afflictions, was unlikely to face another parliament.[120] But the session's main victim was one greater than either, one whom Liverpool was to describe as the administration's right arm. Overworked, overwrought, on 12 August Londonderry ended his existence with macabre surgeon's precision. It was the only, the accumulated, outburst of a man of more than ordinary sensitivity.

III. The Return of Canning

Londonderry's suicide and the vacancies it created in the Commons and the Foreign Office never really revived the antagonisms of the past over Canning's readmission. To be sure, the King still conceived it a matter of private honour to bar the Closet door, and Eldon and Sidmouth readily lent their weight; but among the other ministers who had connived to send him to India, a frank acceptance of his now inestimable value replaced the former feeling that the government could manage well enough without him. Only Canning, they felt, could fill the void to anything near sufficiency. Peel, the single alternative, had undeniable talent and a rising reputation; and yet where he was in the middle of the awkward adolescence from departmental spokesman to front-bench debater, Canning was universally recognised as being at the peak of parliamentary eminence, an eminence enhanced if that were possible by his recent brilliant performances as a private member. Since Canning would never serve under Peel in the House of Commons—how could he after refusing to serve under Castlereagh in 1812?—the government's choice became in reality no choice. If Peel were given the lead, not only would the administration be reduced to 'one individual who could pretend to take a great line in Parliament', and that an individual without

[120] Ibid.

Londonderry's popularity and possibly stamina, but Canning's friends and the Grenvilles, who had already made complaints about his going, would leave in disgust as well, placing the government, as Wellington admitted, 'in respect to parliamentary talents in a situation far inferior to that in which we had been for many years'.

Most of the Cabinet agreed, in fact, that the only debatable point arising from Londonderry's death concerned which office Canning was to occupy. Generally speaking, the lead in the Commons was compatible with the Exchequer or one of the three secretaryships-of-state, though of the latter the War and Colonies was looked upon as a distinctly lesser appointment in time of peace. Everyone knew that were the choice Canning's he would take the Foreign Office, for he had little liking for financial subjects, took the common view that Peel's job was one of endless routine and ever rued the day that he had spurned Castlereagh's generous offer in July 1812. Yet a feeling existed that Wellington was perhaps the more suitable appointment. Probably the King was not alone in thinking that Castlereagh's personal diplomacy had been the foundation of Great Britain's ascendancy among the Continental powers. As Wellington was on equally familiar terms with the crowned heads of Europe, his promotion to the Foreign Office may have been attractive as one guarantee of its continuation. In addition, there were those who detected a tactless streak and a ruthlessness in Canning, a view which his quarrel with Hastings did nothing to diminish, and which if right could quicken the destruction of Castlereagh's handiwork. When all was said and done, though, the Cabinet fully realised that Canning could demand his own price. To offend him would be to incur far too great a risk. Even should he still depart for India it was not unlikely that his friends would go into open hostility, and, thereafter, any change for the worse in the government's parliamentary situation might easily tempt him home to direct in person the opposition's final offensive. On reflection it also seemed that the Exchequer and the Home Office were better left alone. While Castlereagh had once described Vansittart's position as the most important in time of peace, it was difficult to see how a man of Canning's restless energy could strike a working relationship with a premier who was better versed in political economy than he was, and Peel, with his immense knowledge of Ireland and none of Europe, had a natural niche. Quite clearly, 'the full inheritance' became Canning's out of convenience as much as necessity.[121]

The essence of the struggle, then, was to make the King see sense. Liverpool, whose opinion of Canning's desirability had not altered and who after the wrangle of the previous year could not help envisaging 'a more extensive change',[122] must have been pleasantly surprised at his colleagues' change of heart. Wellington, Bathurst and Westmorland, all of whom held Canning in low regard, assumed his accession without a further word spoken, and Melville this time obliged by sending notice from Scotland 'that he would not oppose such a proposition if others deemed it on the whole most desirable'.[123] Since Sidmouth could only threaten resignation from his Cabinet seat and Eldon always exaggerated his political importance, it was the King and the King alone who had to be moved. From past experience the Prime Minister knew that this was a task others could perform better than he could. It seems that he looked to Wellington in particular. Having first summoned him from the Low Countries where he was inspecting the frontier fortresses, he then refrained from sending him to the Congress at Verona in place of Castlereagh, as was originally intended.[124] What made Liverpool change his mind was a letter he received from the King in Scotland on 20 August which left no doubts that George was again meaning to be as awkward as possible. 'The immediate object of my writing to You,' he was told, 'is . . . that You will not interrupt & *on no account impede*, the

---

[121] The most comprehensive ministerial statement of the reasons for appointing Canning is contained in a memorandum Wellington wrote for Londonderry's widow. See *Wellington Desp.* (new series), i. 277–8.

[122] Williams-Wynn to Lord Grenville, 16 August 1822, Coed-y-maen MSS.; Buckingham, *George IV*, i. 364.

[123] For the opinions of various Cabinet ministers see Williams-Wynn to Lord Grenville, 16 August 1822, Williams-Wynn to Thomas Grenville, 20 August 1822, Coed-y-maen MSS.; Buckingham, *George IV*, i. 365–6; Lord Bathurst to Lord Harrowby, 23 August 1822, Harrowby MSS. 14, f. 119; Arbuthnot to Lord Liverpool, 28 August [1822], Add. MSS. 38575, f. 33; *Arbuthnot*, p. 31; *Liverpool*, iii. 198.

[124] Williams-Wynn to Lord Grenville, 16 August 1822, Williams-Wynn to Thomas Grenville, 20 August 1822, Coed-y-maen MSS.; *George IV*, ii. 532–3, 534.

Arrangements which are already settled *respecting India*, as it is *my Decision*, that they should remain *final & conclusive*.'[125] Arriving when this did, on the day of Londonderry's funeral as it happened (20 August), Liverpool knew precisely where he stood. Though he had promised the King, in conveying to him news of the tragedy, that he would do nothing to 'preclude full free and unfetter'd Consideration of the Measures which it might be expedient to adopt', a promise he now repeated,[126] he had already withdrawn to Coombe Wood for a few days with Lord Bathurst, Wellington and the Arbuthnots, and from them he had learnt that the opposition within the Cabinet would fall far short of what he expected. Both Bathurst and Wellington had shown themselves willing to make over the whole inheritance. This had not only coincided with Liverpool's views but had also met Canning's wishes in full, as these had been made known by Huskisson's little confidences.[127]

To complete the picture, the day after Wellington returned to Town (21 August), he received a hardly discreet missive from the Duke of Buckingham, who without having consulted Williams-Wynn or his uncles, demanded Canning's admission or an equivalent accession of 'Catholics' to the Cabinet on pain of terminating his connection with the government.[128] With this threat, despite its clumsiness, the necessity of bringing in Canning was finally driven home, for if the Grenvilles left with Canning's friends the government cart would become dangerously tilted indeed. Apart from Eldon and Sidmouth, the only man now standing in the way of a united Cabinet was Peel. As he was in Scotland with the King, his views were unknown, though George on one occasion tried to sound him out and Liverpool strove continually to wring a drop of significance out of his recurring complaints of ill health.[129] In keeping as quiet as this Peel was merely obeying the Prime Minister's particular

[125] The King to Lord Liverpool, 17 August 1822, Add. MSS. 38190, f. 56.
[126] Lord Liverpool to the King, 20 August 1822, ibid., 38575, f. 50.
[127] Huskisson saw Canning on 15 August and the next day confided his terms to Croker, most likely deliberately for Croker was a notorious gossip. *Croker*, i. 227–8. As if to make absolutely certain that the message got through, not long afterwards Huskisson wrote a similar communication to Arbuthnot. Huskisson to Arbuthnot, 19, 21 August 1822, Add. MSS. 38743, ff. 196–9.   [128] *Wellington Desp.* (new series), i. 261–2.
[129] *Liverpool*, iii. 195–6; *Arbuthnot*, p. 30.

orders; but as soon as he returned to London he would have to unburden his soul, and Liverpool requested an interview at the earliest possible moment for this very purpose.[130] Indeed, everyone appreciated that Peel's decision was crucial. Should he refuse to serve under Canning, and there were many like the Duke of Newcastle who would welcome it,[131] there was little doubt that the government would emerge almost as weak as if Canning had gone and he had remained. Worse, his withdrawal might spark off a run of 'Protestant' resignations and see the total destruction of Liverpool's system of 'Protestant-Catholic' neutrality. It was not long before speculation could cease, however. Leaving Edinburgh a day after the King, Peel hurried to London as fast as horses could carry him, and, arriving at his house in Stanhope Street in the later afternoon of 1 September, he found a note from the Prime Minister appointing the following morning for their tête-à-tête.[132] At it he told Liverpool what he had already written to his closest political friends,[133] that he would in no case oppose what his colleagues thought best for the government's future strength. 'Peel has behaved most handsomely,' Arbuthnot wrote pointedly to Lord Sidmouth. 'Impressed with the benefit to be derived from Canning's Parlty talents it wd be his opinion that, if the King & his own Colleagues shd consent to it, there wd be good sense in endeavouring to avail ourselves of them; & he, Peel, wd under such circumstances be quite ready to stand with respect to Canning in the same position as he stood with regard to our poor friend.'[134] From this moment the way was clear for a straightforward confrontation with the King.

It must be admitted that the ministers had few doubts about what the result would be. Though George was capable of extraordinary vindictiveness, his courage in such cases invariably faltered in a confrontation with personalities stronger than his own. On this occasion, Wellington, who among those sur-

[130] Lord Liverpool to Peel, 23 August 1822, Add. MSS. 40304, f. 63.
[131] *Peel*, i. 330–1. See also Lord Clive to Lord Sidmouth, 22 August [1822], Sidmouth MSS., which conveys the disapprobation of Canning by Holme Sumner and T. S. Gooch, prominent 'country gentlemen'.
[132] Lord Liverpool to Peel, 1 September 1822, Add. MSS. 40304, f. 69.
[133] *Peel*, i. 332–3.
[134] Arbuthnot to Lord Sidmouth, 4 September [1822], Sidmouth MSS.

rounding him probably was the least likely to indulge his huffs
and pets, remained confident that he would eventually allow
himself to be overborne.[135] In trying to reason the King into
compliance, however, Lord Liverpool, on past performances,
was likely to be of little service. A veritable bundle of nerves
before his first audience at Carlton House, he spoke of giving
George twenty-four hours to make his decision, and fortunately
Arbuthnot was at hand to advise him to treat the visit as purely
complimentary.[136] A second meeting a day afterwards only led
to the expected royal tantrum. When told that Wellington,
Bathurst and Westmorland were agreed on the necessity of
having Canning in the Commons, the King immediately
inquired whether they would press their opinion as far as
resignation. This hint of immovability on his part was followed
up by a demand for an alternative, which if not forthcoming
'the King takes for granted that Lord Liverpool and the other
members of the Cabinet are prepared to break up the Government'.[137] But the Prime Minister had proposed and others
would now dispose. No sooner had he left the Closet than
George, thinking to test the Cabinet's solidarity, sent out summons to Peel, Wellington, Sidmouth and Eldon, little guessing
that he was doing Lord Liverpool the service of anticipating
the step he would take next. Of course, Sidmouth and Eldon,
especially the latter who was already thick with the King,[138]
were certain to proffer contrary advice; but the other two could
be trusted implicitly to correct wrong impressions and put the
government's views compellingly and clearly. So it turned out.
Sidmouth unwittingly destroyed the basic premise of the King's
position by refusing to admit that the monarch's personal wishes
were of any account; and when he tried the argument that Peel
and Canning held irreconcilable differences on matters of
policy, Peel himself had probably contradicted him not half an
hour earlier. The Lord Chancellor fared just as badly. He made
no secret of his rooted dislike of Canning, even casting dark
hints of his own retirement if he were appointed. But here
again Peel's behaviour made a telling contrast, for he had had

[135] *Wellington and his Friends*, pp. 28-9.   [136] *Arbuthnot*, p. 31.
[137] *Hobhouse*, p. 95; *George IV*, ii. 535.
[138] *Wellington and his Friends*, p. 28.

every reason to advance his personal claims and yet had waived all in favour of the government's larger interest.[139]

It was Wellington, however, who most trenchantly exposed the weakness of Sidmouth's and Eldon's ground. Himself confined to bed by a fever brought on by barbaric medical treatment, he kept in constant touch with developments through Arbuthnot on the government's side and Knighton on the King's. In the care of the latter, who from being a royal physician had worked his way into a position of confidence and power as George's unofficial secretary, the Duke's advice, more than likely, lost nothing in the passing.[140] From the start George exhibited a willingness to be bullied into acquiescence by a mind more resolute than his. After Knighton's first visit to the bed-chamber at Apsley House, he was pleased to confess that Wellington's counsel 'has produced a stronger conviction on my mind than anything that had been previously urged by others', and before the matter was settled he was to put Liverpool off twice in order to have the Duke deliver his opinion.[141] Apart from urging the necessity on political grounds of Canning's return—the threat of an irresistible surge of reform and the retirement of the Prime Minister loomed over every stage of the negotiation—Wellington got to the heart of the difficulty by tackling head-on the delicate question of the King's private honour. Since the imagined insult had been Canning's refusal to accept the legal guilt of the late Queen, tendering his resignation instead, it was ridiculous for the King to expect any reparation or acknowledgement. But Wellington cleverly drew attention away from the wrong done to the act of honour which could forgive it. In this case, he argued, the essential distinction was between the situation of the King and that of a private individual. Where the latter could call another to account if he felt his honour impugned, the sovereign would only demean

[139] *Hobhouse*, pp. 95–7.

[140] See Knighton's comment that Eldon was an unfit adviser for the King 'from exciting irritation', and his confidence to Arbuthnot that 'we shall soon be right *in all directions*'. Arbuthnot to Lord Liverpool, [7 September 1822], Add. MSS. 38290, ff. 233–4.

[141] Originally, Lord Liverpool expected to receive the King's answer to his proposition on Thursday, 5 September. This was later changed to Saturday, but in the end the King wrote a letter of concurrence on Sunday. Buckingham, *George IV*, i. 372; King to Lord Liverpool, 6 September 1822, Add. MSS. 38190, f. 57.

himself by seeking explanation from one necessarily his subject.
Where others, too, had to demand satisfaction to save their good
name, he could use the royal magnanimity to enhance his royal
character. 'The honour of your Majesty,' Wellington concluded, 'consists in acts of mercy and grace, and I am convinced
that your Majesty's honour is most safe in extending your grace
and favour to Mr Canning upon this occasion if the arrangement in contemplation is beneficial to your Majesty's service.'
This little discourse fully answered the most serious of George's
scruples. Wellington followed it up with further advice through
Knighton, with the result that the King, though Eldon at the
last minute sought a redefinition of the government's Catholic
policy and a joint leadership in the Commons, resigned himself
to the inevitable.[142] On 8 September, when the Lord Chancellor
made his usual Sunday morning call at Carlton House, he
found the letter to Liverpool already written. A few hours later
the Prime Minister, waiting at Coombe Wood with 'philosophical patience', had it delivered into his hands, and early
the next morning Arbuthnot was on his way to Gloucester
Lodge to learn from Mrs Canning her husband's latest
movements.[143]

The royal note accepting the Cabinet's proposal—'the
greatest sacrifice of my opinions and feelings that I have ever
made in my life' said an accompanying letter—also included an
express direction that Canning himself should peruse it, and
this condition was the last of Liverpool's tribulations.[144] One
paragraph in particular was likely to offend Canning, though
the Prime Minister thought that the whole was 'express'd with
as much delicacy as considering the King's strong Personal
Feelings could reasonably be expected'.[145] This paragraph
described the 'brightest ornament' of the Crown to be 'the
power of extending grace and favour to a subject who may have

---

[142] *Wellington Desp.* (new series), i. 272–6; Arbuthnot to Lord Liverpool,
[7 September 1822], Add. MSS. 38290, f. 233.

[143] *Wellington Desp.* (new series), i. 278–9; *Arbuthnot*, p. 32; Arbuthnot to
Canning, 9 September 1822, Canning MSS. It is interesting to note that
while Wellington, in his own words, was being 'of some use in driving the
Nail which we are at present hammering at' the Prime Minister remained at
his place in Surrey, striking evidence of his inability to manage the King.

[144] *Liverpool*, iii. 199–200.

[145] Lord Liverpool to Peel, 8 September 1822, Add. MSS. 40304, f. 70.

incurred his displeasure', and obviously the temptation was for
Canning to inquire in what respect he had so offended. Otherwise there was nothing to mar the government's offer. All along
Canning had needed no persuading that for the sake of his
family's happiness and his obligations as a public man, the
opportunity of honourably succeeding to Londonderry's station
would be improper to pass by, and as soon as the offer was made
on his arrival from Birmingham, with little hesitation but with
genuine reluctance, he turned his back on India and made
ready to re-enter the political roughhouse.[146] As for the insinuation in the King's letter, that was soon got over. On first
reading it, he did not conceal his annoyance, and had it in mind
to write a memorandum denying any disrespect for Lord
Liverpool to read in the Closet. Liverpool, with the help of
Wellington and Arbuthnot, tried to smooth things over by
begging him to remember the political importance of his
acceptance and assuring him that the King would forgive and
forget. But it was not until he had taken a day for consideration,
forcing the Prime Minister to postpone an appointment at
Carlton House, that he contented himself with a formal observation to the effect 'that if he were not restrained by His
Majesty's declared wish from entering into details, he could
make it clear that . . . he had not the remotest intention of
giving any offence. . . .'[147] Three days later, at a ceremony
which was remarkable for the absence of half the Cabinet and
the King's slight awkwardness, the seals of office were handed
over.[148]

Perhaps the greatest anxiety that the government faced after
the King had been reconciled to 'the last calamity' was not so
much whether its offer was good enough but whether Canning,
in the time-honoured fashion, would stipulate men and
measures.[149] Certainly Eldon whispered in the King's ear that

[146] The best account of Canning's feelings, based on an exhaustive survey
of the unpublished material, is to be found in A. Aspinall, 'Canning's Return
to Office in September 1822', *English Historical Review*, lxxviii (1963).
531–45.
[147] *Bathurst*, p. 532; *Liverpool*, iii. 201–2; Arbuthnot to Canning, [12
September 1822], Canning MSS.
[148] Buckingham, *George IV*, i. 375; Canning to Lord Granville, 18 September 1822, PRO 30/29.
[149] See Buckingham, *George IV*, i. 372, 374.

'Canning wod get rid of all his old servants', and that George
was inclined to believe him was apparent when he insisted
vehemently to Arbuthnot 'over and over again . . . that he
would agree to no terms, and that Canning must not be attempting to bring in other persons'.[150] Little did they know that after
'the single transaction' had been carried through, 'the parvenu',
with the full blessing of the Prime Minister, would completely
rebuild the government. In the brief haggle over his own
coming in, Canning made no stipulations except to say that he
had particular interest for Huskisson and one Backhouse, a
protege of his at the Board of Control.[151] Nevertheless, Lord
Liverpool must have known that some weeding-out at least had
soon to take place. Towards the end of the parliamentary session
he himself had sounded Sidmouth on the subject of his brother-
in-law's relinquishment of the Duchy of Lancaster, and, more
than once, the last time indeed in August, he had assured a
thoroughly dissatisfied Huskisson that his claim for higher
office was the first among the junior ministers.[152] Nor could it
be overlooked that Canning, having undertaken the good
government of the House of Commons, would as a matter of
course pursue the changes which would most facilitate that
arduous task. In fact, the new minister made his presence felt
immediately. Wallace was prepared to wager anything that in
no time Canning would establish himself 'not only as the Chief
but the sole depository of L[ord] L[iverpool]'s Confidence',
and, even before the formalities of appointment had been gone
through, he was badgering the Prime Minister with suggestions
that the Speaker might remove to India, Williams-Wynn to the
Speaker's Chair and Huskisson to the thereby vacant Board of
Control.[153] The explanation was that Canning had come to
believe that with Liverpool the desire to avoid giving offence
had come to mean that nothing was ever accomplished. A
smart tug in the right direction would do both him and the
government a world of service. 'He will neither do—not *let* do;
[he once wrote]; is jealous of his authority—but afraid to use it

---

[150] *Hobhouse*, p. 96 n. 2; *Bathurst*, p. 532.   [151] *Arbuthnot*, p. 32.
[152] Huskisson to Canning, 11 August 1822, Canning MSS.; *Hobhouse*,
p. 99.
[153] Wallace to Herries, 2 October 1822, Herries MSS.; Canning to Lord
Liverpool, 14 September 1822, Canning MSS.

himself;—ignorant of the world, but convinced (like our old Dean) that he knows more of it than anyone;—mysterious where he ought to be open; & liable to impressions from quarters against which he ought to be most on his guard; selfish—without absolute heartlessness indeed—but with such nervous intensity of desire to avoid anything that can give him pain—that I am quite sure, if one was to drop down in a fit, or be shot through the head while in his room, he would (if he could unobserved) sneak out of the room & get into his carriage, ringing perhaps for Willimot to take care of one.'[154] The Prime Minister's response to the latest scheming was much in keeping with this character. On the one hand, he mildly encouraged Canning's hopes by letting him visit Dropmore to enlist Lord Grenville's support. On the other, he welcomed Wellington's intention to speak to Canning and warn him 'against the danger of any attempts such as those meditated on former occasions'.[155] Afraid that too much would upset too many, at the outset he was only concerned to achieve the one point of Huskisson's admittedly deserved promotion. This in itself, however, was a blow struck for Canning, for the royal fiat had expressly extended to a man, not a party. Wallace's prophecy that obedience in one thing would shortly become obedience in all already seemed in process of fulfilment.

The first and most essential step of Canning's project was to persuade Williams-Wynn into the Speaker's Chair, for the charge of an empire was not a little flattering to Manners Sutton, its present incumbent, and the India Board had long been an object of Huskisson's. Some time previously Lord Liverpool had casually tested whether Williams-Wynn's ambitions were still parliamentary, but the result had shown rather the reverse. On learning this, to keep two balls in play, Canning cajoled the Prime Minister into writing to Lord Melville to whom an 'Oriental passion' was ascribed, at the same time arranging a visit to Dropmore to get Lord Grenville to bring pressure to bear on his nephew.[156] Both answers were known

[154] Canning to Mrs Canning, 24 August 1822, ibid.
[155] Canning to Huskisson, 21 September 1822, Add. MSS. 38743 ff. 213–214; *Arbuthnot*, p. 32.
[156] Canning to Lord Liverpool, 14 September 1822, Lord Liverpool to Canning, 15 September 1822, Canning MSS.; Canning to Lord Grenville,

by Monday, 23 September. Melville's, probably due to his snug berth at the Admiralty, was a straight refusal, though as far as East India House was concerned the governor-generalship would have been his for the asking. Grenville's came in the form of a letter to Williams-Wynn, which was entrusted to Canning and delivered at a morning meeting at the Foreign Office with Liverpool in attendance. Presumably Grenville advised his nephew to take a kind view of the proposal he was about to hear because Canning went from the conference by no means dissatisfied. However, Williams-Wynn did ask for time to ponder the matter. After sounding a few friends at East India House, he realised that Bengal was out of his reach, but before taking the Chair he had to weigh carefully its expense and labour—'the prolonged debates of the present times under the auspices of Hume make the Speaker's Chair a question of strength of Constitution', his uncle warned[157]—against its honour and political convenience. The last consideration, in fact, turned out to be an empty dream and almost brought the negotiations to an immediate deadlock. For Williams-Wynn himself, appointment to the Speakership was certainly no end of the political road; on important occasions Abbot had participated in debate, Addington was not the only one who had moved from Chair to Cabinet and a posture of neutrality at a time of party turmoil could be distinctly advantageous. But Buckingham it was who reminded him that he was a party man and that the Grenvilles still retained a separate identity though joined with the government. In a letter dated 25 September, followed by another two days later, he put the issue squarely as withdrawal of himself and his friends from 'official connexion' with the government or continued representation in the Cabinet, arguing with some fairness, and indeed as Lord Liverpool had anticipated, that such had been the terms of their original coalition. When informed of this ultimatum, by Williams-Wynn, Canning did not conceal his fury. While he

---

20 September 1822, Grenville MSS.; Lord Liverpool to Lord Melville, 16 September 1822, Canning to Huskisson, 21 September 1822, Add. MSS. 38411, f. 96, ff. 211–14.

[157] Thomas Grenville to Williams-Wynn, 15 September 1822, Coed-y-maen MSS.

agreed that he should visit Coombe Wood to talk the matter over further, he also dashed off notes to the master of that house conveying a scarcely veiled threat that if Huskisson were not advanced his own retirement was imminent. Indeed, Buckingham's awkwardness had brought him to the point where his larger plans could no longer be held back. Already, in writing to the Prime Minister, he had allowed himself to say that Bragge-Bathurst's office should be kept safely away from Grenville hands, and at the first opportunity he resolved to find out whether Liverpool's liking for Vansittart had diminished sufficiently to enable the Exchequer to be opened for Robinson and the Board of Trade for Huskisson. Such a plan showed considerable cunning. Since the Grenvilles had long held that Vansittart was the government's most serious liability, they could not easily stand in the way of his departure by holding on to an adequate inducement, and, should they persist in being uncooperative, means might still be found to reconcile 'poor Van' to administering the affairs of Lancaster rather than India. The 'arch-schemer' was fast proving his capabilities.[158]

Canning's opportunity to set in motion his master plan came almost at once. At his interview with Williams-Wynn on 30 September the Prime Minister made little progress beyond a vague suggestion that Buckingham might be accommodated in the not too distant future,[159] and the day after, in commisserating with Canning over the apparent deadlock, the latter casually, subtly warped the conversation round. 'L[iverpool] does not know of my writing to you,' ran his report to Huskisson. 'Nor had he the smallest notion of mentioning the matter to me, if I had not . . . happened to inquire, hopelessly at the moment, whether he was as much wedded to Van & Van to his Seals as ever. The answer, to my infinite surprize, was "O no! I could get him out, & would, if I saw my way to an arrangement that I was sure would satisfy all parties; but I

---

[158] For the negotiation thus far see Canning to Williams-Wynn, 22 September 1822, Canning to Lord Liverpool, 28, 29 September 1822, Canning MSS.; Canning to Huskisson, 23 September 1822, Add. MSS. 38743, f. 215; Buckingham, *George IV*, i. 381–2, 385–7; Lord Grenville to Williams-Wynn, 24 September 1822, Williams-Wynn to Thomas Grenville, 26 September 1822, Duke of Buckingham to Williams-Wynn, 27 September 1822, Coed-y-maen MSS.

[159] Duke of Buckingham to Williams-Wynn, 1 October 1822, ibid.

could not get him out for H[uskisson] to succeed him, & the
I[ndia] Bd which is H's object would be the surest lure to
Van." This, not in words, but in substance, was L's way of
opening the matter to me. . . . And then we went back to India
& the Speaker &c as if all that had passed had been in paren-
thesis. . . .'[160] Having learnt this much and also that Huskisson
would be content with the Board of Trade, Canning made
ready to harry the Grenvilles mercilessly to a point of outright
capitulation.[161] Here, though, he met with unexpected resistance, much to the timid Liverpool's consternation and his own
barely concealed indignation. Probably through Williams-
Wynn, Buckingham had been invited to come up from the
country to discuss his and his party's position. Instead of
accepting, on the grounds that discussion would only settle his
opinion even further, he produced a letter, ostensibly to his
cousin, proposing the illogical and barely comprehensible course
of so far assisting the interest of government by acceding to the
general arrangement but withdrawing from all 'official connexion' because his party's did not coincide. Though instructed
to do so, Williams-Wynn did not dare show such nonsense to
Canning or the Prime Minister. To explain Buckingham's non-
appearance he merely said that the Duke preferred to convey
his views through him. To give himself time to correct his
cousin's folly, he gave out that he was writing again to render
those views more explicit, also adding, to discourage false hopes,
that a successful termination was 'highly improbable'. Alas, his
diplomacy availed nothing. No sooner had he pointed out the
absurdities and inconsistencies of withdrawal, especially the
invidiousness of deserting the government nine months after
accepting office and a political dukedom, than Buckingham
wrote to Lord Liverpool saying all that he should not have. As
far as Williams-Wynn was concerned, this was the end of the
matter. He had fully made up his mind, and more than once
had told Canning as much, 'to consent to no change of my
official situation which while apparently more advantageous to
myself would loosen the ostensible & real connection of my

[160] Canning to Huskisson, 3 October 1822, Add. MSS. 38743, ff. 217–18.
[161] Huskisson to Canning, 3 October 1822, Canning MSS.; Canning to
Lord Liverpool. 4 October 1822, Add. MSS. 38193, ff. 164–5.

friends'. The appearance of being in open disagreement with his cousin, and possibly of obstructing an arrangement which Buckingham and the government found desirable, made it impossible for him to continue the negotiations.[162]

Even so, Canning refused to take no for an answer. Williams-Wynn had already remarked on 'the manner in which Canning has assumed to himself, even in the presence of Lord Liverpool, the tone and authority of Premier',[163] and, interpreting the Prime Minister's passiveness as tacit approval, Canning was little disposed to concede that he was beaten. As he told Huskisson, when enjoining him not to breathe a word on matters pending: 'I am perfectly confident of L's sincerity: & brought as he is now to a point, which I thought hopeless, it would be a thousand pities to raise any impediments in his way'.[164] The day of the last attempt to persuade the Grenvilles happening to be a Friday (4 October), and it now being clear that the blood of cousins ran thicker than any venom for Vansittart, Canning spent the whole of the weekend feverishly searching for some last minute compromise. On the Saturday he consulted Reid, the Chairman of the East India Company, at his country home, but little came to light that was not already known; with the government's backing, Manners Sutton, the Speaker, could be virtually certain of the Company's favour, but it was most unlikely that Williams-Wynn's selection could be carried. On the Sunday he went on to Coombe Wood, and there a glimmer of hope emerged at least. Talking over the stalemate that had been reached, the Prime Minister, probably thinking aloud, mentioned, none too enthusiastically, the possibility of Buckingham having a Cabinet seat without office, and Canning, desperate for any way out, even one hardly creditable, eventually persuaded him to try the King and abide by his decision. With Williams-Wynn not in the running for the governor-generalship, it was a last despairing throw to open the India Board for Huskisson. In the event, the King's sus-

---

[162] Duke of Buckingham to Williams-Wynn, 2, 3, 4 October 1822, Williams-Wynn to the Duke of Buckingham, 3 October 1822, Coed-y-maen MSS.; Williams-Wynn to Canning, 3, 5 October 1822, Williams-Wynn to Lord Liverpool, 5 October 1822, Canning MSS.
[163] Buckingham, *George IV*, i. 385.
[164] Canning to Huskisson, 4 October 1822, Add. MSS. 38743, f. 228.

picions may well have been aroused. Though Liverpool's letter said nothing of Huskisson, putting the issue rather as a struggle to secure a suitable candidate for India, the King, who was near at hand at Windsor, made no reply for a day and a half. When his answer did come it rejected Buckingham's claim in no uncertain terms and also alluded to the India Board as only a temporary Cabinet office.[165] After this, short of what Canning called an 'act of violence', nothing further could be done except to push Bragge-Bathurst aside and shift Vansittart and Robinson so that room could be made for Huskisson at the Board of Trade. But Canning's zest did not take long to return. On 9 October, a day after the King had spoken the final word, he confessed to being utterly down at heart, 'unless', he added, 'I were to resume my abdicated Empire & embark on the Jupiter after all'.[166] A fortnight later to the day he was telling Huskisson of a forthcoming visit to Walmer when he intended 'to put in motion . . . the other series of machinery by which the Object, of which we have failed through India, is to be achieved'.[167]

Both Liverpool and Canning believed that they had fair prospects of success in trying the more ambitious juggle involving four principals instead of three. Of course, to the Prime Minister's way of thinking, the aim of any reshuffle had to be the greatest happiness of the greatest number, but in this case much of the personal embarrassment was taken away because those concerned had already made known their pretensions. After hearing Bragge-Bathurst's incessant complaints of overwork and ill-health, for instance, Liverpool could not help assuming that a hint of honourable retirement would suffice to open his office.[168] Vansittart too, in giving out that he would go at the end of the parliament, seemed ready for a change, especially when it was remembered that he had offered to relinquish the Exchequer for the India Board in 1820.[169] And Robinson had made it plain that his claims had to be taken

[165] Canning to Huskisson, 9 October 1822, ibid., ff. 235–9; *Liverpool*, iii. 204–7.
[166] Canning to Huskisson, 9 October 1822, Add. MSS. 38743, f. 237.
[167] Canning to Huskisson, 23 October 1822, ibid., ff. 250–1.
[168] Huskisson to Canning, 11 August 1822, ibid., ff. 192–3.
[169] Vansittart to Lord Liverpool, 14 December 1822, Add. MSS. 38291, f. 206.

into account in a letter written after Londonderry's death, in
which he had argued that after Canning he was next in line for
promotion.[170] Indeed, it was ironical that Huskisson, for whose
benefit the new arrangement was principally intended, promised
to be the most difficult party. He had already stipulated that if
the Board of Control were to elude him he would on no account
take the slightly inferior Board of Trade without Cabinet.[171]
Since the King, in Buckingham's case, had been led to remark
that the number of ministers had 'become far too numerous',
to try to force this condition was to run the risk of further
trouble at Carlton House, trouble bound to be accentuated by
the fact that a friend of Canning's was the party involved.
Worse still, the matter might not end there. If the King cried
out that he was being bullied into compliance, the plan to
reshape the government could fail completely. Vansittart, as the
Prime Minister reminded Canning, and he might have added
Bragge-Bathurst's name as well, could not be allowed to suspect
that an approach had been made to him 'at any one's instigation
or as matter of compact'.[172] At all costs, the appearance of an
intrigue, with Canning its master mind, had to be avoided. In
fact, Liverpool needed no prompting to see that the best chance
of success lay in letting Londonderry's ghost preside. He had
been favourable towards Huskisson's pretensions, and Robinson, as Canning remarked, had been his favourite child in the
Commons. By now pretending that the changes were a last act
of respect to him, Canning's enemies were likely to see no
alternative to keeping their worst thoughts to themselves. Only
Huskisson, with his demand for a Cabinet seat, seemed to stand
in the way.

The first moves in the negotiation were made during the last
week of October. On the Tuesday, just before going to Walmer,
Canning wrote to Liverpool suggesting that the time was ripe
to knock on Bragge-Bathurst's and Vansittart's doors.[173] Not
twenty-four hours elapsed before the Prime Minister, presumably in response to this advice, addressed himself to Lord
Sidmouth, who, on the score of family and old friendship, was

[170] Lord Liverpool to Vansittart, 16 December 1822, ibid., 31232, f. 297.
[171] Huskisson to Canning, 3 October 1822, Canning MSS.
[172] Canning to Huskisson, 4 October 1822, Add. MSS. 38743, f. 228
[173] Canning to Lord Liverpool, [29 October 1822], Canning MSS.

personally interested. Of course, the first pass had to be made
at Bragge-Bathurst to ascertain whether a vacancy could be
created. But while Liverpool confined himself to this initially,
what inducements he held out, if any, can only be guessed at.
Whatever he said, it made no impression on Sidmouth. 'I wrote
to sound Sidmouth about his *friend*,' he told Arbuthnot despair-
ingly, 'but I should say that by his answer he appeared more
tenacious of office & situation for himself & friend than he was
before.'[174] After this discouraging start, no more was heard on
the subject until Liverpool returned to Coombe Wood in the
middle of November. However, that he was determined to see
the matter through—the hopelessness of post-bag negotiation
perhaps explained the fortnight's silence—became obvious when
Sidmouth made the short ride over from Richmond Park on the
day of his arrival. Then and there the Prime Minister put the
reasons behind his request; Bragge-Bathurst's ailing health
which with the increasing demands of parliament on ministers
brooked most serious consideration, the importance of promoting Huskisson to gratify Canning and avoid the nuisance of
more than one re-election at prestigious Liverpool, and the
possibility that much could happen in six months or a year to
render a later vacancy more of a curse than a blessing. All this
neatly topped with a cordial assurance that whenever Bragge-
Bathurst should choose to leave 'such an arrangement as to our
Friend's Family as may appear to you & to him to be just &
equitable' would follow immediately.[175] Fortunately, Sidmouth
did all that was desired of him. For a few days, which must have
seemed an eternity to Liverpool and Canning, he pondered the
matter carefully, but once his mind had become reconciled to
the complete extinction of the former Addington glory he lost
no time in conveying to his brother-in-law the Prime Minister's
offer of comfortable and honourable retirement. Nor was
Bragge-Bathurst any less cooperative. Indeed, he was helpful
in a positive way, for in placing Harwich, his parliamentary
seat, at the government's disposal he provided Canning with
perhaps the last of the Treasury boroughs and made it possible

---

[174] *Arbuthnot*, p. 35.
[175] Lord Liverpool to [Lord Sidmouth], 21 November 1822, Add. MSS.
38291, ff. 174–8.

for Huskisson to take over Liverpool simultaneously. The only
favour he did ask, a small enough one, was that the pension
promised to his wife should be inheritable by his daughters
whether or not he survived her, and it was in fact the negotiation
over the legal intricacies involved which alone precluded a
final settlement until a week before Christmas. By then the
Prime Minister had already sought out Vansittart.[176]

In most respects the case of 'poor Van' was much more
delicate than Bragge-Bathurst's. As the figure who, through no
fault of his own, unless it were his peculiar fumbling oratory,
had become publicly identified with the government's financial
embarrassments and an object of ridicule even to his colleagues, the terms of his discharge from the Exchequer had to
be particularly well thought out to be anything not dishonour-
able. In this connection, his replacement by Robinson was
unexceptionable, a much happier choice than say Huskisson,
who, besides being close to Canning, had sat in the 'economic
cabinet', which would have at once smacked of supersession by
command of the Prime Minister. Nonetheless, Lord Liverpool's
offer of the Duchy of Lancaster was not wholly attractive.
Though as an office it was a lucrative post of honour and
though its holder was customarily entitled to a seat in the
Cabinet, what filled Vansittart with dismay was the uncomfortable prospect of being left an elder statesman in the House of
Commons, where from a position of influence he would be
reduced to silence on the floor and hack-work above stairs.
To all appearances, he was immediately conscious of the slight.
In reply to Liverpool's letter, which included the usual patter
about the appropriateness of the changes,[177] he remarked that
his inclination was rather for 'a total retreat', and since the
Prime Minister had invited him to consult Lord Sidmouth on
a matter so personal he excused himself from returning a
definite answer until he had seen him.[178] Canning guessed at

---

[176] Lord Sidmouth to Bragge-Bathurst, 27 November, 1, 5, 17 December
1822, Bragge-Bathurst to Lord Sidmouth, 28 November 1822, Sidmouth
MSS.; Lord Sidmouth to Lord Liverpool, 17 December 1822, Add. MSS.
38291, f. 218; *Hobhouse*, pp. 99–100. It is another indication of Liverpool's
state of mind that he was ready to see Bragge-Bathurst himself if Sidmouth
refused to intercede. *Mrs Arbuthnot*, i. 196–7.   [177] *Liverpool*, iii. 208–10.
[178] Vansittart to Lord Liverpool, 14 December 1822, Add. MSS. 38291,
ff. 205–6.

once that he was after a peerage, and sympathised.[179] But Liverpool had doubts about the propriety of such a request. Always chary of giving away peerages after Pitt's lavish régime, he had tried to make it a rule that any recipient should have the wealth and position to support the title bestowed, and Vansittart's qualifications were sadly lacking in each respect.

However, for the moment both were spared the embarrassment of haggling the matter. Having come to the conclusion that the offer was 'not less honourable than a simple retirement' and its timing 'at least not discreditable', Vansittart first wanted to make certain that Robinson and no other would be his successor. To this end he bombarded Liverpool with advice as to how best to approach him.[180] Most of what he said showed that he knew his man. The ambition in Robinson's soul, reckoned as he was one of the most promising of the younger blood, was diluted by the strain of having a reputation to live up to, and Vansittart's suggestion that Peel, with whom Robinson was staying, should intercede to avoid any nerves was, in the circumstances, eminently sensible. Not that the precaution proved to be necessary. The Prime Minister confided the proposed arrangements 'which our poor Friend Londonderry had very much at heart' to Peel and his house guest on 18 December. Robinson wrote back accepting with alacrity the day after.[181]

With this much settled, Vansittart's one and only concern was to rescue his dignity by escaping from the Commons. When Liverpool communicated the good news of Robinson's acceptance, he replied that his own course was still undecided, while to Sidmouth he complained that continuing in office was an uncertain sort of pension with the added disadvantage that 'any minister in the H of C who would not be utterly insignificant is in a situation very unfavourable to health & comfort'.[182]

---

[179] Canning to Lord Liverpool, 14 December 1822, Canning MSS.

[180] Vansittart to Lord Liverpool, 16 December 1822, Add. MSS. 38291, ff. 211–17.

[181] Lord Liverpool to Peel, 18 December 1822, Lord Liverpool to Robinson, 18 December 1822, Robinson to Lord Liverpool, 19 December 1822, ibid., ff. 219–24.

[182] Vansittart to Lord Liverpool, 21 December 1822, ibid., ff. 225–6; Vansittart to Lord Sidmouth, 22 December 1822, Sidmouth MSS.

A meeting between Liverpool and himself having been arranged
for Boxing Day, he at length resolved to give some indication of
his wishes by speaking to Arbuthnot, often a useful go-between.
Nor did he whisper in the wrong ear. 'I think I have discovered
what the wish is of Vansittart's mind,' wrote his confidant. 'He is
anxious to quit the House of Commons altogether; & it would
I think delight him if you were to propose to him a Peerage
with the Dutchy of Lancaster for immediate Possession. . . . I
did not like to bring him to a precise point, lest I shd seem to
fortify his own notions . . . but he seemed to me to speak
explicitly enough when he repeatedly said that were he a Peer
he shd not hesitate about the Dutchy. . . .'[183] Who broached
the subject on 26 December, or whether Sidmouth did it on
Vansittart's behalf, remains obscure. But both parties certainly
came away with the terms finally settled, 'Van' highly elated
with the promise of a peerage and Liverpool consoled by the
thought that without remainder to his nephews it would
shortly become extinct.[184] To make the jigsaw complete, there
was now only Huskisson to accommodate.

In dealing with Huskisson the greatest difficulty was that,
within the government, his was the classic case of frustrated
ambition. His career had mostly run parallel to Canning's;
since 1816 his official responsibilities had been as slight as his
influence and importance had been large. Soured by nine years'
possession of a near sinecure—the result of too close an attachment to Canning in 1812—he was beginning to act as if every
man's hand was against him, forgetting that in the cruel world
of politics what others thought of him was vastly more important
than what he thought of himself. One outburst in a letter to
Canning showed how agonising his introspection had become:
'My own impression is . . . that L[iverpoo]l has some fanciful
theory of his own about dividing public men into two classes—
those who are, from the outset, destined to be drudges—and
those who are marked for Cabinet:—and that long ago He has
thrown me into the former class: I believe also that He is
backed in this by some Peers in the Cabinet; who think that

---

[183] Arbuthnot to Lord Liverpool, 23 December 1822, Add. MSS. 38291,
ff. 237–40.
[184] Vansittart to Lord Sidmouth, [26 December 1822], Sidmouth MSS.

[that] part of the Govt which belongs to the H of C ought all to be Drudges, subject to their management in their own way.'[185] Neither Canning nor anyone else gave the least encouragement to this mood of self-pity, Canning himself calling it, though not to Huskisson's face, out and out 'perverseness'.[186] If Huskisson thought he was safeguarding his honour as a public man in claiming a seat in the Cabinet, he was alone in that belief. From the start Canning warned him that rank obstruction to the general arrangement would be taken amiss, not only by his superiors but also by the world in general, and for the sake of harmony between Liverpool and the King and between Liverpool and his colleagues, he begged him to be content with the Cabinet in reversion.[187] Though there was little in the claim that the President of the Board of Trade customarily sat in the Cabinet—Robinson's predecessor never did—the argument always came back to the realities of Huskisson's position. Charles Ellis, his friend as well as Canning's, showed him exactly where he stood: '. . . the real practical question now is . . . whether it would be wise on your part— by insisting on the *whole* succession—failing of success, either to defeat altogether an arrangement for many reasons so desirable, or to allow it to take place, another person being placed over your head at the Bd of Trade; or succeeding, to force yourself on the K[ing] & a reluctant & ill disposed Cabt? or whether it is not better Policy, to accept the situation offered to you with perfectly good will on all sides, with the reversion of Cabt on the first vacancy, and the certainty of such Vacancy at the latest by Van's retirement at the end of the Parliam[en]t.'[188]

In the end it took the combined efforts of Wellington and Canning and a fortnight of comings and goings to bring Huskisson to his senses. The other stages of the arrangement being virtually completed, Canning gave him a stern lecture on Christmas Day without any visible effect. Wellington, who seemed to pride himself on his usefulness on such occasions,

---

[185] Huskisson to Canning, 25 October 1822, Add. MSS. 38743, f. 259.
[186] Canning to Lord Liverpool, 28 December 1822, Canning MSS.
[187] Canning to Huskisson, 3, 23 October 1822, Add. MSS. 38743, ff. 219–220, 251.
[188] Charles Ellis to Huskisson, 23 December 1822, ibid., ff. 280–1.

was no more successful the day following.[189] Since Huskisson
had made his position clear weeks before, this much was all
that could be expected.[190] Even so, the delay made everyone's
tempers run short. Liverpool could not 'conceive anything [in]
worse taste than a man endeavouring to *force* himself into a
Cabinet'; Canning remonstrated afresh by letter; and Huskisson angrily retreated to Sussex, broadly hinting that such
ungenerous treatment might easily end in his retirement.[191]
However, a way out of the impasse was soon being sought.
While Wellington hurried off to Brighton to report on 'the
King's state of mind and general disposition to the Govt' before
the whole arrangement was submitted, Canning made a fresh
overture to Williams-Wynn in a last minute endeavour to
charm him from the India Board to the Board of Trade with
its house and a thousand a year less. Neither excursion achieved
its purpose. Williams-Wynn professed himself happy where he
was, and, with mighty conceit, told Buckingham that only the
Admiralty or one of the Secretaryships of State would be
tempting enough to shift him. Wellington on his arrival at
Brighton found Knighton not in attendance, which meant, as
he explained to Mrs. Arbuthnot, that the King would decide
nothing and *'fret and fume'* in the meantime.[192] In deference to
the Duke's advice, Liverpool did agree to wait until the
'Accoucheur' returned; but as he had already made up his mind
to leave Huskisson to 'his M[ajest]y's unfetter'd decision', a
few days' delay made little difference.[193] His thinking was to
coerce the recalcitrant by placing him where to persist he would
have to defy the King's wishes openly; for, after what had

[189] Duke of Wellington to Canning, 26 December 1822, Canning MSS.;
Arbuthnot, p. 35; Huskisson to Arbuthnot, 26 December 1822, Add. MSS.
38743, f. 285.
[190] Wellington's charge that Canning had kept Liverpool deliberately in
the dark about Huskisson's Cabinet pretensions is completely unfounded.
Mrs Arbuthnot, i. 200. The Prime Minister was showing an interest in
Huskisson's state of mind throughout the negotiations. See Arbuthnot to
Huskisson, 2 December [1822], Arbuthnot to Lord Liverpool, 16 December
[1822], Add. MSS. 38743, ff. 265–7, 38291, ff. 209–10.
[191] *Arbuthnot*, p. 37; Huskisson to Arbuthnot, 26 December 1822,
Canning to Huskisson, 27 December 1822, Huskisson to Charles Ellis,
29 December 1822, Add. MSS. 38743, ff. 286, 287–8, 294–5.
[192] Canning to Lord Liverpool, 28, 30 December 1822, Canning MSS.;
Buckingham, *George IV*, i. 406; *Wellington and his Friends*, p. 36.
[193] *Arbuthnot*, pp. 35–6.

passed at the time of Buckingham's suggested preferment, it was highly probable that George would take exception to an arrangement which did not reduce the number of the Cabinet.[194]

Fortunately, the King responded much as Liverpool had hoped. Though George gave his Prime Minister full discretion to do what he considered best 'for the good of the public service', he also said in passing that he was quite right in deploring the Cabinet's present unwieldy size, and this covert suggestion was enough for Canning to make a final appeal to Huskisson.[195] As he explained, after pointing out that his name had been submitted as he had demanded: 'I do think that, *the point of honour thus completely satisfied*, you would do what is right towards the King, what is just & kind towards Liverpool, and what is, beyond all question most expedient for your own comfort, and ultimately (and at no distance of time) for your own reputation, by *yourself proposing* to wave the pressing this point upon the King, at the present moment. I am *sure* it would be politick so far as the King is concerned. I am sure it would set all right with Liverpool—whose agitation has, in some stages of this business amounted almost to illness, and to whom every successive stage has been an effort such as when I came into the Government I thought it utterly hopeless that he should find nerves to undertake. . . . Do not suppose that I wish your sacrifice to be either for a long or much less for an indefinite time. I pledge myself that you will succeed to the first vacancy that happens in the Cabinet: and failing a vacancy, I pledge myself that you shall be called to the Cabinet in the interval between this & the next Session of Parliament.'[196] Rather ungraciously, but acknowledging that a year's abeyance of his claim did not constitute a personal disparagement or mitigate from his argument that the Board of Trade should be a Cabinet office, Huskisson acceded to these terms, and the point to which Liverpool and Canning had most devoted themselves was gained at last.[197] Except for a brief flurry, when Wallace threw up his place at the Board of Trade in disgust, disrupting plans

[194] Ibid., p. 37.
[195] *Liverpool*, iii. 210–11; *Arbuthnot*, pp. 37–8.
[196] Canning to Huskisson, 3 January 1823, Add. MSS. 38744, ff. 2–4.
[197] Huskisson to Canning, 5 January 1823, Canning MSS.; Canning to Huskisson, 6 January 1823, Add. MSS. 38744, f. 9; *Liverpool*, iii. 212.

for the disposal of the minor offices, the jigsaw was now complete.

Without doubt the changes beginning with Canning's elevation and 'Brother Bragge's' dispossession represented a turning point for the administration as a whole. It was not that they ushered in a period of what is usually called 'liberal toryism', for the government had already taken significant steps in this direction; or, more accurately, it had, when faced with new challenges, displayed the old flexibility of aristocratic rule. It was not even that the 'improving' impetus quickened much in consquence; had Wallace continued at the Board of Trade, his achievement, in all probability, would have been as great as Huskisson's, and Peel, of course, was in the midst of preparing his great programme of domestic reforms. Instead of on measures, the emphasis must be on men. Two features were apparent before parliament even reassembled, and almost from the moment that Canning succeeded Lord Londonderry. The first was that henceforth the government would be both stronger and more assertive in the House of Commons, though it is strange to reflect that Huskisson's exclusion left the number of Commons' men in the Cabinet the lowest since 1816. Gone were the days of Londonderry's amiable but lackadaisical régime, when the administration had often lived from week to week in parliament, bullied into action by the Whigs or frantically coming to terms with its own rank and file. Canning appreciated more keenly than his predecessor the need for the executive to have a powerful presence in the legislature, particularly in the popular part. If the authority of government was to be maintained against those dispositions and doctrines contributing towards its subversion, the capability of the holders of power, and therefore the wisdom inherent in the existing political system, had to be demonstrated constantly to the nation. In particular, public opinion was to be gratified with explanation and information. Canning was not loathe to provide this out of parliament, but the fact remained that it was in parliament that the government mostly presented itself to the country. He would have been the first to admit that, by and large, the administration was pursuing right policies; but he wanted it to take a public, which was increasingly interested, into its greater confidence. He wanted a Treasury bench which could 'speechify' and which could firmly check the contrariness of the House by being knowledgeable, well-prepared and alert. It is only against these considerations that the real depth of his interest in recasting the government can be measured.

As early as the beginning of October, Lord Liverpool and Canning decided to hold a week of Cabinets the following month to consider what promised to be the outstanding issues of the forthcoming session; in December they asked the revenue departments and the Home Office for lists of the bills that they intended to sponsor; and a fortnight before parliament reassembled Canning produced a memorandum setting forth the government's 'Engagements or *quasi* Engagements . . . in order that the Cabinet may determine on the course to be pursued . . . & that we may not have to decide upon it on the spur of a call from the opposition, but be prepared to announce it spontaneously'.[198] Always the inference was there that Londonderry had been far too casual for the Commons' good government. 'There is no advantage in avoiding discussion amongst ourselves upon disagreeable subjects, to be taken unprepared when those subjects are forced upon us in Parlt,' observed Canning. 'We all must be sensible of the great disadvantage which accrues from postponing the consideration of subjects which are likely to be brought forward in Parliament to the time of its actual sitting, or even to a short period antecedent to it,' echoed the Prime Minister.[199] A new energy resulting from a different cast of leadership had seized the government. In most respects, after 1822 the issues continued the same—the clamour for economy was as insistent as ever, with the Catholic question still open the Irish problem remained largely administrative, and the struggle went on for a corn law fair to all. In the last years of Liverpool's administration the content of politics did not change so much as the style of government. If overmuch emphasis has been placed on the achievements of 'liberal toryism', it is surely because the government seemed favoured by the opposition's demoralisation and an economic situation

which took much of the sting out of public complaint. Yet the
fact remains that the administration was never stronger in parliament than it was after 1823. Hobhouse, commenting on
Canning's first session as leader, said that he had 'taken less
part in debate than any leader for many years',[200] and with
Peel, Huskisson and a newly conscientious Robinson as his
chief lieutenants it was hardly surprising. By getting rid of the
mediocrities who had ever surrounded Londonderry the balance
of authority and talent between government and opposition was
suddenly put right.

Essentially it was Canning who made all the difference, and
here one is brought to the second feature which distinguished
the period after the reconstruction of 1822. Even if it can be
argued that Canning's qualities as a parliamentary leader were
never tested like Londonderry's, his personality made a decisive
impact inside and outside the Cabinet. One of his subordinates
described him as 'perpetually doing & undoing', in contrast to
Londonderry's habit of doing 'as little as possible consistent
with the proper execution of the business of office'.[201] It was
this unlimited energy, never confined to his own department,
which aroused his colleagues' ire almost immediately.[202] Indeed,
instead of dividing the Cabinet between 'liberal Tories' and
'ultra-Tories' it is probably more meaningful to speak of those
attracted to Canning and those repelled by him, for when the
administration was brought to an end the question of his suitability for the premiership played a large part in determining
new allegiances. Certainly the lines began to be drawn as soon
as Canning became the driving force behind a large-scale reconstruction of the government. A man who enjoyed the manipu-
lative side of politics or who had no great faith in plain dealing,
he never looked like shaking off the reputation for shiftiness and
sly cunning fixed on him in 1809. On this occasion it was the
same old story of having his motives misconstrued and being
abused in many different quarters. Wellington complained of 'a

---

[200] *Hobhouse*, p. 102.   [201] *Mrs Arbuthnot*, i. 209.

[202] In January 1823, for example, he was advocating a plan to relieve the
landed interest by authorising advances from the sinking fund for the repayment of mortgages. Duke of Portland to Canning, 18 January 1823, Canning
to Lord Liverpool, 21 January 1823, Canning MSS. This would have been
completely outside Londonderry's province.

trick played upon us all' in claiming that Lord Liverpool had
been kept deliberately in the dark about Huskisson's Cabinet
pretensions; Eldon was furious that all had been done behind
his back; and the New Year had hardly begun before Bathurst
was convincing himself that 'there is some secret understanding
with Holland House'.[203] The hostility towards Canning, then,
sprang not so much from a conscientious difference of opinion—
he disliked Liverpool's sinking fund policy as much as Wellington disliked his 'foreign politicks'—as from a long-standing
conviction of his deficiencies of character. Canning was a
'charlatan parvenu'—Wellington's words—and all good men
ought therefore to be on their guard against him.

But hence the importance of Liverpool. Though his part in
Vansittart's demotion and the ousting of 'Brother Bragge'
seemed to make him Canning's willing instrument, he became
more indispensable than ever in a Cabinet suddenly become
seriously divided. Canning on his side trusted him implicitly;
in fact, a partnership to last was firmly established during his
first few months in office. As he told Huskisson: 'I will not
deny myself the opportunity of saying that I am quite satisfied
with L's conduct; that he has worked honestly, perseveringly
& sincerely; that each step has been gained separately, with
great dexterity, & (what was essential) without alarm; that each
party necessarily has made the sacrifice exacted of him or taken
the offer proposed to him as of his own free will . . . & that
finally I am perfectly confident that with less management or
with more *brusquerie* the thing would not have been done.'[204]
Naturally, this blameless behaviour also served to mollify those
who would hear nothing good of Canning. But at the same time,
because distrust of the 'parvenu' was so deep-rooted, the notion
that the Prime Minister was his humble obedient servant was
never really dispelled. Indeed, the more his activities went
unchallenged, the more dominant his position became, the
stronger the feeling that Liverpool was grooming him to be
his successor; and with that a possibility not to be discounted,
to stave off the evil hour of political crisis, and, as some feared,

[203] *Wellington and His Friends*, p. 36; *Mrs Arbuthnot*, i. 200; *Eldon*, ii.
468; *Arbuthnot*, p. 42.
[204] Canning to Huskisson, 21 December 1822, Add. MSS. 38743, f. 277.

of Radical triumph, became a foremost responsibility. Canning, therefore, had great need of the Prime Minister, but from the point of view of Wellington and others so did the country. More than ever Disraeli's 'arch-mediocrity' looked irreplaceable.

CONCLUSION

The most frequently encountered interpretation of British politics between Waterloo and Canning's return to power is that of a reactionary government under increasing pressure from outside suddenly making good by bringing in men of more liberal inclination. Among historians it was the liberals of a succeeding generation who first wrote in these terms. To Harriet Martineau writing in the 1840's 'the government had no love from any class—very little respect; intense hate from many—slavish fear from more', and Castlereagh's suicide came 'as a ray of hope in the midst of thickest darkness'.[1] To Spencer Walpole Eldon was 'the genius which withstood all reform', and 'Londonderry regarded a Radical with the feelings with which a Francis or an Alexander regarded a Carbonaro'. 'Englishmen enjoyed less real liberty than at any time since the Revolution of 1688' until 'the Tory party, under new guidance ... deserted its old colours' and for 'the first time in its history ... had the courage to pass over to the popular cause'.[2]

In fact, Liverpool's administration was neither reactionary nor suddenly reformist in 1822. While it did attempt to suppress opinion which it found abhorrent, it acted not so much on behalf of an aristocracy intent on maintaining its privileges as on behalf of a considerable part of society which refused to believe in the political, if not moral, worth of the 'lower sort of people'. An awareness of the importance of 'respectable' opinion not formally represented in the institutions of the state characterised every notable transaction of the government. It encouraged its steady pursuit of economical reform and partly explained the interest it acquired in legal reform; it helped to

[1] Harriet Martineau, *A History of the Thirty Years' Peace, 1816–1846*, i. 88, 385.
[2] Sir Spencer Walpole, *A History of England from the Conclusion of the Great War in 1815*, i. v, 295, ii. 127, 147.

ensure that the inquiry into the currency question would achieve serious results; it, more than anything else, brought about the decision to destroy the bill of pains and penalties against Queen Caroline and to harry her no further; it both made capitulation to the agriculturists impossible and gave representations in favour of 'freer' trade their maximum effect. The ministers knew well that the old order's chances of survival were greatly reduced if once the new forces arising in society found little or nothing to admire in it; and therefore that how they, as the foremost representatives of the ruling class, used their power was of more than passing importance. They had harsh reminders of this in the opening years of peace. The enactment of the corn law of 1815 was really a failure of responsibility on their part, and they paid for their remissness in raising the expectations of the landed interest and suspicions elsewhere. Furthermore, the defeat of the property tax in 1816 occurred when an executive, too confident of its own power and judgement, chose to try its strength against a wrathful country. Never again did the ministers allow themselves to be coerced so obviously into better ways. The charge of 'reaction' levelled against Liverpool and his colleagues is usually based, following the example of Victorian 'Whig' historians, on their opposition to those popular forces which were eventually triumphant. What it overlooks is that, on the whole, they managed to keep the support of those popular forces which were triumphant in the immediate future. Indeed they were not 'reactionary' either in the sense of absolutely resisting the 'progressive' or 'modern' elements in society or in the broader sense of attempting to reverse the general pattern of events. They did not depart from the traditional style of aristocratic government in Great Britain in that they were never insensitive to demands issuing from outside the narrow political establishment. They reformed, albeit slowly and cautiously; with some justification at least, they claimed to prefer a 'national' view over the views of interests and classes; and they came to terms with 'the rise of public opinion' not only with the 'rational part' but with the 'irrational part' insofar as, with the feebleness of the state quite revealed, they would no longer resort to extraordinary persecution.

'Improving' and pragmatic as the administration was, it is probably not amiss to argue that the *ancien régime* was weakened in spite of it rather than because of it. What lay behind the conspicuous growth of middle class radicalism in the 1820's is not easy to determine. But it is clear that many radicals were not at all antagonistic towards the ministers, whom they regarded as 'progressive' and totally out of sympathy with the 'old Toryism' still strongly entrenched in the lower reaches of power, most notably in the corporations and counties. The *Manchester Guardian*, for example, which enjoyed a steadily expanding circulation throughout the decade, confessed in an editorial of 1826 that it did not know 'by whom, among the present race of public men, their places might advantageously be supplied'. Similar sentiments came from the *Leeds Mercury*, the most successful provincial newspaper in the country.[3] Quite possibly the growth of radicalism was most closely linked with the growth of a middle class consciousness. Economic historians are generally agreed that after 1815 the rate of economic growth accelerated,[4] and this must have increased the wealth and self-confidence of the 'middle ranks of society' and also their frustration at political exclusion and social inferiority. The end of the war too may have provided them with greater liberty to voice their resentments, resentments which deepened with the passing of the first generation of the Industrial Revolution and the arrival of a second of established wealth and local prominence. However, the point to be made is that, notwithstanding the progress of radicalism, Liverpool's administration in its last years still had possession of the 'rational part of the community'. It has been postulated that whenever the 'lower sort' became a dangerous presence the 'middling sort' hastened to stand at the aristocracy's shoulder.[5] All that can be deduced from the government's response to what passed between Waterloo and the Queen's trial suggests that this is a simplification. Liverpool's administration was

[3] David Ayerst, *Guardian: Biography of a Newspaper*, pp. 57–8; Donald Read, *Press and People, 1790–1850*, pp. 116–17.
[4] See Phyllis Deane and W. A. Cole, *British Economic Growth, 1688–1959* (2nd ed.), pp. 282–3.
[5] E. P. Thompson, *The Making of the English Working Class*, pp. 177–8, 561.

never more unpopular, and acutely conscious of it, than when it had to contend with 'clamour'. For 'clamour', defined by the 'respectable' as 'an excitement created amongst the uneducated, or amongst those who do not reflect, or do not exercise their judgement',[6] presented such dangers that it was something to avoid more than it was something to silence. While coercion was strongly supported in 1817 and 1819, the feeling that the country had never been nearer to revolution prompted further reflection. In view of the prevalence of the notion that the cause of distress was extravagant government, many no doubt wondered whether the ministers could have averted or reduced the crisis by greater economy. Others must have come to question the wisdom of a policy of repression, since the state could only act with limited effectiveness and the 'irrational' public was antagonised all the more. In general, there must have been a growing conviction that the political consciousness of the lower orders could not be destroyed and that therefore it was idle to pretend that the political situation did not have a new constituent. The fear that aristocratic government would be too provocative and unsympathetic towards the 'inferior sort of people' to guarantee social order was very prominent in 1820. Had popular radicalism not faded away out of sight and, to a lesser extent, out of mind after that date, Liverpool and his colleagues would never have found the favour in the country that they did. As it was, the menace of popular revolution seemed to disappear with economic improvement, which argued strongly that the monster which had terrified the 'respectable' classes was not as formidable as they had supposed. This greatly diminished, if it did not eradicate, the offence of the ministers. What appeared to be a new cordiality towards the public after 1822, most amply expressed in a surge of reform, completed the recovery of a reputation which had steadily dwindled with the passage of the Corn Law, the defeat of the property tax and the post-war disturbances.

But if the administration did enough to maintain the good name of the aristocracy, why did it not do more? The record of the 'liberal Tories' of the 1820's seems mediocre indeed

[6] William Alexander Mackinnon, *On the Rise, Progress and Present State of Public Opinion in Great Britain . . .*, p. 18.

alongside the achievements of the Whigs in the decade following, the more so when it is realised that much of their effort was
devoted to removing patent anachronisms and ambiguities
instead of to bold essays at reform. Apart from their 'freer'
trade legislation and Peel's legal reforms, much of which was
tidying rather than tree-felling, the sum of their success was
virtually that they reduced the expense of government to a
minimum and so rationalised the central administration that
the Whigs found they could do little in the way of 'economical
reform' when they came to power in 1830. Nor could they
blame political difficulties for restricting their achievement.
Except on the question of Catholic emancipation, where for
once the example of his father made a deep impression, George
IV was of a political metal whose malleability and other pro-
perties were fully known to his ministers. On issues connected
with public spending and public establishments, the task of
government was not to avoid checks but to check parliament
and public opinion. In addition, the 'liberals' were never balked
within the Cabinet, and the Whigs often gave valuable assistance
in the legislature. At no time did king, parliament or public
opinion successfully oppose in a large way 'improvement' of
the executive's recommendation; the greatest resistance came
from the House of Lords but even its prejudices could be
melted, as was shown when Peel's criminal legislation was
accepted and, most spectacularly, when Catholic emancipation
was carried in 1829. What was achieved was achieved in such
comfort as to encourage rather than discourage further reforming ventures.

It is not difficult to argue, therefore, that the pace of
'improvement' would have been more rapid but for the ministers themselves. True, they were handicapped by an inefficient
bureaucracy, by a lack of information, and by the public's
concern for economical government which greatly hindered
effective state intervention. But the Whigs in the 1830's were
little better off in these respects. The civil service of those
years was, by and large, still only as useful as the individuals
who comprised it were honest, hard-working and not without
initiative. Many of the great reforms were carried through with
a minimum of information, as was the case with the Reform

Act of 1832, or on the strength of evidence supplied by specially appointed commissioners whose work was hastily done, strongly influenced by their prejudices and sometimes frustrated by local opposition. And it is common knowledge that the legislation amounted to a very hesitant assertion of the central government's authority over its local agencies, and that the inspectorate created by it was, in point of numbers, an insignificant addition to the bureaucracy. Having regard only to the administrative equipment at their disposal, there seems to be no reason why Lord Liverpool and his ministers could not have done what the Whigs did ten years after them.

Mainly the Tory governments of the period after Waterloo were held back by their desire to present reforms which would have the widest possible acceptance. They feared above all the division of society into competing classes or interests, the destruction of the confidence which had formerly subsisted between the nation at large and the ruling class and between the ruling class and the Crown. The Tory party, indeed, based itself on the postulate that if the Whigs were entrusted with power they would wrench at these relationships out of a conviction that the people needed to be accommodated more and the monarch less. The maintenance of social harmony by the state at a time when so much of the old society was being profoundly transformed by agencies other than the state was an exercise full of complication and difficulty. The power which was the traditional possession of the king in person had to be respected, but without bringing the monarchy into public disrepute or obstructing unduly the responsibility the ministers owed to the legislature and the nation. The power which public opinion had obtained in the constitution had to be admitted, but not to the detriment of the executive's superior judgement of the real interest of the state. This need to reconcile past arrangements with present needs generally made reform tentative and expedient instead of bold and doctrinaire. The boldness of the concession of Catholic emancipation in 1828–9 was exceptional, and it was explained by the fact that Wellington and Peel came to the conclusion that the consequences of resistance would be worse than the consequences of submission. Normally a shuffle, not a stride, was found sufficient. Change,

Tory ministers would have argued, had to be carefully regulated, reform had to be the deliberate act of those who were in the best position to calculate its effects. An administration had a duty to be discriminatory towards the past because there were always abuses to eliminate, because knowledge could alter the principles of government, and because the authority of government, in the last resort, depended on those over whom it was exerted. On the other hand, reform which was hasty, ill-considered and intemperate was likely to produce more evil than it removed. The rights of vested interests had to be respected to the extent that their opposition would not be conducted in desperation in the future. Reform at the behest of the public was salutary if it affirmed the executive's flexibility and responsiveness, and unsalutary if it created an impression of subservience. Ideally, reform preserved what was of value and did nothing to disturb the nation's confidence in aristocratic government. The overriding concern of politicians like Lord Liverpool was for the quality of improvement. Belayed by their conservative principles, they proceeded with great caution and great thoroughness, and though their achievements were not spectacular they had a solidity which was not always present in the great Whig reforms of the 1830's. Certainly the least that can be said of such a strategy is that in their own time as the lessees of power, Liverpool and his colleagues had no reason to think that it had failed.

INDEX

abbreviations, xi–xiii
Aberdeen burgh, 167
Acland, Sir Thomas, 126, 142, 240
Addington, Dr., 15
Adelaide, Princess, 139
administration:
  achievements of, 395–6, 401
  as an aristocratic government, 396
  as professional politicians, 14–15
  assessment of, 395–401
  attempt to create broad-bottomed, 2, 8–9, 339–40
  charge of being reactionary, 395, 396
  charge of being suddenly reformist, 395, 400–1
  compared with earlier and later governments, 2, 397, 398–9
  distinction between change and reform, 400–1
  experience of, 15–16
  fear of dividing society, 400
  formation of, 2–3
  in 1812–15, 1–17
  in 1815, 4–5
  in 1822–7, 398–400
  influence of war on, 1–2
  lack of parliamentary talent, 6–7, 284, 307–8
  liberal historians' view of, 395
  limitations on, 398–9
  longevity of, 1
  'middling sort' and, 12–14, 395–6
  mistakes of, 396
  national interest, view of, 10–11, 13–14, 396, 400
  pace and quality of improvement, 399–401
  periods of strength and weakness, 1–2
  popularity of, 4–5
  pragmatism of, 397–8
  prestige of, 7–8, 397

reforms, nature of, 396, 399–401
transition from war to peace, 174–175
youth in, 8
see also Cabinet
Admiralty:
  lordships, 126–8
  pay question, 72–5, 77–8
  reduction of Board, 166
  Whig pressure for reduction, 354, 355
agricultural:
  distress, taxation and, 346–7
  interest:
    conflict with manufacturing interest, 10
    discontent of the, 304–5, 340–1
    the corn laws and, 220–2, 223, 305
    the property tax and, 59, 67, 68
  relief, 346–50
  taxes, 67, 305
agriculture:
  capital for, 92
  credit for, 348–50
  crisis of 1814, 3
  crisis of 1816–17, 90–101
  depression in, 10, 22, 25
  harvests, 90, 304, 340
  overproduction, 95
  protection of, 25–6, 96–7
  state of, in 1821, 304–5
  wartime, 3
  see also corn
aid, foreign, 21, 22–3
alarm, see disaffection of 1819–20
Althorp, Lord, 352, 354
American War of Independence, 29
Arbuthnot, Charles, 75, 83, 142, 159, 166, 189, 265, 278, 283, 284, 294, 313, 315, 325, 326, 345, 351, 386
Arbuthnot, Mrs., 219, 280, 298, 354, 363, 388

Hume, Joseph, 300, 301, 305, 345, 351, 365
Hunt, Henry, 175, 181, 191
Huskisson, William:
  acceptance of office, 389
  as a parliamentarian, 6, 9, 56
  Canning and, 176, 375–6, 378, 379, 380, 382, 387–9
  character of, 386–7
  defence of the corn laws, 304
  membership of committees, 83, 84, 126
  monetary policy, 151, 156–7, 176
  opinions and views on:
    economocal government, 216–17
    economic depression, 96, 117
    1818 election, 142–3, 160
    1820 election, 215–16
    financial system, 168, 169–70, 363
    parliamentary attendance, 166
    property tax, 63
  the Queen's business, 260, 262, 266, 298
  under Canning, 392
Hutchinson, Lord, 205, 231, 233–4, 235, 237

income tax, 68, 69
incomes, standard of, 3
indemnity, 27, 28n
independents, defined, vii–viii
India, 28
individual liberties, 14
industry:
  contribution to public revenue, 14
  property tax and, 67, 68
  prospects under peace, 10, 95
  wartime production, 3, 10
'inferior sort':
  disaffection of, 102, 106–7
  irrationality of, 107
  modified conciliation of, 144
  parliamentary reform and, 66
  political consciousness of, 398
  Radicalism and, 273
  support of the Queen, 248–9, 273, 323
  view of sinecures, 123
Ionian Islands, 30
Ireland:
  Catholic emancipation question, 4

consolidation of the exchequers, 78–80
famine in, 92–3, 102
garrisons in, 28, 31, 49, 119
militia in, 28
outbreak of disorder, 342–3
poor relief, 357
relief measures, 93
state of, during war, 4
Irish members:
  attendance at parliament, 39, 41
  on property tax, 65

'Jacobins', 40
John Bull, 279–80
justices of the peace, 16, 108, 112

Kent, Duke of, 138, 141
Keppel-Craven, R., 274
King, Lord, 156
Knatchbull, Sir Edward, 354
Knighton, Sir William, 275, 276, 278, 372, 388

laissez-faire, role of, 96–7, 349
Lamb, William, 252
Lambton, Lord, 305, 307, 308
Lansdowne, Lord, 163, 237, 250
law reform:
  capital punishment issue, 161, 165, 303
  crime prevention, 164
  criminal convictions, 180
  forgery bills, 302
  government aims, 163–5, 174
  government measures, 162–3
  increase in crime, 162
  inquiry into, 165, 303–4
  larceny bills, 302
  'law improvement', 163
  Mackintosh's committee, 302
  Mackintosh's view, 161
  Peel and, 399
  prison reform, 303–4
  question of, 161–5, 395
  reasons for delay, 302–4
  Romilly's view, 161
  secondary punishment, 161, 164, 303